THE ENTREPRENEUR'S INFORMATION SOURCEBOOK

10/13

THE ENTREPRENEUR'S INFORMATION SOURCEBOOK

CHARTING THE PATH TO SMALL BUSINESS SUCCESS

Second Edition

Susan C. Awe

 **LIBRARIES UNLIMITED**

AN IMPRINT OF ABC-CLIO, LLC
Santa Barbara, California • Denver, Colorado • Oxford, England

Copyright 2012 by ABC-CLIO, LLC

Library of Congress Cataloging-in-Publication Data

Awe, Susan C., 1948–
   The entrepreneur's information sourcebook : charting the path to small business success / Susan C. Awe. — 2nd ed.
       p. cm.
   Includes index.
   ISBN 978-1-59884-786-4 (hardcopy : alk. paper) — ISBN 978-1-59884-787-1 (ebook)   1. New business enterprises.   2. Entrepreneurship.   I. Title.
   HD62.5.A96   2012
   658.02′2—dc23   2011039793

ISBN: 978-1-59884-786-4
EISBN: 978-1-59884-787-1

16   15   14   13   12   1   2   3   4   5

Libraries Unlimited
An Imprint of ABC-CLIO, LLC

ABC-CLIO, LLC
130 Cremona Drive, P.O. Box 1911
Santa Barbara, California 93116-1911

CONTENTS

CONTENTS

ILLUSTRATIONS

INTRODUCTION

Hitch your Wagon to a Star.
—Ralph Waldo Emerson

Welcome to the second edition of *The Entrepreneur's Information Sourcebook.* After six years, many of the resources from the previous edition are out of print, outdated, or, in the case of websites, just plain gone. I've saved the best and added many new print and online resources to help your small business be successful.

How important are small businesses to the U.S. economy during the current recession? Small business, defined generally by the U.S. Small Business Administration (SBA) as firms with fewer than 500 employees, represent over 99.7% of all employer firms, have created 64% of net new jobs in the past 15 years, and employ 44% of all private workers (U.S. SBA Office of Advocacy, *Small Business Economy; A Report to the President*, 2010). Small businesses—that is, entrepreneurs—through the creation of new companies or expansion, generate virtually all new jobs in the U.S. economy. They also fill niche markets, innovate, increase competition, and provide individuals with a chance to succeed. Small businesses play a vital role in our free-market society.

According to the U.S. Department of Commerce, gross domestic investment for private companies fell in 2008 and 2009 due to the shrinking economy and consumer spending. Small firms have shed a significant number of jobs in this recession, and self-employment was also down. In 2009, there were still nearly 6 million small businesses with fewer than 100 employees in the United States, according to the SBA statistics—nearly the same number as in 2005. Small businesses represent 97% of all U.S. exporters. Also, nearly 30% of federal contracts go to small businesses each year. Previously small businesses fought an uphill battle when it came to getting their information out there to compete with larger corporations. Big corporations have more resources, more brand recognition, and, of course, more money. Web 2.0 and now Web 3.0 technologies have significantly leveled the playing field if used efficiently. Tools such as blogs, interactive websites, and social media are powerful marketing tools for small and medium-sized businesses. Even though not all the news is good about small businesses, you still dream of working for yourself and being your own boss. However, you probably have hundreds of questions. Where and how to begin?

INTRODUCTION

WHY ANOTHER BOOK ON ENTREPRENEURSHIP?

Many small businesses fail every year. The Small Business Administration finds that 69% of businesses do not last past seven years, and 56% fail in less than four years. Starting a successful business is not a simple task. Thorough research and planning, resourceful management, and the necessary financial resources are required. Thomas Edison said, "Many of life's failures are people who did not realize how close they were to success when they gave up." Today entrepreneurship is an essential component of a nation's ability to succeed in an ever-changing and more competitive global marketplace. The entrepreneurial spirit is characterized by innovation and risk taking. Entrepreneurs are often technical experts but often fail due to a lack of formal training or experience in management practices and principles. A good product or service fails because the owner could not manage people and things or make the change from technical expert to strategic thinker and did not get the assistance he or she needed. Sometimes entrepreneurs are said to be different from business owners because they create a new product, service, or process, and a small business owner merely manages, but this book will use the terms interchangeably because all small business owners must innovate daily in the way they run, market, and improve their operations. This guide provides help in whatever area or areas the entrepreneur needs to make his or her business thrive and grow.

ORGANIZATION

Find here chapters arranged by functional areas—such as start-up, business planning, marketing, management, franchising, raising capital, and competitive analysis—that take you step-by-step through the process of starting, running, and growing a business; the book is designed to get you the information you need quickly and easily. Subheadings in each chapter highlight important concepts. Each chapter discusses important concepts and resources that are particularly appropriate or useful for that subject area, and resources are described thoroughly. Following the narrative of each chapter is an extensive list of print and online resources that will provide you with advice, guidance, and information to accomplish the tasks described in the chapter. Often resources are listed in more than one chapter if they can help readers accomplish the tasks involved with several different functions. Both the print and online resources are listed in alphabetical, not priority, order. You determine which resources are best for your particular situation and mind-set. The table of contents and index can also direct you to the information you want or need. A glossary explains some of the basic jargon of the business world and also acts as an acronym dictionary.

Besides lack of management skills, one of the top reasons that new enterprises fail is inadequate planning, and poor planning results in undercapitalization and poor cash flow. *The Entrepreneur's Information Sourcebook* gathers in one source a vast amount of information to help new small business owners locate and use data from a wide range of resources to plan every step of their new business. It is imperative that entrepreneurs understand the concepts covered and use current, accurate information for their plans. Small business is eminently important to our nation, and helping small businesses succeed helps us all.

The Entrepreneur's Information Sourcebook begins with an explanation of what it means to be an entrepreneur and ends with ideas and guidance for growing or expanding your business and different exit strategies. Because individuals think and work differently, many different resources have been included as all the issues in starting a small business are covered. When looking for a resource to use for some phase of your business, try several before determining which ones work best for you. Check out the print resources at a library if possible; some materials, if not owned by a local library, may be obtained through interlibrary loan. Libraries lend each other different resources for their patrons. Talk to your local librarian to see what community resources are available. Buy some of the books. Purchase information is provided, though prices change, and these prices are current as of spring 2011. The included books and websites were selected for their quality and availability as well as to represent different approaches to the various aspects of starting a new business. Books were selected for their unique approach, relevancy, authority, organization, and clarity. Websites must provide practical information and/or research data rather than just express opinions or sell products. Sites have been evaluated for authority, currency, objectivity, stability, and usefulness. Many of the websites may be familiar to readers, but new uses and additional important aspects are often identified.

ASK AND PAY FOR HELP!

As you begin to plan, don't be afraid to ask for experienced help. Many free or reduced-fee services are available from the SBA, the Service Corp of Retired Executives, and the Small Business Development Centers, as well as experienced business owners who are willing to act as mentors. Several of these resources can be located and accessed through websites mentioned in this book. Although this book does not focus on e-commerce or home-based businesses, they have not been ignored. A chapter on the Internet and selling globally has been added to this second edition. All of the major websites listed will contain some articles and information on e-commerce, too, because it's such a growing area in the small business world. A technologically enabled future is one of the big trends in business worldwide. The iPhone was a tremendous breakthrough for smart phones and their users. Watch for bigger and better technology advances coming soon involving every service you use. Additionally, chapter 11, "Legal and Tax Issues," lists several resources designed to help start a home-based or e-commerce business and to help navigate the legal world. Check the index to find specific resources.

One important concept that readers will take away from this book is that before any contracts or agreements are signed, they should contact a lawyer and understand all the fine print and points. A small business needs an accountant to help with financial recordkeeping as well. These professionals should be interviewed like any employee, and you should hire one who works well for you and with you.

Now, where and how to begin? Look through the table of contents and find a chapter that interests you or that you know something about. Start reading and learning about starting a small business. Hopefully after working your way through this book, you will have realized your dream of self-employment! Good luck in all your small business adventures.

ARE YOU AN ENTREPRENEUR? 1

CHAPTER HIGHLIGHTS

What Is an Entrepreneur?

What Are the Characteristics Needed?

A Note of Caution

Self-Assessment

Other Resources to Explore

Talk About It!

So, you're considering a small business. Do you have what it takes? At this point in the process, you might ask yourself, "What is an entrepreneur? What are the qualities needed to become a successful entrepreneur? Am I an entrepreneur?"

WHAT IS AN ENTREPRENEUR?

Webster defines an entrepreneur as "one who organizes, manages, and assumes the risks of a business or enterprise." Wikipedia gives this definition: "An **entrepreneur** is a person who has possession of a new enterprise, venture or idea, and assumes significant accountability for the inherent risks and the outcome" (http://en.wikipedia.org/wiki/Entrepreneur). Often described as opportunistic, creative and innovative, and a leader, an entrepreneur differs from a small business person who is an expert at running and growing a business. While both are outcome driven, an entrepreneur is dependent on social and economic factors. Both must be dedicated, innovative, and willing to spend long hours making their business a success.

WHAT ARE THE CHARACTERISTICS NEEDED?

Required entrepreneurial skills include a compelling vision, a driving passion, versatility or flexibility in planning and changing plans, and confident execution. Learn from your mistakes and move on. Curiosity is another necessary attribute, since curious people are creative or innovative—and questioning of current practices, procedures, and methods triggers innovation. See every obstacle as an opportunity and turn it into an advantage.

Lastly, but perhaps most importantly, entrepreneurs are high-energy, ambitious individuals who persevere. A small business revolves around a key person, and that person needs energy, enthusiasm, and drive. And though a successful entrepreneur has a positive attitude toward the business and life in general, entrepreneurship and small businesses involve risk. As an entrepreneur, you will be the engine of a new venture, and its success or failure depends in large measure on you.

A NOTE OF CAUTION

A cautionary note should be added here: if you want to start your own business because you are unhappy with your current job, profession, or personal life, remember that starting, running, and succeeding in your own business takes a lot of work and involves wearing lots of hats and keeping lots of balls in the air at once. "Don't quit your day job" is a hackneyed expression, but testing the waters by starting a business in your spare time is a proven method of discovering whether you have what it takes and whether you might succeed. If you do decide to quit your job to devote yourself full-time to the new enterprise, it's prudent to set aside enough savings to cover your living costs for a year, because it may be at least that long before you can pay yourself a salary.

SELF-ASSESSMENT

To start asking the right questions to find out whether you are or can be an entrepreneur, BizMove.com (www.bizmove.com/other/quiz.htm) has a 10-question quiz that will start individuals thinking about what is involved in starting a business. If you can answer a resounding yes to questions such as "can you lead others?" "are you a good organizer?" and "are you a self-starter?" success is more likely.

Also, consider consulting the Entrepreneur's Guidebook Series at www.patsula.com/businessplanguides/. In guidebook 1, entitled *Personal Planning*, you'll have the opportunity to assess your entrepreneurial talent. This guide discusses what an entrepreneur is and why people become entrepreneurs. It also asks 29 questions to help discover if you have what it takes. Finally, common traits of successful entrepreneurs are succinctly summarized. A good book to look at is Edward Hess's *So You Want to Start a Business?*

Hess, Edward. *So, You Want to Start a Business?* Pearson Education, 2008. 194p. ISBN 0-13-712667-0. $18.99.

This practical, well-organized work begins with a chapter entitled "Can You Be a Successful Entrepreneur?" Learn what it takes and what defines an entrepreneur. Other chapters cover basic rules for success in business, identifying a good business opportunity, hiring and keeping good employees, and how to manage growth. A lengthy list of books by subject and some web resources conclude the work. Use this guide to be successful in any enterprise you undertake.

OTHER RESOURCES TO EXPLORE

If your curiosity has been piqued, or if you want to read and investigate more aspects of entrepreneurship and starting a business, several good books are available. Caitlin Friedman and Kimberly Yorio's *The Girl's Guide to Starting Your Own Business* contains a short quiz to help you discover if you really want to become an entrepreneur. Similar to a job interview, it asks questions about your goals, weaknesses, and how you approach challenges; it prompts you to honestly think about why you want to start a business and helps you focus your energy and motivation.

The updated fourth edition of *Good Small Business Guide 2010* starts with a list of questions to assess yourself and continues with essays on "Deciding Whether to Start a Business" and "Assessing Your Entrepreneurial Profile." Though this title has a slight UK bias, it helps readers develop a mix of hard and soft skills needed to set up and grow a business. Case studies are also featured.

In the third edition of *Starting Your New Business,* Charles L. Martin helps readers understand the nature of entrepreneurship and entrepreneurs and identify whether they have what it takes through self-assessment. Personal computers have become time and money savers and wasters, but they are essential in today's business life. Computer skills are necessary. And leadership and management skills are essential, because you are the key person to the business's success or failure. You need high-level skills in organization, delegation, and coordination to marshal resources and people. The list at the end of this chapter provides more resources that can help you test the strength of your entrepreneurial skills and characteristics.

TALK ABOUT IT!

One last piece of advice in determining if you're entrepreneurial is to discuss your idea with coworkers, family, friends, and neighbors. Networking should begin early. Use social media on the Internet. Find a local role model, someone who is higher up the ladder in the business world such as an established business owner. Find a mentor, someone who will let you bounce ideas off of him or her, give you pointers, and help you learn the ropes. Learn from others' mistakes or setbacks even as you make your own. Observe other businesspeople in action, and ask questions.

Besides tapping your local community, look for a community of like-minded individuals on the Internet. The Entrepreneurs website at About.com at

Figure 1.1 Screenshot of About: Entrepreneurs (http://entrepreneurs.about.com)

http://entrepreneurs.about.com has blogs, forums, newsletters, and other resources that are useful to new entrepreneurs. An article entitled "Is Entrepreneurship Right for Me?" will get you thinking. Talking through your ideas and interacting with a similar group of folks will help you make good decisions and fewer missteps.

If you're a people person or an extrovert who needs to verbalize your ideas, you may want to start your own local group of entrepreneurs or find one at a community college or university in your area. A small business can be a lonely enterprise, and if that is a drawback for you, find a way to interact in a productive way. Trade shows and conferences of like business owners or entrepreneurs is another social and beneficial outlet. Listed below are various resources that will help you determine your entrepreneurial tendencies and what you need to learn to be successful in your own small business.

REFERENCES

Starred titles are discussed in the chapter.

■ Print Resources

Bygrave, William D. and Zacharakis, Andrew (eds.). *The Portable MBA in Entrepreneurship*, 4th ed. John Wiley, 2009. 504p. ISBN 0-470-48131-5. $34.95.

This volume provides practical guidance on the basics of starting and running an entrepreneurial venture effectively. This completely updated and revised edition explores the changing legal, tax, and regulatory climates for small businesses. Using real-life examples and customizable, downloadable forms, the authors help you identify business opportunities and develop a business plan. Written in a clear, scholarly style, it is a reference book that you can refer to when faced with any small business decision or problem.

**Friedman, Caitlin and Yorio, Kimberly. *The Girl's Guide to Starting Your Own Business: Candid Advice, Frank Talk, and True Stories for the Successful Entrepreneur,* rev. ed. Harper Paperbacks, 2010. 272p. ISBN 0-061-98924-X. $15.99.

Covered here are virtually all aspects of owning and managing your own business. The authors provide sound advice to new entrepreneurs. Learn about assessing your finances, writing a business plan, hiring employees, advertising, and more. Interviews with successful women business owners are included as well as budget worksheets. This title is a useful resource for all entrepreneurs.

Gold, Steven K. *Entrepreneur's Notebook: Practical Advice for Starting a New Business Venture.* Learning Ventures Press, 2006. 232p. ISBN 0-976-27904-5. $10.36.

The real-life advice and practical information provided by Gold covers the information you need to get a new venture started. Learn how to build a solid team, make a pitch to possible investors, and choose a lawyer. Strong chapters provide information on understanding cash flow and investments. Understand your strengths and how to put together a useful business plan.

**Good Small Business Guide 2010,* 4th ed. A & C Black, 2010. 581p. ISBN 978-1-4081-2370-6. $24.99.

Besides helping you answer the question, "How can I be sure I've got what it takes to run a business?" this large reference work has sections on "Refining and Protecting Your Idea," "Finding Premises," "Communicating with Customers," "Managing Yourself and Others," and "Working Online." A large section on calculating ratios and creating financial statements as well as amortization, asset turnover, and more is also very useful for the new business owner. This edition has a British slant but has a great deal of useful information for all English-speaking entrepreneurs. The directories in the back contain a collection of print and online resources in a wide variety of business areas. This well-organized resource is a bargain.

**Hess, Edward. *So, You Want to Start a Business?* Pearson Education, 2008. 194p. ISBN 0-13-712667-0. $18.99.

This practical, well-organized work begins with a chapter entitled "Can You Be a Successful Entrepreneur?" Learn what it takes and what defines an entrepreneur. Other chapters cover basic rules for success in business, identifying a good business opportunity, hiring and keeping good employees, and how to manage growth. A lengthy list of books by subject and some web resources conclude the work. Use this guide to be successful in any enterprise you undertake.

**Martin, Charles L. *Starting Your New Business,* 3rd ed. Crisp Publications, 2011. 112p. ISBN 1-426-01946-7. $10.17.

Learn about the pitfalls as well as the opportunities of owning a business. Martin helps you familiarize yourself with the components and jargon involved in getting a business started and navigate the maze of decisions and actions you will need to accomplish.

Michalowicz, Mike. *The Toilet Paper Entrepreneur*. Obsidian Launch, 2008. 199p. ISBN 0-981-80820-4. $24.95.

Michalowicz shows readers how to build their business with a prosperity plan, a quarterly plan, and daily metrics. Entertaining, but not for those who are easily offended, this practical book provides valid, insightful information and will inspire some to take on the challenge of starting and running their own business.

Monosoff, Tamara. *Your Million Dollar Dream: Create a Winning Business Plan*. McGraw-Hill, 2010. 336p. ISBN 0-07-162943-2. $19.95.

Monosoff, founder of Mom Inventors Inc., works with many entrepreneurs and often walks them through the steps to starting and growing their own businesses. The chapter entitled "Making Money Your Way" provides exercises that will help you articulate your dreams, identify skill sets, and broaden your awareness and link to businesses that tap into your strengths and dreams. Learn how to create an effective business plan and use Twitter and Facebook as powerful marketing tools.

Urquhart-Brown, Susan. *The Accidental Entrepreneur: The 50 Things I Wish Someone Had Told Me about Starting a Business*. AMACOM, 2008. 178p. ISBN 0-8144-0167-8. $17.95.

This title includes two outstanding chapters: "What Is an Entrepreneur, Anyway?" asking you to define yourself, your business, and your goals, and "What Do You Bring to the Party?" which asks important questions about accountability and procrastination. Real-life examples illustrate many of the points. Another valuable and interesting chapter is "Get Connected to the Web for Profit." Also, learn what to avoid in starting your new venture.

■ Online Resources

**About.com Entrepreneurs: http://entrepreneurs.about.com (Accessed Spring 2011).

This site contains a wealth of information, such as articles on what states are most supportive of entrepreneurs, best links for entrepreneurs, ethics, professional associations, business mentoring, and more. The four main tabs include "Small Business Information," "Start Up," "Manage and Grow," and "Money Matters." Continually updated and easy to navigate, new and experienced entrepreneurs will visit this site often.

About.com Small Business Information: sbinformation.about.com (Accessed Spring 2011).

This site provides a treasure trove of information, links, books, and other help with improving an entrepreneur's management and coaching skills. Sections cover things to consider before starting a business, business plans, mistakes, goal setting, naming your business, and more. Learn best business practices and leadership skills from experts. A related area of the site helps users learn about human resources issues and managing employees.

**BizMove.com: www.bizmove.com (Accessed Spring 2011).

The wealth of information here covers a variety of topics, including general management, small business marketing, Internet business, and international trade. Worksheets and sample plans help guide users. "Growing a Business on the Internet" covers topics such as search engine positioning, website promotion, and e-mail marketing methods.

Edward Lowe's Entrepreneurs Resource Center: www.edwardlowe.org/ERC/ (Accessed Spring 2011).

This well-known small business site contains a large section on building and inspiring an organization as well as sections on human resources management and legal issues and taxes. Additional resources are often provided at the end of the articles. Also find information on branding, direct mail marketing, social media, and providing a promotional mix for your new business. Use this site frequently when you need help running or marketing your business.

Small Business Administration: www.sba.gov (Accessed Spring 2011).

This official government site offers a wealth of resources and programs for starting and growing a small business. Under "Startup Basics" is an entrepreneurial test of 25 questions that will help you evaluate your possible success in your own business. Other major sections cover business planning, financing, managing, marketing, employees, taxes, legal aspects, and business opportunities. Find here online forms, business plans, loan information, and many publications. Some of the site's content is available in Spanish.

**Small Business Town Network: www.smbtn.com/businessplanguides/ (Accessed Spring 2011).

Defining real entrepreneurs as managers who adopt key behaviors developed by understanding key market concepts and theories and who are successful because of their planning and researching skills, this site discusses why people become entrepreneurs and the type of life entrepreneurs generally lead. Here you will discover what your entrepreneurial talents are and common traits of successful entrepreneurs. Explore this website for good ideas.

Startup Nation: www.startupnation.com (Accessed Spring 2011).

Two brothers founded this site in 2002 to provide one-stop shopping for practical information to help entrepreneurs succeed. Users can access step-by-step advice, easy-to-understand articles, professional groups and forums, expert blogs, podcasts, and member-to-member networking. Learning from peers will help you in many ways, and you can easily connect here. Learn how to use technology efficiently, maximize your niche, acquire growth capital, and more. The eight steps to managing your money will help you plan and organize your business and personal finances. Use this site often to help you and your business succeed.

Wall Street Journal Small Business: http://online.wsj.com/home-page (Accessed Spring 2011).

WSJ's Small Business is an authoritative site that has a section entitled "How-To," where entrepreneurs will find a great deal of help deciding if they are entrepreneurs and how to get started in business. Collected here are many articles about different aspects of starting a business, such as legal structure, finding a name, business plan tools, and more. The sample business plans are very thorough and will help new business owners fill in the gaps in their own plans. Articles on important issues such as "Should You Hire an Accountant" will also get entrepreneurs off on the right foot. Continually updated and well written, this site is useful to all entrepreneurs.

RESEARCH, STATISTICS, AND INFORMATION GATHERING

2

CHAPTER HIGHLIGHTS

Federal Government Statistics

The U.S. Census Bureau

The North American Industry Classification System

FedStats

State Government Agencies

Commercial Publishers

Basic Statistical Concepts

When starting a new business, it's impossible to have too much information. Statistics—the classification, tabulation, and study of numerical data—is vital to making good decisions. Statistics is concerned with both the systematic collection of numerical data and its interpretation. Details on customers, competition, the industry, industry trends, locations, vendors, markets and potential markets, the local and national economy, trends in the economy, and more are necessities. Market research can help the entrepreneur successfully launch a new venture and weed out ideas that are not feasible. Decision making based on intuition and expertise with a thorough (statistical) understanding of the facts available is important to gaining and maintaining a competitive edge.

Because the cost of collecting and analyzing primary statistical data is great, most businesses depend on secondary statistical data generated by a variety of sources, including government agencies, trade associations, commercial publishers, and less often private research firms. Generally you will be able to find the online and print resources listed here at local libraries or for free on the Internet. Some of the sites have free information, but because many are commercial, they will try to sell you their products. This book does not endorse any of these products.

FEDERAL GOVERNMENT STATISTICS

The U.S. government is probably the largest single compiler and publisher of statistics pertaining to U.S. businesses. More than 70 agencies produce statistics of interest to the public, and many of these are useful to entrepreneurs and small business people. Many of the agencies have websites with statistics free to all Internet users, and the various search engines such as Google, Yahoo!, and Alta-Vista have crawled these sites and indexed some of the data. If you search for "small business statistics," you find a wealth of sites: free government ones and, of course, many dot-com sites wanting to sell you a variety of products and services. In this chapter, useful fee and free sites will be included for you to use in your research. The information and sites are presented in as linear fashion as possible, but there is a lot of interconnectivity and crossover. URLs are included whenever confusion seems possible.

One place to start is the U.S. government's official web portal: USA.gov (www.usa.gov/). Users will find a long list of government services and resources under "Explore Topics," many of which will interest and amaze first-timers. The federal government collects and publishes a great deal of data and information. If at any time you decide you'd like to see what paper publications the government has produced, visit a regional government depository at your state library or a large university library in your state. On USA.gov, under the topic of "Business and Economy," clicking on "Data and Statistics" brings up an alphabetical list of links to resources chock-full of statistics. "Economic Indicators" is part of the website for the Census Bureau (www.census.gov/cgi-bin/briefroom/BriefRm), and it provides timely access to the monthly releases and time series of key economic indicators.

The Bureau of Economic Analysis (BEA) website (www.bea.gov) from the Department of Commerce produces a wealth of statistical information on the U.S. economy. The mission of the BEA is to produce and circulate accurate, timely, relevant, and cost-effective statistics and to provide a comprehensive, up-to-date description of U.S. economic activity. The ups and downs of the U.S. economy and regional economic development affect every small business in some way. The cost of a barrel of oil goes up, and it costs more to get supplies to your door; consumers pay more for gas and have less to spend on clothes, food, and other goods and services. As a small business person, you want to keep a close eye on what's happening in the economy. The BEA's "U.S. Economy at a Glance" section will help you do just that. The BEA also produces the *Survey of Current Business,* a monthly publication that provides data on personal income, state and regional economic statistics, and more.

The U.S. Department of Labor's Bureau of Labor Statistics (www.bls.gov) presents the latest numbers on inflation and prices, pay and benefits, and Employment. Quite a few international statistics are also available here. Explore the site to find the Consumer Price Index Inflation Calculator; understanding inflation and how it affects business and prices is essential for an entrepreneur. When you hire employees to help you in your business, you will want to visit this site for information on compensation and working conditions and to review publications such as the *Occupational Outlook Handbook* (www.bls.gov/oco/) for help with job titles and descriptions, training needed, and pay/earnings.

THE U.S. CENSUS BUREAU

The largest statistical agency of the U.S. government is the Census Bureau (www.census.gov); it collects, compiles, and publishes, as mentioned above, economic as well as population statistics. On the home page of the Census Bureau, you will find listed the "American FactFinder." This site has a huge online collection of data on the people, housing, geography, and business of the United States. The American Community Survey (ACS) is a new nationwide survey designed to provide communities a fresh look at how they are changing. It is a critical element in the Census Bureau's reengineered 2010 census plan. The ACS is an ongoing survey that provides data about communities every year, not just census years. In the frame on the left, under Legacy American FactFinder (http://factfinder2.census.gov) is a link to the 2007 Economic Census, which profiles the U.S. economy every five years. Here you can find statistics on the state you live in by Metropolitan Statistical Areas, counties, and even by zip code. Many different publications are a part of the 2007 Economic Census. It contains the Industry Series reports, to which new industries have been added; the *Census of Wholesale Trade,* for example, covers manufacturing, retail, construction, finance and insurance, information, health care and social assistance, service, and many more. Statistics on number of establishments, sales, receipts, revenues, expenses, product, payroll, and more are presented in tables. Find the different parts of the Economic Census listed on the home page. This site may continue to change so you can always just Google "Economic Census" to find it on the Internet.

Another part of the U.S. Census Bureau's data are the *Current Industrial Reports* (CIR) at www.census.gov/manufacturing/cir/historical_data/index.html. Since 1904, the CIR program has provided monthly, quarterly, and annual measures of industrial activity. The program's surveys measure manufacturing activity in commodities such as textiles and apparel, computer and electronic components, consumer goods, and more. Reports can be accessed by subject or NAICS subsectors.

New measures of the way the United States does business are always being added. Data for e-commerce sales are found at www.census.gov/econ/estats/index.html. E-Stats is the U.S. Census Bureau's Internet site devoted exclusively to "measuring the electronic economy." This site features recent and upcoming releases and background papers.

Another publication of the Economic Census is *County Business Patterns;* this is a collection of data by county for every state similar to the Industry Series including number of establishments, payrolls, and employment by industry. *Zip Code Business Patterns* (includes 40,000 five-digit zip code areas) and *Metro Business Patterns* present the same type of data for those areas. The new site is at www.census.gov/econ/cbp/index.html. See chapter 7, "Marketing and Advertising," for a specific example of how to use these data for your small business. Some other examples of how the data in the Economic Census are used include calculating market share, identifying new site locations, and showing or finding new markets for products or services.

THE NORTH AMERICAN INDUSTRY CLASSIFICATION SYSTEM

Many of the U.S. government's statistics are gathered and distributed by the North American Industry Classification System (NAICS). Each business, when it files its taxes, must identify itself by an NAICS number. NAICS has replaced the U.S. Standard Industrial Classification system. NAICS was developed jointly by the United States, Canada, and Mexico to provide new comparability in statistics on business activities throughout North America. The NAICS also introduced a number of new industries, including residential remodelers, electronic shopping and auctions, Internet publishing and broadcasting, and web search portals. The Census Bureau site has a link to NAICS, where you can look up the code for your industry. Many statistical sources present industry ratios and trends by NAICS code.

Another great statistical resource, often called the nation's data book, is produced by the Census Bureau, the *Statistical Abstract of the United States*. It provides statistics such as number of cell phones in the United States, average cost of a home in different regions, educational level in various parts of the country, fastest growing jobs, where population growth is happening, and more in over 1,400 tables and charts.

Also from the Census Bureau, the State Data Center (SDC) program is a cooperative program between the states and the Census Bureau that was created in 1978 (www.census.gov/sdc/). The Business and Industry Data Center was added in 1988 to help meet the needs of local business communities for economic data. The SDC's mission is to provide easy and efficient access to U.S. Census Bureau data through a wide network of lead, coordinating, and affiliate agencies in every state. Today the SDCs are the Census Bureau's official sources of demographic, economic, and social statistics. The SDCs often present training as well as technical assistance in finding and utilizing Census Bureau data. Census data are frequently used to plan and administer new projects as well as to enhance decision making by local governments, businesses, and many types of researchers.

FEDSTATS

FedStats (www.fedstats.gov) is the official website of the Federal Interagency Council on Statistical Policy. This gateway to statistics from over 100 U.S. federal agencies is well organized and easy to use.

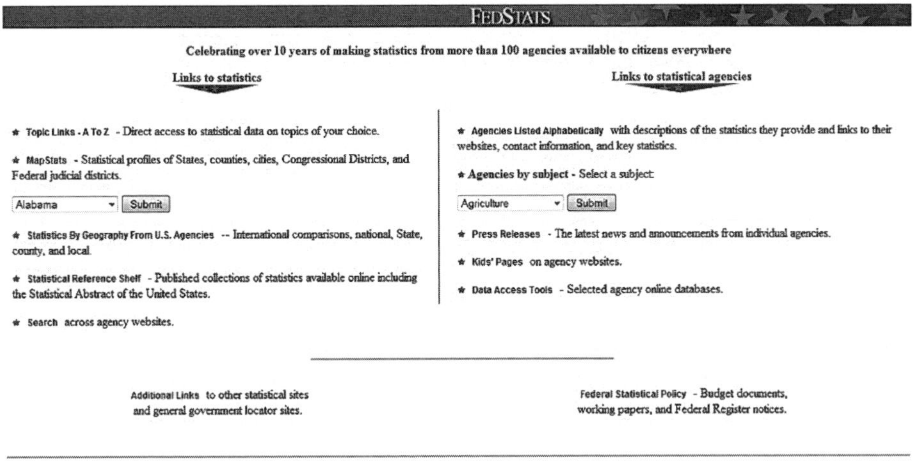

FEDSTATS

Celebrating over 10 years of making statistics from more than 100 agencies available to citizens everywhere

Links to statistics

★ Topic Links - A To Z - Direct access to statistical data on topics of your choice.

★ MapStats - Statistical profiles of States, counties, cities, Congressional Districts, and Federal judicial districts.

[Alabama ▾] [Submit]

★ Statistics By Geography From U.S. Agencies -- International comparisons, national, State, county, and local.

★ Statistical Reference Shelf - Published collections of statistics available online including the Statistical Abstract of the United States.

★ Search across agency websites.

Links to statistical agencies

★ Agencies Listed Alphabetically with descriptions of the statistics they provide and links to their websites, contact information, and key statistics.

★ Agencies by subject - Select a subject:

[Agriculture ▾] [Submit]

★ Press Releases - The latest news and announcements from individual agencies.

★ Kids' Pages on agency websites.

★ Data Access Tools - Selected agency online databases.

Additional Links to other statistical sites and general government locator sites.

Federal Statistical Policy - Budget documents, working papers, and Federal Register notices.

Figure 2.1 Screenshot of FedStats Home Page (www.fedstats.gov)

Users can find statistics and information under "Links to Statistics," "Topic Links A–Z," "MapStats," and "Statistics by Geography from U.S. Agencies." The "Statistical Reference Shelf," a bit farther down on the home page is a large collection of online reference sources such as the *Statistical Abstract of the United States*, which we've already discussed. You will find a variety of other sources, such as the *State and Metropolitan Area Data Book* and *Digest of Education Statistics*, which will provide statistics on many topics of interest to small businesses. On the other half of the page, "Links to Statistical Agencies," under "Agencies by Subject," click "Economic" on the drop-down arrow to lead you to a list of links to agencies with economic data, such as the Small Business Administration and "Small Business Indicators."

The links and descriptions included here also lead users to the U.S. Census Bureau, Bureau of Economic Analysis, Customs and Border Protection, Economics and Statistics Administration, International Trade Administration, Small Business Administration, and National Science Foundation.

Learning to use the many and varied statistical resources of the federal government is no easy task. The Internet has certainly improved the visibility and searchability of these resources, but the enormity of available information is still daunting. When you start your search, have a clear idea of what you need, but be flexible in the vocabulary you use to describe it. Also, ask a librarian to help you get started. Remember that you will probably have to use the data you find to extrapolate, which means you will estimate by projecting from known information or data.

STATE GOVERNMENT AGENCIES

Statistical sources for state data varies greatly. Many state and local government organizations collect the data and then submit them to the federal government

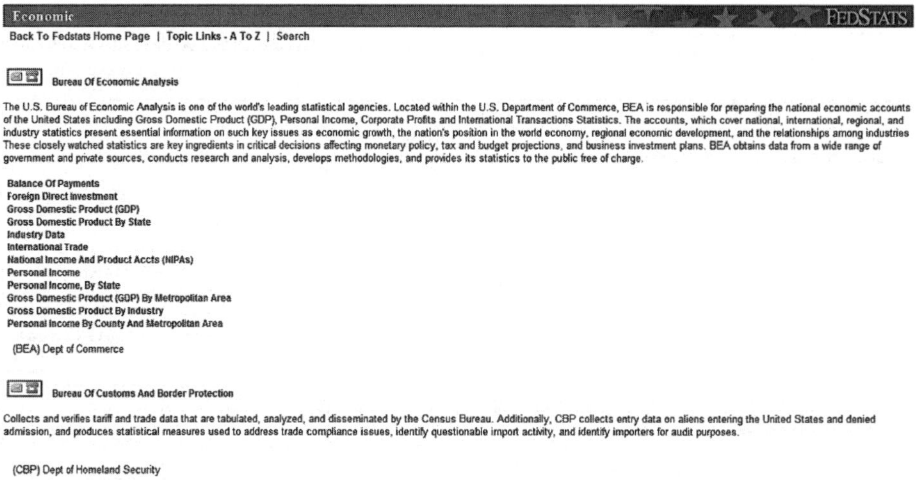

Economic · · · · · · · · · · · · · · · · · · · ★ ★ ★ FEDSTATS

Back To Fedstats Home Page | Topic Links - A To Z | Search

Bureau Of Economic Analysis

The U.S. Bureau of Economic Analysis is one of the world's leading statistical agencies. Located within the U.S. Department of Commerce, BEA is responsible for preparing the national economic accounts of the United States including Gross Domestic Product (GDP), Personal Income, Corporate Profits and International Transactions Statistics. The accounts, which cover national, international, regional, and industry statistics present essential information on such key issues as economic growth, the nation's position in the world economy, regional economic development, and the relationships among industries These closely watched statistics are key ingredients in critical decisions affecting monetary policy, tax and budget projections, and business investment plans. BEA obtains data from a wide range of government and private sources, conducts research and analysis, develops methodologies, and provides its statistics to the public free of charge.

Balance Of Payments
Foreign Direct Investment
Gross Domestic Product (GDP)
Gross Domestic Product By State
Industry Data
International Trade
National Income And Product Accts (NIPAs)
Personal Income
Personal Income, By State
Gross Domestic Product (GDP) By Metropolitan Area
Gross Domestic Product By Industry
Personal Income By County And Metropolitan Area

(BEA) Dept of Commerce

Bureau Of Customs And Border Protection

Collects and verifies tariff and trade data that are tabulated, analyzed, and disseminated by the Census Bureau. Additionally, CBP collects entry data on aliens entering the United States and denied admission, and produces statistical measures used to address trade compliance issues, identify questionable import activity, and identify importers for audit purposes.

(CBP) Dept of Homeland Security

Figure 2.2 Screenshot of FedStats Economic Statistics (www.fedstats.gov/programs/economic.html)

(such as the Census Bureau's State Data Centers) for compilation and publication. Most states do publish some information on the state's economy, economic or industrial development, and employment and unemployment statistics. Once again you can easily find a state website by searching Google, Yahoo!, AltaVista, or other search engine. Another resource is the State and Local Government on the Net website at www.statelocalgov.net/, a site that provides convenient access to all state and local government sites by listing the states alphabetically. Frequently updated, this directory of official state, county, and city government websites also provides a list of topics to choose from plus listings of government grants, with applications.

COMMERCIAL PUBLISHERS

Many commercial publishers produce detailed and high-quality statistical sources. Industry research and averages are an important component of a business plan. Three key resources for operating and financial ratios for many industries are Leo Troy's *Almanac of Business and Industrial Financial Ratios, Dun and Bradstreet's Industry Norms and Key Business Ratios, and RMA Annual Statement Studies;* check your local library to see if they purchase these resources. While available on the Internet, the subscription costs for these services can be substantial. *RMA E-Statement Studies* at www.statementstudies.org/ allows users to purchase single-industry data online for a reasonable price. *Standard and Poor's Industry Surveys* only cover about 50 industries in a three-volume set, but the overview, ratios, and trends data are invaluable. Specific company ratio and balance sheet comparisons are provided under the Basic Analysis section. The financial ratios in the resources listed above are organized by either Standard Industrial Classification or the North American Industry Classification System. *Value Line Investment Survey Standard Edition* is another place to check for industry analysis and company data. Organized by industry, each of the 93 industry reviews contains current and future business environment descriptions and is followed by pages describing and evaluating individual companies. Yahoo! Finance (http://biz.yahoo.com/ic/) organizes its Industry Center alphabetically. Under any given selection, are details on "News," "Leaders & Laggards," "Company Index," "Related Industries," and more. Fee-based research reports are available, and overviews are presented for each industry with some industry ratios such as new profit margin, total debt to equity ratio, dividend yield, and more. The financial ratios in these resources will help you compare your projections with established companies in your industry. Find out more about financial ratios and how to figure them for your business in chapter 9, "Management."

■ BizStats.com

Due to the growth in small and franchised businesses in the United States, the market for popular statistics continues to grow and develop. An outstanding website for financial ratios, business statistics, and benchmarks is BizStats.com, at www.bizstats.com/. Here you can find profitability and operating ratios for corporations, S corporations, and sole proprietorships for industries such as furniture stores, electronics, gas stations, and sporting goods. You can find current ratios and balance sheet ratios by industry and sales by firm structure, for example. This site has financial and operating ratios for some industry segments. Even if your industry is not found here, this site will show you a net-profit risk for many sole proprietorships. The Brandow Company of Camp Hill, Pennsylvania, is a leader in online data analysis and has produced the data on this terrific site for small business statistics.

A wide range of industry directories provides information on industries and specific companies—that is, your competitors. You can also use existing firms' actual performance to validate your projections in your business plan. Listed below are two websites to check for industry information.

■ About.com Business and Finance: www.about.com/money/ (Accessed Spring 2011)

This large site has many parts and is at times a bit difficult to navigate. Use the search feature if you have trouble. This site covers the biotech/biomedical, composites/plastics, metals, nonprofits, and retail industries. The retail industry (retailindustry.about.com/), which is notoriously difficult to locate information about, is especially well done. Articles provide information on current retail trends, retail statistics, retail industry profile, apparel trends, consumer trends, and more. Also included are articles on retail strategy, store operations, store design and atmosphere, and branding.

 Market Research, Industry Research, Business Research:
www.virtualpet.com/industry (Accessed Spring 2011)

This major portal for researching companies and industries presents a step-by-step process to begin researching an industry. Here you can find sources to help you learn about legal issues, regulatory issues, competition, markets, and even a history of the industry for your new business. Additional links to industry portals are also available. Another linked site offers help on how to learn about a company.

BASIC STATISTICAL CONCEPTS

Every businessperson needs to be familiar with some key statistical concepts to use in business planning and projections. Above we have seen that the government and commercial publishers present us with both *descriptive statistics,* which utilize numerical and graphical methods to look for patterns and summarize and present that information in a set of data, and *inferential statistics,* which utilize sample data to make estimates or predictions about a larger set of data as an aid to decision making. Below I briefly define some of the concepts relevant to business statistics in general.

Sampling and Probability

Sampling is the process of selecting units (e.g., people, organizations) from a population of interest so that by studying the sample we may fairly generalize the results back to the population from which they were chosen. A sample is anything less than a survey of the full population. Population statistics are important to business owners and researchers, and while it would be best to collect information from each person in the population being studied, surveying each individual is usually not possible. Therefore, sampling is used to select a small but representative sample and make inferences or conclusions about the entire population. A good source to learn more about sampling, especially in relation to market research, is the *Marketing Research Kit for Dummies* by Michael Hyman and Jeremy Sierra.

Hyman, Michael and Sierra, Jeremy. *Marketing Research Kit for Dummies.* For Dummies, 2010. 408p. ISBN 0-4705-2068-X. $29.99 (with CD-ROM/DVD).

Hyman and Sierra present clear, concise advice with short, real-life examples on the topic of market research. Tools and techniques are described and explained, and a highlight of this work is that readers will learn how to write and design good questionnaires. The book contains advice on how to select and use a sample to see trends in your business or industry and local area.

Sampling is based on the theory of probability and can only be understood in those terms. Probability is the basis of sampling; it shows the likelihood or chances for each of various potential outcomes based on a set of assumptions about how the world works generally. Using the data from a random sample, you can infer knowledge or probability about the population from which the sample was drawn. The objective of sampling is to select a part that is representative of the entire population. For example, the television rating service Nielsen tracks the TV-watching behavior of a sample of viewers and makes inferences about the popularity of shows to the majority of TV viewers.

Earlier in this chapter we've looked at statistical sources produced by the Census Bureau. The Census Bureau uses sampling extensively to produce many of its publications. To be aware of when and how sampling is used to produce statistics, careful readers always check the introductory matter and footnotes to ascertain what methods were used for the statistics presented. When checking the source of statistics, ask yourself: (1) are the statistics self-serving, and (2) is the source biased? The government doesn't have any vested interest in presenting the population statistics, but when you use other sources for statistics, forecasts, or ratios, remember to keep the above questions in mind. Statistics work best when you combine them with your own judgment and common sense.

Forecasts, Projections, and Estimates

Forecasting is the use of known measurements to predict the value of unknown measurements that will occur at a later date generally no more than two years into the future. Forecasting always applies to the future, but is based on information about the ways in which variables have behaved in the past. In forecasting it is assumed that the behavioral patterns traced in the past will continue in the future. Business forecasting is a process that seeks to answer a variety of forward-looking questions about the operations of a company and the demands that will be placed upon it. Business forecasting cannot deliver absolutely accurate, error-free forecasts, but it can have a reasonably small margin of error and will reduce future uncertainty to a manageable level.

Statistical projections don't always yield accurate forecasts, because any analysis of trends depends on the assumption of stable political, economic, and social conditions. Projections are predictions made about the distant future, so they are more speculative and prone to error than forecasts. Projections cannot always take into account the effect of technological advances and manmade and natural disasters. Small business owners need to understand forecasting and projections because they are important elements in planning and control in any business. Management decisions must often be based on what is likely to happen in the future, which may be tomorrow, next week, or next year. To arrive at a sales forecast, the owner may start with an economic forecast, which considers trends in the whole economy.

An estimate is an approximation of an unknown value based on an extrapolation from a known value. Estimates may apply to any time—past, present, or future measurements. Statistical estimation finds a statistical measure of a population from the corresponding statistics of the sample. It's an estimate because it's not certain that the sample is an exact reflection of the entire population. An estimate draws a conclusion from the study of representative cases.

This quick overview of research sources and definitions will help you gather the information you need to decide what business you want to be in, a good location, how much money it will cost to start, and more. The following resources will help you understand business concepts more and find statistical sources.

REFERENCES

Starred titles are discussed in the chapter.

Print Resources

Boettcher, Jennifer C. and Gaines, Leonard M. *Industry Research Using the Economic Census: How to Find It, How to Use It.* Greenwood, 2004. 305p. ISBN 1-57356-351-X. $85.

This guide will help beginners use the Economic Census to recognize trends in different industries, provide help for marketing and targeting sales, and understand the key economic indicators of the U.S. economy. This handbook explains the census's concepts, methods, and vocabulary in everyday language and will help users locate needed census data. The authors also explain how business executives and researchers use the industry data. Use this resource as a place to begin researching your industry.

Burton, Virgil L. III. *Encyclopedia of Small Business,* 4th ed. Gale Cengage, 2010. 2v. 1,414p. ISBN 1-4144-2028-5. $631.

Arranged alphabetically, over 500 essays cover topics such as advertising media on the web, business start-up, employee compensation, franchising, health insurance options, e-commerce, product development, and tax planning. How those topics affect small business is, of course, emphasized. Bibliographic citations at the end of each topic point to additional sources of information. The master index at the end of volume 2 provides additional subject, organization, government agency, and legislation access. Written in a relevant and accessible format and manner, all types and ages of entrepreneurs will find this a useful reference.

**Dun & Bradstreet. *Industry Norms and Key Business Ratios,* annual.

This annual resource is very expensive, but some libraries still purchase it for their business collections. D&B analyzes nearly 800 business lines and can help small businesses make financial projections. If you haven't been able to find financial norms for your industry, try this resource.

**Hyman, Michael and Sierra, Jeremy. *Marketing Research Kit for Dummies.* For Dummies, 2010. 408p. ISBN 0-4705-2068-X. $29.99 (with CD-ROM/DVD).

This useful resource and companion CD provide hands-on tools to identify, obtain, record, and analyze secondary data. Hyman and Sierra present concise instructions and customizable forms for conducting your own primary research. You will understand fully the process of sampling, analyzing data, and reporting results. Find here tips on developing questionnaires for face-to-face, Internet, and mail surveys and how to identify techniques used by your competition and analyze their research. Tools and techniques are described and explained, and a highlight of this work is that readers will learn how to write and design good questionnaires. The book teaches readers how to select and use a sample to see trends in their business or industry and local area.

Leach, Robert. *Ratios Made Simple: A Beginner's Guide to the Key Financial Ratios*. Harriman House, 2010. 196p. ISBN 1-9066-5984-2. $22.99.

Ratios provide an effective method of understanding company accounts. Leach shows readers how to look at ratios to accurately to analyze a company. This book is divided into nine chapters on the topics of profitability ratios; investment ratios; dividend cover; margins; gearing; solvency ratios; efficiency ratios; policy ratios; and volatility. For each ratio, Leach provides a detailed definition, explains how it works, and describes its use. Learn how to calculate each ratio, what the ratio means, and how to apply the answers to business decisions.

**RMA Annual Statement Studies. Robert Morris Associates, annual.

These studies compile current and historical financial data for almost 350 industries by company asset and sales size. An annual volume is expensive, so check your library or its website for information on buying data for one industry (www.rmahq.org). The website is also described below in online resources. Banks use this information for analyzing business loan applications. Libraries have traditionally purchased these data for their business collections, but subscription costs keep rising.

**Small Business Sourcebook. Gale, 2v, annual.

This directory provides a wealth of information for the small business owner or manager. The small business profiles cover 340 different small businesses. Businesses profiled include catering, cooking schools, fish farms, antique shops, bookstores, and car washes, for example. Entries contain as many as 17 subheadings, such as start-up information, educational programs, reference works, sources of supply, statistical sources, trade periodicals, trade shows and conventions, consultants, and franchises and business opportunities. The "Small Business Topics" section covers budgets and budgeting, retailing, service industry, franchising, insurance, seasonal business, and more. Like the small business profiles, these entries have the same 17 subheadings and lead readers to many resources related to the topics. The sections on state listings and federal government assistance list programs and offices that provide information and support to small businesses. Check your library for this practical, well-organized source.

Strawser, Cornelia J. *Business Statistics of the United States*, 16th ed. Bernan Associates, 2011. 690p. ISBN—1-59888-486-9-. $154.

This comprehensive, classic business resource contains all kinds of data relevant to the economic performance of the U.S. economy. Historical data, over 77 years, including statistics on production, manufacturers' stocks, exports, and prices, are provided for a variety of U.S. industries. Over 3,000 economic time series, mainly from federal government sources, are included. This huge compilation of data enables users to observe past trends and provides the basis for projecting trends in the future. Part B presents a general description of

NAICS and its differences from SIC before presenting detailed industry data on the NAICS basis as far back as possible, usually the early 1990s. Part D includes state and regional data on personal income and employment back to 1972.

**Troy, Leo. *Almanac of Business and Industrial Financial Ratios.* Aspen, 2009. 801p. ISBN 0-8080-1898-1. $201.

This updated business reference standard covers 50 operating and financial factors in 195 industries. Troy derives the data from Internal Revenue Service figures on U.S. and international companies. Data for each industry have been subdivided into 13 categories based on company size. The variety of factors relating to operations, operating costs, financial performance, and an array of financial factors in percentages includes debt ratio, return on assets, return on equity, and profit margins. Tables are divided into 13 asset sizes to help with making comparisons.

**U.S. Department of Commerce. Bureau of the Census. *Statistical Abstract of the United States.* U.S. Government Printing Office, annual. Web version atwww.census.gov/compendia/statab/ (also available on CD-ROM).

This collection of statistics on U.S. social, political, and economic conditions provides statistics on things like the number of cell phones in the United States, average cost of a home in different regions, educational level in various parts of the country, fastest growing jobs, where population growth is happening, and more in over 1,400 tables and charts. First published in 1878, the data are collected from over 220 government and private agencies. Each chapter begins with a description of the data being presented and definitions of terms and concepts. Use the subject index to quickly locate the statistical tables you need. Most tables present information for the past 5 to 10 years. Footnotes under the tables provide source information.

■ Online Resources

About.com Business & Finance: www.about.com/money (Accessed Spring 2011).

This site provides a treasure trove of information, links, books, and other assorted help in learning new research and management skills and improving those an entrepreneur has already developed. Finding industry research is easy as well as articles on industries. Sections cover "Business Practices," "Industry," "Small Business" (sbinformation.about.com/), and more. Learn best business practices and leadership skills from experts. The area of the site under "Human Resources" will especially help users learn about human resources issues and managing employees.

American FactFinder: http://factfinder2.census.gov/home/ (Accessed Spring 2011).

This federal government source for information on population, housing, economic, and geographic data is easy to use and well designed. You can get a fact sheet for your community by just entering town, county, or zip code. A quick link gets you to the Decennial Census of Housing and Population, American Community Survey, Economic Census, or the Population Estimates program. A couple clicks under "Subjects A to Z" will get you to County Business Patterns, information on the NAICS codes, statistics about small business from the Census Bureau, the characteristics of business owners' database, and more. A glossary, FAQs, and search feature will also help you use this great, free resource.

**Bureau of Economic Analysis (BEA): www.bea.gov (Accessed Spring 2011).

This government website from the Department of Commerce produces a wealth of statistical information on the U.S. economy. Its mission is to produce and circulate accurate, timely, relevant, and cost-effective statistics and to provide a comprehensive, up-to-date description of U.S. economic activity. The ups and downs of the U.S. economy and regional economic development affect every small business in some way. The BEA's "U.S. Economy at a Glance" section will help you keep a close eye on what's happening in the economy. The BEA also produces the *Survey of Current Business*, a monthly publication that provides data on personal income, state and regional economic statistics, and more.

BEOnline: Business and Economics Online: www.loc.gov/rr/buisness/beonline/ (Accessed Spring 2011).

Compiled by the Library of Congress Business Reference Services for researchers, under "Subject Guides," you will find a lengthy list of business topics such as associations, business plans (forms), companies by industry, data sets, e-commerce, franchises, economic indicators, legal resources, and more. If you click on "Associations," you will enter an associations database that includes contacts, descriptions, addresses, and events data for the organizations listed. Over 10,000 business organizations in the United States are listed. Find here a link to the Herb Growing and Marketing Network or the Association of Bridal Consultants. Under the "Title Listing," you will find "Airlines of the Web," "America's Business Funding Directory," "American Chambers of Commerce Abroad," "American City Business Journals," and more.

**BizStats.com: www.bizstats.com/ (Accessed Spring 2011).

Find profitability and operating ratios for S corporations, partnerships, and sole proprietorships for industries such as furniture stores, electronics, gas stations, and sporting goods. This site has financial and operating ratios for many industry segments. Even if your industry is not found here, this site will show you a net-profit risk for many sole proprietorships. The Brandow Company of Camp Hill, Pennsylvania, is a leader in online data analysis and has produced the data on this terrific site for small business statistics.

**Bureau of Labor Statistics: http://stats.bls.gov/ocohome.htm (Accessed Spring 2011).

Find here publications such as the *Dictionary of Occupational Titles* and the *Occupational Outlook Handbook* online. The *Handbook* provides training and education needed, earnings, and expected job prospects for a wide range of jobs. Here's help to write job ads, job descriptions, and more. Also find out about current government regulations and legislation in regard to employees.

Department of the Treasury Internal Revenue Service (IRS): www.irs.gov (Accessed Spring 2011).

The IRS's Market Segment Specialization Program focuses on particular market segments, which may be an industry like auto body and repair, a profession like ministers, or an issue like aviation tax. These guides discuss common and unique industry issues, business practices, and industry terminology. These guides are produced and updated on an as-needed basis, so some are quite old; but you may find (in the overview of the bars and restaurants industry from April 2003, for example) that the information presented is very useful for your business.

**FedStats: www.fedstats.gov/ (Accessed Spring 2011).

The official website of the Federal Interagency Council on Statistical Policy is a gateway to statistics from over 100 U.S. federal agencies and is well organized and easy to use. Users can find information under "Links to Statistics," "Topic Links A–Z," "MapStats," and "Statistics by Geography from U.S. Agencies." MapStats provides statistical profiles of states, counties, cities, congressional districts, and federal judicial districts. The "Statistical Reference Shelf," a bit farther down on the home page is a large collection of online reference sources such as the *Statistical Abstract of the United States.* You will find a variety of other sources, such as the *State and Metropolitan Area Data Book* and *Digest of Education Statistics,* which will provide statistics on many topics of interest to entrepreneurs. On the other half of the page, "Links to Statistical Agencies," under "Agencies by Subject," click "Economic" on the drop-down arrow to lead you to a list of periodic economic censuses." Below this area, you'll find "Data Access Tools," which link users to agency online databases.

**Market Research, Industry Research, Business Research: www.virtualpet.com/industry (Accessed Spring 2011).

This major portal for researching companies and industries presents a step-by-step process to begin researching an industry. Here you can find sources to help you learn about legal issues, regulatory issues, competition, markets, and even a history of the industry for your new business. Additional links to industry portals are also available. Three other linked sites offer help on "How to Learn about a Company by Examining Its Products," "How to Review, Evaluate, Critique a Web Site," and "How to Conduct a Patent Search."

Plunkett Research, LTD. Plunkett's Industry Research Center: www.plunkettresearch.com (Accessed Spring 2011).

Plunkett Research offers business intelligence, industry trends, statistics, marketing research, and corporate profiles that give researchers and business owners a variety of statistics and information. For example, the section on advertising, branding, and marketing broadly covers data and areas of interest ranging from branding strategy and trends to emerging technology and an in-depth analysis of "The Advertising 350." Included are data on radio and TV, direct mail, and online advertising as well as public relations. Trends in areas like advertising agencies, marketing consultants, and global markets are reviewed. Contacts for business and industry leaders, industry associations, Internet resources, and magazines are provided. Examples of statistics included are worldwide advertising growth from 2000 to 2015, advertising spending of U.S. top 10, cable and pay TV revenues and expenses, and annual television advertising expenditures in the United States from 1970 to 2007. The company profiles are a major section, and companies are arranged alphabetically. Details for each company contain rankings within industry grouping, business description, major brands, divisions and affiliations, officers, addresses, phone and fax numbers, URLs, number of employees, locations, and growth plan statements. If your industry is covered by Plunkett Research, these authoritative reports will help you make good business decisions.

**RMA E-Statement Studies: www.statementstudies.org/ (Accessed Spring 2011).

After 85 years in the business previously known as Robert Morris and Associates, Risk Management Association's *Annual Statement Studies* are one of the standards in business ratios. This resource will help you show investors that you understand your business and are prepared to compete. Financial ratio benchmarks are included for over 700 industries, now using the NAICS codes. Trend data are available for five years. Using these data, you can make more informed decisions for your new business.

SBDCNET: www.asbdc-us.org/ (Accessed Spring 2011).

The Small Business Development Center National Information Clearinghouse provides timely, web-based information to entrepreneurs. Small Business Development Centers (SBDCs) are located in all 50 states, and they offer free, confidential business counseling. This website provides information on business start-up, e-commerce, industry research, marketing, trends, and more. Templates for business plans and marketing tools are also available. A free newsletter will help you keep up on trends in small business. Entrepreneurs will find plenty of links and information here to help them plan and run their new business.

Small Business and Entrepreneurship: http://libguides.unm.edu/small_business (Accessed Spring 2011).

This web page was created and is maintained by me. Some of the resources, especially under the "I need to find ..." tab, are specific to the University of New Mexico. However, under the tab "Selected Internet Resources," you will find links to many free small business gateways and legal and government sites. Use my guide as a gateway to many of the websites—such as Business Owners Idea Café, Entrepreneur.com, and MoreBusiness—listed in this resource. My colleagues and I also publish other research guides on business topics such as marketing and advertising, company and industry information, and business basics. Use all of these guides to help you find more information to start and run your new business.

**State and Local Government on the Net: www.statelocalgov.net/ (Accessed Spring 2011).

This site provides convenient access to all state and local government sites by listing the states alphabetically. Frequently updated, this directory of official state, county, and city government websites also provides a list of topics to choose from plus listings of government grants, with applications. Links are provided to even the smallest counties or state agencies if they have a web presence. The directory lists 10,792 websites and can be searched by state, topic, or local government name.

The Thomas Register, now Thomas Net: www.thomasnet.com/ (Accessed Spring 2011).

This well-known, multivolume set is now available online. It lists data on more than 150,000 manufacturing companies in the United States and Canada by type of product, company name, and location. Find your competitors and suppliers in this comprehensive listing of North American manufacturers; search by product, service, company, or brand.

**U.S. Census Bureau: www.census.gov/ (Accessed Spring 2011).

This web page is the best place to start searching for the multitude of data produced by Census Bureau programs, publications, and statistics. The home page groups the data under "Census 2010," "People," "Business," "Geography," "Newsroom," "At the Bureau," and "Special Topics." Under "Business," you can click on the "Economic Census," "NAICS," "Survey of Business Owners," "E-Stats," and "Foreign Trade." Under "People," business owners will be interested in income statistics, housing data, and more. Analyzing the demographic trends in the United States allows businesses to forecast future demands for their products or services. The "New to Using Census Bureau Data" page is very helpful for locating information quickly. A catalog, a search feature, and links to related sites are also accessible on the left side of the home page. Use this site frequently to help start and grow your business.

**USA.gov: The U.S. Government's Official Web Portal: www.usa.gov/ (Accessed Spring 2011).

The "Explore Topics" tab will interest and amaze first-timers. Topics include "Environment, Energy and Agriculture," "Money and Taxes," "Reference and General Government," and "Science and Technology." On USA.gov, under "Business and Economy," clicking on "Data and Statistics" brings up a long list of links to resources chock-full of statistics. "U.S. Economic Indicators" (http://Economic Indicators.gov) is brought to you by the Economics and Statistics Administration at the U.S. Department of Commerce. Its mission is to provide timely access to the daily releases of key economic indicators from the Bureau of Economic Analysis and the U.S. Census Bureau, and it provides timely access to the daily releases of key economic indicators from the Bureau of Economic Analysis. Also, under "Data and Statistics," find health statistics, labor statistics, searchable government databases, and searchable bibliographies. Spanish translation of the site is also available. You can e-mail questions about the site and the statistics or telephone for help, too. Your taxes pay for the collection, compiling, and publishing of these statistics, and they are available for your use.

Valuation Resources.com: www.valuationresources.com (Accessed Spring 2011)

This commercial site provides links to many industry information resources for many industries. It pulls together industry resources from trade associations, industry publications, and research firms. Topics included are industry outlook, financial ratios, salary surveys, economic data, and public market data. Check here to see what information is available on your industry.

START UP 3

To this point, you've decided you have entrepreneurial talents and you now know where to find many different types of business and industry information, statistics, economic indicators, and so on. In this chapter, we'll examine some of the sources you'll want to consult as you begin your business planning—sources that will help you in everything from selecting a type of business and determining structure to how to get licenses and permits. Only one chapter completely focuses on e-commerce or e-business; but keep in mind that if you are starting a dot-com business or e-commerce, basically everything that is needed for a successful brick-and-mortar business is needed for an e-business to be successful as well. Let the decision making begin.

SELECT YOUR BUSINESS

What type of business should you start? Many people already have an idea and just need to determine if it's viable. Experts advise that you choose something related to what you love, enjoy, and won't mind spending thousands of hours and dollars working on. The first question to ask yourself is, If you could do anything in the world, what would you truly like to do with your time, daily, twelve or more hours each day? There are probably a number of things that will occur to you. Make a list of them, and prioritize the list.

Other leading questions that may help you in the decision-making process are, What don't you want to do? and What did you hate about previous jobs? These questions may help you rule out some of the ideas swimming in your head.

Another important, even vital, question is, Does the market need your product or service? Most businesses provide a service to individuals or companies or they manufacture a product for individuals or businesses. Can you provide something better or more affordable than what is already being offered by other businesses?

Finding the perfect fit for you with a business may be difficult, but if you lack the drive and passion to overcome challenges and obstacles, success will be elusive. Time spent determining what business you want to start is time well spent.

A CAUTIONARY NOTE

There are five common mistakes that entrepreneurs often make when choosing their business. Review the list, and remember them.

1. Overestimating demand for your product or service; be realistic as well as optimistic.

2. Inadequate planning. One of the main reasons businesses fail is that the entrepreneur has not researched and planned every step of the way. Never guess, and always do the research.

3. Not asking for help and advice and not listening to it. It is essential that you fully appreciate your own strengths and weaknesses. It is vital that you recognize who can best help you with each step of developing your business plan. Get free help when possible, but don't be afraid to pay a consultant, lawyer, or accountant.

4. Inadequate funding. Seek and obtain an adequate amount of financing because inadequate funding is a difficult problem to overcome. Opening on a shoestring may sound romantic, but it's not sound business practice.

5. An unsuitable legal structure. Utilizing the appropriate legal structure is essential to limit potential liability for the new business owner.

If you have several business ideas and want to check a resource that will give you an overview of them, try the *Small Business Sourcebook* from Gale Publishing. This annual directory provides a wealth of information on nearly 350 different choices for the small business owner/manager. Each profile provides start-up information sources, associations, educational programs, reference works, sources of supply, statistical sources, trade periodicals, trade shows and conventions, consultants, franchises, and libraries and research centers relating to businesses such as coffee shops, dry cleaners, car washes, home furnishings stores, and many more. This excellent first source of current, relevant information should be consulted by every new business owner.

Small Business Sourcebook. Gale, annual. $405.

This directory provides a wealth of information for the small business owner/manager. In the over 300 small business profiles, users will find a long and complete list of resources including trade associations, licensing, trade publications, trade shows, franchises, sources of supply, etc. about the type of business from bagel shops to restaurants. Each resource in a profile has a complete citation as well as a short description. Often URLs or e-mail addresses are provided. The two-volume set helps entrepreneurs start up, develop, and grow their businesses.

A website that allows you to explore different businesses is Entrepreneur.com (www.entrepreneurmag.com) from *Entrepreneur Magazine.* Under the "Businesses Ideas" tab, you will find many ideas of current hot businesses, new ideas for businesses, and information on starting or growing established business lines such as restaurants or interior decorating. If you need ideas or help developing an idea, here's a great place to start.

RESEARCH YOUR BUSINESS AND INDUSTRY

Now that you've determined what you want to do and that the market needs this product or service, you need to start asking questions and doing some research to form a start-up plan. As mentioned previously, failure to plan is one of the most frequently cited reasons for small business failures. You will need to extrapolate the information on your industry, market, and competition from government reports, newspaper and magazine articles, trade associations, university studies, and other research. Some of this material is available online, and some will only be found by visiting a business research library.

Interviewing potential customers and suppliers and people already in the same or a similar business is an additional method of collecting current data. Before conducting interviews, you will probably want to identify a list of questions to ask. For example,

1. Would the interviewee be interested in this product/service that you're thinking of offering?

2. How much might they pay for it?

3. Could the product or service they currently use be improved, and how?

4. What do they see as trends in this industry/business?

If you know of people already in this type of business, you might approach them and ask if they can give you a few hours of their time to help you learn the ropes or offer to pay them as a consultant. Besides conducting personal interviews, a survey can also be used to ask questions of potential customers or your target market. If you can identify a product or service that is similar to your idea, find out everything you can about the companies involved. One way to learn from possible competitors is to become a customer and identify what they do well and what needs improvement.

To learn more about the industry your business is in, explore the Small Business Development Center (SBDCNet) National Information Clearinghouse website at www.sbdcnet.org/. Here you will find industry information links on many smaller and developing industries and businesses, including the arts, energy/fuels, e-commerce, pets, and more. You can easily identify your North American Industry Code to use when you research your industry in many sources. Start your industry research at this user-friendly site.

FIND TRADE ASSOCIATIONS

Trade associations are an important resource for any new business. Everyone needs contacts or a network, and you'll be no exception when you are running your own business. Joining a trade association, such as the National Retail Federation for small retailers, that is relevant to your industry (and nearly every industry has one) is a great way to get access to any research they have conducted on your industry as well as a way to network with seasoned professionals. Trade association members usually receive a copy of a monthly or quarterly newsletter; this will help you find out what's happening in the industry as well as within the association. These associations exist to provide networking, pooling of resources, sponsoring of conferences, and, of course, publishing special reports and statistics on the industry. They also devote time and resources to keeping tabs on and influencing what's going on at all levels of government. Trade associations can even help you find professionals, like lawyers and accountants, who specialize in your industry. As mentioned above, the *Small Business Sourcebook* is a good resource for trade associations, and below is an outstanding print source for locating trade associations with contact information. Many libraries will have copies of one or both of these sources:

Encyclopedia of Associations. Gale, annual. $2,500.

This annual is a comprehensive list of national organizations provides a brief entry for each one, including names, addresses, telephone numbers, URL, cost of membership, and a short description of the organization's publications and members. Organizations are grouped in general subject areas. Indexes provide access to the organizations by name, keyword, and geographic area. An international directory is also available. This work is a standard in the field and one that any small business owner should know about.

Trade associations can also be located online. Using any search engine, such as Yahoo! or Google, you will find a wide variety of associations. A sample search might include "trade associations" and the name of your state or "business associations" and the name of your state. If too many irrelevant associations surface this way, add your industry, such as "retail grocer" or "construction" to narrow the search.[1] Another approach is to use a subject directory, such as Yahoo!'s, which can be found at the following lengthy address: http://dir.yahoo.com/Business_and_Economy/ Organizations/Trade_Associations/. This directory lists national and international associations alphabetically, and it can be searched by keyword. The Library of Congress also sponsors Business and Economics Online+ (BEOnline+) at http://lcweb. loc.gov/rr/business/beonline/. BEOnline began in 1996 as an experimental project to provide access for Internet resources related to the practice or study of entrepreneurship and small business. BEOnline+ expands the project to include additional subject areas in the humanities and social sciences. You will find a short page of links for associations. More associations can be found under the "Industries" page.

A few specific URLs for small business general associations as examples are listed below alphabetically with a short description:

Entrepreneurship Institute: www.tei.net (Accessed Spring 2011).

Established in 1976, this institute provides encouragement and assistance to entrepreneurs and unites financial, legal, and community resources to foster success of their companies. A monthly newsletter and periodic president's forums are available to members.

Minority Business Development Agency (MBDA): www.mbda.gov (Accessed Spring 2011).

Through its minority regional and district business development centers, the MBDA helps new ventures and established businesses seek working capital, start-up business financing, and access to markets. Key sections include "BizDev Central," "Opportunities and Partnerships," "Press and Media," and "Research Library." It publishes *Demographic Trends*, *Industry Trends*, and *Finance*. The "BizDev Central" tab will help users locate local minority business resources, business tools, and more. Another MBDA development program is the Native American Business Enterprise Centers or American Indian Enterprise Development (www.ncaied.org/default.php).

National Association for the Self-Employed: www.nase.org (Accessed Spring 2011).

The self-employed and microbusinesses (up to 10 employees) join this group for support and advocacy. Use the "Tax Resource Center" for updates on changes and tips on filing your taxes. The *Self-Employed Magazine* has articles on various topics related to small businesses.

National Federation of Independent Businesses (NFIB): http://nfib.com (Accessed Spring 2011).

This long-established and well-known national advocacy organization represents small, independent businesses in Washington, D.C. The NFIB aims to impact public policy at the

---

1. When you put quotation marks around a phrase in a search engine, the search will look for the phrase instead of each individual word. Therefore, "trade associations" would be searched by Google instead of "trade" and "associations." Hopefully, you will get fewer hits and fewer false hits with such a search.

state and federal level and be a key resource for small businesses. On its site, you can see what impact the approximately 400,000 members have and read other articles of interest to small businesses. Members have access to discounts on business products and services. Anyone can access the "Business Resources" section with helpful, practical articles for entrepreneurs on financing, franchises, business structure, and more.

Below are listed a couple of sites for special sectors of small business owners:

National Association for Women Business Owners: www.nawbo.org (Accessed Spring 2011).

This group has chapters located throughout the United States and sponsors national and regional conferences, provides networking opportunities, and sponsors awards. The Center for Women's Business Research, part of the National Foundation for Women Business Owners, produces original groundbreaking research to show the economic and social contributions of women-owned firms.

FIND NEWSPAPER AND MAGAZINE ARTICLES, TRADE PUBLICATIONS, AND NEWSLETTERS

Start your research by doing an industry overview and then move to specific companies in that industry. Periodicals are one of the best resources for current industry statistics as well as trends in the industry and the economy that are affecting companies. For some lists of trade publications grouped by business type, visit the Business Owners Idea Café at www.businessownersideacafe.com, and some of the publications will give you a free one-year trial subscription to see if you can use the information they provide. At the top of the page, you'll see the "Business Ideas" tab. Near the bottom of the list is "Discuss Your Ideas in CyberSchmooz." If you click on it, you will see business ideas discussions, and on the left side of the screen about halfway down, you'll see "Take Out Info" and below that "Free Trade Publications." The number of publications listed under each subject varies, but you'll probably find something of interest related to your new business.

Another way to find trade journals online by industry is to use Direct Contact PR at www.directcontactpr.com/jumpstation/index.src. Just select a media type, magazine, and then a magazine subject. It brings up a list. Sometimes a website is cited or the entire journal is available or sometimes just some of the articles. Thousands of publications can be located here. For example, *All About Beer* (under "Beverages") brings up the website http://allaboutbeer.com/. Another example is *Beverage World International* at www.beverageworld.com/, which features lists and rankings of soft drinks, bottled water, and beer plus many links about alcoholic and nonalcoholic drinks.

Large periodical indexes are generally available through local libraries and are usually online. Check with your local librarian to see if the library subscribes to ProQuest, EBSCO's *Business Source Complete*, or Gale's *Business and Company Resource Center*. If you are familiar with searching the Internet, you will have no problem

Figure 3.1 Screenshot of Small Business Help: Business Owners Idea Café (www.businessownersideacafe.com). Used with permission.

searching these databases. Articles on new developments and trends in industries or companies can be found by searching company names or the industry. Major business publications such as the *Wall Street Journal* will provide information on economic and business trends that may impact your new venture. Large city newspapers such as the *Los Angeles Times, Washington Post,* or *New York Times* are also indexed in large periodical indexes and can be searched in the same way. Local business journals and newspapers can provide you with data on your area; usually either local indexes or the large indexes will help you find information on subjects.

Another good resource to help you investigate business ideas is John Mullins's book, *The New Business Road Test.* Use his practical advice and real-world examples to give your new business idea a better chance at success. Learn what makes a viable business model and why good business ideas fail.

Mullins, John. *The New Business Road Test: What Entrepreneurs and Executives Should Do Before Writing a Business Plan,* 3rd ed. FT Press, 2010. 336p. ISBN 0-273-73279-X. $19.99.

Before writing a business plan or investing any money, use Mullins's new version of the seven domains model for assessing new business ideas. Learn how to run a customer-driven feasibility study to assess that new business opportunity. Updated case studies use real businesses like Honda and Starbucks to illustrate industry trends and opportunities. What are critical success factors and niche markets? Avoid the "me too" trap and more. Chapter 13 has been rewritten to make the Industry Analysis Checklist more understandable. Use his practical advice and guidance to help your new business succeed.

Determine who is your market before you invest time and money in a business with a shrinking market or no market at all.

See chapter 2 for more sources of statistics and industry data. Also, if during this planning phase of starting a new business, you decide that maybe you'd like to purchase an established business, one resource you might try is BizBuySell (www.bizbuysell.com). Here you will find a great deal of information about buying and valuing an established business. Also, check chapter 5 on franchising.

DETERMINE YOUR BUSINESS STRUCTURE

After deciding what type of business you're going to start and researching the industry, competition, and economy, you must decide the legal or business structure. This determination is one of the most important decisions that the new business owner can make. Depending on your choice of business structure, you may be personally liable if your business is sued for tax liabilities, tortious injuries (slip and fall), or other problems. This decision can also determine your ability to sell your interest in the business, influence the ease of later capital infusions, and affect the relationship between co-owners.

The primary forms of ownership in the United States include sole proprietorship, general partnership, limited partnership, C corporation, S corporation, and limited liability company (LLC). These forms will be briefly discussed here. If you have any doubts about which one best fits your needs, the number of owners in your business, and financial exposure you can accept, research the forms more thoroughly (check the References for print and online resources), and consult an attorney.

Sole Proprietorship

This simplest, most common form of legal structure means you are the business and the business is you. The main advantages of the sole proprietorship are:

1. The owner has complete authority and control, and it's the easiest and cheapest form to set up and terminate.

2. It can easily be changed to a partnership or corporation.

3. The government tends not to regulate.

The disadvantages of a sole proprietorship include:

1. As owner, your personal assets are at risk, and all business obligations remain on you.

2. The business ends with death or departure of the owner.

Partnership

A partnership is a business relationship involving two or more owners who share management responsibilities, profits, and all liability. A partnership agreement has been compared to a prenuptial agreement, but it is usually more complicated. This complex agreement should be created by a lawyer and typically covers:

1. Financial contribution of each partner.

2. Management and control of each partner.

3. Profit/loss sharing.

4. Responsibilities and duties.

5. Term of the partnership.

6. Guidelines for admitting new partners.

7. Right of first refusal (other partners have the right to purchase withdrawing partner's interest before that partner can offer it to someone else).

8. Stated policy on how a deceased partner's interest will be handled.

A partnership is not considered as a separate taxpayer so profits or losses are passed through individual income tax returns proportionate to the ownership percentage (see chapter 11, on legal and tax issues, for more information). Two types of partnerships exist: a general partnership and a limited partnership. A limited partnership is based on a general partnership and consists of one or more general partners and one or more limited partners who have restricted or limited responsibilities and liabilities. *Silent partner* is a term that is often used to describe these agreements because limited partners have no voice in the day-to-day business operations and management. Limited partnerships are a method of obtaining investments in a business with limited financial exposure as well as limited exposure to lawsuits for the investor.

Advantages of partnerships include:

1. Shared power and responsibility along with complementary skills.

2. Partners' investments bring additional funds.

3. Tax rate is lower than corporate rate.

4. Partnerships can easily be incorporated.

5. Partnerships are relatively inexpensive and easy to start and operate.

Disadvantages of partnerships are:

1. All partners are responsible for all the other partners' liabilities and debts for the partnership.

2. The partnership terminates upon the death of a member unless prior arrangements are made in the initial agreement.

3. Disagreements between partners can affect the success and operation of the business.

Corporations

A C corporation is a legal entity whose organizational structure has been established in accordance with state laws and given certain rights and responsibilities. In its simplest form, a corporation can have one shareholder or stockholder who owns 100% of the stock, is chair of the board, and president of the company. The sole voting stockholder can nominate and elect individuals to serve on the board of directors. For specifics on state requirements for C corporations, check with the secretary of state in your state. Corporations must conform to numerous regulations and file certain forms in a timely manner, so verify your state and federal procedures with a local lawyer.

Under S corporation structure, income losses, deductions, and credits of the corporation are passed through its shareholders to be included on personal income tax returns. Organizational requirements for corporate structure must still be met and maintained. The S status exists only for reporting taxes and can easily be changed to a regular corporate tax structure. Not all states recognize the S corporation, which means that you would pay federal individual taxes, but state taxes would be paid at the corporate rate. Check with an accountant and lawyer for recommendations on your specific situation. The advantages of corporations are:

1. Your business has a legal life of its own.

2. It's easy to raise capital by selling stock or shares in the company or transferring stock to key employees as an incentive or benefit.

3. A corporate structure allows each owner to separate personal assets from company assets.

4. Corporations are granted tax deductions not available to other forms of businesses.

Disadvantages of corporations include:

1. Corporations have more complex start-up procedures and maintenance with higher costs to meet legal requirements.

2. If shareholders are involved, decision making can be more complex.

3. Taxes may be higher as corporate tax rates are higher than individual ones, and dividends are taxed as profits and then as income to the shareholder.

Limited Liability Company

Limited liability company is the newest business structure in this country. An LLC contains the tax advantages of a partnership with the limited personal liability of a corporation. An LLC must issue stock but can issue two classes of stock—for voting and nonvoting members. Advantages of an LLC include:

1. It allows an unlimited number of stockholders who need not be U.S. citizens.

2. It requires less paperwork than corporations and limits the liability of the owners.

3. It avoids being taxed twice like C corporations are.

Disadvantages of a limited liability company are:

1. The organizing costs are as high as corporations.

2. The states are interpreting the legalities of an LLC differently, which sometimes involve high fees and additional taxes.

Below are several resources to check first when you're deciding on your business structure.

Harrington, Judith. *The Everything Start Your Own Business Book,* 3rd ed. Adams Media, 2010. 320p. ISBN 1-440-50407-5. $19.95.

With Harrington's straightforward advice, you can make sure your business flourishes. This third edition is completely revised and updated. Learn about business structures and which might work best for your business and why. Here you will find information on green businesses and making your business greener, how to use the latest social media to market your business, using leased employees, and more about your tax and payroll responsibilities. The accompanying CD is loaded with business-plan examples, useful lists, sample letters, and important forms.

Tyson, Eric and Schell, Jim. *Small Business for Dummies,* 3rd ed. John Wiley, 2008. 432p. ISBN 0-470-17747-0. $21.99.

This enterprising guide explains how to write a business plan, manage your costs and your time, create the right legal framework for your business, find financing, and understand financial statements. Financial ratios and how to determine them is also well covered in plain, simple language. Develop a winning marketing strategy, and hire the right employees. The For Dummies format includes tear-out cheat sheets, top 10 lists, and dashes of fun and humor.

ESTABLISH YOUR BUSINESS IDENTITY

Naming or identifying your business holds it together and should be a fun, personal, and professional activity that uses your creative powers to the max. Try to find something that represents the feel of your business and is infused with your personality. Be sure to consider these aspects or issues as you brainstorm:

1. Alphabetical placement (as in the Yellow Pages and other directories) should be considered, because a name at the beginning of the alphabet has major benefits since people often start at the top of a list and work their way down.

2. Personalization, or whether you should include your name. Whether you choose to use your name or someone else's probably depends on personal preference and the type of industry.

3. Depictive or representational names that connect to the kind of business you are in are sometimes helpful. People associate the name with the product or service.

4. A play on words such as puns can help or hurt your cause, but try to stay away from too cute. A clever name that sets you apart from competitors is a real plus, but often a straightforward, informative name works best.

5. Expandability is important, so don't get too specific. Adding "Etc." or "and More" can give one room for diversification.

6. Trademark-ability is a complex process, but in the future you might want to consider it. See more information about trademarks below and in chapter 11.

7. Internet domain availability is important even if you have no immediate plans to use the Internet. Check to see if [the name you want].com has been registered and, if not, register it immediately. One good website to use in this search is www.internic.com. If you are new to the world of domain names, this site can provide some basic information on domains and has been designed to provide the public with information regarding Internet domain name registration. See chapter 11, on legal and tax issues, for information on registering a domain name and checking to see what ones are available. If your domain name has already been registered, you might want to consider changing it slightly or find a variation that you can register as a dot-com.

In any case, you must pay attention to the laws of business names and trademarks in selecting your name. To begin learning the basics about trademarks (and patents), a good place to start is by reading the information on the U.S. Patent and Trademark Office website at www.uspto.gov. Here you will find FAQs and guidelines to help you understand the basic ideas and types of trademarks available. You can search trademarks to see if your idea has already been trademarked. You can e-mail or call the Trademark Assistance Center with your questions too. It's possible to apply for a trademark online, but a lawyer is useful in guiding you through this tricky procedure. The site also provides a list of trademark lawyers. Depending on your chosen legal structure, you will have to follow some specific rules for registering your business's name and protecting its identity. And, in today's world of the Internet, growing national chains, and mail order, checking local sources in your state is not enough.

In Peri Pakroo's *The Small Business Start-Up Kit*, you will find an excellent chapter on "Picking a Winning Business Name." Nolo Press is the publisher of this book, and on its website (www.nolo.com) you will find an article under "Business Name, Location & Licenses" entitled "Registering Your Business Name" by attorney Richard Stim. This article is short but thorough and will help you cover your bases. Readers are also referred to Peri H. Pakroo's e-guide from Nolo: *Trademark Basics for Naming a Business*. Keep in mind that if you choose a business name that has no part of your name, then you will need to file a fictitious business name statement, sometimes called an assumed business name or doing business as (DBA) name with your county or city clerk and with your state's secretary of state. Resources in chapter 11 cover the legalities of name more thoroughly. In most books about starting a business, there is some information on business names, but be as thorough as you can to save yourself grief later when your business is established.

FINANCIAL STATEMENTS

As you begin the process of estimating your sales and expenses for your new business, keep in mind that, at this time, these numbers are guesses. You must conduct your research and make your best estimates based on that research. The basics are provided here, and it is recommended that you consult several of the sources at the end of the chapter and/or an accountant to help you develop your financial plan. You will need to develop three critical financial statements as part of the planning process, and most experts suggest projecting for three years.

Start with the cash flow statement. This statement monitors the changes in your cash during a set period of time. Estimate here your gross receipts on sales for the first year and then break it down into monthly income. If you know of any seasonal highs or lows for your business, include those in your estimates. Also list any invested capital. Below this, estimate your monthly expenses. Just like a home budget, you will need to include utilities, insurance, supplies, raw materials, taxes, any loan payments, travel, and so on. Then subtract your expenses from your income each month. This tool is very important because if you run out of cash, you could be out of business. Monitor your cash flow at least monthly, if not weekly, when you first begin your business.

The income statement is similar to the cash flow statement and presents the proverbial bottom line. It is sometimes referred to as a statement of profit and loss and is really quite simple. Write down the total revenue you expect to receive from selling your products or services, and then subtract the total cost of operating your company. This number is your net profit. This statement will show your company's financial performance over a period of time.

Finally, the balance sheet details a company's assets (cash, inventory, equipment), liabilities (accounts payable, loans), and capital (equity in the business). It tells you how much money you'd have left if you sold absolutely everything and then paid every last one of your debts. Everything your company owns are its assets, the amounts you owe are your liabilities, and the difference between the two is the equity in your business. Financial information will help you develop a realistic budget and develop a vision for growth. With these three financial statements, you can also compare your company with other companies and with industry averages through financial ratios.

The best resource for help in preparing these three important financial statements is by Peri Pakroo.

Pakroo, Peri. *The Small Business Start-Up Kit,* 6th ed. Nolo Press, 2010. 368p. ISBN 1-41331-099-0. $29.99.

The chapter on financial statements is particularly helpful. Additionally, chapter 3, "Picking Winning Business Names That Won't Land You in Court," is a well-written collection of information and advice on trademarks, names, and domain names. The chapter on financial management is also very useful and thorough, as is the chapter on choosing a legal structure. Chapters on federal, state, and local start-up requirements, on insurance and risk management, and on taxes are also treasure troves of practical, useful information for every new business owner. A CD-ROM that is included with the book contains useful forms and a partnership agreement. Pakroo's outstanding book is mentioned many times throughout this book because it provides essential advice to new entrepreneurs in many areas of starting a new business and is a worthwhile purchase.

BREAK-EVEN ANALYSIS

In addition to financial ratios, every small business owner needs to know how to conduct a break-even analysis. When planning a new business or making decisions about offering new products or services, entrepreneurs need to find out at what point they will begin making money. The break-even point is where the income from sales exactly equals all the fixed and variable costs incurred in doing business. More sales will result in profit, and fewer sales will result in loss. Once you know all your costs and have estimated the selling price, you can calculate how many products or hours of your time you will need to sell to break even, or cover all your costs. When you know what you need to sell, you can look at market demand and competitors' market shares to determine whether it is realistic to expect to sell that much. Break-even analysis helps you think through the impact of price and volume relationships. A higher price for your product or service will achieve breakeven with fewer sales, but a lower price may attract more customers.

The further above breakeven that a business can operate, the greater its margin of safety is. Once you have determined your price and defined the break-even volume that you need to sell, you can set an annual target, broken down by monthly targets, to determine how to generate a reasonable profit.

Financial calculators from Dinkytown.net (www.dinkytown.net) will help you calculate many different financial ratios and break-even analyses. This large collection of financial calculators is brought to you by KJE Computer Solutions. Here you'll find current information on many business calculators like break-even analysis, cash flow calculator, working capital needs, and inventory analysis. Tax planning and calculators are also available for self-employment taxes and payroll deductions.

To monitor the progress of your business, you might want to plot targets for sales and actual sales on a graph. If your business is not achieving its targets, you can take remedial action immediately. A business owner should review sales volumes and income regularly to ensure that you are making a profit. Adjusting your sales price and increasing marketing efforts are two actions that can affect your business's profitability. Once again refer to Peri Pakroo's book, *The Small Business Start-Up Kit*, for more help on estimates to figure your break-even point. A good website for all things accounting is BusinessTown.com at http://businesstown.com/accounting/projections.asp. The article "Break-Even Analysis" thoroughly explains why an analysis is important and then walks you through an example using fixed and semivariable expenses. It will also help you find ways to lower your break-even volume.

BUSINESS LICENSES AND PERMITS

The list of businesses and professions that must be licensed varies by state, as does the list of businesses needing a permit to operate. Virtually every business owner will have to acquire a county, city, state, and/or federal license. You may need a seller's permit and federal ID number depending on your industry and local requirements. Seller's permits are required in states that impose sales tax. Each state uses a different agency to issue such permits. You may also need a permit to handle flammable materials, a food service license, or others. Don't think that if you have an e-commerce or Internet business that you are exempt from business licenses and permits; check with these agencies to see what's required.

Start by calling your city or county clerk's office or checking with your local chamber of commerce, and these may lead you to a state office. Securing the appropriate licenses for your business can be a challenging task. Most entrepreneurs will need a local or municipal license and some type of filing with their state. Call or visit the appropriate licensing departments in your area for information on fees and necessary forms. Planning and zoning departments often review license applications to determine whether the area's zoning ordinances permit your type of business in that jurisdiction. Besides providing government agencies with a tax-collecting strategy, licensing and permits shows your customers that you have complied with local regulations. Generally speaking, it can take from two to eight weeks to obtain the necessary permits and licenses.

BUSINESS LOCATION

Business location can be a major issue for retail operations and restaurants, so if you're planning one of these types of businesses, you must determine if your customers will be coming to you and how visible you need to be. For some businesses, success is based on choosing a strong, visible, accessible, and high-traffic location. On the other hand, some businesses are not impacted by location, and you can work from your home or any rented location. If your business has special needs (e.g., catering or mail-order food business), or if you've outgrown your basement or garage, you might look into a small business incubator. Incubators offer commercial space to start-up businesses at a below-market rate in order to foster entrepreneurism. They have different sponsors—usually universities, economic development groups, or state and local governments. New incubators open every month, and some are now located in rural areas as well as in cities. The basic services offered vary by locale but generally include:

1. *Low-cost flexible space and leases.* Keywords here are low cost (usually below-market rate) and flexibility, giving a new business space to grow if needed quickly.

2. *Shared business equipment and services.* Expensive equipment such as fax machines, copiers, computers, and services such as bookkeeping, reception, and word processing are often among the choices offered. Sometimes access is included in the rent, and sometimes it is pay as you use.

3. *Business and technical assistance.* A team of experts or network of community support may help entrepreneurs in areas such as business planning, engineering, patent protection, and marketing.

4. *Financial assistance.* Expert help in preparing to secure a loan or gain access to federal and state research and development funds may be provided.

5. *Networking.* Associating with other small business owners in the incubator allows you to bond with people facing the same problems and issues your company may face. The mentoring and access to business contacts provided may be the most important value of an incubator. Partnerships with other businesses in the facility may be advantageous to your business.

To see if an incubator might be a fit to help your business off to a good start, analyze the costs and services, as well as policies and procedures. Business incubators screen new businesses and accept companies that are likely to succeed, have sufficient financing, are committed to success, will benefit from the incubator's help, and are able to build a growing business. Check out the website of the National Business Incubation Association at www.nbia.org for more information on incubators, locations in your area, and help in determining whether one is right for your business.

If you're a dot-com entrepreneur, keep in mind that operating an e-business from home or an office does not mean you can skip licensing. Like a brick-and-mortar business, a license will legitimize and establish your business in the view of local, state, and federal governments. If you have an income, you must pay taxes, and if you have a loss, you will want to use it to save you taxes. Local licenses are easy to obtain and inexpensive. For more information on starting an e-business, check out *Entrepreneur Magazine*'s website at www.entrepreneur.com. Tim W. Knox's article on "No Exemptions for E-Businesses" is excellent, and the section on online businesses includes how-to guides and information on building a website, expanding your online presence, and more.

INSURANCE

All businesses need business insurance to protect against losses. Uninsured losses will threaten your financial situation, so don't cut corners here. The type of insurance you buy depends on the specific coverage you need. Ask other business owners in your area which insurance agents or brokers they would recommend. Get quotes from several agents to compare quotes and gain a perspective on which types of insurance your business needs. Some types of insurance include business owner's policy, property, malpractice, liability, product liability, health, and business interruption. Property insurance usually covers vehicle damage, comprehensive damage, fire, crime, and inland marine. Liability covers general liability, but there's also product liability, automobile, and umbrella-type insurance to consider. To learn more about the types of insurance that would apply to your business, check out the Insurance Information Institute's website at www.iii.org or check with an insurance agent. The institute's site answers questions about how to save money on business insurance, whether you need professional liability insurance, what a business owner's policy covers, and more.

Everyone has different ways of thinking and working. Below is a list of resources that can help you work through the procedures of kick-starting your first business venture. Try several to see which ones work best for you. For researching your industry, go back and look at references listed in chapter 2 for additional assistance. Remember, planning is the key to a successful business. Good luck!

REFERENCES

Starred titles are discussed in the chapter.

■ Print Resources

Barrow, Colin. *Starting a Business from Home: Choosing a Business, Getting Online, Reaching Your Market and Making a Profit,* 2nd ed. Kogan Page, 2011. 306p. ISBN 0-749-46264-7. $24.95.

Barrow's second edition includes more exercises and end-of-chapter advice. Learn how to identify a business structure, how to do market research, ins and outs of building a website, and even hints on going global. Appendices provide ideas for home-based businesses, sources of help and advice, and ideas on raising necessary capital. The slight British slant may confuse some.

Broadsky, Norm and Burlingham, Bo. *The Knack: How Street-Smart Entrepreneurs Learn to Handle Whatever Comes Up.* Portolio, 2008 (and Kindle). ISBN 1-59-184221-2. $18.99.

This thoughtful guide stresses the thinking necessary to deal with many different situations and uses engaging examples and case studies to illustrate how their advice works. Find out how to learn the basics of accounting, establish goals, spot problems in the numbers, why you need cash to survive, and keep your perspective when dealing with challenges. Learn also the importance of gross profit.

Cagan, Michele. *Streetwise Incorporating Your Business: From Legal Issues to Tax Concerns.* Adams Media, 2007. 352p. ISBN 1-59-86909-41. $19.95.

Cagan educates readers on critical issues and long-term implications of the legal structure of your new business. Learn what state and federal regulations affect your corporation, find hidden costs associated with incorporation, and find out from the get-go the necessary tax planning strategies and required accounting practices. Also covered is information on choosing the best location and how to organize a board and shareholders meeting.

Castell, John. *Big Ideas for Small Retailers: Discover New Ways to Improve Your Business.* Global Management Enterprises, 2010. 146p. ISBN 1-934747-11-4. $21.95.

This comprehensive, excellent book will help you establish a new retail business and covers major issues like company image, financing, trade associations, finding and keeping customers, competitors, security, hiring and keeping good staff, using the Internet, and more.

Cooney, Scott. *Build a Green Small Business.* McGraw-Hill, 2008. 256p. ISBN 0-07-160293-3. $19.95.

The highlight of this work is the load of green start-up ideas, including green wedding planning and green travel planning. Find expert advice on market research, financing, key legal and insurance issues, and green franchises. Use the marketing, advertising, and networking techniques described here to build a loyal customer base. Learn how to create a business that builds your local community, heals the environment, and feeds the growing green demands. Also find valuable resources such as web links and contacts to help you succeed.

Croston, Glenn. *Starting Green: An Ecopreneur's Toolkit for Starting a Green Business from Business Plan to Profits.* Entrepreneur Press, 2009. 324p. ISBN 1-599-18355-2. $21.95.

Learn how to create new green businesses for the coming global green economy of conservation. Croston, a green scientist and entrepreneur, outlines how to discover eco-friendly opportunities, build a sustainable business plan, and attain a competitive advantage in today's green market. Many of Croston's ideas for marketing, funding, and basic operations are applicable to all new small businesses. Get your business off the ground and growing from day one.

daCosta, Eduardo. *Global E-Commerce Strategies for Small Business.* MIT Press, 2001. 230p. ISBN 0262041901. $24.95.

daCosta lays out the steps for beginning a global small business. Using examples from seven companies located in six different countries, he details the purchasing process and customer service, explains how to research new business opportunities and markets, recommends ways to utilize the web and other forms of new technology, and provides ideas for overcoming obstacles to international trade for small companies. Written in a casual, readable style, readers of all levels will gain something from this optimistic view of the global marketplace.

Davis, Charlene. *Start Your Own Senior Services Business.* Entrepreneur Press, 2010. 242p. ISBN 1-59918-359-5. $17.95.

In the next 25 years, the senior population in the United States will double. This work covers adult day care, relocation services, home care, transportation services, concierge, and travel services. Learn how to choose which opportunity is right for you, get licenses and certifications, set rates, and develop a business that fits your area's demographics and needs. The chapter on concierge service includes many of the smaller needs, such as companion, personal shopper, cleaning, personal chef, and more. Nicely organized and well written, you will find many similar books on specific industries or types of business, but this one stands out.

DeBaise, Colleen. *Wall Street Journal. Complete Small Business Guidebook.* Crown, 2009. 272p. ISBN 0-307-40893-0. $15.

This practical guide covers all the basics, such as business plans, funding, using technology, marketing, managing, and how to hire the right employees. The "Better Business Bureau's Worksheets for Estimating Start Up Costs" in the back are easy to use and well organized. Additionally, find secrets to locating extra money to support expansion or maintenance, executing an exit strategy, and managing vacations. DeBaise provides useful help for turning your dreams into a profitable business.

Dion, James E. *The Complete Idiot's Guide to Starting and Running a Retail Store.* Alpha, 2008. 368p. ISBN 1-59-257726-1. $19.95.

This industry is particularly attractive to entrepreneurs and small business owners. Dion is a well-known expert and consultant for companies like Maytag and Harley-Davidson. Provided here are practical, hands-on tips for many aspects of retail business, including choosing the right business model and finding an ideal location. With this well-organized and thoughtful book, learn some of the psychology and human behavior connected to buying and selling.

***Encyclopedia of Associations.* Gale, annual.

This comprehensive list of national organizations provides a brief entry for each, including names, addresses, telephone numbers, URL, cost of membership, and a short description of publications and members. Organizations are grouped in general subject areas.

Indexes provide access to the organizations, by name, keyword, and geographic area. An international directory is also available. This work has become a standard in its field.

Encyclopedia of Small Business Legal Forms and Agreements. Atlantic, 2010. 288p. ISBN 1-60138-248-1. $29.95.

This encyclopedia and CD-ROM identify the issues and problems that you, as a small business owner or manager, may face daily. Covered are the issues of incorporation, partnerships, business plans, insurance, employment policies, employee termination, job descriptions, sales and service contracts, bills of sale, invoices, venture capital, license agreements, letters of intent, domain names, and e-commerce contracts. Over 250 essential documents—including lists, forms, sample contracts, and human resources procedures—are included to help your business succeed. Organize your business and manage it while increasing your bottom line.

Entrepreneur Press. *Start Your Own Business,* 5th ed. Entrepreneur Press, 2010. 704p. ISBN 1-599-18387-0. $24.95.

Offered here are critical start-up essentials and tips on how to survive the first crucial three years. Commonsense solutions to common challenges when starting a new business are presented in a well-organized format. You will find useful forms, worksheets and checklists. Find out the secrets of successful entrepreneurs, and discover new digital and social media tools and how to use them effectively. Pinpoint your target market and find your niche.

Friedman, Caitlin and Yorio, Kimberly. *The Girl's Guide to Starting Your Own Business.* HarperResource, 2004. 272p. ISBN 0-06-052157-0. $21.95.

Full of practical, frank, and useful advice and presented in a straightforward, breezy style, this guide covers all the basics using charts, quizzes, checklists, worksheets, and interviews. In addition, the authors cover proposals, presentations, payroll taxes, selecting a lawyer and an accountant, and venture capital, with an emphasis on networking and public relations. Their knowledge and zeal are contagious.

Gegax, Tom. *The Big Book of Small Business.* HarperBusiness, 2007. 448p. ISBN 0-06120-669-5. $29.99.

This lively, practical guide will help you start, fund, and get your new business off the ground as well as craft a mission statement and create processes for continuous innovation. Gegax explains and illustrates the importance of effective leadership. The business plan can easily be adapted to a web-based company as well as a retail or service brick-and-mortar. Great for the beginner and also useful to those who have started a successful company but want to expand and enjoy their business life.

Good Small Business Guide 2010, 4th ed. A & C Black, 2010. 581p. ISBN 978-1-4081-2370-6. $24.99.

Besides helping you answer the question, "how can I be sure I've got what it takes to run a business?" this large reference work has sections on "Refining and Protecting Your Idea," "Finding Premises," "Communicating with Customers," "Managing Yourself and Others," and "Working Online." A large section on calculating ratios and creating financial statements as well as amortization, asset turnover, and more is also very useful for the new business owner. This edition has a British slant but has a great deal of useful information for all

English-speaking entrepreneurs. The directories in the back present a collection of print and online resources in a wide variety of business areas. This well-organized resource is a bargain.

Goodridge, Walt. *Turn Your Passion into Profit,* 2nd ed. Passion Profit, 2010. 338p. ISBN 0-9745313-2-4. $24.95.

Updated annually since 1999, this inspiring work advises readers to follow their passion. Goodridge, a writer for *Entrepreneur Magazine, Black Enterprise,* and others, motivates readers and provides the steps needed to achieve success as an entrepreneur. All the basic areas of starting and growing a small business are presented. Practical, down-to-earth advice to make the move from employee to self-employed businessperson is provided in a logical, well-organized format.

Gordon, Michael E. *Trump University Entrepreneurship 101: How to Turn Your Idea into a Money Machine,* 2nd ed. Wiley, 2009. 304p. ISBN 0-470-4671-83. $24.95.

Gordon, an entrepreneur, shares his lifetime of wisdom and covers all the bases. Pertinent topics in this new edition include Web 2.0, cloud computing, technopreneurship, and opportunity recognition in turbulent economic times. Also new in this edition are various analysis tools briefed in charts and exhibits that can be downloaded from the website for personal use. An "Action" section follows each chapter to motivate new small business owners to begin using what they learn.

Gottry, Steve. *Common Sense Business: Starting, Operating, and Growing Your Small Business— In Any Economy!* HarperBusiness, 2005. 368p. ISBN 0-06-077838-5. $19.95.

Gottry started and ran a large Minneapolis-based ad agency and video production firm, which failed after 22 years in business. You can learn from his mistakes. Well organized and clearly written, Gottry's book includes specific how-tos, such as ways to prioritize bills for payment when cash flow is limited. He explains how to find solutions to the questions and challenges you're facing daily. Learn how to begin to understand yourself, your employees, your vendors, and your customers. Using humor, Gottry will help you successfully manage your business through good times and bad.

Handelsman, Joel. *Launching Your First Small Business: Make the Right Decisions during Your First 90 Days,* 3rd ed. Toolkit Media Group, 2009. 216p. ISBN 0-8080-0211-5X. $14.95.

The purpose of this work is to lead entrepreneurs through the process of starting their first business. The first part, "Clearing the Preliminary Hurdles," helps readers answer questions such as, what do you want from self-employment, is there a market for your business idea, and can you afford to go into business. Chapters cover the topics of matching your skills with current opportunities in the marketplace, selecting professionals, marketing your business concept, and equipping and staffing the right facility and location. Especially useful is chapter 10, "Figuring the Cost of Opening Your Doors." A companion website, Business Owner's Toolkit Online at www.toolkit.com, provides a wealth of interactive forms and spreadsheets to customize for your business. There is a lot of free information here, but there is a charge for premium membership.

**Harrington, Judith. *The Everything Start Your Own Business Book,* 3rd ed. Adams Media, 2010. 320p. ISBN 1-440-50407-5. $19.95.

With Harrington's straightforward advice, you can make sure your business flourishes. This third edition is completely revised and updated. Here you will find information on green businesses and making your business greener, how to use the latest social media to market your business, using leased employees, and more about your tax and payroll responsibilities. The accompanying CD is loaded with business-plan examples, useful lists, sample letters, and important forms.

Hess, Edward G. and Goetz, Charles F. *So, You Want to Start a Business?* FT Press, 2008. 224p. ISBN 0-137-12667-0. $21.99.

Using real-life experiences, case studies, and research, the authors present 55 simple but indispensable rules for success. Especially important is their insight into the art and science of managing people, operations, and growth. Learn to set priorities, know your competitors, and create practical and efficient processes. Written in a simple but academic style, you will find help here to realize your business goals.

Holden, Greg. *Starting an Online Business for Dummies*, 6th ed. For Dummies, 2010. 432p. ISBN 0-4706-0210-4. $24.99.

As in other books of this series, readers find the basics of starting a business on the Internet. Holden's work is particularly helpful if you're thinking of adding an online element to your brick-and-mortar operation. E-commerce survival stories, best practices, and other resources to help you develop your new business are provided. The book contains good tips on selecting an online host, understanding website design, establishing a graphic identity, providing customer service, and providing various payment options. Some coverage of legal matters, trademarks, copyrighting, and taxes are included. If you like the For Dummies format and are thinking of joining the e-commerce world, this book will work for you.

Horn, Thomas W. *Unlocking the Value of Your Business: How to Increase It, Measure It, and Negotiate an Actual Sale Price—in Easy Step-by-Step Terms*, 3rd ed. Charter Oak Press, 2008. 273p. ISBN 0-8752-1016-3. $39.95.

A good way to really examine how your business is doing is to analyze it as a potential buyer would. Horn explains in simple, everyday language how to calculate the value of your business and how to maximize its market value. Practical advice on negotiating the acquisition contract and how to prepare and present your business to potential buyers is included. Buyers and sellers of a business will use this knowledge to negotiate price much more effectively. Horn clearly presents tried-and-true formulas for valuing your business.

Kaplan, Jennifer. *Greening Your Small Business*. Prentice Hall, 2009. 304p. ISBN 0-7352-0446-1. $19.95.

This practical guidebook will help your company become more competitive, profitable, and eco-conscious. Find ideas on reducing waste, saving energy, and green marketing. Find out how to tell your customers and stakeholders about your sustainable mission and keep your core customers happy while attracting a whole new group of eco-conscious consumers to your service or product. Learn about 50 ways to make your workplace greener as well. Develop a green business plan and be part of saving the planet.

Kawasaki, Guy. *Reality Check: The Irreverent Guide to Outsmarting, Outmanaging, and Outmarketing Your Competition*. Portfolio, 2011. 496p. ISBN 1-59184-394-4. $11.99.

Kawasaki has a solid business background, and this new book covers all aspects of starting and operating a great organization. With humor, the 12 sections deal with the realities of starting, raising money, planning and executing, innovating, marketing, communicating, competing, hiring and firing, and working in your own organization. Divided into lots of short chapters, you can sample ones that interest you at the time so it's an easy read for busy entrepreneurs.

Levonsky, Rieva. *Start Your Own Business,* 4th ed. McGraw-Hill, 2007. 700p. ISBN 1-599180-81-2. $14.95 (Kindle ed.).

Full of worksheets, tip boxes, charts, graphs, and illustrations, Levonsky's book provides practical, hands-on techniques to get you started in your own business. Learn how to conduct market research, develop a system for keeping your books and doing your taxes, create a winning business plan, harness the power of the Internet and social media, and learn about choosing a name and leasing versus buying equipment. Chapters are short and to the point. If you're a new entrepreneur with little or no business education or experience, this book will help you with the basics.

Mohr, Angie. *Financial Management 101: Get a Grip on Your Business Numbers.* Self-Counsel Press, 2004. 176p. ISBN 1-55180-448-4. $14.95.

Mohr helps new entrepreneurs plan the financial end of their business from the first financial statements through budgeting for advertising. Learn to measure your business success and how to find new opportunities. The chapter on ratio analysis will help readers learn what basic ratios tell them, what to do when ratios indicate a problem, and how to integrate ratios into your management reporting system. Case studies are presented throughout the book to help readers understand the importance of the concepts presented.

Morris, Michael. *Starting a Successful Business: Start Up and Grow Your Own Company,* 7th ed. Kogan Page, 2011. 176p. ISBN 0-74-94614-9. $24.95.

This new edition takes readers through all the important steps necessary to complete the start-up process. Morris discusses many of the challenges facing new businesses, selecting the best marketing strategies, ideas for an online presence, finding financing, and finding and training the best staff. Included are international case studies, an introduction to cloud computing, and suggestions on starting and running a green business.

**Mullins, John. *The New Business Road Test: What Entrepreneurs and Executives Should Do Before Writing a Business Plan,* 3rd ed. FT Press, 2010. 336p. ISBN 0-273-73279-X. $19.99.

Before writing a business plan or investing any money, use Mullins's new version of the seven domains model for assessing new business ideas. Learn how to run a customer-driven feasibility study to assess that new business opportunity. Updated case studies use real businesses like Honda and Starbucks to illustrate industry trends and opportunities. What are critical success factors and niche markets? Avoid the "me too" trap, and more. Chapter 13 has been rewritten to make the industry analysis checklist more understandable. Use his practical advice and guidance to help your new business succeed.

**Pakroo, Peri. *The Small Business Start-Up Kit,* 6th ed. Nolo Press, 2010. 368p. ISBN 1-41331-099-0. $29.99.

Besides comprehensively covering the basics, chapter 3, "Picking Winning a Business Name," is a well-written collection of information and advice on trademarks, names, and domain names. The undated chapter on financial management is also very useful and thorough, as is the chapter on "Choosing a Legal Structure." Chapters on federal, state, and local start-up requirements, insurance and risk management, and taxes are also treasure troves of practical, useful information for every new business owner. The updated e-business chapter covers how to use social media to promote business, and search engine optimization strategies will help readers drive traffic to their websites. Additionally, a CD-ROM is included with the book and contains useful forms and a partnership agreement. Pakroo's outstanding book is mentioned many times throughout this book because it provides essential advice to new entrepreneurs in many areas of starting a new business and is a worthwhile purchase.

Paauwe, Theresia M. and Gilkerson, Linda D. *Self-Employment: From Dream to Reality,* 3rd ed. JIST Works, 2008. 198p. ISBN 1-59-357-520-3. $29.99.

Highlights of this new edition include guidance on writing a business plan, marketing on a shoestring, understanding financial statements, and keeping accurate records. The authors have a thorough and helpful style of writing that readers will find refreshing and easy to understand.

Pease, Tom. *Going Out of Business by Design: Why Seventy Percent of Small Businesses Fail.* Morgan James, 2009. 188p. ISBN 1-60037-672-X. $29.95.

Pease is very good at analyzing business processes and procedures and determining how to creatively deal with many types of business trouble. From finances to human resources, he describes methods to ensure success and avoid small business failure. His book explains how to establish cash flow, how to price correctly for the market, how to select products, and more. Learn what Pease believes is "the great secret to making a small business last and retain employees."

Reid, Gail Margolies. *Complete Idiot's Guide to Low-Cost Startups.* Penguin Group, 2010. ISBN 1-5925-7994-9. $18.95.

Reid provides readers with innovative ideas for new businesses from hi-tech service to low-tech selling. Businesses are grouped under "Home Maintenance," "Home Makeovers," "Personal Touch," "Hospitality Beckons," and "Business Goods and Services." She discusses the basics of starting a business or a home business. An appendix presents a lengthy list of websites and resources arranged by the chapters in the book. Find tips on essential recordkeeping and taxpaying as well as how to invest in smart advertising and promotion.

Reuting, Jennifer. *Limited Liability Companies for Dummies.* For Dummies, 2007. 384p. ISBN 0-47-01723-8-9. $24.99.

Find here winning strategies for protecting your assets and passing your business on to heirs. Learn the pros and cons of forming a limited liability company. Create and file your articles of organization, and create an outstanding operating agreement. Get guidance on converting an existing company to an LLC and how to save on taxes. Chapters are autonomous and cross-referenced, so you can easily find the information you need when you need it.

Sitarz, Daniel. *S-Corporation: Small Business Start-up Kit,* 4th ed. Nova, 2010. 235p. ISBN 1-89294-53-0. $29.95.

You will learn through this complete guide what an S corporation is, how it benefits small businesses, and exactly how to form an S corporation. Sitarz is good at simplifying a very complicated process. The accompanying CD is loaded with PDF documents and worksheets to help you through the process. A worthwhile purchase if you choose to incorporate this way.

Slaunwhite, Steve. *Starting a Web-Based Business.* Alpha Books, 2009. 350p. ISBN 1-59257-889-4. $19.95.

Learn how to create and operate a successful cyberspace venture step-by-step. Slaunwhite looks at the basics of doing business online and then helps you identify online trends, create a game plan and a website, market your site, and then provides tactics for turning clicks into customers. Appendix B helps you locate free and nearly free online tools and resources. Well written and organized, use this reference to help you with day-to-day issues.

**Small Business Sourcebook.* Gale, annual. $405.

You'll find a wealth of information for the small business owner/manager in this guide, but here we'll concentrate on trade associations. In the small business profiles, the second part of the entry is entitled "Associations and Other Organizations," and listed here are trade and professional associations that gather and disseminate information and statistics of interest to association members. This resource lists association's name, address, phone, toll-free and fax numbers, company e-mail address, URL, contact name, purpose and objective, description of the membership, and a listing of its publications with frequency. Also in the small business profiles, users will find a long and complete list of resources grouped under categories such as licensing, trade publications, trade shows, franchises, and sources of supply about any type of business from bagel shop to restaurant. Each resource in a profile has a complete citation as well as a short description. Often URLs are provided or e-mail addresses. The two-volume set helps entrepreneurs start up, develop, and grow their businesses.

Stephenson, James and Mintzer, Rich. *Ultimate Homebased Business Handbook: How to Start, Run and Grow Your Own Profitable Business.* Entrepreneur Press, 2008. 400p. ISBN 1-599-1818-5-1. $29.95.

This handy guide will help you start your own venture in your kitchen or spare room. Every stage of business creation is covered, but the chapter on setting up your business legally is especially noteworthy. Stephenson and Mintzer provide how-to tips, ideas, and tools to organize and develop a winning business strategy. Operations, collections, taxes, licenses, and increasing sales are presented thoroughly and in layperson's language. And, if you haven't determined what kind of business to start, good ideas are also available here. This useful book will help many new entrepreneurs.

Strauss, Steven D. *The Small Business Bible,* 2nd ed. John Wiley, 2008. 544p. ISBN 0-470-26124-2. $19.95.

Strauss's massively expanded and updated edition teaches an entrepreneur what steps to take to start, run, and grow a successful business. Included here are proven strategies, tips, tools, and forms to fill out. The first chapters concentrate on how to choose and do what you love, and new chapters cover green businesses, online advertising and marketing, mobile technology, and many aspects of e-commerce. Learn about how to write an outstanding business plan and financial planning for your start-up. Thorough coverage of this complex challenge is presented clearly.

Thaler, John. *The Elements of Small Business: A Lay Person's Guide to the Financial Terms, Marketing Concepts, and Legal Forms That Every Entrepreneur Needs.* Silver Lake, 2005. 354p. ISBN 1-56343-784-4. $24.95.

Specializing in small business law, this lawyer and small business owner presents tools, tips, and advice to help you get your business off to a smooth and legal start. Chapters are thorough and cover topics such as business formation, insurance, computers and e-commerce, marriage and divorce, retirement planning, and exit strategies. Each chapter concludes with a list of resources. Over 20 appendices provide forms and sample reports, such as registration for a fictitious business name, operating agreement for an LLC, and financial statements. This well-written book will help entrepreneurs.

Thomas, Matt and Wasmund, Shaa. *The Smarta Way to Do Business: By Entrepreneurs, for Entrepreneurs.* Capstone, 2011. 334p. ISBN 1-907312-52-8. $34.95.

This title has a definite British slant but still brings you real-life case studies providing insider knowledge from those who have built successful businesses. Connected to the website Smarta.com (see Online Resources), the authors work with entrepreneurs every day and so are aware of current trends and issues. Learn how to use emerging technologies and social media to help your small business grow.

Tracy, Tage C. *Small Business Financial Management Kit for Dummies.* For Dummies, 2007. 384p. ISBN 0-470-12508-X. $24.99.

Tracy will help you plan a budget, streamline your accounting process, raise capital, and generally keep your business solvent. Learn how to avoid common management pitfalls and use the bonus CD's reproducible forms, checklists, and templates. Tracy explains the financial foundations of a sound business.

**Tyson, Eric and Schell, Jim. *Small Business for Dummies,* 3rd ed. John Wiley, 2008. 432p. ISBN 0-470-17747-0. $21.99.

This enterprising guide explains how to write a business plan, manage your costs and your time, create the right legal framework for your business, find financing, and understand financial statements. Financial ratios and how to determine them is also well covered in plain, simple language. Develop a winning marketing strategy, and hire the right employees. Also find help here to determine your start-up costs and find your niche and time to start up. The For Dummies format includes tear-out cheat sheets, top 10 lists, and dashes of fun and humor.

Willams, Beth and Murray, Jean. *The Complete Guide to Working for Yourself: Everything the Self-Employed Need to Know about Taxes, Recordkeeping, and Other Laws.* Atlantic, 2008. 288p. ISBN 1-601-38048-8. $29.95 (with CD-ROM).

Starting your own business is a genuine and attainable goal. Williams and Murray will help you make the right decisions and will also prevent you from making the wrong ones. If you truthfully answer a few questions, you can forecast your own success. Other areas covered include legal concerns, tax implications, liability, naming your business, marketing, location, human resources issues, and so on. The authors cover the basic and the more advanced challenges to starting your own business. Find ready-to-use forms, ideas on cutting costs, and a sample business plan here.

Online Resources

**BEOnline: Business and Economics Online: www.loc.gov/rr/business/beonline/ (Accessed Spring 2011).

Compiled by the Library of Congress Business Reference Services for researchers, under "Subject Guides," you will find a lengthy list of business topics like associations, business plans (forms), companies by industry, data sets, e-commerce, franchises, economic indicators, legal resources, and more. If you click on "Associations," you are in an associations database that includes contacts, descriptions, addresses, and events data for the organizations listed. Over 10,000 business organizations in the United States are listed. Find here a link to the Herb Growing and Marketing Network or the Association of Bridal Consultants. Under the "Title Listing," you will find "Airlines of the Web," "America's Business Funding Directory," "American Chambers of Commerce Abroad," "American City Business Journals," and more.

**BizBuySell: www.bizbuysell.com (Accessed Spring 2011).

This very useful, practical website not only lets you find businesses for sale on the Internet but provides a wealth of articles on valuing and buying a business. Search for a business to buy here if you've decided through the planning process that you'd like to start with an established business. The "Community" section covers many common questions and answers questions about seller financing, how you can help your business sell, and what business brokers really do. Business brokers can be located from the site. Also find franchises for sale.

BizStats.com: www.bizstats.com/ (Accessed Spring 2011).

Find profitability and operating ratios for S corporations, partnerships, and sole proprietorships for industries like furniture stores, electronics, gas stations, and sporting goods. This site has financial and operating ratios for many industry segments. Even if your industry is not found here, this site will show you a net-profit risk for some sole proprietorships. The Brandow Company of Camp Hill, Pennsylvania, is a leader in online data analysis and has produced the data on this terrific site for small business statistics. This site may help you do a financial and industry analysis using the figures you have gathered.

BFI Business Filings Inc.: www.bizfilings.com (Accessed Spring 2011).

This large site provides detailed information on incorporating, listing advantages and disadvantages, forms needed, advice on where to incorporate, and publication requirements. LLCs are also discussed in detail. The "Small Business Information" section covers many subjects related to start-up, taxes, and legal issues. "Business Tools" provides sample forms and agreements from CCH Incorporated. "Ask Alice!" is a series of columns where small business owners ask questions about issues they've encountered from computer encryption to finding a business incubator. Learn how to select an accountant and an attorney.

Bloomberg Businessweek: www.businessweek.com/small-business/ (Accessed Spring 2011).

This large site has an abundance of current articles on many phases of starting and running a small business. Financing, sales and marketing, management, and more are covered as well as research and special reports. Keep current on what small businesses need to keep up with the competition.

Business Know-How: www.businessknowhow.com/startup/businessplanning.htm (Accessed Spring 2011).

This large business website has a great page under "Start Business." One article is on "10 Tips to Ignore When You're Starting a Business," and handy checklists help you remember what to do and when to do it. Also included is information on business loans, employment forms, templates and productivity tools, and web design and content. Check out this site when starting your business and working on your business plan.

**Business Owners Idea Café: www.businessownersideacafe.com (Accessed Spring 2011).

Developed by successful entrepreneurs and authors of published guides on starting a business, this large site presents short articles on all aspects of small business or entrepreneurial life. The main divisions are "CyberSchmooz," "Starting Your Biz," "Running Your Biz," "Small Business Tax Center," "Take Out Info," "Classifieds," "De-Stress and Have Fun," "About Idea Café," and "Join Idea Café." Here you can find experts to answer your questions or discuss your current business crisis. You'll find sample business plans, financing help, business forms, and business news.

Business Owner's Toolkit: http://toolkit.com (Accessed Spring 2011).

The section of this large site under "Small Business Guide" has a great deal of information about break-even analysis, planning your business, getting financing, going green, Internet marketing, and more. Learn to use the Internet to market, promote, and finally sell your products or services. Use "Win Government Contracts" to find out what the government needs, define the rules, and locate case studies of small businesses that have been successful in their efforts to sell to the federal government. Check this site when seeking any kind of small business help and advice.

**BusinessTown.com: www.businesstown.com (Accessed Spring 2011).

This extensive business information site has sections on managing a business, home businesses, Internet businesses, accounting, selling a business, and more. The articles are not lengthy but thoroughly cover their subjects. Under "Home Business," you will find ideas for home businesses, how to set one up, and articles on getting started right. Under "Accounting," you will learn basic concepts, how to budget, how to plan and project, and more. The site also has links to a variety of financial calculators at www.dinkytown.net. Useful site and not commercial, use it to help you in any area where you need more information.

**Direct Contact Publishing's Media Jumpstation: www.imediafax.com/jumpstation/ (Accessed Spring 2011).

This large site is terrific for locating trade journals. Just select an industry under "Magazine Subject," and it brings up a list. Sometimes the entire journal is available and sometimes just some of the articles. Thousands of publications can be located here.

eHow.com—Business: www.ehow.com/business/ (Accessed Spring 2011).

This huge site contains articles on every phase of starting and running a business from incorporating a business, creating a market survey, filing for a copyright, finding cheap advertising, deciding when to quit your day job, and leasing office space to opening particular types of businesses such as garden centers, catering, pet care, and online businesses. Articles are short and to the point to get you started in the right direction. Links to related or relevant topics expand on the basic article.

Entrepreneur's Reference Guide: www.loc.gov/rr/business/guide/guide2/ (Accessed Spring 2011).

The Library of Congress's Business Reference Services staff originally compiled this guide, updated by Robert Jackson. Although it's getting a bit dated, this large collection of how-to books, reference books, and directories covers a number of topics, including start-up, raising capital, managing your business, human resources, and more. Find classic resources here to help you get started and manage your small business.

Entrepreneur's Resource Center: www.edwardlowe.org/ERC/ (Accessed Spring 2011).

This nonprofit organization promotes entrepreneurship by providing information, research, and education. Use this site to find practical articles on marketing, acquiring and managing finances, human resources management, and legal issues and taxes. Networking possibilities include conferences and educational seminars listed here. Now aimed at entrepreneurs, this site from the Edward Lowe Foundation provides good basic help too.

**Entrepreneur.com: www.entrepreneurmag.com (Accessed Spring 2011).

Maintained by *Entrepreneur Magazine,* this site supports new businesses and growing companies. Under "First Steps," learn how to evaluate your idea and determine if there's a market for your business. "Start Up Topics" include location, naming your business, and business structure. Especially strong in franchising and home-based businesses, you can get expert help on a variety of topics, including toolkits for specific kinds of businesses like herb farms, bed and breakfasts, and consulting firms. Find ready-made business forms here, too, in the "FormNet" section.

**Entrepreneurship Institute: www.tei.net (Accessed Spring 2011).

Established in 1976, this institute provides encouragement and assistance to entrepreneurs and unites financial, legal, and community resources to help foster success of their companies. Case studies and audio presentations are available here, too. Podcasts and forums of interest to small business members are also included.

Entreworld: www.entreworld.org (Accessed Spring 2011).

Sponsored by the Kaufman Center for Entrepreneurial Leadership at the Ewing Marion Kauffman Foundation, this free, online international resource is focused on growing entrepreneurship and continuing to expand entrepreneurial economies. Entrepreneurship.org is very content rich, with resources to assist entrepreneurs, business mentors, policy makers, academics, and investors through each phase of the entrepreneurial process. The content will help small business owners launch a company, write policies, and find research on entrepreneurship. Easy to navigate and updated daily, in the "Sandbox" find online tools and entrepreneurial resources. The "Resource Center" contains various forms of content and even user feedback, with the information you need for every level of the entrepreneurial process. This site contains no advertising; the only agenda here is to promote the growth and understanding of entrepreneurship internationally.

**Financial Calculators from Dinkytown.net: www.dinkytown.net (Accessed Spring 2011).

This large collection of financial calculators is brought to you by KJE Computer Solutions. Here you'll find current information on many business calculators like break-even analysis, cash flow calculator, working capital needs, and inventory analysis. Tax planning and calculators are also available for self-employment taxes and payroll deductions.

Home Business Magazine: www.homebusinessmag.com (Accessed Spring 2011).

The "Start-Up" category accessible through the frame on the left side of the screen or tab at the top provides a wealth of articles on starting various types of small businesses in your spare room or kitchen. Advice and ideas on business start-up, management, and marketing and sales are also included. Technology issues are presented clearly, and telecommuting is also explored thoroughly. "Find a Business" is a large directory of home-based businesses, franchises, and other opportunities.

**Insurance Information Institute: www.iii.org (Accessed Spring 2011).

This site has plain English answers to questions about how to insure a home business, what's the difference between cancellation and nonrenewal, and how to find the right agent. Look under "Business" at the site, then "Business Insurance General" and find a list of questions on business insurance. Find information on annuities, health, disability, life, home, and auto as well. The Insurance Information Institute provides basic information not slanted toward a particular company.

**InterNIC.com: www.internic.com (Accessed Spring 2011).

This website was established to provide public information in regard to Internet domain name registration services and is updated frequently. A directory lists the ICANN-accredited (Internet Corporation for Assigned Names and Numbers) registrars; for more information on ICANN, go to www.icann.org. Though the site needs updating, InterNIC will answer many of your questions about registering a domain name and the competitive registration environment.

**The Minority Business Development Agency (MBDA): www.mbda.gov (Accessed Spring 2011).

Through its minority regional and district business development centers, the MBDA helps new ventures and established businesses seek working capital, start-up business financing, and access to markets. Key sections include "BizDev Central," "Opportunities and Partnerships," "Press and Media," and "Research Library." It publishes *Demographic Trends, Industry Trends,* and *Finance.* The "BizDev Central" tab will help users locate local minority business resources, business tools and more. Another MBDA development program is the Native American Business Enterprise Centers or American Indian Enterprise Development (www.ncaied.org/).

MoreBusiness.com: www.morebusiness.com (Accessed Spring 2011).

Basic sections on this site include "Startup," "Marketing," "Management," and "Online Business." A "Legal and Insurance" section provides sample business contracts and agreements, sample business plans, liability insurance information, and business checklists. Users will find sample marketing plans for specific businesses such as car washes, rental clothing stores, catering, and health fitness programs; some plans are free and some are offered for a fee.

**National Association for the Self-Employed: www.nase.org (Accessed Spring 2011).

The self-employed and microbusinesses (up to 10 employees) join this group for support and advocacy. Use the "Tax Resource Center" for updates on changes and tips on filing your taxes. The *Self-Employed Magazine* has articles on various topics related to small businesses.

National Association for Women Business Owners: www.nawbo.org (Accessed Spring 2011).

This group has chapters located throughout the United States and sponsors national and regional conferences, provides networking opportunities, and sponsors awards. The Center for Women's Business Research, part of the National Foundation for Women Business Owners, produces original groundbreaking research to show the economic and social contributions of women-owned firms.

National Business Incubation Association: www.nbia.org (Accessed Spring 2011).

This organization aims to advance business incubation and entrepreneurship by providing education, information, advocacy, and networking resources for professionals helping early-stage companies. Entrepreneurs will visit this site to find a business incubator in their state or city where they can rent space to start their new business venture. Use "Find a Business Incubator" to search your locale for an incubator. The "Tips for Entrepreneurs" is also useful in the "Resource Library."

National Federation of Independent Businesses (NFIB): http://nfib.com (Accessed Spring 2011).

Since 1943, this long-established and well-known advocacy organization has represented small, independent businesses in Washington, D.C. The NFIB aims to impact public policy at the state and federal level and be a key resource for small businesses. On the site, you can see what impact its 350,000 members have and read other articles of interest to small businesses. Members have access to discounts on business products and services. Anyone can access the "Business Resources" section with helpful, practical articles for the entrepreneur on financing, franchises, business structure, and more.

Nolo Press: www.nolo.com (Accessed Spring 2011).

This commercial site provides a good collection of free articles written by lawyers generally. Nolo's legal self-help books, now often accompanied by CD-ROMs, are outstanding, and you will find useful information and advice on the site as well as invitations to buy their products. Just click on "Patent, Copyright, and Trademark" for answers to your questions. Free online books are also available on a variety of topics.

SBDCNET: http://sbdcnet.org (Accessed Spring 2011).

The Small Business Development Center National Information Clearinghouse provides timely, web-based information to entrepreneurs. Small Business Development Centers are located in all 50 states and offer free, confidential business counseling. This website provides information on business start-up, e-commerce, industry research, marketing, trends, and more. Entrepreneurs will find plenty of links and information here to help them plan and run their new business.

SmallBusinessTV.com: http://sbtv.com (Accessed Spring 2011).

This web-based network provides information and advice of interest to entrepreneurs and small business owners and managers. Various channels such as "Money," "Marketing," "Legal," "Real Business," "Women," and "Technology" contain a list of short videos where experts present practical advice. Sign up for the newsletter to keep current on what's happening.

Service Corp of Retired Executives (SCORE): www.score.org (Accessed Spring 2011).

SCORE (Counselors to America's Small Business) is an organization of volunteer members that provides business advice to small businesses throughout the nation. Visiting the website, you can receive free counseling via e-mail. Click on "Ask SCORE," search the specialties of the counselors, and select a counselor with the specific expertise you need. "Business Tools" provides important links and a template gallery with many templates to help the new business owner. Business counseling and workshops are offered at 389 SCORE chapter offices across the United States. To find a SCORE office near you, visit the website.

Small Business Administration: www.sba.gov (Accessed Spring 2011).

This official government site offers a wealth of resources and programs for starting and growing a small business. Under "Starting and Managing a Business," users will find an "Is Entrepreneurship for You?" quiz that will help them evaluate their possible success in their own business. Other major articles cover business plans, financing, managing, marketing, employees, taxes, legal aspects, and business opportunities. Find here online forms, business plans, financing and loan information, and many publications. Some contents are available in Spanish.

Small Business Advisor: www.isquare.com (Accessed Spring 2011).

This large site has lots of articles and advice for entrepreneurs just getting started in business. The "Biz FAQs" answer many basic questions such as, do I need a federal ID number, how do I buy a franchise, and do I need a business license. "Tax Advice" is another major section as is "Checklists for Success." Find articles on pricing your product or service, steps to improve sales, how to choose a partner, and how to build customer loyalty. The U.S. government and state information is also very helpful. Use this site to help you get started.

Small Business Notes: www.smallbusinessnotes.com (Accessed Spring 2011).

Here you will find articles on starting or buying your first business as well as planning, management, and legal issues. Explore articles on business incubators as well as marketing and choosing a business name. Basic articles contain links to fuller explanatory articles on a wide variety of topics such as business models and recordkeeping. A useful site for many topics related to small business and entrepreneurship; come here for answers to basic and more complex questions.

Smarta.com: www.smarta.com/ (Accessed Spring 2011).

Under "Advice, Guides," you will find over 40 useful guides on things like how to prove your business idea will work, how to start a toy shop, five reasons to start a business at university, and more. More than 600 videos and 343 guides are available on many short topics. Case studies are provided also. The "Tools Directory" covers ideas like finding a franchise, creating your brand identity, finding a location, shipping goods, and more. The slight British bent is not a barrier.

SmartMoney Magazine's Small Business site: www.smsmallbiz.com/ (Accessed Spring 2011).

This large site covers small business by focusing on the entrepreneur as a quick-thinking take-charge type of person who turns his or her passion for a product or a service into a successful business. Regular columns focus why and how you should run your business. Sections include "Work & Life," which advises entrepreneurs on issues such as taking vacations or dealing with sickness or creating family time, and "Starting Up," which helps entrepreneurs through the early stages of launching a business with case studies and articles. Other sections cover marketing, technology, taxes, best practices, and more. Also included are streaming video reports from SmartMoney TV, which showcase a topic of interest to entrepreneurs. Special emphasis is given to women and minorities, which are the fastest growing subsets of entrepreneurs.

Startup Nation: www.startupnation.com (Accessed Spring 2011).

Two brothers founded this site in 2002 to provide one-stop shopping for practical information to help entrepreneurs succeed. Users can access step-by-step advice, easy-to-understand articles, professional groups and forums, expert blogs, podcasts, and member-to-member networking. Learn how to use technology efficiently, maximize your niche, acquire growth capital, and more. The eight steps to managing your money will help you plan and organize your business and personal finances. Use this site often to help you and your business succeed.

**U.S. Patent & Trademark Office: www.uspto.gov (Accessed Spring 2011).

This large, easy-to-use site will help entrepreneurs gain a basic knowledge of the trademark and patent processes. Find tips on conducting a search for registered patents and trademarks plus those pending or rejected. Use this site to begin your search for a unique business name.

Wall Street Journal Online: http://online.wsj.com/public/page/news-small-business-financing.html (Accessed Spring 2011).

The *Wall Street Journal*'s website is authoritative and has a section entitled "Tools and How-To Guide." Entrepreneurs will find a great deal of help deciding if they are entrepreneurs and how to get started in business. Collected here are many articles about different aspects of starting a business, such as legal structure, business plan tools, and more. The sample business plans are very thorough and will really help new business owners fill in the gaps in their plans. Articles on important issues such as "Should You Hire an Accountant" will also get entrepreneurs off on the right foot. Continually updated and well written, this site is useful to all entrepreneurs.

**Yahoo! Business and Economy: http://dir.yahoo.com/Business_and_Economy/ (Accessed Spring 2011).

Especially important categories are organizations, e-commerce, software, and use tax issues. This large site includes a wealth of information with good international coverage on a wide variety of topics. Under "Organizations" and then "Small Business," users will find listings for trade associations in many industries. Under its small business site (http://smallbusiness.yahoo.com/), the e-commerce section covers online shopping centers, privacy seal programs, and digital money. For industries, it covers manufacturing as well as the retail industry. The information on sales and marketing is large and very helpful. Check this site for current, accurate business information.

Young Money: www.youngmoney.com (Accessed Spring 2011).

This informative and user friendly website focuses on but is not limited to money management, entrepreneurship, careers, investing, technology, and travel for young adults. Across the top of the home page numerous tabs link to the main sections: "Calculator/

Tools," "Careers," "Entrepreneurship," "Investing," "Personal Finance," and more. The "Entrepreneurship" tab links to articles under, for instance, "Start a Business." Here you will find "Entrepreneurship 101" listed in the left column; blogs and videos in the center column; and in the right column is a "Tag Cloud," a box with most-read, most-e-mailed, and most-comments sections on the articles for the whole website. Use the Googlelike search box to get right to what you need. A free e-mail newsletter is available as well as the ability to subscribe through Facebook, Twitter, and an RSS feed.

YOUR BUSINESS PLAN 4

Writing a business plan is not an event—it's an ongoing, essential process. Remember the adage: "failing to plan is planning to fail." It can be a daunting, time-consuming task, but creating a business plan is crucial to the success of your business. Find the method of creating and maintaining a business plan that works for you. Planning is a strategy for survival. The real value of creating a business plan is the process of researching and thoroughly thinking through your plan for a new business in a systematic manner. Remember, a business plan is a living document and should continually be revised and updated.

WHAT IS A BUSINESS PLAN?

What is in this essential document, and why must it be written down? The well-prepared plan raises numerous critical questions and then discovers answers to those questions. It provides owners with a business advantage over industry rivals. Because it describes the basics of your business's operations and forecasts, the format should be easy to read, understand, and change.

Your business plan requires market research on an ongoing basis. The world of business, your industry, and your business will constantly change, and you must be alert and aware of trends and economic changes that affect your business. Your business plan communicates your vision and ideas to others, and it will continually change and grow with you and your business. Obviously, it cannot be kept in your head but must be committed to paper. Don't worry about writing complete sentences or using perfect grammar; just start writing down your thoughts and ideas, and use the plan as an organizing tool. Tim Berry advocates not writing a formal plan until you need it.

Berry, Tim. *The Plan-As-You-Go Business Plan.* Entrepreneur Media, 2008. 269p. ISBN 1-59918-190-8. $19.95.

Berry, the manufacturer and principal author of the software *Business Plan Pro*, presents a flexible, modular tool for writing and maintaining a business plan. Berry takes what is important from the traditional business plan idea and applies it practically to today's world. Berry's book is flexible and practical; find the chapter you need today and use it to help you start or continue your business planning.

Occasionally, potential dot-com entrepreneurs ask if they must do a business plan. The answer is an emphatic yes. Just remember that today's plan is quicker, easier, more flexible, more practical, and more useful overall. In the whole scheme of things, nothing is different in starting a dot-com business than a brick-and mortar business. See chapter 8, "The Internet and Selling Globally," for more about doing business on the Internet. Remember, whether you're dot-com or brick-and-mortar, there is no substitute for business planning to ensure your success.

How to begin? Take an objective and unemotional look at your business idea. State the mission of your business. Why does or should your business exist? What is the purpose of your business? Conversely, state what your mission is not. Profit is not a goal or a mission but an outcome of the successful achievement of your mission. Emphasize the things that set your business apart from others.

SAMPLE PLANS: WHERE TO FIND AND HOW TO USE

Now is a good time to look at some resources specifically designed to help you make and write your business plan. One of the best places to start on the Internet is Bplans.com (www.bplans.com). Here you'll find over 50 free, sample business plans as well as helpful tools and know-how for creating a business plan. Sample plans, even if they are for the same business you plan to open, should not be simply copied. A sample plan suggests categories of things for you to consider. A business plan defines and reveals the relationship between the business and the entrepreneur, you. A sample plan tells you what must be included in a well-written document. Take a careful look at the financial section in the sample plan because it can help you in developing your financial plans.

Another good site for business plan guidance is sponsored by *Inc.* magazine (www.inc.com/guides). This site provides two plans for business planning: one is an in-depth look at each section of a plan, and the other is a quick guide to building and improving your plan. Also, you may find the Small Business Administration sample business plan at www.sbaonline.sba.gov useful. Its business plan section was written by Linda Pinson, who is a well-known author on business

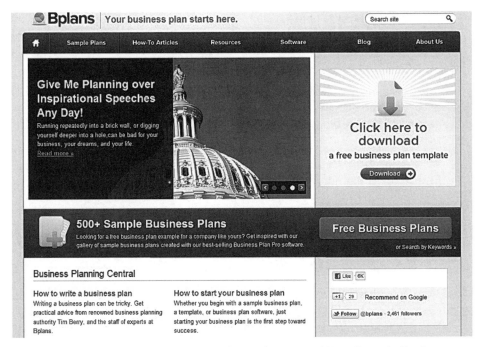

Figure 4.1 Screenshot of Business Plan Software and Free Sample Business Plans (www.bplans.com)

planning. You'll also find her business plan book listed in the References at the end of this chapter. In the For Dummies series, the *Business Plans Kit for Dummies* (with a CD-ROM) is an easy-to-use, easy-to-follow, humorous work. The authors lead you through the steps of writing a business plan for all types of businesses, including nonprofits, as well as plans for businesses in later stages of development or those that need restructuring. The CD-ROM contains lots of forms, government documents, sample by-laws, and more. This package will help new entrepreneurs along the path to success.

ESSENTIAL ELEMENTS OF A BUSINESS PLAN

The essential parts of a business plan include:

1. *Cover page* contains the name of the business, a brief description or mission statement, the title "Business Plan," the date written, your name (and contact information if you want to list different ones from your business), and the address and phone number for the business. If you have a business logo, it should be included here.

61

2. *Table of contents* is the name of each section, the page number where each section begins, and subheadings if needed for clarity. The purpose of this page is to get your readers to the section that they are most interested in reading.

3. *Executive summary* identifies the key ideas you want to emphasize (write this after your plan is finished). Summarize all sections briefly; this should be just a page or two. Many readers will only read this section, so it is very important that it be done well. This section is expanded upon later in this chapter.

4. *Business overview* describes the services and/or products you'll be selling, legal structure, and some short-term and long-term goals. Focus here on customer benefits.

5. *Business environment* identifies all the major aspects that affect your company's situation that are beyond your control, such as how your industry operates, industry regulation, intensity of your competition and who they are, and the movement and trends of the marketplace.

6. *Marketing plan* describes how to get the products or services to your targeted consumer or market. Also describe your pricing philosophy and competitive advantage, if any. Describe how you will promote your business and its wares (advertising).

7. *Financial plan* tells your story in numbers. You will include a projected balance sheet and a profit-and-loss statement, which shows when you anticipate profits to start and how long you can afford to absorb losses. Here is where you show your start-up and operating cash needs.

8. *Outside advice* lists those individuals you plan to hire, such as insurance agents, lawyers, accountants, and bankers.

9. *Supporting documents* include any contracts, agreements, or leases that you feel are important to the operation of your business.

After reading through the list of sections in a business plan, start a list of things you need to research in connection with your business and for preparing your business plan. Set a deadline for completion. Ask someone to read it and comment on your work, so you'll have a reason to write and complete your plan in a timely fashion. Professional business planners often suggest that a short section on exit strategies be included for a complete business plan. Check chapter 14, "Growing Your Business and Moving On," for suggestions on possible contingencies to plan for when leaving your business. Life does not follow our plan but occasionally throws a curve such as a death, divorce, upturn or downturn in the economy, and so on, and you should be prepared to consider your business options.

If you would like to compare your plan to other business plans, try Alice Magos's *Business Plans That Work: For Your Small Business*. She presents useful plans for a video production company, yard care, and coffee cart, for example. Several other business plans are also included to help you compare and develop your own plan.

Magos, Alice H. *Business Plans That Work: For Your Small Business,* 3rd ed. Toolkit Media Group, 2008. 244p. ISBN 0-8080-1793-4. $19.95.

This new edition updates and revises the elements of a professional business plan in accordance with new laws and regulations. Magos also uses common language to interpret complicated marketing and financial concepts, providing down-to-earth advice along the way. Sample business plans are particularly useful. Learn how to analyze the competition and create outstanding sales and marketing plans. Operations and management plans are also included. Continue using your business plan as a management tool as you grow your new business.

FORMAT YOUR PLAN

Keep your audience in mind as you prepare your formal business plan. In order to make your plan more readable and improve the readers' comprehension of your vision, use headings and subheadings. When you begin a new topic area and for key or important points, let the reader know. This practice improves the visual appeal and readability of your plan. Numbered lists are also effective in breaking up long blocks of text and increasing impact. Bulleted lists bring information across clearly and concisely. If you can produce or obtain good graphics, use pie charts, graphics, or other pictorial devices to illustrate the numerical parts of your plan. Be succinct and to the point, but completely describe your business vision and include all the necessary parts of a good business plan.

REVIEW, UPDATE, AND CHANGE YOUR BUSINESS PLAN

Be committed to continually reviewing and updating your plan. Note in your calendar to review the business plan in six months (or less if you know things will change sooner). Business events that should trigger an update of your business plan include:

1. Something in your business changes, such as you hire an employee, you add a new product or service, or you take on a partner.

2. Your target market or customer base changes, and you make a change in your product line or price or inventory that reflects this change and meets a new need or request.

3. Technology continues to change, and some of its changes will affect the way you do business, such as new software packages, Internet resources, desktop environments, or new hardware.

Experts who critique business plans frequently state that entrepreneurs are not realistic. Try not to be overly enthusiastic and inflate your potential or expectations.

Be precise, concise, and clear, but demonstrate a thorough knowledge of the market and the competition and your industry as a whole. Emphasize what is different or unique about your venture, and find a niche. For help with keeping your plan current, use Mike McKeever's book, *How to Write a Business Plan.*

McKeever, Mike. *How to Write a Business Plan,* 9th ed. Nolo Press, 2010. 256p. ISBN 1-4133-1280-2. $34.99.

This logically organized, thoughtfully presented book uses examples and worksheets to help entrepreneurs prepare a successful business plan. Included are business plans for a small service and a manufacturing business. A business plan is a dynamic document that needs constant revision to keep you and your business current. His explanation of the break-even analysis and sales forecasting are very thorough and easy to understand. The chapter on selling your business plan will especially help those interested in obtaining financing for their new venture. This new edition has good new online and offline resources to help the new entrepreneur plan her or his business.

THE EXECUTIVE SUMMARY

This snapshot of your company's history, objectives, financial status, industry overview, and marketing plan is sometimes the only section people will read carefully. It must be a complete, yet brief, overview of your entire plan, and it must be very well written. It should be specific, exciting, and succinct in order to grab your readers' attention. Cover the type of business you have or want, what you hope to achieve, how you hope to achieve it, and your capabilities.

First, outline your business's philosophy, goals, and commitments. Identify the type of business you have, such as a new or existing business or a franchise. Define your legal structure with name, location, hours of operation, and years in operation, if any. Name the principal owner(s). State the objective of the business plan. What do you need to help you accomplish your business goals? What business opportunity have you identified? If you need start-up capital or a bank loan, state the amount and explain generally how the money will be used. Don't forget to include the potential return on investment along with the proposed payback period. Also mention the industry overview, target market, and competitive advantage.

Although this document appears at the beginning of your business plan, you should prepare it last, because it summarizes the deep learning that has taken place through the planning process. You have identified your niche in the market, researched and analyzed your industry, and are ready to launch and grow a business. If you're having trouble writing the executive summary, take a look at Linda Pinson's book *Anatomy of a Business Plan* for help in writing this snapshot of your business so that it will capture the attention and interest of your readers.

Pinson, Linda. *Anatomy of a Business Plan,* 7th ed. Out of Your Mind . . . and Into the Marketplace, 2008. 352p. ISBN 0-944-2053-72. $22.95.

This user-friendly handbook includes sample business plans, plus blank forms to help you write a thoughtful, thorough, and professional business plan. Pinson believes that the executive summary should grab attention, and she presents ways for you to do just that. This edition includes a resource section to help businesses research financial and marketing information, so essential for an outstanding plan. Also find guidelines for updating and packaging your plan. Appendices at the end provide full-length business plans for wholesale, restaurant, service, and manufacturing businesses.

Below are resources to help you learn how to write a business plan and where to get help in preparing your plan. Sample several different resources and find one that helps you work through the process.

REFERENCES

Starred titles are discussed in the chapter.

■ Print Resources

**Berry, Tim. *The Plan-As-You-Go Business Plan.* Entrepreneur Media, 2008. 269p. ISBN 1-59918-190-8. $19.95.

Berry, the manufacturer and principal author of the software *Business Plan Pro,* presents a flexible, modular tool for writing and maintaining a business plan. Berry takes what is important from the traditional business plan idea and practically applies it to today's world. Berry's book is flexible and practical; find the chapter you need today and use it to help you start or continue your business planning.

Calvin, Robert J. *Entrepreneurial Management: Creating Successful Business Plans, Raising Capital and Structuring Deals, Maximizing Profits and Growth.* CreateSpace, 2010. 304p. ISBN 1-4392-7231-X. $14.94.

Combining decades of experience and real-world knowledge, Calvin will help you spot the right opportunity, find your niche, price your product or service right, and reach out to customers. Learn techniques for targeting, evaluating, and obtaining alternative sources of financing. Learn how to create and run a successful business.

Cooney, Scott. *Build a Green Small Business.* McGraw-Hill, 2008. 256p. ISBN 0-07-160293-3. $19.95.

The highlight of this work is the load of green start-up ideas, including green wedding planning and green travel planning. Find expert advice on market research, financing, key legal and insurance issues, and green franchises. Learn how to create a business that builds your local community, heals the environment, and feeds the growing green demands. Also find valuable resources such as web links and contacts to help you succeed.

DeBaise, Colleen. *Wall Street Journal, Complete Small Business Guidebook.* Crown, 2009. 272p. ISBN 0-307-40893-0. $15.

This practical guide covers all the basics, such as business plans, funding, using technology, marketing, managing, and how to hire the right employees. The "Better Business Bureau's Worksheets for Estimating Start Up Costs" in the back are easy to use and well organized. Additionally, find secrets to locating extra money to support expansion or maintenance, executing an exit strategy, and managing vacations. The chapter on business plans and the sample business plan are excellent as well. DeBaise provides useful help for turning your dreams into a profitable business.

Hazelgren, Brian and Covello, Josep. *The Complete Book of Business Plans: Simple Steps to Writing Powerful Business Plans,* 2nd ed. Sourcebooks, 2006. 512p. ISBN 1-4022-0763-8. $24.99.

The authors present step-by-step instructions for writing business plans as well as tips on avoiding common mistakes. They help you understand and plan for the challenges in owning and running your own business. They teach readers how to read and understand financial statements along with illustrating how they are developed. Understand how starting a business will impact your family, your income, your personality, and generally your life.

**Magos, Alice H. *Business Plans That Work: For Your Small Business,* 3rd ed. Toolkit Media Group, 2008. 244p. ISBN 0-8080-1793-4. $19.95.

This new edition updates and revises the elements of a professional business plan in accordance with new laws and regulations. Magos also uses common language to interpret complicated marketing and financial concepts, providing down-to-earth advice along the way. Sample business plans are particularly useful. Learn how to analyze the competition and create outstanding sales and marketing plans. Continue using your business plan as a management tool as you grow your new business.

**McKeever, Mike. *How to Write a Business Plan,* 9th ed. Nolo Press, 2010. 256p. ISBN 1-4133-1280-2. $34.99 (with CD).

In this updated edition of McKeever's logically organized, thoughtfully presented book, examples and worksheets help entrepreneurs prepare a successful business plan. Included are updated business plans for a small service and a manufacturing business, for example. Many new online resources have been added. The chapter on writing your marketing and personnel plans is particularly helpful for the marketing section of a business plan. Before proceeding with the marketing plan, McKeever suggests that you return to your written business description to see if it still is an accurate statement of how you view your business or if the thinking and writing experiences between chapters have changed your current ideas. A business plan is a dynamic document that needs constant revision to keep you and your business current. His explanations of the break-even analysis and sales forecasting are very thorough and easy to understand. The chapter on selling your business plan will especially help those interested in obtaining financing for their new venture.

Monosoff, Tamara. *Your Million Dollar Dream: Create a Winning Business Plan.* McGraw-Hill, 2010. 336p. ISBN 0-07-162943-2. $19.95.

Monosoff, founder of Mom Inventors Inc., works with many entrepreneurs and often walks them through the steps of starting and growing their own business. The chapter entitled "Making Money Your Way" provides exercises that will help you articulate your dreams, identify skill sets, and broaden your awareness and link to actual businesses that tap into your strengths and dreams. Learn how to create an effective business plan and use Twitter and Facebook as powerful marketing tools.

Moran, Gwen and Johnson, Sue. *The Complete Idiot's Guide to Business Plans,* 2nd ed. Alpha Books, 2010, 360p. ISBN 1-59257-973-0. $19.95.

This basic writing guide will help new entrepreneurs understand what decisions they need to make before writing a business plan and will help them put together a good plan. Chapters cover the industry overview, analyzing your market, the sales plan and forecast, financial statements, and how to use your business plan. Sample plans in common categories of businesses and industries and resources are included. Keep your plan current and stay ahead of the competition.

**Peterson, Steven, et al. *Business Plans Kit for Dummies.* For Dummies, 2010. 384p. ISBN 0-4704-3854-1. $34.99.

This kit helps you put your business plan to work. Every chapter has checklists and forms. The examples in the case studies illustrate how real-life businesses succeed. The analysis of business plans for businesses that didn't make it is an unusual and useful feature. An excellent sample business plan is included in chapter 16. Chapter 17 lists 10 final questions to ask about your business plan before you show it to anyone or decide it is complete. Every entrepreneur will want to test his or her plan. Plus, the CD-ROM with its wealth of forms and useful documents will help entrepreneurs in many areas of their business.

**Pinson, Linda. *Anatomy of a Business Plan,* 7th ed. Out of Your Mind . . . and Into the Marketplace, 2008. ISBN 0-944-2053-72. $22.95.

This user-friendly guide includes sample business plans, plus blank forms to help you write a thoughtful, thorough, and professional business plan. Pinson believes that the executive summary should grab attention, and she presents ways for you to write one that will do just that. This edition includes a resource section to help businesses research financial and marketing information, so essential for an outstanding plan. Also find guidelines for updating and packaging your plan. New chapters on financing resources and business planning for nonprofits add value to this practical, well-written resource.

Stutely, Richard. *The Definitive Business Plan,* 2nd ed. FT Press, 2007. 336p. ISBN 0-273-71096-6. $34.99.

This excellent work has a more international focus and viewpoint, and is written by a British businessman. Some of the terminology is slightly different, but the basics are the same. Stutely presents many short case studies to illustrate the use or importance of sections or strategies in business planning, which often target misconceptions. Stutely also includes many quotes and proverbs, which will help the important ideas and concepts of business planning stick in your mind. Stutely takes you from the beginning to the end on the operating principles of a business and the reasons behind each process. This outstanding work will help you write a great business plan.

Tyson, Eric and Schell, Jim. *Small Business for Dummies,* 3rd ed. John Wiley, 2008. 432p. ISBN 0-470-17747-0. $21.99.

This enterprising guide explains how to write a business plan, manage your costs and your time, create the right legal framework for your business, find financing, and understand financial statements. Financial ratios and how to determine them are also well covered in plain, simple language. Develop a winning marketing strategy, and hire the right employees. The For Dummies format includes tear-out cheat sheets, top 10 lists, and dashes of fun and humor.

Online Resources

About.com Small Business Information: http://sbinformation.about.com (Accessed Spring 2011).

This large site has many different parts, but the "Small Business Information" and "Business Plan Writing" sections are especially well done. Find articles about the importance of writing a plan and how to complete a useful plan. There's a business plan FAQ and more. Location selection advice is provided, as well as many downloadable business forms. Some industry information can be accessed here as well. Continually updated and well organized, this site will help you write your business plan and continue to plan your business activities.

**Bplans.com: www.bplans.com (Accessed Spring 2011).

This well-established, frequently updated site, sponsored by Palo Alto Software, Inc., is the best for help in writing your business plan. The section entitled "Write a Business Plan" contains articles, calculators on cash flow, starting costs, breakeven, a business plan template, executive summary and mission statement help, plus access to expert advice. Currently 60 free plans are viewable online. Fully searchable, users can quickly find topics that they need, such as getting your plan funded and business plan legalities. Another nice feature is a "Business Planning Audio" for auditory learners. Other sections include "Finance and Capital," "Marketing & Advertising," "Buying a Business," "Market Research," and a monthly newsletter. Bplans.com is a useful, practical site that also offers fee-based experts and assistance.

Business Know-How: www.businessknowhow.com/startup/businessplanning.htm (Accessed Spring 2011).

This large business website has a great page under "Start Business." One article is on "10 Tips to Ignore When You're Starting a Business," and handy checklists help you remember what to do and when to do it. Also included is information on business loans, employment forms, templates and productivity tools, and web design and content. Check out this site when starting your business and working on your business plan.

Business Owners Idea Café: www.businessownersideacafe.com (Accessed Spring 2011).

Developed by successful entrepreneurs and authors of published guides on starting a business, this large site presents short articles on all aspects of small business and entrepreneurial life. The main divisions are "CyberSchmooz," "Starting Your Biz," "Running Your Biz," "Take Out Info," "Classifieds," "The 'You' in Your Biz," "De-Stress and Have Fun," "About Idea Café," and "Join Idea Café." Here you can find experts to answer your questions or discuss your current business crisis. You'll find sample business plans, financing help, business forms, and business news.

Business Plan Center: www.businessplans.org (Accessed Spring 2011).

The main sections of this website include "Business Plan Software," "Sample Business Plans," "Planning Guidelines," "Web Resources," and a list of consultants. The library of business plans was compiled from the finalists and winners in the University of Texas's student business plan competition. The sample plans are grouped by type: Internet services, services, and products. The "Guidelines for Business Planning" links users to articles written by experts who analyze business and marketing strategies and the parts of business plans, such as the mission statement, pricing, financial statements, and marketing strategy.

Entrepreneurs' Help Page: www.tannedfeet.com/bizplan.htm (Accessed Spring 2011).

Find here help with business plans, financial statements, legal structure and legal forms, marketing and public relations, human resources, and strategy. Parts of the site are becoming dated, but details on things that really matter when preparing your business plan and the 10 "painless" steps to writing a business plan are still useful. Articles are usually not long but ask questions to help the new businessperson start thinking about what is needed and what questions will be asked of him or her. Down-to-earth advice from peers is often the most valuable.

Entrepreneur.com: www.entrepreneur.com/businessplan/index.html (Accessed Spring 2011).

Under "Starting a Business, Business Plans," *Entrepreneur Magazine* provides a wealth of information and assistance to the new entrepreneur. A thorough understanding of the need and finding the right type of business plan to fit your business and your style of planning and working is very important; this site guides you through the process. Learn how to determine your goals and objectives and how a plan will help you achieve them. Assess your company's potential and plan for growth. Besides a sample plan, Entrepreneur.com leads you to consultants, associations, government agencies, and software to help you develop the best business plan possible. Additionally, the site helps users find free places for start-up help and mentors for advice during the start-up phase. Use this outstanding site often during the planning and opening of your new business.

**Inc.com: www.inc.com (Accessed Spring 2011).

The publishers of *Inc.* magazine present a large directory of articles by topic targeting many problems, concerns, and decisions confronting new business owners and managers. The "Start-Up" section on business plans is precise and practical. Particularly strong is the article on writing your business description, which advises you to write out the problem your business solves for its customers and then describe how your business solves your customers' problem. As stated earlier, the executive summary is a critical section in the business plan, and the article at Inc.com is right on target. Get advice here on what not to include in the executive summary. Simple but effective advice is the hallmark of this outstanding, easy-to-use site.

PowerHomeBiz.com: www.powerhomebiz.com (Accessed Spring 2011).

This large site for small business has many outstanding sections, including "Starting a Business," "Success Stories," and "Resources." It has one of the longest lists of links to free sample business plans on the Internet. Under "Business Calculators," the starting costs calculator is practical and well done. The article "How to Raise Money to Start a Business" will give entrepreneurs ideas and help in trying to finance their new business. Use this site to help you plan and manage your new business.

SBDC Network: www.asbdc-us.org/ (Accessed Spring 2011).

The Association of Small Business Development Centers provides timely, web-based information to entrepreneurs. Small Business Development Centers are located in all 50 states and offer free, confidential business counseling. This website provides information on business start-up, e-commerce, industry research, marketing, trends, and more. Entrepreneurs will find plenty of links and information here to help them plan and run their new business.

Service Corp of Retired Executives (SCORE): www.score.org (Accessed Spring 2011).

SCORE (Counselors to America's Small Business) is an organization of volunteer members that provides business advice to small businesses throughout the nation. Visiting the website, you can receive free counseling via e-mail; ask to have a counselor look at the first draft of your plan. The "Business Tools" section provides important links and a template gallery with many templates to help the new business owner with several parts of a good business plan. Like the Small Business Administration site, solid business planning help is available here.

**Small Business Administration: www.sba.gov (Accessed Spring 2011).

This official government site offers a wealth of resources and programs for starting and growing a small business. Under "Starting & Managing a Business," check out the areas you need help with while doing your business planning. Other major sections cover business planning, financing, managing, marketing, employees, taxes, legal aspects, and business opportunities. Find here online forms, sample business plans, loan information, and many publications. Some contents are available in Spanish. Parts of the Small Business Administration program are the Small Business Development Centers (SBDCs) at www.sba.gov/sbdc. SBDCs are located in every state and deliver counseling and training for small businesses in the areas of management, marketing, financing, and feasibility studies.

WebSite 101 (Expanding Your Business to the Web): http://website101.com (Accessed Spring 2011).

This huge, helpful site is focused on the online entrepreneur. Very useful articles cover many areas of e-commerce and domain names. WebSite 101 surveys its users and other groups, tallies the results, and presents them on the website; it also collects surveys with results from other researchers and presents them. This site is very dynamic and contains a wide variety of practical, realistic data. Many free, online tutorials are available here. Learn how to buy health insurance and use social media for marketing and growing your business.

WebSite MarketingPlan: www.websitemarketingplan.com (Accessed Spring 2011).

This site contains a wealth of information for small businesses. A large assortment of articles and sample marketing plans are available as well as sample business plans, a newsletter, Internet marketing articles, marketing strategy articles, and more. Featured directory categories include articles grouped under "Search Engine Marketing," "Marketing Strategy," "Marketing Plan," and "Public Relations." Learn about the four seasons of public relations. Lengthy articles on advertising, using public relations for communicating to customers and finding new ones, and customer retention are outstanding. The site has many commercial links but plenty of free help for the new entrepreneur, too. Many sample business plans are also available. This site is especially helpful for those interested in e-commerce. Easy to navigate, this site will definitely help you develop a marketing plan that you can use.

Yahoo! Small Business Resources: smallbusiness.yahoo.com (Accessed Spring 2011).

Under "Resources" on the far right-hand side of this large site, the "Getting Started" section has information on business plans and is full of good links to articles on the basics, the risks, the need for updating, the financials, and the importance of a good executive summary. Under "Ecommerce," articles are presented for online businesses and e-businesses, which are very popular today. The site is fully searchable, and the listing of new articles covers a wide range of relevant information, including choosing an e-mail marketing firm and a web host. In fact, Yahoo! presents a whole section on e-commerce and the many decisions involved in setting up a store online. This useful site is a good place to start learning about planning your new business.

FRANCHISING OPTIONS 5

A franchise is not a separate type of small business entity. A franchise is a contractual licensing and distribution arrangement between two businesses, in which the franchisor (the owner of a business concept) gives the franchisee (another businessperson) the right to own and operate a business based on that concept. Franchisees borrow from another entrepreneur's success and pay for his or her experience. So, if you don't have the experience and expertise to start a business from scratch, another option is buying a franchise, utilizing another business owner's established business idea and plan. Franchisees rarely go bankrupt, and franchises can be found in nearly every industry in the United States and globally, in various sizes and requiring varying amounts of financial investment. Franchising is very popular and continues to expand. The two major reasons franchisees fail are undercapitalization and absentee ownership.

TYPES OF FRANCHISES

Two main types of franchise operations exist for the independent entrepreneur. The first one is the entire business format (EBF), or turnkey package, where the franchisor grants the franchisee a license to use the logos, trademarks, business know-how, copyrights, trade secrets, standard operating procedures, and purchasing power of the franchisor. The franchisee is required to pay a franchise fee plus start-up costs, ongoing royalty fees, and operating expenses (inventory, rent, and so forth). The franchisor provides site selection assistance, job training, an operating manual, volume purchasing, and advice on marketing, management, personnel, and finance issues. Some franchisors offer workshops, newsletters, a toll-free telephone number for technical assistance, and other services. In an EBF, the business identity of the franchisor and franchisee are merged so the public perceives each outlet as a part of a large chain of identical outlets all offering the same goods and services. The franchisor exercises a great deal of control over the business operations of the franchisees.

The second type of franchise is the product and trade-name franchise, which involves the distribution of a product through a dealer, usually limited to an exclusive geographic distribution area. This franchise is limited to selling only the products included, such as ice cream, soft drinks, or candy, but does utilize the recognition and notoriety accompanying the franchise name and history. Some tire stores are a good example of this type of franchise. Some other support services may be offered to the franchisee, but generally assistance is limited and only minor control over the franchisee's business operation is exerted. Each franchisee is free to use its own business style and distribution techniques. In the end, franchising is a relationship business with franchisor, customers, other franchisees, suppliers, attorneys, bankers, and family.

You will find specific types of franchises and lists of the 75 industry categories at the International Franchise Association (www.franchise.org/). Use this excellent site, further described in the online resources at the end of the chapter, for more detailed information on specific franchise opportunities.

UNIFORM FRANCHISE OFFERING CIRCULAR

The exact services provided to franchisees are described in the Uniform Franchise Offering Circular (UFOC). Under the Federal Trade Commission (FTC) Franchising and Business Opportunity Ventures Trade Regulation Rules (FTC rules) franchisors must provide franchisees with full disclosure of all the information they need to make an informed and rational decision about purchasing the franchise in the UFOC document. Under the FTC rules, franchisors must supply the complete franchise agreement at least five days before the franchisee signs any forms or issues any money. The terms in this document are uniform and nonnegotiable. Read and understand it thoroughly. The UFOC contains 23 items of information about the franchise. A few key points to identify include:

1. When the company was founded and date of incorporation

2. Franchise fees

3. Litigation history

4. Renewal dates

5. Start-up costs

6. Earnings claims

7. Territory rights

8. Grounds for termination

Much of this same information will be in the franchise agreement, but you may want to know these things before you even consider this franchise. *The Better Business Bureau's Buying a Franchise* book lists key questions that franchisees need to know, such as what are the fees; is the territory you're buying exclusive; can the franchisor bypass the franchisee's outlet; what happens if the franchisor merges with another business; what are the online issues, exactly what training and support are provided; does the franchise sponsor an association of franchisees; and what happens if you die, become disabled, or you want out of the franchise agreement. Be clear on what you want from a franchise before you make any commitments. The information and citation for the book is below:

The Better Business Bureau's Buying a Franchise. Planning Shop, 2007. 200p. ISBN 1-933-8950-12. $19.95.

The Better Business Bureau guides you through every step of choosing a franchise. Worksheets and checklists will help you ask the right questions, discover the meaning of terms, and what red flags and warning signs you should be alert to in avoiding a rip-off. Use this guide early in your decision-making process.

Another useful resource for finding a franchise is Robert Bond's directory, now in its 22nd edition.

Bond, Robert E. (ed.). *Bond's Franchise Guide 2011,* 22nd ed. Source Book Publications, 2011. 488p. ISBN 1-88713-775-0. $34.95.

Covering 29 distinct business categories, profiles of franchises describe the business, with number of operating units and geographic distribution; capital requirements, including initial investment and total investment; detailed space needs and staffing levels; initial training and start-up assistance as well as ongoing support; evaluation statements from current franchisees; and specific areas of geographic expansion. For this new edition, profiles of franchise attorneys and consultants have been added. This directory is one of the first places a prospective franchise buyer should search.

RESEARCHING FRANCHISE OPPORTUNITIES

One outstanding resource for entrepreneurs and new franchisees that I have found useful is Franchise.com, which provides information for franchise buyers, franchise owners, franchisors, and suppliers. You can search or view by category, license, or franchise name. Find lists such "Star Opportunities," "New Arrivals," and "Premier Listings." Also provided are "Green Franchises," "Resale Franchises," and "Lenders, and Attorneys." "Small Business and Franchise Events" can also be useful to new franchisees. This site is international, so you can find opportunities globally. The "Small Business Articles" section covers topics such as finding financing, new franchises success rate, and how to choose the right franchise. Use this site to investigate franchising.

The FTC does not require that franchisors register with the commission in order to conduct business. Some states impose registration rules; check with your secretary of state office for requirements in your state. States usually grant or deny a franchisor the right to franchise its operations in their state. This state approval only means that the state could not find any reason to refuse the franchisor's application. Because buying a franchise involves considerable risk on your part, you will want to research a franchise opportunity thoroughly.

ADVANTAGES AND DISADVANTAGES

Looking at the big picture, what are the advantages and disadvantages of purchasing a franchise? Advantages of purchasing a franchise include:

1. Business ownership

2. The economic power of immediate name recognition

3. Assistance in finding financial support or even providing financial assistance

4. Reduced risk of failure

5. Advertising assistance and publicity both locally and nationally

6. Reduced costs for equipment and inventory through bulk buying power

7. Help with site selection and possibly development of your facility

8. Basic business training plus sometimes advanced training in marketing, management, and training for employees

9. The provision of an operations manual

Disadvantages of buying and running a franchise include:

1. The high cost of purchasing, plus the ongoing costs

2. Loss of control and inflexibility over such things as facility look and layout; method of operation, including hours of operation; vendors; pricing; advertising campaigns; and facility location

3. The requirement to follow the restrictive franchise agreement

4. Sharing the parent company's image when things go wrong

Again, you have to ask yourself what is most important to you. Do you follow the rules? Realize and accept that franchisees are not rebels or independent thinkers but team players.

FRANCHISING AND YOU!

If you have decided that you want to investigate franchising further, how do you begin? Well, if you know already exactly what kind of franchise you want to acquire, contact a franchisee in your community or state to see if it might be interested in selling its outlet, or contact the franchisor directly. Also check out the franchise on some of the websites listed in the resources at the end of this chapter to see what different organizations and other franchisees are saying about it. Another important resource is the business and trade press. Has an article on the franchise appeared in the *Wall Street Journal* or other business publication? Search the Internet. Visit your local library.

Attend seminars sponsored by the International Franchise Association; find locations on its website for upcoming franchise seminars and shows with dates for events all over the country at www.franchise.org. Besides seminars, users will find sections like "Franchise Basics," "Franchise Resources," and the "FTC Guide to Buying a Franchise." This large site links to specific companies that sell franchises as well as to information about franchising in general. Use this site to start your search for information on a franchise.

Call the Better Business Bureau to see if there are complaints about the franchisor, or contact the attorney general in your state, neighboring states, or the state where the franchisor is based. Be sure to thoroughly research any franchise you are seriously interested in, because research now will save time and money in the future.

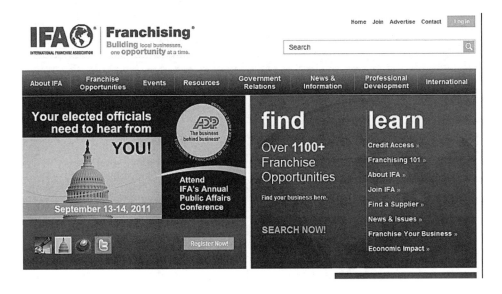

Figure 5.1 Screenshot of International Franchise Association (www.franchise.org). Used with permission.

VISIT A FRANCHISE TRADE SHOW

To talk to many different franchisors and industry experts in one location, attend a franchise trade show or exposition. These shows often offer workshops and seminars to teach you about the industry and explore its advantages and disadvantages. Some exhibitors may use hard-sell tactics, so it's probably worth your time to do some preliminary investigation before attending one of these shows. Develop a budget or investment range and some business goals. At the show, comparison shop for opportunities that meet the criteria you've developed. Remember, you are just investigating possibilities and will need to do a great deal more research before making a decision and selecting a franchise to purchase. Your local chamber of commerce may be aware of trade shows coming to your area or state.

Another place to check is FranchiseHandbook.com (www.franchise1.com). This site lists shows by date and covers the world. Shows are sponsored by different vendors, so if you have several franchises you want to research, see if they'll be exhibiting at the show you're thinking of attending. Research beforehand can always save you time and money.

A FINAL CAUTIONARY NOTE

Some basic guidelines for franchise buyers include the following:

1. A large industry does not assure success; careful planning, research, training, site selection, and marketing are essential for any business to be successful.

2. If you are the first franchisee for a company, be extra careful. If, after a good deal of research, sign on only if you are very confident that the business can replicate its success.

3. Always hire a lawyer to read the agreement with you before you sign; lawyers are necessities, not luxuries.

4. All franchise systems are not the same, so find one that fits your philosophy of doing business, investment limits, and management style.

5. Every business venture involves risk, so plan to work long hours to implement the franchisor's business plan and succeed.

If you want to use books or the Internet to find a franchise that matches your talents, tastes, and investment capital, below are many places to check. The business of franchising has really proliferated on the web, and with the explosion of U.S. exports of franchises to many other countries, international opportunities are also often listed. Find and use several of the resources listed below.

REFERENCES

Starred titles are discussed in the chapter.

▌ Print Resources

Bennett, Julie and Babcock, Cheryl R. *Franchise Times Guide to Selecting, Buying, and Owning a Franchise.* Sterling, 2008. 416p. ISBN 1-402-7439-39. $17.95.

Five sections and 18 chapters cover topics such as finding your perfect franchise fit, the UFOC, franchise attorneys, training, and franchising's future. Find out the pitfalls and drawbacks of franchises here as well as the advantages. Using anecdotes and advice from franchisees and franchisors, the practical tips here will help you enter an agreement with knowledge from a trustworthy source. This book is franchising in a nutshell.

**The Better Business Bureau's Buying a Franchise.* Planning Shop, 2007. 200p. ISBN 1-933-8950-12. $19.95.

The Better Business Bureau guides you through every step of choosing a franchise. Worksheets and checklists will help you ask the right questions, discover the meaning of terms, and learn what red flags and warning signs you should be alert to in avoiding a rip-off. Use this guide early in your decision-making process.

Bisio, Rick. *The Educated Franchisee: The How-To Book for Choosing a Winning Franchise.* Bascom Hill, 2008. 212p. ISBN 0-979-84677-3. $24.99.

Bisio has been a franchise consultant and owned franchised and nonfranchised businesses. Bisio will show you how owning a franchise can create wealth, where to find quality franchisors, what qualities franchisors most often look for, and how you can gather information from franchisees. A summary concludes each chapter. In this well-written book, you will learn the five keys to success from Bisio.

Burton, Virgil L. III. *Encyclopedia of Small Business.* 4th ed. Gale Cengage, 2010. 2v. 1,414p. ISBN 1-4144-2028-5. $631.

Arranged alphabetically, over 500 essays cover topics such as "Advertising Media on the Web," "Business Start-up," "Employee Compensation," "Franchising," "Health Insurance Options," "E-commerce," "Product Development," and "Tax Planning." How those topics affect small business is, of course, emphasized. Bibliographic citations at the end of each topic point to additional sources of information. The master index at the end of volume 2 provides additional subject, organization, government agency, and legislation access. Written in a relevant and accessible format and manner, all types and ages of entrepreneurs will find this a useful reference.

**Bond, Robert E. (ed.). *Bond's Franchise Guide 2011*, 22nd ed. Source Book Publications, 2011. 488p. ISBN 1-88713-775-0. $34.95.

Covering 29 distinct business categories, profiles of franchises supply a description of the business, with number of operating units and geographic distribution; capital requirements, including initial investment and total investment; detailed space needs and staffing levels; initial training and start-up assistance as well as ongoing support; evaluation statements from current franchisees; and specific areas of geographic expansion. For this new edition, profiles of franchise attorneys and consultants have been added. This directory is one of the first places a prospective franchise buyer should search.

Keup, Erwin J. *Franchise Bible: How to Buy a Franchise or Franchise Your Business,* 6th ed. Entrepreneur Press, 2007. 342p. ISBN 1-599180-98-7. $22.95.

Franchise lawyer Keup explains how to assess your suitability for running a franchise, investigate franchisors, interview existing franchisees, and understand the legal terms and documents associated with franchising. The checklists and worksheets Keup has prepared will be useful to readers as well. The appendices contain sample franchise documents for UFOCs, franchise agreements, background data for circulars and agreements, state franchise information guidelines for many states, and UFOC guidelines. The second half of the book tells readers how to franchise their business, but this section is also of interest to new franchisees.

Levonsky, Rieva and Conley, Maria Anton. *Ultimate Book of Franchises,* 2nd ed. Entrepreneur Press, 2007. 540p. ISBN 1-5991-8099-5. $29.95.

Over 1,000 companies, 400 of which are described as "up-and-coming," are listed for the prospective franchisee to browse. The authors provide in-depth facts and figures, such as company size, financial ratings, training and support provided, qualifications needed to obtain a franchise, and contact information. Top 10 lists rank franchises in numerous industries. Practical, how-to advice on buying your first franchise is presented in an easy-to-understand, organized manner.

Luther, William M. *The Marketing Plan: How to Prepare and Implement It,* 4th ed. AMACOM, 2011. 304p. ISBN 0-8144-1693-4. $21.95.

This classic teaches you how to navigate the new landscape involved in producing a working marketing plan. Each chapter contains questions that will help you identify your marketing objectives and provides specific strategies for every stage of a marketing cycle, including market analysis, branding, forecasting, and management. Case studies and examples from major brand successes illustrate good marketing strategies. Online software is available to help in decision making, pricing, budgeting, and sales projections. This practical resource is very useful to all entrepreneurs and particularly to owners of chain franchises.

Norman, Jan. *What No One Ever Tells You about Franchising.* Kaplan, 2006. 193p. ISBN 1-41-95061-37. $18.95.

Norman interviews numerous franchisors and franchisees who provide very practical advice about franchising. Her book is well organized and extremely helpful; she asks good questions and gives a broad and fair representation of the view from both the franchisor's position and the franchisee's position. Find here information on getting good help, the importance of good marketing skills, how to evaluate the franchisor's stability, how to research a franchise before buying, and more.

Purvin, Robert and Purvin, Robert L. Jr. *The Franchise Fraud: How to Protect Yourself Before and After You Invest.* BookSurge, 2008. 332p. ISBN 1-419-6886-21. $18.99.

This critical evaluation of the franchising industry may be enlightening to some who are new to franchising. The Purvins explore the frauds and abuses that some companies perpetrate on their franchisees. Potential franchise owners can learn what to look out for, what questions to ask, and what agreements to make or not make before signing a contract. Find a worthwhile franchising opportunity that suits you and your situation.

Seid, Michael and Thomas, Dave. *Franchising for Dummies,* 2nd ed. For Dummies, 2006. 408p. ISBN 0-47004-581-7. $24.99.

Yes, that's Wendy's International late owner, Dave Thomas, who was the coauthor of this useful guide that outlines in typical fashion the basics, development procedures, running the business, and moving forward. One highlight of this practical guide is the approach to franchisor/franchisee disagreements. Seid and Thomas suggest sitting down with the franchisor, discussing your concerns, and negotiating a way to settle the problem instead of hiring a lawyer. Thomas recommends that training is an ongoing activity for employees and franchisees, because you can always improve. This book will help new franchisees make the most of the time and money invested in a franchise.

Small Business Sourcebook. Gale, annual.

This directory provides a wealth of information for the small business owner/manager. The small business profiles cover 340 different small businesses. Businesses profiled include catering, cooking schools, fish farms, antique shops, bookstores, and car washes, for example. Entries contain as many as 17 subheadings, such as start-up information, educational programs, reference works, sources of supply, statistical sources, trade periodicals, trade shows and conventions, consultants, and franchises and business opportunities. The "Small Business Topics" section covers general ideas like retailing, service industry, franchising, and more. Under restaurants, the sourcebook lists nearly 200 franchises. The "State Listings" and "Federal Government Assistance" sections list programs and offices that provide information and support to small businesses. Check your library for this practical, well-organized source.

Online Resources

America's Best Franchises: www.americasbestfranchises.com/ (Accessed Spring 2011).

Learn about franchises and franchise opportunities on this large site. A newsletter is available for updates, and tabs list "Featured Franchises" and "Franchises Just Added." Find information on using your 401(k) to finance a franchise. Also find attorneys specializing in franchises and information on franchising your own business.

American Franchisee Association: www.franchisee.org (Accessed Spring 2011).

Founded in 1993 and now with more than 16,000 members, this association promotes the economic interests of small business franchisees, assists in the formation of franchisee associations, and provides support and assistance to its members. It provides information on legislation such as the Small Business Franchise Act and other legislative activities affecting franchisees. Resources for legal and business issues are provided. The article on buying a franchise is outstanding, and the article on how to find a franchise attorney is useful also. A monthly newsletter is provided to members. This trade association is useful for all new franchisees.

Bison1.com: www.bison1.com (Accessed Spring 2011).

This well-researched and organized site helps would-be franchisees learn about purchasing a franchise, profiles many franchises in a variety of industries, and even provides a franchise self-test. Franchises are grouped alphabetically, by categories, or premium opportunities. Under "Franchise News," find brief but informative articles on trends and specific franchises from industry experts who give advice. Under "Franchise List," find opportunities listed alphabetically, and under "Top Franchises," find rankings. Under "Franchise Categories," also find franchises by state. This worthwhile, useful site is sponsored by a variety of advertisers.

Entrepreneur.com: www.entrepreneurmag.com (Accessed Spring 2011).

Maintained by *Entrepreneur Magazine,* this site supports new businesses, franchisees, and growing companies. Under "Grow Your Biz," learn how to evaluate your idea and determine whether there's a market for your business. Other topics include location, naming your business, and business structure. Especially strong in franchising and home-based businesses, you can get expert help on a variety of topics, including tool kits for specific kinds of businesses like herb farms, bed and breakfasts, and consulting firms. A unique feature under "Franchises & Opportunities" is a look at franchises by the training they offer. Also, search franchises organized in categories such as low cost, top global, and fastest growing.

FindAFranchise.com: www.bizquest.com/findafranchise/ (Accessed Spring 2011).

This user-friendly site calls itself "The Internet Franchise Search Engine" and is sponsored by BizQuest. Here users can browse 1,200 franchises; find the hottest or trendiest franchises; find franchises for sale; and search through a wide variety of categories, locations, and investment amounts. Categories include "Children's Franchises," "Educational Franchises," and "Home Services Franchises." An alphabetical list is also available. Franchise financing information as well as other franchise resources are also provided. A list of low-cost franchises is available. "Sell Your Business" is a place to list a business or franchise. Lots of well-organized, balanced information is presented. Several newsletters are also available to help in your search for a business or franchise.

**Franchise.com: www.franchise.com (Accessed Spring 2011).

This large site provides information for franchise buyers, franchise owners, franchisors, and suppliers. You can search or view by category, license, or franchise name. Find lists such "Star Opportunities," "New Arrivals," and "Premier Listings." Also provided are sections on "Green Franchises," "Resale Franchises," "Lenders," and "Attorneys." "Small Business and Franchise Events" can be useful to new franchisees. This site is international, so you can find opportunities globally. The "Small Business Articles" section covers topics such as finding financing, new franchise success rates, and how to choose the right franchise. Use this site to investigate franchising.

Franchiseexpo.com: www.franchiseexpo.com (Accessed Spring 2011).

This well-researched and organized site helps would-be franchisees learn about purchasing a franchise, profiles many franchises in a variety of industries, and suggests franchises for seniors, veterans, women, etc. Franchises are grouped alphabetically, by categories, or premium opportunities. Find franchises grouped under home based, low cost, part time, and more. Under "Franchise By State," find franchises by state or click one of the international flags at the top of the page to find franchises in other countries. This worthwhile, useful site is sponsored by a variety of advertisers.

FranchiseGator.com: www.franchisegator.com (Accessed Spring 2011).

Search here for conventional franchises and multiunit franchise opportunities. Besides franchise offerings and franchise FAQs, users can access franchise services and brief articles on a range of franchising topics. Search by state and/or by industry. Frequently updated and easily searchable, users will return to this site to learn more about franchises.

**FranchiseHandbook.com: www.franchise1.com (Accessed Spring 2011).

This online directory lists franchising shows by industry and covers the world. Shows are sponsored by different vendors, so if you have several franchises you want to research, see if they'll be exhibiting at the show you're thinking of attending. Franchise opportunities and companies are described with contact information. Franchise industry news and a list of franchises for sale are also available. The "Expert Advice and Resources" section is worth a look for articles and information. Like most sites today, it is linked to Facebook and Twitter.

Franchise Info Mall: www.franchiseinfomall.com (Accessed Spring 2011).

Another large franchise directory, Franchise Info Mall has over 100 franchise categories that can be searched. It lists "Franchises Best Suited for Women," "Fastest Growing Franchises," the top 100 franchises, the top 500, and the top 200 international franchises. Franchise expos are listed as well as franchise attorneys and consultants. Franchise-related articles are also presented.

The Franchise Millionaire: www.thefranchisemillionaire.com (Accessed Spring 2011).

This large site wants to give you free coaching to learn about franchising and provides a great deal of useful information when investigating franchises. Under the main menu, you will find franchise statistics and facts, advantages, financing, why buy a franchise, and categories of franchises like automotive, dry cleaning, home care, senior care, and many others. Gathered here are short articles about many different possible franchise opportunities.

Franchise News Center: www.franchisenewscenter.com/ (Accessed Spring 2011).

The "Franchise Buyer Resources and Information" teaches users about franchising, franchisors, and being a franchisee. Also available here is a franchise directory. One excellent article is "Top Reasons Why Some Franchises Fail." Information to help users find out about a franchise before signing an agreement is included. Use to find business opportunities, especially franchises for sale and how to sell your franchise.

Franchise Opportunities: ww.franchiseopportunities.com/ (Accessed Spring 2011).

This site identifies, creates, and distributes information regarding franchising and small business opportunities and was created to promote high-quality franchising and business resources in a secure, collegial, professional, and ethical business environment. This large directory of franchise opportunities is searchable by industry, state, and investment. Under "Franchise Resources" and the "Franchise Network" find more information and resources to help you become a successful franchisee. Be sure to check out the "Consumer Guide to Buying a Franchise" to help you make the best decision.

Franchise Solutions: www.franchisesolutions.com (Accessed Spring 2011).

This unique site lists franchise resales, plus allows franchisees to sort franchise opportunities by cash requirements and industry category. Users can also check out the "New Owners Club" and home-based franchises. The "Franchise Business News" section includes franchise success stories and advice on starting and managing a successful franchise. Franchises for veterans are showcased. This site also highlights green business franchises. Sign up for the free newsletter for updates. A wealth of information is available and nicely organized.

Franchising: Franchise411: www.franchise411.com (Accessed Spring 2011).

This online library and resources center will help you understand what franchising is and how to take advantage of everything it has to offer. Find here an explanation of UFOCs, the FTC's rules, state registration information, and international franchising. Upcoming franchise seminars and shows and events with dates around the country are listed. Included are links to sites presenting franchise opportunities in the United States and internationally and information about franchising in general and specific franchises. It is infrequently updated and losing its usefulness right now.

Franchoice: www.franchoice.com (Accessed Spring 2011).

The FranChoice program is a consultation program that is similar to working with a realtor when you buy a house. An industry expert works with the prospective franchisee to find a good match in terms of the type of franchise to buy and run. Fees are paid by franchisors. Franchise consultants help you select and evaluate a franchise opportunity, including reviewing and explaining the UFOC.

FranNet: www.frannet.com (Accessed Spring 2011).

A similar service to Franchoice is FranNet. This site is a bit larger with testimonials, events, helpful tips, news, and links to other sites. If you want to use one of these services, it's probably good to shop around on the Internet and find the best deal you can for the service you need.

Inc.com: www.inc.com (Accessed Spring 2011).

The publishers of *Inc.* magazine present a large directory of articles by topic targeting many problems, concerns, and decisions confronting new business owners/managers. The section on business plans is precise and practical and applies to a franchise business plan, too. The section "Start Up, Franchises" includes "Should You Consider an International Franchise," and articles under "Understanding a Franchise Agreement" should be read by every prospective franchisee. Simple but effective advice is the hallmark of this outstanding, easy-to-use site.

**International Franchise Association: www.franchise.org (Accessed Spring 2011).

If you are thinking of purchasing or have purchased a franchise, this site contains a comprehensive database with links to over 800 companies. Many details about buying and running an individual franchise are provided. Its publication, *Franchise Opportunities Guide,* is outstanding. The Franchise Discussion Forum allows users to discuss best practices, answer questions and share ideas for new and existing franchisees, locate and contact international franchise groups, and exchange ideas and news on technology. Under "Guidance," find a free franchise basics course and a list of key questions to ask. Here you can also search franchises by investment dollar amount needed. You will find educational opportunities here as well as news affecting the franchise industry. This easy-to-use, large site spotlights all information related to franchising.

Small Business Administration: www.sba.gov (Accessed Spring 2011).

This official government site offers a wealth of resources and programs for starting and growing a small business. Search "franchises," and you will find a "Consumer Guide to Buying a Franchise." Also read "How Can I Go about Investigating a Franchise?" This authoritative site covers many of the major concerns when choosing a franchise. Other major articles cover business plans, financing, managing, marketing, employees, taxes, legal aspects, and business opportunities. Find here online forms, business plans, financing and loan information, and many publications. Some contents are available in Spanish.

USA Franchise Directory: www.franchisedirectory.com (Accessed Spring 2011).

This large directory allows you to request brochures directly from franchises that interest you, send e-mails to sales representatives, and access the franchises' websites. The "Franchise Guide" is very useful, as is the featured franchise. Franchising statistics provided are current and interesting. A Canadian franchise directory is also provided.

RAISING CAPITAL

6

CHAPTER HIGHLIGHTS

What Will It Cost?

Sources of Seed Capital

Traditional Sources of Loans

As a new business owner, a key factor in starting or growing your business is your ability to obtain financing. You need start-up capital or "seed money" to finance every aspect of this venture, from securing a location to printing business cards. Start by carefully analyzing these costs to determine how much money you'll need. Remember that undercapitalization is one of the most common reasons small businesses fail.

WHAT WILL IT COST?

Using the business plan that you're developing and your own instincts about what is the least you can do and the most you can afford, make a list to start deciding what you already have and what you will need to rent or purchase. The list will include:

- Office equipment
- A space in which to conduct business
- Computer
- Furniture
- Telephone service
- Utilities
- Product inventory
- Business licenses and permits
- Insurance
- Advertising

- Professional fees
- Miscellaneous expenses

As in figuring any budget, you'll have priorities to establish and choices to make, but figuring a budget first and deciding where to cut corners will help you in the day-to-day management of your business. Collect the information to make these figures as accurate as possible. If you completed your three financial statements for your business plan already, you should have most of this data at your fingertips. If you're still having trouble estimating start-up costs, try consulting the Entrepreneur's Guidebook Series at (www.smbtn.com/business planguides/). Under the "Accounting Help Center" you will see *Start-up Costs*, guidebook 78. Find a lengthy and thorough guide and worksheet to help you estimate start-up costs.

If your opening estimate is greater than your available resources, you will have to consider different sources for the necessary capital. Be very careful about using retirement savings to fund your new business. There's always a risk to any new venture, so consider every possibility, and then weigh your alternatives carefully. You know your financial needs; prepare to present your financial request in the most professional manner you can devise, regardless of how you decide to pursue the necessary capital.

SOURCES OF SEED CAPITAL

Family and Friends

A variety of methods can be used to raise seed capital. Probably the least expensive route is to tap family and friends. If your business is too small or too new to get other financing, this may be the best route. Inform them as to how much interest you can pay and when they will be paid back. Put the loan terms in writing, and treat this loan as any other. Also tell investors how much of your own funds are invested in the business.

> *A note of caution:* Be sure motives and expectations are clear with family and friends—the price of losing a valuable relationship is very high. Treat them as professionally as you would a banker or a potential partner. Clearly outline the repayment schedule, and keep updating them as your business situation changes.

Partner

Acquiring a partner is often used as a means to bring into the business someone who has the funds needed for start-up. Go back to the section in chapter 3 on business structure to see if this type of financing would work for your business.

Life Insurance

Life insurance policies that have a cash surrender value are a source of money that you can borrow, and sometimes the interest rates are lower than market rates. However, before you borrow against your policy, be sure you understand all the conditions outlined in the policy.

Home Equity Loan

If you own your own house, a home equity loan can be a source of capital for your new business. Call several lenders for the lowest rates, and find out if there are any hidden costs you'll have to pay at closing. If you use a home equity loan, consider it a business loan that uses your house as collateral that will enable you to write off the interest as a business expense. Check with your accountant to see if you can and how to do this correctly.

TRADITIONAL SOURCES OF LOANS

Debt Financing

Financing is generally grouped into two types. First decide if you are looking for debt financing, which is money you borrow, or equity financing, which is money acquired from investors and/or savings. If you decide to convince a bank or credit union to lend you the money for your business, present your financial needs and expectations precisely, showing exactly where the money will be used and how and when it will be repaid. If you have collateral to offer to guarantee the loan, include that information. Also include financial information about you, any partners, or any key employees.

Most financiers check five criteria, known in the banking industry as the five Cs of credit, when reviewing your request for a loan:

1. *Cash flow* or the money coming in to and going out of your business is a major consideration. Provide projected cash flow statements as well as historic financial reports if possible.

2. *Capital* or how much of your own money is invested in your business. The standard amount that banks usually require is 30% of the total projected start-up costs.

3. *Collateral* or what property can be used to secure this loan that could be seized by the lender if the borrower defaults or fails to repay the debt. Among the personal assets you could use as collateral are inventory, life insurance policies, real estate, and stocks and bonds.

4. *Credit* or your current credit history, both business and personal. As in personal credit history, lenders like to see four or five years of credit experience before considering your business for a commercial loan.

5. *Character* or your personal financial investments or past and present lender relationships. Sometimes banks will ask for references from other professionals such as lawyers or accountants with whom you have worked in the past.

Obtaining a bank loan is a challenging task for a new business owner, but with a solid, well-documented business plan, persistence, and patience, your chances of success improve greatly.

Even though you make a presentation for a business loan, banks are more likely to give you a personal loan to use for business purposes. One strategy that may work is to ask for a very small business loan that you agree to pay back in 180 days or a year. This type of short-term business loan, which needs to be repaid with interest within a set period of time, is sometimes called a demand loan, as the lender can call it in at any time. Just as in your personal credit history, your business credit history is established by having a record of prompt payments. *Entrepreneur Magazine*'s website (www.entrepreneur.com/bestbanks) presents a list of best small-business-friendly banks that are more likely to lend you the funds you need. You will also find a list of top 20 nationwide micro loan lenders. Another section of Entrepreneur.com presents a guide to raising money for more assistance in obtaining the capital you need. More information about venture capital is provided later in this chapter.

After you have established a business credit history, a bank may provide a line of credit that you can draw against. Through this type of agreement, your business has a set amount of credit, called revolving credit, that you can draw upon. A line of credit provides you with the flexibility to meet cash flow crises and day-to-day expenses, but it, of course, has to be paid back, and you pay interest on the outstanding balance. Revolving credit is replenished every time you make a payment. There is no charge for having a line of credit, just for using it.

Today some financial institutions offer small businesses credit cards to finance start-up and operating expenses. However, due to their interest rates, credit cards are often the most expensive type of small business financing. Financing your business on credit cards may save time and allow you to keep business expenses separate from personal ones. But be forewarned, without very careful management, credit card debt can quickly put you out of business.

The Small Business Administration (SBA) has numerous guaranteed loan programs available for start-ups and small businesses, but they are generally associated with banks so you still have to apply for the loans through banks. Visit the SBA's home page at www.sba.gov and select the "Loans & Grants" tab at the top of the page, under "SBA Loan Programs," to learn about programs like the 7(a) Loan Guaranty, Microloan Program, Minority Prequalification Loan Program, and others. In recent years, the SBA loan package process has been simplified for loans less than $100,000, so you may want to check them out. The Microloan Program provides short-term loans of up to $35,000 and is only available in selected locations in most states. Small business investment companies (SBICs) are government-operated investment firms that provide venture capital to small businesses. SBICs are licensed by the SBA, and you will find information about them on the SBA's website by searching for "SBIC."

A CAUTIONARY NOTE ABOUT SBA LOAN GUARANTEES

SBA loan guarantees differ in a few important ways from loans made by other lending institutions; when you consider what type of loan to apply for, it's good to keep these items in mind:

1. These loans take longer and require more paperwork.

2. The loan funds won't be released in one check. Canceled checks, invoices, or purchase orders may be required before funds are released.

3. Personal assets or jointly owned assets may have to be used as personal guarantees to get the loan.

4. An SBA-guaranteed loan may carry a higher interest rate than a conventional bank loan; the benefit of an SBA guarantee is that the lender extends the term of the loan beyond the usual time period—for example, seven years instead of five.

5. The SBA charges lenders an annual servicing fee and a guaranty fee, and those percentages may be passed on to the borrower by the lending institution.

6. The SBA makes a special effort to make minority-owned, women-owned, and veteran-owned businesses aware of SBA programs, but there is no special pot of money or special considerations for those enterprises.

Equity Financing

Since debt financing is often difficult for small start-up businesses to obtain, let's now look at equity financing. Equity financing is an exchange of money for a share of business ownership. Equity capital gives its contributor an ownership interest in the assets of the business and a share of its future income. You do not incur debt with this form of financing, and you do not have to repay a set amount of money at a particular time. The contributor often wants a voice in how the business is run, so you do give up some control over your business. Two main sources for equity financing are angel investors and venture capital firms.

Angel Investors

An angel investor is a wealthy private individual or groups of businesspeople or professionals who provide early-stage capital to new companies, especially companies that can improve the community, and who usually invest in regional or local companies within a specific industry or area of business interest or expertise. Generally speaking, these investors are more patient than venture capitalists, who often want to make back 10 times their investment in less than five years. Prepare a pitch to an angel in the same manner as you approach a bank. Once again, an outstanding business plan can help you succeed.

How does one locate an angel investor? This step can be difficult, because angel investors don't advertise. Start by networking with local entrepreneurs, lawyers, and accountants. Show your business plan to many local individuals and follow every lead you're given to connect with leaders of the community. Angel investors are beginning to create a network, and the place to start looking is at the website www.angelsummit.org. This site lists these groups by state and also lists their websites. Another resource for learning about angel investors and investing is *Raising Venture Capital for the Serious Entrepreneur,* by Dermot Berkery. Here you'll find out how to match your new business to angel investors as well as additional sources of information.

Berkery, Dermot. *Raising Venture Capital for the Serious Entrepreneur.* McGraw-Hill, 2007. 288p. ISBN 0-071-49602-5. $49.95.

Berkery covers the major topics for obtaining financing in a well-organized, readable style. This complete toolbox details how venture capitalists arrange the funding for a company. Particularly useful chapters include "Developing a Financing Map" and "Creating a Winning Business Plan." An entire chapter is devoted to "Setting Terms for Splitting the Rewards." Venture capital firms are described in detail along with a description of how they evaluate a business. Three extensive case studies are provided to illustrate points made by Berkery. This comprehensive reference guide will help new and old entrepreneurs obtain financing.

Other sites at the end of the chapter list sources where you may be able to locate an angel investor.

Venture Capital

Venture capital is the money invested in young, rapidly growing businesses. Venture capital firms pool money from private investors and expect a high annual return (20% to 40%) on their investment and usually invest in companies for a period of three to seven years. Venture capital firms often focus on a certain industry and invest at a particular stage of the company's development. Seed capital is needed at the start-up stage. Early stage financing is designed to fund the early growth stage after the company is delivering a product or service. The final stage is expansion-stage financing, when the company needs funds to expand into new markets or product lines. As your business grows, you may need venture capital to help you finance changes that you need to make to expand your operation. The cost of this type of financing is high and may require you to sell off large portions of your business with a resulting loss of control. Sometimes when a venture capitalist decides to exit a business, an initial public offering of your company's stock is used to continue financing the business. Investigate the pros and cons of venture capital very carefully before seeking this type of financing. When you want to find a venture capitalist or venture capital firm, check with your attorney, banker, or other local business owners to get a personal recommendation if possible.

You may also want to check the National Venture Capital Association at www. nvca.org. This trade association provides advocacy, education, and networking opportunities for the U.S. venture capital industry. The directory provides access to venture capital organizations regionally throughout the United States. Another classic reference on venture capital is David Gladstone's *Venture Capital Handbook*. Learn how to obtain venture capital as he walks you through the process and the forms, including commitment letters, loan agreements, promissory notes, and stock purchase warrants.

Gladstone, David. *Venture Capital Handbook,* rev. ed. Prentice Hall, 2002. 424p. ISBN 0-13-065493-0. $39.

Gladstone explains the venture capital process for entrepreneurs, using insights and actual examples gained from his experience as a venture capitalist. Learn how to develop a business plan with obtaining venture capital in mind. Each step in the process to obtain venture capital funding is discussed. Advice on attracting investors, accelerating the investment process, and building long-term relationships with investors is included. Many checklists are included to help you keep track of all the homework and paperwork needed to work with venture capitalists. This revised edition also considers the impact of the Internet and new technologies on the marketplace and the venture capitalist industry. Well written and to the point, the information here is easy to understand and well organized. This handbook is a classic on venture capital.

Listed in the resources at the end of the chapter are more sources of information on venture capital.

If you would like to read further about sources that can help you obtain many types of financing, the *Inc.* magazine site (www.inc.com/) has very good articles under the "Finance" tab, including "How to Raise Start-up Capital in 2011" and "How to Raise Venture Capital."

REFERENCES

Starred titles are discussed in the chapter.

▮ Print Resources

Amis, David and Stevenson, Howard. *Winning Angels: The 7 Fundamentals of Early Stage Investing.* BookSurge, 2009. 390p. ISBN 1-439-22546-X. $49.99.

This practical, well-organized guide reduces the art of angel investing to the basics. Entrepreneurs will benefit from reading this work before they seek funding. Learn what investors are looking for in new businesses and how to provide it. Many venture capitalists and entrepreneurs were interviewed to provide the advice. Learn how to attract financing to your business venture. Find a collection of advice, examples, and venture capital contact information in this insightful primer.

**Berkery, Dermot. *Raising Venture Capital for the Serious Entrepreneur.* McGraw-Hill, 2007. 288p. ISBN 0-071-49602-5. $49.95.

Berkery covers the major topics for obtaining financing in a well-organized, readable style. This complete toolbox details how venture capitalists arrange the funding for a company. Particularly useful chapters include "Developing a Financing Map" and "Creating a Winning Business Plan." An entire chapter is devoted to "Setting Terms for Splitting the Rewards." Venture capital firms are described in detail along with a description of how they evaluate a business. Three extensive case studies are provided to illustrate points made by Berkery. This comprehensive reference guide will help new and old entrepreneurs obtain financing.

Calvin, Robert J. *Entrepreneurial Management: Creating Successful Business Plans, Raising Capital and Structuring Deals, Maximizing Profits and Growth.* CreateSpace, 2010. 304p. ISBN 1-4392-7231-X. $14.94.

Combining decades of experience and real-world knowledge, Calvin will help you spot the right opportunity, find your niche, price your product or service right, and reach out to customers. Learn techniques for targeting, evaluating, and obtaining alternative sources of financing. Learn how to create and run a successful business.

Carlini, Ronald J. and Moss, Therese Carlini. *Smooth Sailing to Venture Capital Funding.* Venture Capital Strategies, 2005. 174p. ISBN 0-9760908-5-6. $19.95.

The authors focus on teaching entrepreneurs and companies how to evaluate their business model and measure it against what the financial community is currently funding. Identify your company's strengths and eliminate the weaknesses to attract investors and build a strong, profitable company. This book identifies the obstacles to obtaining financing and helps entrepreneurs and small businesses in general overcome them and successfully obtain the needed financing.

DeBaise, Colleen. *Wall Street Journal, Complete Small Business Guidebook.* Crown, 2009. 272 p. ISBN 0-307-40893-0. $15.00.

This practical guide covers all the basics, such as business plans, funding, using technology, marketing, managing, and how to hire the right employees. The "Better Business Bureau's Worksheets for Estimating Start Up Costs" in the back are easy to use and well organized. Additionally, find secrets to locating extra money to support expansion or maintenance, executing an exit strategy, and managing vacations. DeBaise provides useful help for turning your dreams into a profitable business.

**Gladstone, David. *Venture Capital Handbook,* rev. ed. Prentice Hall, 2002. 424p. ISBN 0-13-065493-0. $39.

Gladstone explains the venture capital process for entrepreneurs, using insights and actual examples gained from his experience as a venture capitalist. Learn how to develop a business plan with obtaining venture capital in mind. Each step in the process to obtain venture capital funding is discussed. Advice on attracting investors, accelerating the investment process, and building long-term relationships with investors is included. Many checklists are included to help you keep track of all the homework and paperwork needed to work with venture capitalists. This revised edition also considers the impact of the Internet and new technologies on the marketplace and the venture capitalist industry. Well written and to the point, the information is easy to understand and well organized. This handbook is a classic on venture capital.

Gordon, Michael E. *Trump University Entrepreneurship 101: How to Turn Your Idea into a Money Machine,* 2nd ed. John Wiley, 2009. ISBN 0-47-04671-85. $24.95.

The second edition adds three new chapters, teaching you how to build a technology venture, how to use social networking for competitive advantages, and how to exploit opportunities during recessionary times. Using a systematic approach and interactive learning, this comprehensive guide also covers writing an effective business plan and how to negotiate with investors and provides visual models, case studies, worksheets, and personal stories from Donald Trump.

Green, Charles H. *The SBA Loan Book.* Adams Media, 2011. 232p. ISBN 1-5806-2202-X. $12.95.

Green answers questions such as how to increase your odds of getting a loan, how to present your business to lenders, and how to appeal the lender's denial. This down-to-earth, logical resource walks readers through the process of loan applications. Find out how to be successful no matter what type of loan you need or want to obtain.

Hashemi, Sahar and Hashemi, Bobby. *Anyone Can Do It: Building Coffee Republic from Our Kitchen Table—57 Real Life Laws on Entrepreneurship.* Capstone, 2007. 224p. ISBN 1-8411-2765-5. $17.95.

This sister-brother team (she a lawyer, he an investment banker) built Coffee Republic, the original high street coffee chain in the United Kingdom. They left the security of well-paying jobs to follow the entrepreneurial dream. Here they chronicle the development of the business plan, raising money, opening the first store, taking the company public, and finally today's inspirational success, where Coffee Republic has over 100 outlets and thousands of employees. Small business ownership is time-consuming, but this book is very motivating and inspirational.

Lee, Trent and Lee, Chad. *Unlimited Business Financing.* Xeno Press, 2008. 134p. ISBN 1-934-2750-54. $14.95.

Use the Lees' suggestions to establish credit in the name of your company with their legal and ethical methods. Cash flow fuels your business growth according to the Lees. This book will help you understand the business credit system better.

Mohr, Angie. *Bookkeepers' Boot Camp: Get a Grip on Accounting Basics,* 2nd ed. Self-Counsel Press, 2010. 204p. ISBN 1-55180-449-2. $14.95.

This handy title walks readers through the essentials of recordkeeping for a small business and explains why it's so necessary to track this information. Learn how to sort through paperwork, how to record and file what is important for your business, and how to use that information to help your business succeed. The basics of balance sheets, income statements, cash flow statements, inventory management, and monitoring budgets and cash flow are thoroughly explained so readers can understand what the accountant is telling them. Brief case studies are used to illustrate the use of financial data in your business.

Also covered are tax planning, choosing an accountant, and the role of an accountant in running your small business. Chapter summaries highlight important concepts in each chapter. Learn how to manage the financial part of your business and personal life as an entrepreneur.

Mohr, Angie. *Financial Management 101: Get a Grip on Your Business Numbers,* 2nd ed. Self-Counsel Press, 2010. 161p. ISBN 1-55180-805-6. $14.95.

If you are new to the complexities of finance and want to competently analyze financial data, study this book. Mohr helps new entrepreneurs plan the financial end of their business from the first financial statements through budgeting for advertising. Learn to measure your business success and how to find new opportunities. The chapter on ratio analysis will help readers learn what basic ratios tell them, what to do when ratios indicate a problem, and how to integrate ratios into your management reporting system. Case studies are presented throughout the book to help readers understand the importance of the concepts presented.

Ochtel, Robert T. *Business Planning, Business Plans, and Venture Funding.* Carlsbad Technology Group, 2009. 232p. ISBN 0-615-25714-3. $49.95.

Ochtel provides concrete examples of business planning documents and plans as well as detailed descriptions of various types of funding available for start-up companies. Learn how to efficiently and effectively introduce your company's product, service, or new technology into the right marketplace at the right time.

Pratt, Stanley E. *Pratt's Guide to Private Equity Sources.* Venture Economics, annual. $750.

This comprehensive, classic library reference, formerly known as *Pratt's Guide to Venture Capital Sources* and now combined with the *Directory of Buyout Financing Sources,* includes both venture and buyout sources of financing. The 2004 edition contains more than 4,500 listings, including U.S.-based and foreign-based firms. Information on the venture capital industry and guidelines for companies seeking financing are provided in the sections on "Background on Private Equity" and "How to Raise Private Equity." Perspectives provide insight into the characteristics private equity investors look for in their clients as well as an entrepreneur's view of the private equity process. Following the text is a directory with detailed information about private equity companies. An index of firms by location and an executive index follow the directory.

Preston, Susan L. *Angel Financing for Entrepreneurs.* Jossey-Bass, 2007. 384p. ISBN 0-787-9875-06. $39.95.

Learn how angel investors think and what their expectations are from entrepreneurs. Business plans must be well written and detail financial forecasts for three to five years. Learn how to determine your capital requirements. Preston explains how to put together and what to include in a 10-minute presentation that will grab investors. This invaluable resource is easy to read, practical, and nicely organized to help you get the information you need.

Reiss, Bob. *Bootstrapping 101: Tips to Build Your Business with Limited Cash and Free Outside Help.* R&R, 2009. 190p. ISBN 0-57-802413-6. $19.95.

Reiss presents a variety of different ways to kick-start a new enterprise without spending a lot of cash. Follow his advice to learn about getting and keeping customers, bartering, outsourcing, and networking. Detailed and clear, find many resources that illustrate the concepts and applications he offers. From spreadsheets and advertising to fiscal management and meeting hard-to-reach contacts, this book is useful for all small business owners and managers.

Richards, Rene V. *How to Buy and/or Sell a Small Business for Maximum Profit.* Atlantic, 2006. 288p. ISBN 0-910-6275-35. $24.95.

Richards's book is a roadmap of suggestions, insights, and techniques for both buyers and sellers. Covered here is the entire selling process. Learn how best to decide when to sell or buy by figuring out how to market the company and learn to understand the various legal and financial documents involved in a sale. Find here hints on closing the deal and handling the transition afterward. The first-time entrepreneur, deciding whether he or she wants to buy a small business, will find plenty of help here. Areas Richards covers include finding and evaluating a business to buy and/or sell, how to value a business, raising the funds for purchase, evaluating a business financial condition, asset valuation and income capitalization, leveraged buyouts, letters of intent, and legal and tax concerns.

Sigmon, Patricia. *Six Steps to Creating Profit: A Guide for Small and Mid-Sized Service-Based Businesses.* John Wiley, 2010. ISBN 0-470-55425-8. $34.95.

Learn how to change your business and measure the results of each change so your business is more profitable. Learn more about and understand cash flow, management costs, and how important selling is for all your employees. Find out more about visibility in the marketplace, marketing, and financing. Keep the cash flowing, know your budget, and manage for profit. Sigmon presents useable, practical, and easily implemented tactics to improve your bottom line.

Tracy, Tage C. *Small Business Financial Management Kit for Dummies.* For Dummies, 2007. 384p. ISBN 0-470-12508-X. $24.99.

Tracy will help you plan a budget, streamline your accounting process, raise capital, and generally keep your business solvent. Learn how to avoid common management pitfalls and use the bonus CD's reproducible forms, checklists, and templates. Tracy explains the financial foundations of a sound business.

Warner, Ralph E. and Laurence, Bethany. *Save Your Small Business: 10 Crucial Strategies to Survive Hard Times or Close Down and Move On.* Nolo Press, 2009. 316p. ISBN 1-4133-1041-9. $29.99.

The basic thrust of this book is covered by chapters about concentrating on what is really profitable for your business, controlling your cash flow, minimizing your liability, bankruptcy and its alternatives, and not wasting money on ineffective marketing. Chapter 12 is about closing down your business and is very thorough. If you feel the business has run its course, learn how to shut down operations while protecting your personal assets. The appendix, "How to Prepare a Profit and Loss Forecast and Cash Flow Analysis," is very comprehensive.

Wyszkowski, Eric P. *All You Need to Know about SBA Loans from a Lender.* E-Book Time, 2009. 68p. ISBN 1-6086-2003-4. $8.95.

Wyszkowksi will help you gather the information you need to successfully apply for and receive an SBA loan. With this simple and straightforward book, you will be able to meet the requirements and find out about the many different formats you can use for a loan proposal. You will know when you should contact the lender. When writing your proposal, be sure to familiarize the lender with your industry or your individual business. Industry-specific details provided to the lender can help you understand how your particular business is run and what industry trends affect it.

▌ Online Resources

About.com: http://sbinformation.about.com/od/creditloans/u/moneymatters.htm (Accessed Spring 2011).

This large site has many different parts, but the "Small Business Money Matters" section contains good articles on getting a loan, cash flow management, finding an angel investor, and sources of equity financing. Also find tips on insurance and tax questions or decisions. Many downloadable business forms as well as some industry information can be accessed here as well. Continually updated and well organized, this site will help you find information on financing options as well as budgeting and planning your finances.

AllBusiness: www.allbusiness.com (Accessed Spring 2011).

This huge site contains articles and advice on any area of business law, including legal structure, property leases, patents, trademarks, employment law, taxes, and even how to work with your lawyer. The finance section includes articles on budgeting, credit, pricing, and taxes. The articles on green businesses are also very useful. Links to many directories are also provided as well as news and business information sites. The tax articles discuss topics such as barter tax and accounting issues and tax strategies for keeping the family business in the family. Use this well-organized, functional website often.

Angel Capital Association: www.angelcapitalassociation.org/ (Accessed Spring 2011).

Looking for an angel investing group in North America? Start your search here. This peer organization of angel investing organizations holds annual summits and regional meetings to develop best practices and encourage collaboration. ACA is not a source of capital but provides information to investors and entrepreneurs. Under "Entrepreneurs" you will find a link to "Listing of ACA Member Angel Groups: in the U.S., Canada, and Mexico."

Business Finance: www.businessfinance.com (Accessed Spring 2011).

This large, well-organized website includes more than 4,000 business loan and capital sources. You can search the "Small Business Loans" or "Working Capital" sections with sources categorized for you. Microloans, business credit cards, equipment leasing, Small Business Administration small business loans, venture capital, construction loans, and investment banks are all included. Search the "Business Funding Management Center" and the how-to e-books sections for tools and resources. This site is easy to use and provides financing information.

Business Know-How: www.businessknowhow.com/bkhstartup.htm (Accessed Spring 2011).

This large business website has a great page on starting a business as well as lots of information on small business finances, cash flow, taxes, and business loans. A handy checklist helps you remember what to do and when to do it. Also included is information on human resources training and tools, employment forms, templates and productivity tools, and web design and content. Check out this site when starting and running your business.

Business Owner's Toolkit: http://toolkit.com (Accessed Spring 2011).

Commerce Clearinghouse, now a Wolters Kluwer business, started the Small Business Guide, which provides pages of information and tools to help individuals start, run, and grow a successful small business. Business tools provided include sample letters, contracts, forms, and agreements ready for you to customize for your business and use. Financial spreadsheet templates are available in the "Financial Planning Toolkit," and checklists help you stay organized in completing necessary tasks. IRS tax forms, state tax forms, employee management forms, and more are all linked to this site. Also find articles on how tax law changes could affect your business.

Entrepreneur.com: www.entrepreneurmag.com (Accessed Spring 2011).

Maintained by *Entrepreneur Magazine,* this site supports new businesses and growing companies. Find many good articles on financing your new business. Two important areas of this site are listed at the top: "Management" and "Business Coaches." Here you'll find lists of articles covering various topics in management such as trends in management, time management, managing employees, and more. "Business Coaches" can help you through difficult times in your business life. "Start Up Topics" includes organization and managing, finding a location, naming your business, and business structure. Find ready-made business forms here, too. Use this site whenever you need help in determining what to do next.

**Entrepreneur's Guidebook Series: www.smbtn.com/businessplanguides/ (Accessed Spring 2011).

Defining real entrepreneurs as managers who adopt key behaviors developed by understanding key market concepts and theories and who are successful because of their planning and researching skills, this site discusses why people become entrepreneurs and the type of life entrepreneurs generally lead. Here you will discover what your entrepreneurial talents are and common traits of successful entrepreneurs. Explore this website for good ideas.

Financial Calculators for Business: www.dinkytown.net/business.html (Accessed Spring 2011).

This lengthy list of calculators will help you with break-even analysis, cash flow, inventory, taxes, business valuation, ratios, and more. Use to help you with payroll deductions, self-employment taxes, and more.

**Inc.com: www.inc.com (Accessed Spring 2011).

The publishers of *Inc.* magazine present a large directory of articles by topic targeting many problems, concerns, and decisions confronting new business owners/managers. Especially outstanding are the current articles on financing your new business. The articles on marketing and advertising are informative and practical. Simple but effective advice is the hallmark of this outstanding, easy-to-use site.

**National Venture Capital Association (NCVA): www.nvca.org (Accessed Spring 2011).

This trade association provides advocacy, education, and networking opportunities for the U.S. venture capital industry. The NVCA supports entrepreneurial activity and innovation and aims to increase the visibility and awareness of the industry as well as its importance to the U.S. economy. The NVCA membership directory provides access to venture capital organizations regionally throughout the United States. Another section of the directory covers venture capital organizations outside the United States. Each entry includes a brief description and the web address. Its affiliate group, the American Entrepreneurs for Economic Growth, is the nation's largest network of emerging growth companies with 14,000 members.

PowerHomeBiz.com: www.powerhomebiz.com/Index/financing.htm (Accessed Spring 2011).

This small business site has an outstanding section on how to finance your business. The section includes start-up expenses, managing business finances, finance tools, and controlling your taxes. There is a special section on bank loans and microloans. "Must-Have Books" are listed with some articles and recommended tools and software as well. This large, established, and well-organized site will help new entrepreneurs with financing and other aspects of starting a new business.

**Small Business Administration: www.sba.gov (Accessed Spring 2011).

This official government site offers a wealth of resources and programs for starting and growing a small business. Under "Starting and Managing a Business" users will find an entrepreneurial test that will help them evaluate their possible success in their own business. Other major sections cover business planning, financing, managing, marketing, employees, taxes, legal aspects, and business opportunities. Find here online forms, business plans, loan information, and many publications. Some contents are available in Spanish.

Small Business Town Network: www.smbtn.com/businessplanguides/ (Accessed Spring 2011).

This large site has links to business plan samples, software, services, and various other small business e-guides. Under "Bplan" you will find accounting help, with information on start-up costs, cash flow projections, financing, and reducing your taxes. Under the step-by-step planning is the "Company Plan," where you will find information tailored to your industry, business laws and regulations, information on hiring personnel, and more.

Startup Nation: www.startupnation.com (Accessed Spring 2011).

Two brothers founded this site in 2002 to provide one-stop shopping for practical information to help entrepreneurs succeed. Users can access step-by-step advice, easy-to-understand articles, professional groups and forums, expert blogs, podcasts, and member-to-member networking. Learn how to use technology efficiently, maximize your niche, acquire growth capital, and more. The eight steps to managing your money will help you plan and organize your business and personal finances. Use this site often to help you and your business succeed.

vFinance.com: www.vfinance.com (Accessed Spring 2011).

This commercial site allows visitors to search for venture capital or angel investors. Free business plan sample templates are provided for entrepreneurs in the "Business Plan Center." Users can post business plans for viewing by potential investors. Also, users can research lists of lenders, investment banks, and angel investors, as well as get information on venture capital sources, accountants, lawyers, and others. The *Venture Capital Resource Directory* is continually updated and checked for accuracy.

Women's Business Development Center: www.wbdc.org/ (Accessed Spring 2011).

This site of the Women's Business Development Center strives to help women business owners but provides a great deal of information free to all. Under "Getting Started," you will find various resources and tools for starting a business. Under "Already in Business" are numerous topics about financing that will help you determine whether you can qualify for a loan, a loan package checklist, and more. A wealth of information and workshops will help you develop a financial plan, budget, and learn more about most financial issues in running your own business.

Young Money: www.youngmoney.com (Accessed Spring 2011).

This informative and user-friendly website focuses on but is not limited to money management, entrepreneurship, careers, investing, technology, and travel for young adults. Across the top of the home page, numerous tabs link users to the main sections: "Calculator/Tools," "Careers," "Entrepreneurship," "Investing," "Personal Finance," and more. The "Entrepreneurship" tab links to articles under, for instance, "Start a Business." Here you will find "Entrepreneurship 101" listed in the left column, blogs and videos in the center column, and in the right column is a "Tag Cloud," a box with most read, most e-mailed, and most comments sections on the articles for the entire website. Use the Googlelike search box to get right to what you need. A free e-mail newsletter is available as well as the ability to subscribe via Facebook, Twitter, and an RSS feed.

MARKETING AND ADVERTISING

7

Marketing is about how you communicate with customers and prospective customers, often called your audience or target market. Most marketing involves promoting a combination of products and services. The most important word in marketing is *consistency*. Decide up front on how you want to be perceived and remembered so you can create a consistent look and presence. Send a clear message describing how your product or service will improve or simplify your customer's life. In today's multitasking, dual-income households, saving time often outweighs saving money. If your product or service can save both, it's a good bet for success.

The purpose of marketing is to plan and carry out a variety of strategies to inspire new customers to give you a try and encourage current customers to return. Remember that creativity is more important than money in marketing a new venture. Marketing includes research, distribution, pricing, advertising, and promotion as well as sales. If you are new to market research, find a copy of *Marketing Research Kit for Dummies* by Hyman and Sierra to get you started. This book and accompanying DVD walk you through the basics of market research from finding the data through analyzing and interpreting your data to developing a marketing plan. Worksheets, case studies, and samples help you along the way.

Hyman, Michael R. and Sierra, Jeremy J. *Marketing Research Kit for Dummies.* John Wiley, 2010. 392p. ISBN 0-4705-2068-X. $29.99.

Market research is described by the authors as a process of asking questions or finding existing information about the market, the competition, and potential customers. Written for the first-time, do-it-yourself market researcher, the authors guide readers step-by-step through marketing your first business. Worksheets and checklists on the bonus DVD and explanations in nontechnical language help you decide when to consult a professional, how much you want to spend, and help you gather and analyze data to create a marketing strategy. Learn how to write a questionnaire, decide on a sample size and type, and more. Learn how to use in-depth interviews and focus groups. Discover how to find and use secondary data. The authors assert that the most difficult part of market research is that it can burst your bubble, demolish a cherished idea, but it will save you money and point you in the right direction.

YOUR MARKETING PLAN

Your marketing plan is a key component of your business's strategy for success. The well-prepared marketing plan specifies what is unique about your product and/or service. It identifies the size of your expected or target market by segment and the share you can reasonably expect to capture. It lists major competitors, why customers buy from them and why they don't (strengths and weaknesses), their sales, growth rates, and market shares. It also describes your most likely customers, why they will or should buy from you, what sets you apart from your competitors, and which forms of promotion and advertising will most effectively reach them. Lastly, it includes a timetable, budget, and means for measuring results. Marketing without a plan wastes money and time.

Defining your competition is very important. What companies are currently selling something similar if not exactly the same as what you want to offer? It's important to identify them and research everything you can about them. Chapter 13, "Competitive Analysis," delves deeply into competitive intelligence and competitive advantage. Knowledge of your competitors is important, because you can learn how to get more customers, learn how they impact your business, and learn from their mistakes. Competitors influence your position in the market and how quickly or slowly your business grows.

FOUR PS OF MARKETING

Marketing research is an integral, essential part of business planning. It can be gathered by both statistical research and observation or, ideally, a combination of both. Remember to answer the questions relating to the four Ps of marketing:

1. *Product or service.* What are you offering and what do consumers want? Market research determines what consumers are buying and why; identify why consumers will buy your product over your competitors'.

2. *Pricing.* How much must you charge for your product or service, and is it a competitive price? Market demand must be considered. Pricing is closely regulated and subject to public scrutiny. Can you balance sales volume and price to maximize income?

3. *Place.* This identifies not only the geographic area where you will market your product or service but what sales channels you will employ to promote and sell your product or service. This item is also often called distribution.

4. *Promotion.* How will you position your product or service in the market? It involves personal selling, sales promotion, and advertising in print, broadcast, or other media. Market research will help you define the media to which your customers are most receptive.

WHERE TO FIND MARKET RESEARCH

To know your market, start with observation and use what are called primary market research sources. Look closely at what products and services consumers purchase, and find out when, where, why, and how they buy them. Define your information needs. What do you need to know about your potential market?

■ Observation

Now start collecting data and then analyze your findings. Talk to other individuals in your industry. Talk to the competition and find out how they got started. Ask what trends they see happening in the industry. Talk to potential suppliers. Get a good feel for your industry and the market in your state, county, or city. This process is ongoing as long as you're in business; keep tabs on what is happening in the market and the industry. Market research takes time.

Secondary market research is extracted from industry studies, books, magazines or trade publications, and other published sources. Look for basic demographic information as a starting point.

■ Local, State, and Federal Government Agencies

As discussed in chapter 2, use American FactFinder, produced by the U.S. Census Bureau (www.factfinder2.census.gov). You can find statistics on age, sex, geographic region, marital status, income, and more. See how many people live in a particular county or zip code. You can also find the median age and median household income. You can see how many households earn over $10,000 a year or $75,000 a year. Find out how many families of four live in a particular zip code. Knowing income statistics and the size of the household can indicate the buying power of consumers in your area. If your product or service is family oriented, you want to know how large the possible market is now and the possibilities for growth. Using industry studies, though not tailored to your specific needs, can give you insights into the customers in your industry. Find trends in your industry—how much it has changed in the past five years. From the American Fact-Finder page, check out the Economic Census (produced every five years) for your industry and the Survey of Current Business. Sales and employment statistics are indicators of market size and company performance.

Another great resource from the U.S. Census Bureau is County Business Patterns. Learn about the businesses in your area. Below is a detailed example of how this web resource can be used.

Start at http://censtats.census.gov/cbpnaic/cbpnaic.shtml and select a zip code.

This section is called "Zip Code Business Patterns" and presents data on the total number of establishments, employment, and payroll for over 50,000 five-digit zip code areas throughout the nation. Let's say 87059 for Tijeras, New Mexico. What comes up are the statistics for the most recent year available, 2008; but you can go back 10 years. First you'll see a table with the total number of establishments, number of employees, first-quarter payroll, and annual payroll. Now, look below that at the larger table and the column labeled "Industry Code Description." If we want to start a bed and breakfast, we'll look at "Accommodation & Food Services, Industry Code 72" (72 is the first two digits of the NAICS code). We see that there are four establishments in this zip code, and the next columns tell us the number of establishments by employment size class: 1 to 4 employees, 5 to 9 employees, 10 to 19 employees, and so on. Clicking on the far left column, "Detail," breaks the NAICS code down into RV parks and campgrounds, full-service restaurants, limited-service restaurants, and drinking places (alcoholic beverages). So there are no bed and breakfasts in this zip code, which may be good news. On the "Detail" page, another column has popped up which is "Compare." Click on "Compare" for "Accommodation & Food Services." "Compare" shows us how many accommodation and food services businesses are in nearby zip codes. There we see that Cedar Crest, a town about 10 miles away, has 8 establishments; Edgewood, 10 miles away in another direction, has 10; and so on. Use these statistics to help determine the viability of your new business idea.

Because a bed and breakfast is a tourism business, you would want to explore the tourism industry statistics for New Mexico and Bernalillo County to track the number of overnight visits or visitors to continue your market research. The State Data Center (SDC) program (as discussed in chapter 2) is a cooperative program between the states and the Census Bureau; at the URL www.census.gov/sdc/network.html, you can click on your state and see a list of Census State Data Centers, where you will find people to help you access and use your state's data. Contact the SDC in your state for training and technical assistance in accessing and using Census Bureau data for your market research.

For local information, don't forget the chamber of commerce, county or city clerk, other local business organizations, and, of course, the local library. If you're marketing a service business, you might check with other service-type businesses in the area to see if they would share some of their local data, or try local media sources.

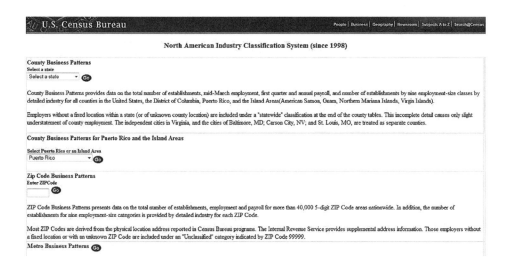

Figure 7.1 Screenshot of CenStats Databases (http://censtats.census.gov/ cbpnaic/cbpnaic.shtml)

Creativity in finding sources of information is always helpful. Network with other business owners to see what sources they have used.

■ Trade and Professional Associations and Trade Journals

Refer back to chapter 2, "Research, Statistics, and Information Gathering," to locate many sources to find and use trade publications. Joining a trade association will provide you with access to industry data and trends as well as provide opportunities to network with business owners with similar interests.

■ The Library

Besides the federal government online, visit the business section of a local library or a larger public or public university library in your state. Ask what industry, company, or market share resources are available for the public to use. Visit several times and ask for help. If the library purchases the *Editor and Publisher Marketing Guide* (Editor & Publisher, annual), you will find statistical data for U.S. and Canadian cities that publish one or more daily newspapers. Tables based on publisher estimates include disposable income per household and more.

Another well-known commercial publisher of marketing statistics and data is Standard Rate and Data Service. While it publishes a number of outstanding volumes, the *Lifestyle Market Analyst* correlates demographic characteristics with consumer behavior patterns. This volume takes interests, hobbies, and activities such as bicycling, fishing, gambling, and reading and combines them with demographic and geographic data. *The Survey of Buying Power* published each year as a special issue (September) of *Sales and Marketing Management* magazine contains regional and state summary data, retail sales, media statistics, and effective buying income of households. Parts of the 2009 survey are now on the Web at www.surveyofbuyingpower.com/sbponline/index.jsp or use a search engine to locate it. Effective buying income, developed by *Sales and Marketing Management,* is defined as personal income less personal income tax and nontax payments or disposable income. Many of these publications are very expensive, but some are now putting the older editions up free on the Web.

Most libraries will have some good resources for you to use or check out on market research or marketing small businesses. See the list of resources at the end of this chapter and in chapter 3, "Start Up," to get started.

■ Local Media and Organizations

Don't forget that local newspapers, radio stations, television stations, and business-related magazines are great resources for gathering demographic information about potential target markets. They can provide you with information and statistics about economic trends, tax issues, advertising, and readership or viewership.

Look for networking opportunities by joining the local chamber of commerce and volunteering for committees. Share information and ask questions. Community groups often have information concerning local habits and markets. Find other local merchant associations or trade groups. Be active in your community.

WRITE YOUR MARKETING PLAN

Now, having gathered your research, it's time to write down your plan. Generally, a marketing plan contains the following sections:

1. *Business environment:* Describe your company's and your competition's strengths and weaknesses and the key to success in your industry today. (Sometimes called a SWOT analysis, read more about this in chapter 13, "Competitive Analysis.")

2. *Overview of the marketplace:* Identify how fast the market is growing, what's causing the growth, and present your forecast for the immediate future.

3. *Market opportunities:* Identify the opportunities in the industry and market that you will use to your advantage.

4. *Business description:* Outline current products or services and the demographics of your customer base as well as your vision of how your business will grow.

5. *Sales:* Set sales targets for the coming year, including number of customers or unit sales and projected total sales dollars.

6. *Marketing program:* Describe here your planned methods of marketing your product or service. For each tool, indicate monthly activities for the coming year with estimated costs.

For some practical, detailed help in writing your marketing plan, use *Marketing Your Product* by Donald Cyr and Douglas Gray. The authors provide a step-by-step guide to preparing and executing your first plan.

Cyr, Donald and Gray, Douglas. *Marketing Your Product,* 5th ed. Self-Counsel Press, 2009. 192p. ISBN 1-55180-859-8. $21.95.

Covering all the essentials of marketing, this expanded edition of a marketing classic demonstrates how your business can carve a niche for its products or services. Learn about market researching, market positioning, planning a marketing strategy, product launching, and competitor awareness. One highlight in this edition is a chapter on the value of the Internet as a marketing tool. Good worksheets help entrepreneurs and new small business owners develop their own marketing plan.

A good website for help with marketing is Edward Lowe's Entrepreneur's Resource Center at www.edwardlowe.org/ERC/. The section entitled "Defining and Serving a Market" explains how to anticipate customer needs, keep an eye on your competition, and write a practical marketing plan. Once again, the *Entrepreneur Magazine* site (www.entrepreneur.com) proves to be very useful, with sales and marketing plan forms as well as articles to help the new entrepreneur. For dot-com businesses, the WebSite MarketingPlan.com website at www.websitemarketingplan.com is highly recommended for help in getting started. See the resources at the end of the chapter for more books and websites with sample plans and more help and advice. Don't forget to review and update your marketing plan on a regular basis, just as you would your business plan. What would you do differently? What new goals does your business have or need?

MARKETING ACTIVITIES

As a new business, attracting customers is critical. The first and free option is word-of-mouth marketing. Work with your current customers and encourage them to spread the word. Good customer service will generate repeat business, and happy customers will talk to their friends and relatives. Ask your customers for referrals. Keep the concerns of your customers in mind, and let them know you care. Keeping your customers happy will make your business successful.

■ Public Relations

Publicity in a local publication is another way to generate discussion. Send out press releases to all such publications announcing your new enterprise and what it offers. Whenever your company wins an award, introduces a new product, or hires a new employee, send a press release. Help promote a community event. Send a pitch letter to editors suggesting that you write an article on a subject related to your new business. Marcia Yudkin has written a book entitled *6 Steps to Free Publicity* in which she details many different ways to attract media attention. Use this book and brainstorm with family and friends about how you can generate publicity for your new business.

Yudkin, Marcia. *6 Steps to Free Publicity,* 3rd ed. Career Press, 2008. 287p. ISBN 1-60163-027-1. $15.99.

This small guide is packed with inspirational ideas and tips to bring visibility to your new venture. Chapters explain how to create and distribute a news release; write "advertorials"; cope with reports and information overload; concoct creative angles, images, and exploits; and make time to publicize. Well written with more than a touch of humor, this book will help you learn how to get media attention at no cost to you.

◼ Advertising and Promotion

Advertising is a type of marketing where a business pays for a certain amount of space in a newspaper or magazine, or airtime on radio or television in order to present its message to an audience. If you open a retail store or restaurant, you will want to make advertising a priority. Otherwise, try to hold off on placing ads, and try other forms of promotion. Take some time to establish goals for your ads and to create a budget. Determine what publication or publications would be most effective in generating customers for your business. Remember to run at least six ads, or you'll be wasting money. People need to see something at least three times in print before it makes an impression. Be consistent—companies often change their ads just when customers are beginning to read, remember, and possibly act on the message. Also, try to develop a method or response mechanism to analyze the results of your advertising efforts.

Direct mail is another vehicle of advertising, but it is very expensive and has really fallen out of favor, especially for younger target groups. If you have a targeted group of people or businesses, such as baby boomers between the ages of 50 and 65 with an annual income of more than $50,000 (rather than just anyone over 50), direct mail can be more cost-effective. Focus on the three Ms when using the mail to market your product or service. The three Ms are:

1. *The Market,* which is the number of identifiable people who need your product or service enough to make a purchase.

2. *The Message,* which is the words, images, or special offers used to get attention and get the customers to take action.

3. *The Mailing List,* which is the people who receive the mailing and closely matches the types of people who have a need or desire for your product or service.

If all these three Ms are in sync, the mailing is likely to get good results. Do a series of smaller test mailings before you consider a large bulk mail effort to determine the effectiveness of your marketing piece and your mailing list. Keep testing with small samples until you have a handle on what copy, offers, and mailing list works for your business. Be sure to include a response mechanism in each mailing to help you track the results of the mailing. For example, "mention this flyer for a 20% discount." Coupons, discounts, and giveaways are the most frequently used methods. Be sure to weed out those names from future mailings that respond the least or not at all.

Like ads, a series of direct mail pieces sent to a select group generates a better response than a single flyer or postcard sent indiscriminately. Another form of direct mail is marketing via e-mail. Though cost-effective, remember that unsolicited e-mail is viewed as junk mail and may irritate your prospects rather than interest them. One way to avoid this is to buy advertising space on e-mail newsletters and e-zines (online magazines) that are sent out from websites to your target audience.

Here is a brief list of inexpensive promotional ideas for a new business: leafleting house to house; posters; hiring a sandwich board person; offering discounts for launch week; giving away freebies such as rulers, bookmarks, any type of small item with the business name, address, phone number, and URL on it; sending e-mail messages; providing free samples; and placing a window display in a local business. Use a mixture of marketing and promotional methods to generate sales and get your business noticed.

■ The Internet

Small businesses have been at a disadvantage for decades when it comes to marketing; large corporations have more resources, brand recognition, and money. However, Web 2.0 and emerging Web 3.0 technologies are leveling the playing field and are giving small businesses an equal voice. Tools such as blogs, interactive web pages, and social media networks can be extremely powerful marketing tools for entrepreneurs and small businesses.

Let's start by discussing the importance of using a website to market a business. Many consumers and businesspeople use the Internet to research a company before deciding to patronize it. When creating a website, be clear about providing information about your business, products, or services. Remember, it is the message that matters, not the slickness of the medium; but be sure your website is usable, attractive, and easy to navigate. Start simple, build, and see what happens. As in other forms of advertising, develop a method to count visitors and, if possible, actual sales that result from seeing or using your web page. Be sure to use the speed and flexibility of the Web to immediately adapt to changing market conditions and customer demands as a way to seize a competitive advantage. A website that's only updated annually or when the spirit moves you is very nearly worthless; on the Web, timeliness is what it's about. If customers seek information on the Internet and find it on your competitor's site, you will lose customer loyalty. Research and understand search engine optimization and pay-per-click ads to increase the effectiveness of your web page and your advertising budget. See the section on technology in chapter 9, "Management," for more information and ideas on creating a web page for your small business. One resource that will help you use and develop your web presence is Jantsch's *Duct Tape Marketing.*

Jantsch, John. *Duct Tape Marketing.* Thomas Nelson, 2008. 304p. ISBN 1-59-555131-X. $15.99.

This collection of proven tools and tactics is presented as a step-by-step marketing system to show entrepreneurs and small business owners what to do to market and grow their businesses. Learn ways to inspire customers to stick to your company, make your website work for you, and hone your message. Jantsch also explains how to automate your marketing with technology tools and produce marketing materials that educate.

Social Media Marketing

Social media marketing is a relatively new marketing trend, and, in order to be successful, you must understand the mind-set of people who are using social media and use it to your advantage. What is social media? It is multiple online media controlled by the people who participate in them by having conversations, sharing resources, and forming new communities. Social media is not passive like television, print, or radio, but full of constant activity with no one in control. To use social media for marketing a business, you will need to learn how to make your website fit into social media and make it the focus of your online marketing efforts; use media like Facebook, Twitter, and LinkedIn in an ethical way; drive traffic to your site; build a community of fans; and measure your social media marketing efforts. Use Kabani's book *The Zen of Social Media Marketing* to help you.

Kabani, Shama. *The Zen of Social Media Marketing: An Easier Way to Build Credibility, Generate Buzz, and Increase Revenue.* BenBella Books, 2010. 200p. ISBN 1-93525-173-2. $16.95.

This step-by-step guide to using social media like Facebook, Twitter, and LinkedIn to market and create buzz about your new business is well written and easy-to-use. Use proven marketing strategies to make your business succeed in today's social media world. Case studies help you understand how to lay and build on an effective social media marketing foundation. Buying the book provides access to regular updates and video extras.

Another good print resource for information on internet marketing and social media marketing is VanRysdam's *Marketing in a Web 2.0 World;* full information for it is listed in the resources at the end of the chapter. And an exceptional website for marketing with social media is an online magazine called *Social Media Examiner.* See the complete information below (including a screenshot) and in the list of resources.

Figure 7.2 Screenshot of Social Media Examiner (www.socialmediaexaminer.com). Used with permission.

Social Media Examiner: www.socialmediaexaminer.com/

This free online magazine will help you learn how to use social media tools like Twitter and Facebook to increase sales and generate brand awareness. Find out about Foursquare, Facebook Places, Gowalla, and others. Learn how to use automation tools and which ones are better and why. Also download the "2011 Social Media Marketing Industry Report" by Michael A. Stelzner (www.socialmediaexaminer.com/social-media-marketing-industry-report-2011/) and use it to maximize your social media activities and learn about trends in social media marketing.

■ Trade Shows

Trade shows can be a very effective way to market your new business. Find the right one, and you have the opportunity to sell to people who have already identified themselves as interested in your product or service. Attend several shows before signing up and paying to be a vendor. See what other businesses in your industry are doing and what's effective. Benefits of exhibiting at a trade show include meeting with users of your product or service and getting feedback, selling merchandise or services, developing sales leads, keeping current on trends in the industry, showing your new products, and building your company's image.

However, exhibiting at a trade show is expensive, so be selective and keep the following ideas in mind:

- Keep your booth small, especially in the beginning, or consider sharing a booth with someone who sells a complementary product or service.
- Don't print too many brochures or handouts.
- Collect names and mail or e-mail contact information so you can follow up leads immediately after the show.
- Offer a show special, hold a contest, and/or hand out something related to your product or service or a sample.
- Try to be memorable or stand out; wear a costume or T-shirt with a catchy phrase or eye-catching logo.

Find more ideas and advice on Trade Show News Network (www.tsnn.com). Setting up a booth at a trade show is a great way to make contacts, find people, and even sell products or services, and this comprehensive site provides information on more than 15,000 trade shows that you can find by industry, month, city, state, or country. Trade show planning is also featured.

Like the business plan, a marketing plan is essential for a successful small business. Develop a consistent look and message for your business, and use it to market your business every day. Word-of-mouth marketing and public relations are inexpensive and effective methods of gaining visibility and credibility; use them to your advantage. Listed below are many resources to help you learn how to market and advertise your new business.

REFERENCES

Starred titles are discussed in the chapter.

▇ Print Resources

Barrow, Colin. *Starting a Business from Home: Choosing a Business, Getting Online, Reaching Your Market and Making a Profit,* 2nd ed. Kogan Page, 2011. 306p. ISBN 0-749-46264-7. $24.95.

Barrow's second edition includes more exercises and end-of-chapter advice. Learn how to identify a business structure, how to do market research, ins and outs of building a website, and hints on going global. Appendices provide ideas for home-based businesses, sources of help and advice, and ideas on raising necessary capital. The slight British slant may confuse some.

Berkley, Holly. *Low-Budget Online Marketing: For Small Business,* 3rd ed. Self Counsel Press, 2010. 136p. ISBN 1-55-18089-01. $20.95.

Full of good, basic, and up-to-date ideas on e-mail marketing, co-branding strategies, good web design, and working with a web developer, Berkley writes short and to the point. If you are new to the business uses of the Internet and small business, you will find this precise tome very useful.

Block, Robbin. *Social Persuasion: Making Sense of Social Media for Small Business.* Block Media, 2010. 258p. ISBN 0-98-26013-03. $24.95.

Learn how to fit social media into your business's marketing and overall business strategy. Find out which sites to use and how to make the most of your time and money for effective marketing. One highlight is the glossary of key marketing and social media terms. What is your target audience, and who needs your products and services? Real-world, practical advice is presented in a well-written and well-organized format.

Brennan, Bridget. *Why She Buys: The New Strategy for Reaching the World's Most Powerful Consumers.* Crown Business, 2009. 336p. ISBN 0-307-4503-84. $26.

Brennan will help you market and sell to women, who not only purchase more goods but are also key influencers for about 80% of consumer products in the United States. She shares the five important global demographic changes affecting female consumerism; for example, one is the divorce economy, which necessitates the purchase of things for two households instead of one. Well organized and very pragmatic, this book will help you learn why and how to market to women.

Calkins, Tim. *Breakthrough Marketing Plans.* Palgrave Macmillan, 2008. 184p. ISBN 0-23-060-7578. $25.

This title will help you understand why marketing plans are necessary, where they go wrong, and how to create a powerful plan and successful business. Calkins's key message for marketing plans is to keep it focused to maximize its effectiveness. Find a good, practical template in this organized, useful handbook.

Cooney, Scott. *Build a Green Small Business.* McGraw-Hill, 2008. 256p. ISBN 0-07-160293-3. $19.95.

The highlight of this work is the load of green start-up ideas, including green wedding planning and green travel planning. Find expert advice on market research, financing, key legal and insurance issues, and green franchises. Use the marketing, advertising, and networking techniques described here to build a loyal customer base. Learn how to create a business that builds your local community, heals the environment, and feeds the growing green demands. Also find valuable resources such as web links and contacts to help you succeed.

Crane, Frederick G. *Marketing for Entrepreneurs: Concepts and Applications for New Ventures.* Sage, 2009. 240p. ISBN 1-412-9534-72. $41.95.

This practical work provides insights, strategies, and tips on how to apply entrepreneurial marketing concepts to a new business. Find out how marketing can be used to find, evaluate, and exploit the right business for you. Crane walks readers through the steps of the marketing process and goes beyond the four Ps to address the external marketing environment. Real-life examples and exercises are also provided.

**Cyr, Donald and Gray, Douglas. *Marketing Your Product,* 5th ed. Self-Counsel Press, 2009. 192p. ISBN 1-55180-859-8. $21.95.

Covering all the essentials of marketing, this expanded edition of a marketing classic demonstrates how your business can carve a niche for its products or services. Learn about market researching, market positioning, planning a marketing strategy, product launching, and competitor awareness. One highlight in this edition is a chapter on the value of the

Internet as a marketing tool. Good worksheets help entrepreneurs and new small business owners develop their own marketing plan.

DeMao, Sherre L. *50 Marketing Secrets of Growth Companies in Down Economic Times*. Green-Castle, 2010. 242p. ISBN 0-984-10511-5. $24.95.

Success stories from more than 60 companies that realized huge growth during the recession are presented by DeMao. This practical how-to guide contains documented tactics and strategies such as offering what no one else does in quite the same way. Learn to use market planning tools that are flexible and to put high touch with your high tech. Use DeMao's work to spend your marketing dollars right.

****Editor and Publisher Marketing Guide*. Editor & Publisher, annual. $200.

Statistical data are arranged alphabetically by state and city for the United States and by province and city for Canada. Cities included publish one or more daily newspapers. Information collected is wide ranging, and examples include passenger auto registrations, residence electric meters, number and sales of furniture and home furnishings stores, and principal industries, number of employees, and average wage. Many libraries cannot afford to purchase annually but very useful data even if a few years old.

Entrepreneur Press. *Start Your Own Business*, 5th ed. Entrepreneur Press, 2010. 704p. ISBN 1-599-18387-0. $24.95.

Offered here are critical start-up essentials and tips on how to survive the first crucial three years. Common-sense solutions to common challenges when starting a new business are presented in a well-organized format. You will find useful forms, worksheets, and checklists. Find out the secrets of successful entrepreneurs and discover new digital and social media tools and how to use them effectively. The chapters titled "Market" and "Engage" will help you discover ways to brand and take advantage of social media networking. Learn to pinpoint your target market and find your niche.

Frazier, Shirley George. *Marketing Strategies for the Home-Based Business*. Globe Pequot, 2008. 192p. ISBN 0-762-742-402. $18.95.

Providing an array of worksheets, sample marketing plans, sample direct mail items, and a product creation chart, Frazier shares her advice and expertise on focusing your energies to get the media on your publicity bandwagon to setting up an Internet presence and rewarding customers for their business. She uses case studies and real-life examples to provide you with effective marketing methods.

Friedmann, Susan. *The Complete Idiot's Guide to Target Marketing*. Alpha, 2009. 352p. ISBN 1-592-57903-7. $19.95.

If you want to learn about demographics, psychographics, and your customers, this is the place to start. Friedmann provides practical, easy-to-use tips and ideas to get your business noticed. She gives powerful pointers on viral marketing, blogging, webinars, online surveys, and many similar web marketing ideas and tools. Consult this guide for new and quick marketing ideas.

Godin, Seth. *Purple Cow: Transform Your Business by Being Remarkable*, 2nd ed. Portfolio, 2009. 224p. ISBN 1-591-843-170. $21.95.

What do Starbucks, KrispyKreme, HBO, and JetBlue have in common? They've created new ways of doing old business, and, like a purple cow in a field of Holsteins, they stand out. Godin uses case studies of real businesses to illustrate his points in each chapter. Godin provides new uses for the "ideavirus" concept that he's written about previously. Powerful, fun, and simple—look at your marketing strategies with new eyes.

Hiebing, Roman G. and Cooper, Scott W. *The One Day Marketing Plan: Organizing and Completing a Plan That Works,* 3rd ed. McGraw-Hill, 2004. 344p. ISBN 0-07-139522-9. $24.95.

Learn how to quickly design a marketing plan for any type of business with the authors' streamlined, 10-step process. Templates and helpful checklists lead new marketers to complete an effective plan. Learn how to use Internet marketing tactics and learn to accurately evaluate bottom-line results.

Hoxie, Mark. *90 Days to Success Marketing and Advertising Your Small Business.* Course Technology, 2010. 288p. ISBN 1-4354-5828-1. $19.99.

Identify the various forms of advertising available today, select the forms most appropriate for your business and customers, and develop marketing and advertising strategies to make your business successful. The chapter on "Tracking and Follow-Up Marketing" is a highlight of this work, because so often small business owners don't know what works and why or why not. Hoxie suggests that, even when you're comfortable with your marketing strategy, you should track your ads on a rotating monthly basis. Each chapter ends with a suggested action plan. Case studies for specific businesses in specific industries are also very useful. Make marketing decisions that will help your new business grow.

****Hyman, Michael R. and Sierra, Jeremy J. *Marketing Research Kit for Dummies.* John Wiley, 2010. 392p. ISBN 0-4705-2068-X. $29.99.

Market research is described by the authors as a process of asking questions or finding existing information about the market, the competition, and potential customers. Written for the first-time, do-it-yourself market researcher, the authors guide readers step-by-step through marketing your first business. Worksheets and checklists on the bonus DVD and explanations in nontechnical language help you decide when to consult a professional, how much you want to spend, and help you gather and analyze data to create a marketing strategy. Learn how to write a questionnaire, decide on a sample size and type, and more. Learn how to use in-depth interviews and focus groups. Discover how to find and use secondary data. The authors assert that the most difficult part of market research is that it can burst your bubble, demolish a cherished idea, but it will save you money and point you in the right direction.

Jacobson, Jennifer L. *42 Rules of Social Media for Small Business.* Super Star Press, 2009. 122p. ISBN 1-60-773014-9. $19.95.

Find social media that fits your business, and get the most out of your social media presence. This comprehensive guide addresses many of the questions and concerns many business owners and managers have about this new form of communication. Practical examples and how to use time-tested marketing concepts are included for this new format.

****Jantsch, John. *Duct Tape Marketing.* Thomas Nelson, 2008. 304p. ISBN 1-59-555131-X. $15.99.

This collection of proven tools and tactics is presented as a step-by-step marketing system to show entrepreneurs and small business owners what to do to market and grow their businesses. Learn ways to inspire customers to stick to your company, make your website work for you, and hone your message. Jantsch also explains how to automate your marketing with technology tools and produce marketing materials that educate.

Jarvis, Jackie. *85 Inspiring Ways to Market Your Small Business.* How to Books, 2010. 244p. ISBN 1-84528-396-1. $26.

Jarvis cleverly gets across her ideas for marketing through a series of special response questions and the vital thinking behind their application. She helps you understand your marketplace, your customers, and your competition. Learn to build your business profile to make it work for you 24/7. Chapter 15, on "The Simple Things That Make a Big Difference," is particularly outstanding. Chapters are short and to the point, easy to understand and put into practice.

**Kabani, Shama. *The Zen of Social Media Marketing: An Easier Way to Build Credibility, Generate Buzz, and Increase Revenue.* BenBella Books, 2010. 200p. ISBN 1-93525-173-2. $16.95.

This step-by-step guide to using social media like Facebook, Twitter, and LinkedIn to market and create buzz about your new business is well written and easy to use. Use proven marketing strategies to make your business succeed in today's social world. Case studies help you understand how to lay and build on an effective social media marketing foundation. Buying the book provides access to regular updates and video extras.

Kennedy, Dan S. *The Ultimate Marketing Plan: Target Your Audience!* 4th ed. Adams Media, 2011. 240p. ISBN 1-4405-118-45. $14.95.

Kennedy provides a basic, solid manual for beginning marketing practitioners and small business owners/managers. He covers all the familiar fundamentals, from developing a unique selling proposition to practicing target marketing and online marketing to using testimonials and celebrity endorsements. His book is well organized and carefully thought out. Small business owners will learn to conduct in-house marketing and get a practical overview of marketing methods and strategies for today's consumers.

Kobliski, Kathy J. *Advertising without an Agency,* 3rd ed. Entrepreneur Press, 2005. 240p. ISBN 1-932531-28-9. $19.95.

This thorough reference guide will inform small business owners about the ins and outs of advertising and how to use it effectively. Kobliski covers radio, television, print, direct mail, and outdoor advertising. She provides worksheets to take the guesswork out of buying ad space or time and defines advertising jargon in easy-to-understand language with descriptive analogies. She discusses methods for finding out who your customers are and how to keep track of them on paper. This book will help you advertise more effectively.

Kotler, Philip. *Ten Deadly Marketing Sins: Signs and Solutions.* John Wiley, 2004. 132p. ISBN 0-471-66206-2. $19.95.

Well-known and respected marketing expert Kotler identifies and describes the 10 glaring deficiencies companies make in their marketing efforts. Each mistake is covered thoroughly in its own chapter. Kotler explains how to remain customer driven, understand your customers, track the competition, find new opportunities, and develop effective marketing plans. He also includes ideas for using technology to the fullest in your marketing plan. Find out if you're making any of these marketing mistakes and how to avoid or reverse them.

Levine, Michael. *Guerrilla PR 2.0: Wage an Effective Publicity Campaign without Going Broke.* Harper, 2008. 368p. ISBN 0-06-143832-9. $14.99.

This collection of low-cost publicity techniques includes sample press releases and attention-getting strategies targeted for the wired environment. Focused on the Internet, Levine's theories are steeped in specifics, and readers will find his examples of highly successful campaigns (such as the launch of Mothers Against Drunk Driving) and flops (remember New Coke?) instructive and entertaining. Levine has many years of experience in public relations, and entrepreneurs will benefit from this discussion and hints gathered from his experiences.

Levinson, Jay Conrad and Gibson, Shane. *Guerrilla Social Media Marketing.* Entrepreneur Press, 2010. 240p. ISBN 1-5991-8383-8. $21.95.

This thorough guide presents sample materials including "100 weapons to grow your online influence." Learn how to use public relations tools such as press releases, e-mail, radio, direct mail, and more in the new world of social media. Learn the basic skill of online relationship building here. Ideas are summarized in an easy-to-understand and easy-to-read format. This field guide is for any business wanting to do things right the first time and get engaged in the social media space quickly.

Levy, Justin. *Facebook Marketing: Designing Your Next Marketing Campaign,* 2nd ed. Que, 2010. 216p. ISBN 0-789-74321-3. $24.99.

Levy presents real experiences of companies and individuals who have used Facebook to reach customers on and outside of Facebook. Learn how to use widgets and apps to communicate and build communities that promote loyalty and innovation. The chapter on best practices is outstanding. Discover traffic builders like sweepstakes and prepare for the future of Facebook and other social media.

Luther, William M. *The Marketing Plan: How to Prepare and Implement It,* 4th ed. AMACOM, 2011. 304p. ISBN 0-8144-1693-4. $21.95.

This classic teaches you how to navigate the new landscape involved in producing a working marketing plan. Each chapter contains questions that will help you identify your marketing objectives and provides specific strategies for every stage of a marketing cycle, including market analysis, branding, forecasting, and management. Case studies and examples from major brand successes illustrate good marketing strategies. Online software is available to help in decision making, pricing, budgeting, and sales projections. This practical resource is very useful to all entrepreneurs and particularly to owners of chain franchises.

Margolis, Jonathan and Garrigan, Patrick. *Guerrilla Marketing for Dummies.* For Dummies, 2008. 384p. ISBN 0-470-28967-9. $21.99.

This informal, fun approach to marketing guides readers to powerful and effective approaches for increasing the customers' knowledge and interest in your business. Learn why it is important to have a cohesive campaign, how to write an outstanding press release, budget-friendly ways to market, and when and how to hire a pro. The authors also include 10 "practically perfect" campaigns.

Monosoff, Tamara. *Your Million Dollar Dream: Create a Winning Business Plan.* McGraw-Hill, 2010. 336p. ISBN 0-07-162943-2. $19.95.

Monosoff, founder of Mom Inventors Inc., works with many entrepreneurs and often walks them through the steps to starting and growing their own businesses. The chapter entitled "Making Money Your Way" provides information and exercises that will help you articulate your dreams, identify skill sets, and broaden your awareness and link to businesses that tap into your strengths and dreams. Essential how-to chapters include ideas on using e-mail marketing, blogs, social media, and social networking for your business. Learn how to create an effective business plan and use Twitter and Facebook as powerful marketing tools

O'Connor, Jason P. *The Ultimate Guide to a Successful Business Website.* Brandon Oak, 2008. 196p. ISBN 0-980-19120-3. $39.

O'Connor, a professional web designer and marketer, will teach you how to go from an outdated site or simple website to a fully functional and money-generating user-friendly one. Learn how to hire a good web designer for a fair price and how to tell the designer what you want the site to do. Learn how to plan your business website and then how best to market it. Written in easy-to-understand, nontechnical language, one highlight of the book is the "Great Website Rules," which describe everything a website needs to be successful.

Parasuraman, A. and Colby, Charles L. *Techno-Ready Marketing: How and Why Your Customers Adopt Technology.* Free Press, 2007. 240p. ISBN 1-416-57663-0. $17.95.

Parasuraman and Colby's compelling framework for "measuring the propensity of customers to welcome and use technology-intensive products and services" is presented clearly and concisely. Learn to determine each customer's technology readiness, motivate customers to use the new and emerging technologies you're providing, and understand why customers either embrace or resist technology. Find out if you need to divide your customers into five distinct groups. Small business owners and marketing professionals can learn about the technology-driven future from these authors.

Phillips, Michael and Rasberry, Salli. *Marketing without Advertising,* 6th ed. Nolo Press, 2008. 398p. ISBN 1-41330-632-2. $20.

This book takes readers on an in-depth, practical journey through marketing strategies. One valuable section illustrates how to design and implement a marketing plan. Other topics include the physical appearance of your business, educating and helping prospective customers find your business, and using the Internet to market your business. Also plan marketing events that will keep customers involved, and encourage the media to comment positively on your business. Sections on the importance of good relations with your employees and how they influence the perception of your business are interesting and informative. Questionnaires, checklists, and worksheets help readers understand important points.

Pinson, Linda. *Anatomy of a Business Plan,* 7th ed. Out of Your Mind . . . and Into the Marketplace, 2008. ISBN 0-944-2053-72. $22.95.

This user-friendly guide includes sample business plans and blank forms to help you write a thoughtful, thorough, and professional business plan. Pinson believes that the executive summary should grab attention, and she presents ways for yours to do just that. Pinson also includes the latest marketing strategies and how to incorporate the Internet into your marketing plan. Forms, worksheets, and examples for guidance in writing your plans are also very useful. This edition includes a resource section to help businesses research financial and marketing information, so essential for an outstanding plan. Also find guidelines for updating and packaging your business plan. New chapters on financing resources and business planning for nonprofits add value to this practical, well-written resource.

Pool, Jeanna. *Marketing for Solos.* 3 Bar Press, 2011. 242p. ISBN 0-976-9962-79. $19.95.

Pool delivers practical, step-by-step guidance to marketing strategies that really work. She'll show you how to stand out from the competition, consistently attract new customers, attract more lucrative customers, and avoid some big marketing mistakes. Pool shares many examples of marketing plans and strategies, and they are all tailored to small business owners. Marketing is a process, and you can have success using her "situation or solution" template.

Powell, Guy R. *Marketing Calculator: Measuring and Managing Return on Marketing Investment.* Wiley, 2008. 300p. ISBN 0-47-08239-58. $32.

Powell demystifies how marketers can significantly improve their measurement and management infrastructure to understand the key issues and improve the return on marketing effectiveness. Case studies cover many industries, including home repair services, travel, software, restaurants, and others. Learn how to collect data meaningful to improving your marketing effectiveness. Visit the marketing-calculator.com website for more information.

Poynter, Ray. *Handbook of Online and Social Media Marketing Research.* John Wiley, 2010. 462p. ISBN 0-47-071-040-3. $66.

This volume will provide e-commerce companies and those interested in marketing their businesses on the Internet with comprehensive information about understanding, using, acquiring, and conducting market and marketing research online. Important chapters thoroughly cover sampling, questionnaire design, target markets, and tracking (feedback systems). The second half of the book covers the process of applying online marketing research to all phases of online product development and marketing. Poynter provides his views on "how to be better with people" and "how to maximize response rates." Use this information to assist you in developing every stage of an online venture.

Scott, David Meerman. *The New Rules of Marketing and PR,* 2nd ed. John Wiley, 2009. 320p. ISBN 0-47-054781-2. $19.95.

If you're trying to survive and be successful in the new media jungle, Scott's work will help you establish a social media marketing strategy and create effective web content. Learn how to be a thought leader and how to target a small niche market first. Scott will help you develop a step-by-step plan for harnessing the power of online marketing.

Sigmon, Patricia. *Six Steps to Creating Profit: A Guide for Small and Mid-Sized Service-Based Businesses.* John Wiley, 2010. 208p. ISBN 0-470-55425-8. $34.95.

Learn how to change your business and measure the results of each change so your business is more profitable. Learn more about and understand cash flow, management costs, and how important selling is for all your employees. Find out more about visibility in the marketplace, marketing, and financing. Learn how to put online networking to work for you. Sigmon presents practical and easily implemented tactics to improve your bottom line.

Singh, Shiv. *Social Media Marketing for Dummies.* For Dummies, 2009. (Kindle ed. available.) 288p. ISBN 0-470-2893-41. $24.99.

Thought-provoking and practical, this book covers the basics, strategic concepts, and practicalities of social marketing topics. Learn how to create your own online spokesperson for your brand or business, optimize your page to attract clicks and customers, and measure what is successful by results. Take steps to get your message to mobile users, and discover strategies to get employees involved.

Slaunwhite, Steve. *Starting a Web-Based Business.* Alpha Books, 2009. 350p. ISBN 1-59257-889-4. $19.95.

Learn how to create and operate a successful cyberspace venture step-by-step. Slaunwhite looks at the basics of doing business online and then helps you identify online trends, create a game plan and a website, and market your site, and then he provides tactics for turning clicks into customers. Learn how to get started with PayPal and mobile apps. Appendix B helps you locate free and nearly free online tools and resources. Well written and organized, use this reference to help you with day-to-day issues.

Solis, Brian. *Engage, Revised and Updated: The Complete Guide for Brands and Businesses to Build, Cultivate, and Measure Success in the New Web,* rev. ed. John Wiley, 2011. 336p. ISBN 1-11800-37-64. $18.95.

Solis examines the social media landscape and how to effectively use social media to succeed in business, one network and one tool at a time. He leads you through the detailed and specific steps required for conceptualizing, implementing, managing, and measuring a social media program. Understand the psychology, behavior, and influence of the new social consumer. Using Solis's techniques, your business will gain the ability to increase visibility, build communities of loyal brand enthusiasts, and increase profits. Learn how to create a space online that really represents your business and cultivates customer loyalty and trust.

Stasch, Stanley F. *Creating a Successful Marketing Strategy for Your Small New Business.* Praeger, 2010. 224p. ISBN 0-313-38246-8. $44.95.

Understand how to create a complete, synergistic marketing strategy with the characteristics and elements associated with successful start-ups. Full of lists, guidelines, warnings, and rules, Stasch's book presents good examples of both marketing successes and failures but the author's style is more inspiration than practical.

Sterrett, Paddy and Sterrett, Patricia. *Marketing Ideas for the Small Business: 45 Actions, Ideas, and Promotions to Increase Your Business.* Global Management Enterprises, 2010. 144p. ISBN 1-934747-25-4. $19.95.

This compendium of simple promotional ideas is ideal for small businesses to create buzz and awareness of their products or services and themselves. Follow the authors' guidelines to avoid marketing pitfalls and develop the confidence to undertake the sorts of ventures you haven't dared to tackle before now in social media, consumer competitions, and more.

Stevenson, Jim and Thurman, Courtney. *Ultimate Small Business Marketing Guide,* 2nd ed. Entrepreneur Press, 2007. 478p. ISBN 1-599180-37-5. $24.95.

Written with small businesses in mind, this book presents cost-effective but innovative and time-tested ways to market a small business. Chapters cover research, planning, competition, customer service, advertising, networking, websites, and trade shows. Checklists and sample forms help readers understand concepts and put them into practice. Internet resources that provide more marketing ideas are listed. This small business marketing library of information will help most entrepreneurs think of new ways to sell their products or services and win new customers.

****Survey of Buying Power.* Sales and Marketing Management Magazine, annual. $52 (accompanies subscription to *Sales and Marketing Management* magazine).

Published in September, this classic library resource provides regional and state summary data on retail sales, media statistics, and its own measure of effective buying income of households, which is defined as personal income less personal income tax and nontax payments or disposable income. Well known in the marketing industry, this source is expensive and may not be available at all libraries.

Sweeney, Susan. *101 Ways to Promote Your Web Site,* 8th ed. Maximum Press, 2010. 392p. ISBN 1-93164-478-0. $29.95.

Sweeney's practical guide is filled with checklists, templates, and forms to help entrepreneurs make their website more successful and productive by enticing surfers to check out the site, absorb what it offers, and return at some time in the future. Learn how to use the latest Web 2.0 trends and techniques to get more visitors and more repeat visitors to their site. Use RSS feeds, blogs, podcasts, and mobile marketing for online success. Use these techniques to improve your small business website.

Tasner, Michael. *Marketing in the Moment.* FT Press, 2010. 256p. ISBN 0-13-708109-X. $24.99.

Tasner introduces readers to Web 3.0 and the many marketing tools available under the Web 3.0 umbrella. He presents practical tips and techniques to derive maximum value from online, mobile, and social marketing. His innovative marketing techniques will help you move beyond the hype to successful entry and ground-level execution. Learn how to capitalize on content marketing, microblogging, voice broadcasts, and more as well as how to systematically optimize everything you're already doing online.

Tuten, Tracy L. *Advertising 2.0.* Praeger, 2008. 216p. ISBN 0-313-35296-6. $24.95.

Tuten approaches social networking, blogging, mobility, and branding with an analytical mind. Learn about the habits and needs of contemporary consumers. See how companies are using web options and the web environment, and find guidelines for their application from Tuten. Learn how to effectively and efficiently use social media marketing.

Urquhart-Brown, Susan. *The Accidental Entrepreneur: The 50 Things I Wish Someone Had Told Me about Starting a Business.* AMACOM, 2008. 178p. ISBN 0-8144-0167-8. $17.95.

This title includes two outstanding chapters. "What Is an Entrepreneur, Anyway?" asks you to define yourself, your business, and your goals. "What Do You Bring to the Party?" asks important questions about accountability and procrastination. Real-life examples are often included to illustrate the author's points. Learn here the six secrets of marketing a business. One other valuable and interesting chapter is "Get Connected to the Web for Profit." Also, learn what to avoid in starting your new venture.

**VanRysdam, Peter. *Marketing in a Web 2.0 World.* Atlantic, 2010. 288p. ISBN 1-60138-317-7. $24.95.

Web 2.0 technologies with tools like blogs, interactive websites, and Facebook have leveled the playing field between large corporations and small businesses. These technologies allow businesses to reach out and touch their target demographics. Learn how your customers use the social media websites, and then establish your website as your marketing hub by drawing visitors in through the best search engine optimization practices, webinars, and blogs. Social media is not a fad but a fundamental shift in the way business is done today.

**Yudkin, Marcia. *6 Steps to Free Publicity,* 3rd ed. Career Press, 2008. 287p. ISBN 1-60163-027-1. $15.99.

This small guide is packed with inspirational ideas and tips to bring visibility to your new venture. Chapters explain how to create and distribute a news release; write "advertorials"; cope with reports and information overload; concoct creative angles, images, and exploits; and make time to publicize. Learn to use the author's publicity writing tips that ensure you'll be easily found online through search engines. Well written with more than a touch of humor, learn how to get media attention at no cost to you.

■ Online Resources

About.com: http://marketing.about.com (Accessed Spring 2011).

This large site has many different parts, but the "Marketing" section is particularly well done. The section on "Marketing Plan and Strategy" includes ideas and articles on using blogs to market your business, how to find your target market, sponsoring events to increase your credibility and prestige in your target market, and how to set the right prices. Learn more about Internet and e-mail marketing. The "Plan Tutorials and Samples" section is particularly helpful. Continually updated and well organized, this site will help your marketing efforts. Another section of the About.com site is called "Advertising" at http://advertising.about.com. This site contains interesting promotional ideas and materials. Public relations and social media marketing are covered thoroughly as well. Learn why and how you should use promotional products and giveaways to advertise your business effectively.

All About Market Research: www.allaboutmarketresearch.com/ (Accessed Spring 2011).

This directory is a guide to outstanding tools, tips, resources, and services for your e-commerce Internet marketing research. This well-organized site has areas listed across the top, including "Blog," "Academic Market Research," "Associations," "Directories," "Internet Growth," "Library," "e-Commerce," and "Links." The "Library" has coaching-type articles on search engine optimization, Internet writing, Internet online advertising, and more. "Associations" has an extensive list of links to international market research organizations. "Internet Growth" has a wealth of informative statistics. Use this site to improve your online marketing efforts.

AllBusiness: www.allbusiness.com (Accessed Spring 2011).

This huge site contains articles and advice on any area of business law, including legal structure, property leases, patents, trademarks, employment law, taxes, and even how to work with your lawyer. Links to many directories are also provided as well as news and business information sites. The sales and marketing section has many articles on techniques, advertising, and publications. Forms and agreements are also covered in detail. The tax articles discuss topics such as barter tax and accounting issues and tax strategies for keeping the family business in the family. Use this well-organized, functional website often.

**American FactFinder: http://factfinder2.census.gov/home/saff/main.html?_lang=en (Accessed Spring 2011).

This federal government source for information on population, housing, economic, and geographic data is easy to use and well designed. You can get a fact sheet for your community by just entering town, county, or zip code. A quick link gets you to the Decennial Census of Housing and Population, American Community Survey, the Economic Census, or the Population Estimates program. A couple of clicks under "Subjects A to Z" will get you to county business patterns, information on NAICS codes, statistics about small business from the Census Bureau, the characteristics of business owners' database, and more. Use the Economic Census Factsheets to find industry statistics such as retail trade, then type of store, and you'll find number of establishments, sales, payroll, and ratios. A glossary, FAQs, and search function will also help you use this great, free resource.

American Marketing Association: www.marketingpower.com (Accessed Spring 2011).

This website has many articles that will help you start and continue learning how to market your small business. Search "marketing plan" to find a great article in the "Resource Library" that asks users questions to help them start thinking about the plan, their target consumers, the product, and so on. The structure of a marketing plan is discussed. Other areas of the site provide articles on best practices in marketing, trends in marketing, networking opportunities, and practitioner resources. Joining the association gives you access to additional member-only resources. A directory of marketing suppliers as well as excellent marketing tools and templates are also available for free.

**Edward Lowe's Entrepreneurs Resource Center: www.edwardlowe.org/ERC/ (Accessed Spring 2011).

This well-known small business site contains a large section on "Defining and Serving a Market." One of the articles here is "Gathering Market Research," and it walks users through identifying data sources, gathering customer and competitor information, and gathering information on suppliers with real-life examples of successful marketing. Additional resources are often provided at the end of the articles. Find also information on branding, direct mail marketing, social media, and, in general, providing a promotional mix for your new business. Use this site frequently when you need help running or marketing your business.

eHow.com—Business: www.ehow.com/business/ (Accessed Spring 2011).

This huge site contains articles on every phase of starting and running a business, from incorporating a business, creating a market survey, filing for a copyright, finding cheap advertising, deciding when to quit your day job, and leasing office space to opening particular types of businesses such as garden centers, catering, pet care, and online businesses. Articles are short and to the point to get you started in the right direction. Links to related or relevant topics expand on the basic article.

**Entrepreneur.com: www.entrepreneur.com (Accessed Spring 2011).

Entrepreneur Magazine provides a wealth of information and assistance to the new entrepreneur. A thorough understanding of the need for a marketing plan and finding the right type of marketing plan to fit your business and your style of planning and working is very important, and this site guides you through the process. Learn how to determine your marketing goals and objectives and how a plan will help you achieve them. Under

"Sales & Marketing" you will find tips on building buzz, branding, word-of-mouth advertising, and marketing materials. Learn about the "10 Laws of Social Media Marketing," for example. Discover how to build an ad budget and find ad inspiration as well as how to reassess your ad strategy. Use this outstanding site often during the planning and opening of your new business.

Entrepreneurs' Help Page: www.tannedfeet.com (Accessed Spring 2011).

Find here help with business plans, financial statements, legal structure and legal forms, marketing and public relations, human resources, and strategy. Designed, created, and published by a group of young professionals in Chicago, Entrepreneurs Help page does not claim to substitute for professional advice and judgment but provides information to entrepreneurs to get them started in the right direction. Experts offer advice on finding the right customers, how to select and work with an advertising agency, and marketing budgets. Articles are usually not long but ask questions to help the new businessperson start thinking about what is needed and what questions will be asked of him or her. Down-to-earth advice from peers is often the most valuable.

Entrepreneurs Resource Center: www.edwardlowe.org/ERC/ (Accessed Spring 2011).

This nonprofit organization promotes entrepreneurship by providing information, research, and education. Use this site to find practical articles on marketing, acquiring and managing finances, human resources management, and legal and tax issues. The "Defining and Serving a Market" section contains articles on public relations, market strategy, niche marketing, sales techniques, and more. Networking possibilities include conferences and educational seminars listed here. Now aimed at entrepreneurs, the Edward Lowe Foundation provides good basic help too.

Home Business Magazine: www.homebusinessmag.com (Accessed Spring 2011).

The "Marketing" category accessible through the frame on the left side of the screen provides a wealth of articles on marketing any type of small business. Short courses on marketing success, information on how you could be hurting your sales, and other articles as well as subcategories on direct marketing, web marketing, publicity, and selling provide inexpensive but effective marketing ideas. Advice and ideas on business start-up, management, and money are also included.

Ideas-for-Marketing.com: www.ideas-for-marketing.com/ (Accessed Spring 2011).

This large site presents an overview of Internet marketing by entrepreneur Paul Taylor. Here you will find ideas about a systematic approach to Internet marketing, detailed step-by-step guides to some of the most important actions that you need to take, tools to help automate your electronic marketing activity, and templates for organizing and tracking your marketing. There is a wealth of information here, but it is a commercial site that also offers products for sale.

Inc.com: www.inc.com (Accessed Spring 2011).

The publishers of *Inc.* magazine present a large directory of articles by topic targeting many problems, concerns, and decisions confronting new business owners/managers. The "How To" section has many articles related to marketing, such as "The New Rules of Event Marketing" and "Developing a Holiday E-mail Marketing Strategy." The articles on marketing and advertising are informative and practical. Simple but effective advice is the hallmark of this outstanding, easy-to-use site.

KnowThis.com: www.knowthis.com/index.php (Accessed Spring 2011).

This information and resource website for those involved in marketing, market research, advertising, selling, promotion, and other marketing-related areas includes blog postings, tutorials, marketing stories, and links to industry resources. One of the marketing tutorials is "How to Write a Marketing Plan," and it walks you through developing and formatting a plan for your company. Use this large site for learning more about marketing anything.

MoreBusiness.com: www.morebusiness.com (Accessed Spring 2011).

Basic sections on this site include "Startup," "Marketing," "Management," and "Online Business." A "Legal and Insurance" section provides sample business contracts and agreements, sample business plans, liability insurance information, and business checklists. Users will find sample business and marketing plans for specific businesses such as personal fitness, retail clothing stores, corporate event planning, and retail bike shop; some plans are free, and some are offered for a fee. The article on "Build Your Own Website" is very useful. Many of the articles are lengthy and thorough. Use this site to help improve your marketing and management skills.

Mplans.com: www.mplans.com (Accessed Spring 2011).

This site wants to sell you marketing software and more, but it also provides interesting and useful articles for free. Articles will help you understand your competition, learn about target marketing, and develop a market forecast for your business. Articles are timely and well written. The free newsletter may help you market your business.

Plunkett Research, LTD. Plunkett's Industry Research Center: www.plunkettresearch. com (Accessed Spring 2011).

Plunkett Research offers business intelligence, industry trends, statistics, marketing research, and corporate profiles that give researchers and business owners a variety of statistics and information. For example, the "Advertising, Branding and Marketing" section broadly covers data and areas of interest ranging from branding strategy and trends to emerging technology and an in-depth analysis of "The Advertising 350." Included are data on radio and TV, direct mail, and online advertising as well as public relations. Trends in areas like advertising agencies, marketing consultants, and global markets are reviewed. Contacts for business and industry leaders, industry associations, Internet resources, and magazines are provided. Examples of statistics included are worldwide advertising growth from 2000 to 2015, advertising spending of U.S. top 10, cable and pay TV revenues and expenses, and the annual television advertising expenditures in the United States from 1970 to 2007. The company profiles are a major section, and companies are arranged alphabetically. Details for each company contain rankings within industry grouping, business description, major brands, divisions and affiliations, officers, addresses, telephone and fax numbers, URLs, number of employees, locations, and growth plan statements. If your industry is covered by Plunkett Research, these authoritative reports will help you make good business decisions.

PowerHomeBiz.com: www.powerhomebiz.com/Index/financing.htm (Accessed Spring 2011).

This small business site has an outstanding collection of marketing advice. Featured articles include "Promotions That Build Profit," "The 7 Commandments of Marketing," and "Top Ten Steps to Tweak Your Business Image." If you are new to marketing, the article "First Steps to Picking the Perfect Marketing Method for You" should help you get started. Must-have books are listed with some articles and recommended tools and software as well. Recommended magazines include several marketing classics. This large, established, and well-organized site will help new entrepreneurs with financing and other parts of starting a new business.

Small Business and Entrepreneurship: http://libguides.unm.edu/small_business (Accessed Spring 2011).

This web page was created and is maintained by me. Some of the resources, especially under the "I need to find …" tab, are specific to the University of New Mexico. However, under the tab "Selected Internet Resources," you will find links to many free small business gateways and legal and government sites. Use my guide as a gateway to many of the websites—such as Business Owners Idea Café, Entrepreneur.com, and MoreBusiness—listed in this resource. My colleagues and I also publish other research guides on business topics such as marketing and advertising, company and industry information, and business basics. Use all of these guides to help you find more information to start and run your new business.

SmallBusinessTV.com: sbtv.com (Accessed Spring 2011).

This web-based network provides information and advice of interest to entrepreneurs and small business owners and managers. Various channels such as "Internet Marketing," "Marketing," "Law for Business," "Sales Strategies," "Women in Business," and "Technology" contain a list of short videos where experts present practical advice. Sign up for the newsletter to keep current on what's happening. A high-speed Internet connection is a real bonus for viewing the videos.

Smartbiz.com Small Business Resource: www.smartbiz.com (Accessed Spring 2011).

This large site is organized into five major sections: "Sales & Marketing," "Online Business," "Business Strategy," "Bits & Bytes," and "Forums & Resources." Users will find business forms like Daily cash flow, employee disciplinary action, employee time sheets, sample business and marketing plans, and collection letters. Continually updated, new articles on public relations and marketing appear with some regularity. Find articles on the positive and negative attributes of radio, expanding your public relations program, e-mail marketing, outdoor advertising media, social media marketing, and how to ask your customers for their opinions. Marketing is vital to any small business, and this site helps you find new methods to improve your marketing and, thus, improve sales.

**Social Media Examiner: www.socialmediaexaminer.com/ (Accessed Spring 2011).

This free online magazine will help you learn how to use social media tools like Twitter and Facebook to increase sales and generate more brand awareness. Find here current articles and tools along with case studies, reviews of industry research, and advice from industry experts. Find out about Foursquare, Facebook Places, Gowalla, and others. Learn how to use automation tools and which ones are better and why. Also download the "2011 Social Media Marketing Industry Report" by Michael A. Stelzner (www.socialmediaexaminer.com/social-media-marketing-industry-report-2011/) and use it to maximize your social media activities and learn about trends in social media marketing.

**SRDS Media Solutions: www.srds.com (Accessed Spring 2011).

Compiled from 12 million households, the *Lifestyle Market Analyst,* an annual market analysis tool, is now part of the SRDS database. It provides demographic, lifestyle, and consumer segment profiles to help users locate where consumers live and how they spend their money and free time. This volume takes interests, hobbies, and activities such as bicycling, fishing, gambling, and reading and combines them with demographic and geographic data. Use it to help you find regional buying powers, find your target audience(s), and analyze 40 demographic segments.

**Trade Show News Network: www.tsnn.com (Accessed Spring 2011).

Though the Internet definitely has had an impact on the trade show market, sometimes setting up a booth at a trade show is a great way to make contacts, find people, and even sell products or services. This comprehensive site provides information on more than 15,000 trade shows that you can find by industry, month, city, state, or country. The Small Business Guide also provides short articles on franchising, incorporating, Internet ads, temporary help, bartering, and home-based businesses. Also find advice on virtual trade shows, trade show planning, convention centers, online service providers, and more.

U.S. Census Bureau: www.census.gov/ (Accessed Spring, 2011).

This website is the best place to start searching for the multitude of data produced by Census Bureau programs, publications, and statistics. The home page categorizes the data under "Census 2010," "People," "Business," "Geography," "Newsroom," "At the Bureau," and "Special Topics." Under "Business," you can click on the "Economic Census," "NAICS," "Survey of Business Owners," "E-Stats," and "Foreign Trade." Under "People," business owners will be interested in income statistics, housing data, and more. Analyzing the demographic trends in the United States allows businesses to forecast future demands for their products or services. The "New to Using Census Bureau Data" page helps users locate what they need quickly. The "Catalog," a search feature, and links to related sites are also accessible on the left side of the home page. Use this site frequently to help start and grow your business.

VerticalResponse Marketing Lounge: lounge.verticalresponse.com/ (Accessed Spring 2011).

This large site includes groups, case studies, articles, business tools, and videos to help you successfully market your small company. Learn how to increase your social media clicks, how to blog as a marketing tool, use e-mail marketing, how to improve your search engine optimization, and more. Learn about new software through webinars, live demos, and other events.

**WebSite MarketingPlan: www.websitemarketingplan.com (Accessed Spring 2011).

This large site contains a wealth of information for small businesses. A large assortment of articles and sample marketing plans are available as well as sample business plans, a newsletter, Internet marketing articles, marketing strategy articles, and more. Featured directory categories include articles grouped under "Search Engine Marketing," "Marketing Strategy," "Marketing Plan," and "Public Relations." Learn about the four seasons of public relations. Lengthy articles on advertising, using public relations for communicating to customers and finding new ones, and customer retention are outstanding. Many commercial links but plenty of free help for the new entrepreneur, too. Many sample business plans are also available here. This site is especially helpful for those interested in e-commerce. Easy to navigate, this site will definitely help you develop a marketing plan that you can use.

THE INTERNET AND SELLING GLOBALLY

8

Expanding your operations outside your home country is a proposition that's obviously exciting and scary. Worldwide, the total number of people using the Internet will reach 1.9 billion in 2012, and the number of devices accessing the Internet will double to 3 billion, according to forecasters. Also by 2012, the number of mobile devices accessing the Internet will surpass the number of online PCs. China has more Internet users than any country in the world—nearly 35% of its population and more than India and the United States. U.S. homes and businesses with broadband access now total over 100 million. Adjusting for the effect of exchange rates, international sales grew nearly 30% in 2010. By 2012, there will be more than 1 billion online buyers worldwide making business-to-consumer transactions worth $1.2 trillion.

We now take for granted the role of technology and the Internet and its impact on communication. The fundamental issue that separates the Internet from other support tools used to build international trade is that time and distance do not matter or impact costs. In other words, businesses no longer have to worry about how far away a customer is or what time of day it is in the local time zone. With the Internet, all communication is immediate and distance has no impact on cost. Internet-enabled cell phones are easy to use and become less expensive every day. The duration of the communication does not impact costs either. The full impact of the advantages of the Internet over other forms of communication is just being understood by international and domestic companies. The web is uniting the world! Today product manuals, price lists, software patches, training materials, and audio/video materials are all only a click away for users. Information is available on demand.

Therefore, one way to ease the stress of expanding your business and getting into international business is to use the Internet and e-commerce to test the waters and not risk investing in hiring staff, international travel, and financial investment. Selling wares globally is a growing niche for many e-commerce sites. Now you can serve customers directly and bypass the middle of the supply chain—distributors, wholesalers, and brick-and-mortar stores—to reach potential customers in every nook and cranny of the world. A partner who has experience in working outside the United States or using the Internet for international business would also make this leap less scary and risky. The return on investment in going international can be lucrative, especially as the ever-competitive U.S. market becomes oversaturated with products and services. Overseas, the product may be relatively new and sought after, with few, if any, distributors; and you may find untapped markets in dozens of countries.

In spring 2010, Forrester Research predicted that e-commerce sales will keep growing in the United States at a 10% compound annual growth rate through 2014. The Department of Commerce predicts that online overall retail sales in the United States for 2011 will be up 7.9% compared to 2010. The Department also predicts that e-commerce sales will represent 8% of all retail sales in the United States by 2014. In 2010 the business-to-consumer e-commerce market grew nearly six times faster than total retail sales. In 2009 nearly 154 million people in the United States (or 67% of the online population) bought something online. Eighty-two percent of online consumers are happy with their experience, compared to just 61% of store consumers.

Therefore, looking at the pros and cons of taking your e-commerce business international, you may find that the pros are:

- More opportunity for growth in customer base and increased sales in foreign countries

- Global name recognition and inexpensive advertising

- Low financial investment

- The ability to move ahead of your competition

- Inexpensive and immediate translation

- Full control over information flow

The cons may include:

- Language barriers may complicate the process.

- Selling products on a large scale may require setting up foreign distributors and manufacturing plants.

- Laws and regulations vary by country, which adds another layer of compliance and complexity.

GETTING STARTED

The Internet connects buyers and sellers in most countries around the world. Experts believe that international markets are growing at nearly twice the rate of domestic markets and that this trend will continue for some time to come. When you start selling on the Internet, you become part of the global e-commerce market, and international customers may seek you out whether you're ready for them or not. Remember that international trade rules are complicated, and even accidental violations of policy can get you in trouble. Consult with government agencies, trade organizations, or a lawyer who practices international law before you make your first international sale. A great website to start at is the SBDCNet's E-commerce Guide.

Figure 8.1 Screenshot of SBDCNet E-commerce Guide (www.sbdcnet.org/e-commerce-guide.html)

This well-organized guide provides information about the current technologies to use, online training, building a website, finding a web host, security issues, and more.

QUICK CHECKLIST FOR MAKING
THE E-COMMERCE DECISION

If what you've learned so far makes you hesitate, here's a list of questions to help you consider more details and implications:

1. *Level of experience:* Have you already done business in another country? Have you received inquiries from other countries? Make a list of potential buyers by product for each country. Is there a trend? Who are your domestic and foreign competitors?

2. *Management and personnel:* Who will be responsible for e-commerce exports and imports? What are the expected outcomes? What changes in the organization are needed to ensure export sales are adequately serviced? Who will lead the follow-through after the planning stage?

3. *Production capability:* Is there a commitment to international sales for the long term, not just as a short-term measure to boost a domestic downturn or slump in sales? Will filling export orders negatively affect domestic sales? What are the new costs? What about employment effects? What design, packaging, and labeling changes are needed?

4. *Financial capacity:* What capital, if any, is available for developing an international market? Are there operating costs? List the initial expenses. Is there a deadline for making this business expansion become self-supporting?

INVESTIGATE MORE POSSIBILITIES

Use the Internet to perform the following business functions for expanding into international trade: market research; identifying, profiling, and communicating with potential agents and distributors; customer and market support services; advertising; trade leads; and logistics such as tracking package status, pricing freight movements, routine communications with customers, and more.

One of the keys to successfully using the power of the Internet is to properly plan the whole company's Internet effort. Go back to chapter 4 to work through developing a business plan, keeping the needs and limitations of international Internet buyers in mind. Other questions to consider include: What training is needed for company staff to ensure that use of the Internet is appropriate and efficient? How will your needs for the Internet change as your international business changes? Is there a need for an intranet website for internal users?

Sometimes there is confusion between the roles of outside companies when providing that provide Internet solutions. An Internet service provider (ISP) is the company that supplies your company with connectivity to the Internet, arranging for equipment and special phone lines to ensure that your company's computers can access the Internet. Many companies have a third party host their websites. This company may be the same one that designs the website, or it may be the company that provides access to the Internet, or there may be three separate companies. The company that is paid to store the data and images of the website is the host.

Involve the webmaster early in the initial stages of planning the company's website; it is the webmaster's responsibility to turn your ideas and goals for your company into reality. Be sure the webmaster is aware of the international component because these international needs will impact decisions about the technical specifications for the website. Learn how to work with and supervise your web designer. Find and visit the websites of companies that have the function and design that you believe will fit your requirements, and share your list of sites with the webmaster to help ensure that he or she understands your vision for your site. The webmaster may be a company employee or an outside contractor; however, an employee in the company should be always trained in updating and making simple changes to the website. Be sure to maintain your site and keep it current, with the latest product or service support information, so foreign agents and distributors can consult it for information and assistance. Make it a priority to keep your site up to date by continually changing the product and company information.

OTHER TECHNICAL CONSIDERATIONS

Besides implementation and website development issues, discuss the following issues with your webmaster:

- *Internet speed connections.* Some countries have slower Internet connections, connect through older software, and have limited access to high-speed Internet. These conditions are changing, but remember them and take into consideration that some foreign customers will have lower modem speeds and/or lower-quality phone connections. The connection between the ISP and the Internet network itself also can affect Internet performance. Minimizing the use of graphics can help sites load faster, so users can navigate more quickly to the information they need.

- *User statistics.* Data about who accessed your website and when will help you understand your customers better and provide the service needed. These data may help track the effectiveness of your advertising or marketing campaigns and measure the interest in your products overseas.

- *Site registration.* Asking visitors to register prior to providing full product or service details is a well-known method for tracking visitors' interests.

- *Site security.* If your company wants to protect sensitive information such as pricing or technical manuals, ask the Webmaster to use some type of security to block unauthorized visitors from parts of the site. Passwords are one option. Remember that probably anything online can make its way into the hands of a competitor.

To learn how to plan your website and successfully work with your web designer, use resources on developing a business website, such as O'Connor's *The Ultimate Guide to a Successful Business Website.*

O'Connor, Jason P. *The Ultimate Guide to a Successful Business Website.* Brandon Oak, 2008. 196p. ISBN 0-980-19120-3. $39.

O'Connor, a professional web designer and marketer, will teach you how to go from an outdated site or simple website to a fully functional and money-generating user-friendly one. Learn how to hire a good web designer for a fair price and how to tell him or her what you want the site to do. Learn how to plan your business website and then how best to market it. Written in easy-to-understand, nontechnical language, one highlight of this book is the list of "Great Website Rules," which describe everything a website needs in order to be successful.

One source of competitive advantage for your website is sustainable traffic. How does one build sustainable traffic?

1. First-time visitors should be able to find your site easily.

   Use search engine metatagging and search engine optimization techniques.

2. Most visitors should be happy with their first experience.

   Find companies that are related to yours in some way, and use reciprocal links to share visitor traffic. Also use pay-per-click ads.

3. Make visitors want to return frequently.

   Learn how to encourage repeat purchases by asking visitors to opt in to receive communications from your business, providing current content or contests, giving coupons on future purchases, or offering free shipping on future orders.

Researching how to improve your website and its traffic is an ongoing project for the successful small business owner. Learn to use techniques that build sustainable online traffic such as writing dynamic web copy, traffic conversion, automation and multimedia, and develop an interactive web presence.

THE LANGUAGE BARRIER

This obvious cultural distinction is the first one you'll need to overcome to do business in a non-English-speaking country or region. While English is the recognized language of business in many countries, not everyone speaks it. Using graphic features can be difficult because they typically make sense only for users who read left to right. For populations that read right to left, the graphics' meaning may be changed or incomprehensible. Graphics can also slow down the connection. The choice of colors for your site is also difficult. Understand that different colors mean different things in different cultures, and research before you design your web pages. Current estimates are that only about 68% of Internet users speak English. Obviously, if you can communicate in the local language, you'll have a distinct advantage. The most basic detail of online business involves understanding the written word. What will you do if you receive an e-mail from a customer in a language you don't understand? You actually have several possible solutions to this dilemma:

1. *Translation software:* One popular solution is to purchase a good software program that lets you convert standard business applications into a foreign a language. These software packages may translate just one language, or a more comprehensive program will translate multiple languages. They generally are as easy to operate as a common word-processing program. Translation.net has been in business since 1994 on the Internet and so has a long history of helping people communicate. SysTran Software Inc. (www.systransoft.com) is another well-established company.

2. *Web-based translations:* The Internet expedites many things, including the availability of real-time translation services and products. You and your customers can translate information by using a Web browser. Pricing is generally based on the size of your company or number of users, number of transactions monthly or yearly, or on the product type. To find out more about these services, try Translation Services USA (www.translation-services-usa.com/service.php) or Translation Experts (www.tranexp.com).

3. *Free online translation tools:* Several companies offer free translation software through the Internet. FreeTranslation.com is a powerful and popular instant translation service powered by SDL's Enterprise Translation Server. The translation is generated by a computer and is displayed instantly. Affiliated with Click2Translate, the user is dynamically shown the cost of having the same text professionally translated, too. PROMPT Translator from Smartlink Corporation (www.online-translator.com/Default.aspx/Site) is another free online translation service, and it also provides automated translation software.

Whether every business should have its entire website translated into other languages is an issue still up for debate. Most companies that are thinking about getting involved in international trade should consider translating a welcome or introductory page into three or four languages such as German, French, and Spanish or, depending on the products or services, Chinese, Japanese, or Hindi. At least provide a link to Yahoo's Babelfish (free online web page translation service: babelfish.yahoo.com/) to help foreign visitors. Let potential customers know if you offer a translation service locally to translate their e-mails into English. If you have forms on the website, be sure they conform to the conventions of international addresses, titles, surnames, postal codes, and so forth. Be careful about making too many fields obligatory because they may not apply. Don't forget the country field. Keep your target market in mind when developing forms. Remember that companies that are new to international e-commerce often cannot fill international orders simply because their systems can't register international addresses or price total delivery costs.

Another important step after you've invested in a website is making sure customers know it exists and how to find it: in other words, marketing. Put your URL and e-mail address on all brochures, flyers, billboards, ads in many types of publications, stationery, and business cards. Get your web address listed in Internet business directories and possibly join a virtual mall. Last but definitely not least is to be certain to get your address on as many search engines as you possibly can. Today social media marketing is a very inexpensive and important way to meet your customers where they are every day. Check chapter 7 for marketing ideas.

EXPANDING YOUR BUSINESS ONLINE

You may be very happy to keep your company small, but for some, the challenge of growth is irresistible, and often e-commerce really makes a company take off. Remember, the key to successful expansion in any business is planning. Before moving your small e-commerce business to the next level, you need to determine what that level is. Start by closely analyzing your options, and determine the advantages and disadvantages of the common paths.

1. An obvious way to expand your business is to offer more products or services on your existing site, which will attract a wider customer base and bring in larger revenues. This strategy is implemented by many companies regularly whether they realize it or not. However, if you consciously identify this as your first growth strategy, your actions will be more targeted and aggressive.

   Here's a start on identifying pros for expanding your e-commerce business by adding products or services:

   • You continue to retain full control of your company.

   • The exploration of different areas, products, services, or markets may increase your enthusiasm for the business.

   And, of course, the cons include:

- It takes time to see results.

- It may take a larger financial investment to support back-end systems for added inventory or providing expanding services.

2. Another way to expand your e-commerce business is to acquire other sites. Start by identifying competitors' sites that may prove profitable for your company. Also look at complementary business sites because they may offer products and services that are different but still a good fit for your business. Pros of acquiring other sites include:

- It's a quick way to expand and diversify.

- Other sites expand your site's customer base easily.

On the other hand, cons include:

- Expansion requires an infusion of cash.

- Negotiations for the sale may drag on and be a drain on time and resources.

3. Another well-recognized way to expand your company is to partner opportunities for affiliate programs. Partnerships could be with a national organization to provide a product or service or with other businesses that will expand your product line and customer base. Pros of affiliate programs or partnerships include:

- Another entity shares the financial burden and associated risks.

- More staff and business knowledge may be available.

- There may be tax or legal advantages.

Cons may include:

- You must share the profits.

- You lose some control and power in making decisions.

- Negotiations take time, and decision making is slow.

- Raising funds may be more difficult.

Find more ideas for growing your business in chapter 14.

E-COMMERCE PITFALLS

Although the Internet offers many benefits and all companies need to use it to enhance their domestic and international expansion, potential downsides and concerns do exist:

- Don't use the Internet as a substitute for all foreign travel. Travel should sometimes still be included in your company's overall international business plan.

- Remember that not everyone in the world has as much access to the Internet as most Americans do. We accept it as reliable, inexpensive, and accessible to all, but some regions of the world remain shut out or limited, while others (like most of the population of South Korea) enjoy high-speed access, and financial transactions are most often conducted via a PC or cell phone.

- Be wary and keep security measures current and active. All companies as well as individuals should maintain a certain level of scrutiny and suspicion about Internet correspondence, especially in relation to financial issues because a strong potential for fraud does exist.

- Remain vigilant about information posted on the company website. The more competitors know about your products or pricing details, the easier it is to compete against your company. Security and control on the Internet are important for a variety of reasons.

As you've learned from reading this chapter, e-commerce is rapidly expanding throughout the world; this often profitable type of business is also available to more entrepreneurs than ever before. The world is shrinking, and consumers are enthusiastically embracing the possibilities of getting the products and services when they need them, at a price they can afford, and when they want them. Planning, as in any new business venture, is still the key to success. Leap into the e-commerce world, but plan for success.

REFERENCES

Starred titles are discussed in the chapter.

▮ Print Resources

Awe, Susan C. *Going Global: An Information Sourcebook for Small and Medium-sized Businesses.* Libraries Unlimited, 2009. 265p. ISBN 9-78-15915-8. $45.

This resource guide outlines how business owners can become global companies. Learn how to get involved in international trade and international selling, how to use the Internet to sell globally, and find foreign customers for your products or services. In this well-organized book, also find out about risks of international expansion, ins and outs of exporting and importing, and various as aspects of e-commerce today.

Barrow, Colin. *Starting a Business from Home: Choosing a Business, Getting Online, Reaching Your Market and Making a Profit,* 2nd ed. Kogan Page, 2011. 306p. ISBN 0-749-46264-7. $24.95.

Barrow's second edition includes more exercises and end-of-chapter advice. Learn how to identify a business structure, how to do market research, ins and outs of building a website, and hints on going global. Appendices contain ideas for home-based businesses, sources of help and advice, and ideas on raising necessary capital. The slight British slant may confuse some.

Basic Guide to Exporting: Official Government Resource for Small and Medium-sized Businesses, 10th ed. U.S. Department of Commerce, 2008. 254p. ISBN 0-16079-20-4-5. $18. Also available online: www.unzco.com/basicguide/index.html

Conventional wisdom once held that U.S. businesses should be content selling within their domestic market, because international markets were too difficult and too expensive to penetrate. However, in the past decade, barriers to trade have been lowered, and tremendous advances in communications technology have been achieved. Now exporting is seen as a prime growth area, and this title describes the costs and risks associated with exporting, how to develop a strategy for success, and where to get the knowledge to enter exporting. Assistance from the federal and state government is also discussed.

Belew, Shannon and Elad, Joel. *Starting an Online Business All-in-One Desk Reference for Dummies,* Kindle ed. For Dummies, 2009. 840p. $29.99.

As in other books of this series, readers find the basics of starting a business on the Internet. E-commerce survival stories, best practices, and other resources to help you develop your new business are provided. The book contains good tips on selecting an online host, understanding website design, establishing a graphic identity, providing customer service, and providing various payment options. The chapters on "Niche E-Commerce" and "E-Commerce Advances" are especially useful. Learn to build a customer-friendly site as well as market with Facebook and MySpace and set up a shop on Second Life. Some coverage of legal matters, Internet security, trademarks, copyrighting, and taxes are included.

Burgess, Stephen et al. *Effective Web Presence Solutions for Small Businesses: Strategies for Successful Implementation.* Information Science Reference, 2008. 352p. ISBN 1-605-66224-0. $165.

This holistic approach to designing and implementing a small business web presence advises owners to identify the website content that matches their business strategy. This text is based on many years of research and provides practical guidance to new business owners and managers. Learn how to use the web to gain new customers and effectively sell your products or services there.

Capela, John J. *Import/Export for Dummies.* For Dummies, 2008. 360p. ISBN 0-470-26094-7. $19.99.

This clear, practical primer provides businesses with necessary information to begin exporting their products around the world and importing goods to the United States to sell. Covering the ins and outs of developing or expanding operations to capture a share of this developing market, Capela details the top 10 countries with which the United States trades. Well organized and inexpensive, this title is a good purchase for new exporters and importers.

Cooper, Ian et al. *Smarta Way to Do Business.* John Wiley, 2011. 334p. ISBN 1-907312-52-8. $34.95.

This British title is brought to you by Smarta.com, the United Kingdom's ultimate resource for business advice, networking, and tools. The emphasis here is tied to the consumer's and the company's online experience; use and learn how to use networking and interactive tools such as giveaways, vouchers or coupons, and codes to access restricted areas of the website. Discover here strategies for survival, expansion, and exiting your business. This step-by-step guide provides practical advice and tips to help you start and grow a successful business.

Culwell, Lori. *Million Dollar Website*. Prentice Hall, 2009. 288p. ISBN 0-7352-0441-6. $19.95.

Learn how to pinpoint what your business website needs, and take the steps to improve it and get it noticed. Detailed advice by a website consultant can help the business owner ramp up a web presence and use the right tools to gauge its success. Find out how to enhance brand awareness, write web-savvy content, and use social networking sites to increase traffic.

daCosta, Eduardo. *Global E-Commerce Strategies for Small Business*. MIT Press, 2001. 230p. ISBN 0262041901. $24.95.

daCosta lays out the steps for beginning a global small business. Using examples from seven companies located in six different countries, he details the purchasing process and customer service, explains how to research new business opportunities and markets, recommends ways to utilize the web and other forms of new technology, and provides ideas for overcoming obstacles to international trade for small companies. Written in a casual, readable style, readers of all levels will gain something from this optimistic view of the global marketplace.

Exporters' Encyclopaedia. Dun & Bradstreet, annual.

A comprehensive world reference guide, this encyclopedia is divided into 220 country-specific sections; firms specializing in international business, laws, and legislation; international trade associations; government agencies; shipping practice; and reference data on weights and measures for overseas ports. Find key contacts, trade and safety regulations, and information on documentation needed. Marketing data include legal requirements for importers/agents, procurement standards, environmental protection/pollution control, marking, and labeling. The encyclopedia also provides passport regulations and business etiquette guidelines.

Funk, Tom. *Web 2.0 and Beyond: Understanding the New Online Business Models, Trends, and Technologies*. Praeger, 2008. 192p. ISBN 0-313-35187-2. $34.95.

Web 2.0 can describe many things—including websites; cultural trends such as social networking, blogging, or podcasting; or the technology underlying today's newest and coolest web applications—so it's really a series of trends, not a collection of things. Pioneered by giants like Amazon, YouTube, and Google, even the smallest companies can take advantage of new, open-source programming tools, new social software, and new networks. The Web 2.0 landscape is really about users controlling their online experience and influencing the experiences of others. Small companies can gain customers and competitive advantage by putting these new technologies to work for them. This nontechnical guide will help readers understand recent developments in the online world and put them to practical business uses.

Gendron, Michael P. *Creating the New E-Business Company*. South-Western, 2005. 304p. ISBN 0-32-4224-85-0. $34.95.

This book discusses how emerging technologies should be viewed in a total corporate context as an intrinsic part of the organization's structure and mission. Learn how new technologies will revamp the way we do business and learn to use them to maximize your company's potential. Management in all sizes of businesses will have to think about how organizations and industries can adapt to the electronic future. E-thinking in day-to-day business tactics and strategic plans is essential. Discover how this conversion to e-commerce thinking can boost the bottom line.

Holzner, Steven. *Small Business Web Sites Made Easy.* McGraw-Hill Osborne Media, 2009. 272p. ISBN 0-07-161481-8. $21.99.

Holzner explains how to take your business online and generate additional revenue by using search engine optimization and pay-per-click advertising, marketing on Facebook, creating a shopping cart, enabling credit card transactions, and more. He advocates using cascading style sheets and JavaScript elements to establish a solid online presence.

Jacob, Sherice. *Get Niche Quick! The Definitive Guide to Marketing Your Business on the Internet.* 162p. CreateSpace, 2009. ISBN 1-44-04353-08. $16.50.

This clear, straightforward book details many secrets of online marketing. The first chapter clears up what exactly niche marketing is and the importance of using keywords. Chapter 2 explains how to use Word Tracker (an important tool for finding out which keywords are used most). Chapter 3 explains how to check out competitor websites in the same niche. Each chapter covers an in-depth process involved in online marketing, and chapter 9 is outstanding as it guides you through creating an online marketing plan. The final chapter gives you many more tips, such as writing articles and where to submit them, how to use blogs and RSS feeds, and more. The effective strategies presented here will help you more effectively market your online business.

Jagoe, John R. *Export Sales and Marketing Manual 2008: The Bible of Exporting.* Export Institute of the United States, annual. 520p. ISBN 0-943677-66-1. $295.

Having been updated annually for 21 consecutive years, this international trade publication has achieved longevity and global reach. This manual covers all the steps involved in selling products in world markets. Over 120 illustrations, 85 graphs, 40 flow charts, and 60 sample international trade documents lead readers through the process. Jagoe helps readers conduct market research through 1,200 website addresses providing information on various markets and products and services. A lengthy glossary of export terms and detailed index for quick access to important information are also provided.

Jantsch, John. *Duct Tape Marketing.* Thomas Nelson, 2008. 304p. ISBN 1-59-555131-X $15.99.

This collection of proven tools and tactics are presented as a step-by-step marketing system to show entrepreneurs and small business owners what to do to market and grow their businesses. Learn ways to inspire customers to stick to your company, make your website work for you, and hone your message. Jantsch also explains how to automate your marketing with technology tools and produce marketing materials that educate.

Johnson, Thomas E. *Export/Import Procedures and Documentation,* 4th ed. AMACOM, 2010. 640p. ISBN 0-81441-550-4. $85.

The world of international rules, laws, and regulations is complex and always changing, and this comprehensive work provides a clear view of the entire process. Find out here about currency exchange, dealing with banks and contracts as well as customs, and, of course, transportation issues. Johnson provides 140 sample contracts, documents, and forms. Written in clear, nontechnical language and providing checklists and question-naires, this large reference will help anyone getting into the import or export trade.

Levine, Michael. *Guerrilla PR 2.0: Wage an Effective Publicity Campaign without Going Broke.* Harper, 2008. 368p. ISBN 0-06-143832-9. $14.99.

This collection of low-cost publicity techniques includes sample press releases and attention-getting strategies targeted for the wired environment. Focused on the Internet, Levine's theories include specific campaigns, and readers will find his examples of highly successful campaigns such as the launch of Mothers Against Drunk Driving and flops like New Coke instructive and entertaining. Levine has many years of experience in public relations, and entrepreneurs will benefit from this discussion and hints gathered from his experiences.

Levinson, Jay Conrad and Gibson, Shane. *Guerrilla Social Media Marketing.* Entrepreneur Press, 2010. 240p. ISBN 1-5991-8383-8. $21.95.

This thorough guide presents sample materials including "100 weapons to grow your online influence." Learn how to use public relations tools such as press releases, e-mail, radio, direct mail, and more in the new world of social media. Learn the basic skill of online relationship building here. Ideas are summarized in an easy-to-understand and easy-to-read format. This field guide is for any business wanting to do things right the first time and get engaged in the social media space quickly.

Manresa, Maritza. *How to Open and Operate a Financially Successful Import Export Business.* Atlantic Publishing Group, 2010. 288p. ISBN 1-601-38226-X. $39.95.

This comprehensive manual will help any business start or expand its business into the international arena. Learn how to draw up a winning business plan; find out about government regulations, tax laws, and customs requirements; and discover where to find foreign trade leads. Find out before you begin how to meet Internal Revenue Service requirements and build your business by using low-or no-cost ways to satisfy your customers. The companion CD-ROM contains many forms and templates. A lengthy list of resources provides more information and help.

Marshall, Perry and Todd, Bryan. *Ultimate Guide to Google AdWords,* 2nd ed. Entrepreneur Press, 2010. 304p. ISBN 1-599-18360-2. $24.95.

Learn the fundamentals, techniques, tools, and tricks that will get your business in front of thousands every day. Google is searched more than 250 million times a day, and Marshall and Todd will help you develop a high-quality keyword list, earn high rankings in Google's organic search results, and determine what's working with Google's conversion tracking. The second section covers marketing topics such as customer relationship management, positioning, and e-mail marketing so you will have a better understanding of the role AdWords plays in a marketing plan. The numerous examples in the third section will help you create short yet successful ads. This work is very useful to those who are new to marketing.

McFadyen, Thomas. *Ecommerce Best Practices: How to Market, Sell, and Service Customers with Internet Technologies.* McFadyen Solutions, 2008. 366p. ISBN 0-9815951-0-3. $34.95.

This title provides tools for companies in any stage of developing a web presence to market and sell their products or services to global customers. McFadyen is a frequent speaker and consultant on e-commerce matters. Learn how to make navigation easy for your customers, the latest in shopping carts, and how to make visitors into buyers. Use this well-written and well-organized resource to improve your website.

Meyerson, Mitch and Scarborough, Mary Eule. *Mastering Online Marketing.* Entrepreneur Press, 2007. 211p. ISBN 1-59918-151-7. $21.95.

This 12-step system teaches readers how to build and sustain a thriving e-commerce business. These strategies and tactics will help owners get targeted traffic to their websites, turn visitors into buyers, and generally help build a successful business on the Internet. Find help in understanding why your website is underperforming. Worksheets, resources, and case studies from successful businesses are highlights of Meyerson and Scarborough's bible for online marketing.

Monosoff, Tamara. *Your Million Dollar Dream: Create a Winning Business Plan.* McGraw-Hill, 2010. 336p. ISBN 0-07-162943-2. $19.95.

Monosoff, founder of Mom Inventors Inc., works with many entrepreneurs and often walks them through the steps to starting and growing their own businesses. The chapter entitled "Making Money Your Way" provides information and exercises the will help you articulate your dreams, identify skill sets, and broaden your awareness and link to businesses that tap into your strengths and dreams. Learn how to create an effective business plan. An important section on "Making the Most of Today's Marketing and Sales Tools" will help you use Twitter and Facebook as powerful marketing tools.

Morrison, Terri. *Kiss, Bow, or Shake Hands: The Bestselling Guide to Doing Business in More than 60 Countries.* Adams Media, 2006. 592p. ISBN 1-59-33736-86. $24.95.

This encyclopedic resource presents information on history, type of government, languages, religions, business practices, titles, and forms of address for 60 countries. A cultural orientation for each country with negotiation strategies and value systems is included. Learning to do business in a foreign country will be easier using this well-organized and concise guide. This guide is now available by subscription online.

Nelson, Carl A. *Import/Export: How to Take Your Business across Borders,* 4th ed. McGraw-Hill, 2008. 352p. ISBN 978-0-07-148255-5. $21.95.

As in previous editions, Nelson demystifies international trade, including basics such as writing the business plan, choosing a product or service, sample for customs and duties, financing international transactions, and more. He uses examples and success stories to illustrate his points. Hot-button issues such as the World Trade Organization, doing business with North American Free Trade Agreement, Africa, India, China, and the European Union and the changing world of e-commerce are explored. His step-by-step guidance will help entrepreneurs succeed in international ventures and use the Internet to their advantage.

**O'Connor, Jason P. *The Ultimate Guide to a Successful Business Website.* Brandon Oak, 2008. 196p. ISBN 0-980-19120-3. $39.

O'Connor, a professional web designer and marketer, will teach you how to go from an outdated site or simple website to a fully functional and money-generating user-friendly one. Learn how to hire a good web designer for a fair price and how to tell the designer what you want the site to do. Learn how to plan your business website and then how best to market it. Written in easy-to-understand, nontechnical language, one highlight of the book is the list of "Great Website Rules," which describe everything a website needs to be successful.

Olsen, Kai A. *The Internet, the Web, and EBusiness: Formalizing Applications for the Real World.* Scarecrow Press, 2005. 432p. ISBN 0-810-85167-9. $57.

This introductory book to the online world includes case studies and exercises about the human-computer interface and presents a concise overview of the fundamental principles of computer applications on the Internet. Learn the distinction between formal and informal processes and their relationship to virtual environments. Tables and graphics illustrate Olsen's ideas in an easy-to-understand manner. This basic knowledge will help you understand and utilize the online environment.

Parasuraman, A. and Colby, Charles L. *Techno-Ready Marketing: How and Why Your Customers Adopt Technology.* Free Press, 2007. 240p. ISBN 1-416-5766-30. $17.95.

Parasuraman and Colby's compelling framework for "measuring the propensity of customers to welcome and use technology-intensive products and services" is presented clearly and concisely. Learn to determine each customer's technology readiness, motivate customers to use the new and emerging technologies you're providing, and understand why customers either embrace or resist technology. Find out if you need to divide your customers into five distinct groups. Small business owners and marketing professionals can learn about the technology-driven future from these authors.

Phillips, Michael and Rasberry, Salli. *Marketing without Advertising,* 6th ed. Nolo Press, 2008. 398p. ISBN 1-41330-63-22. $20.

This book takes readers on an in-depth, practical journey through marketing strategies. One valuable section illustrates how to design and implement a marketing plan. This new edition uses updated real-world examples and resources. Other interesting and informative topics include the physical appearance of your business, educating and helping prospective customers find your business, good relations with your employees and how they influence the perception of your business. Questionnaires, checklists, and worksheets help readers understand important points and make decisions about expanding their marketing efforts by using the Internet.

Poynter, Ray. *Handbook of Online and Social Media Marketing Research.* Wiley, 2010. 462p. ISBN 0-47-071-040-3. $66.

This volume will provide e-commerce companies and those interested in marketing their businesses on the Internet with comprehensive information about understanding, using, acquiring, and conducting market and marketing research online. Important chapters thoroughly cover sampling, questionnaire design, target markets, and tracking (feedback systems). The second half of the book covers the process of applying online marketing research to all phases of online product development and marketing. Poynter provides his views on "how to be better with people" and "how to maximize response rates." Use this information to assist you in developing every stage of an online venture.

Regnerus, Bob. *Big Ticket Ecommerce: How to Sell High-Priced Products and Services Using the Internet.* Innovation Press, 2008. 181p. ISBN 0-9764624-9-4. $16.95.

Learn techniques and methods of selling high-priced products and services through the new technologies available to e-commerce leaders and innovators. Regnerus provides practical hints about blogging, setting up online communities, Google AdWords, reciprocal links, and more. Learn how to plan and market products to the clients who need them.

Rich, Jason R. *Design and Launch Your eCommerce Business in a Week*. Entrepreneur Press, 2008. 260p. ISBN 1-59918-183-5. $17.95.

This step-by-step guide will help you build a website quickly and with little frustration. Using inexpensive, turnkey solutions like Yahoo!, GoDaddy, Google, and eBay, beginners can design and build a professional, easy-to-navigate e-commerce site. Learn how to reach potential customers, accept payments from all over the world, and process simple orders. Discover ideas on how to keep customers coming back.

Risdahll, Aliza. *Streetwise eCommerce: Establish Your Online Business, Expand Your Reach, and Watch Your Profits Soar!* Adams Media, 2007. 371p. ISBN 1-59869-144-9. $19.95.

This handy guide teaches readers how to create and manage an e-mail list, design a website, build an online community, and market and sell online. Early chapters discuss the uses of various online communication tools like e-mail, blogs, and message boards and compares online marketing to traditional marketing efforts. Risdahl, an author of several books on entrepreneurship and Internet marketing, discusses building and maintaining your online presence, how to sell online, and evaluating techniques for your successes. Learn how to develop company policies, negotiate a web deal, and the basics of web design. In this well-organized and user-friendly book, most readers will discover strategies and tools useful for developing and expanding their e-commerce business.

Rognerud, Jon. *The Ultimate Guide to Search Engine Optimization: Drive Traffic, Boost Conversion Rates and Make Tons of Money,* 2nd ed. Entrepreneur Press, 2010. 240p. ISBN 1-5991-839-23. $24.95.

Search engine optimization (SEO) brings you fast results, and you can reach your target audience with the most cost-effective method on the Internet today. Rognerud explains the secrets of executing a successful, cost-effective online campaign using social media solutions, SEO, and pay-per-click advertising. Succeeding in online advertising is accomplished by knowing what you are doing, constructing a comprehensive advertising plan, and knowing the relationships between your website, many search engines, and advertising campaign methods.

Sharp, Julien. *Design and Launch an Online Social Networking Business in a Week.* Entrepreneur Press, 2009. 200p. ISBN 1-59918-268-1. $17.95.

Practical guidance is provided by Sharp on starting a social networking business and includes tips on setting goals; developing an inviting, interactive website; generating traffic and membership; and building advertising and other revenue streams while using online resources to stay on the cutting edge. Very well organized and well written, use this book to get you started.

Slaunwhite, Steve. *The Complete Idiot's Guide to Starting a Web-Based Business.* Alpha Books, 2009. 350p. ISBN 1-59257-889-4. $19.95.

Learn how to create and operate a successful cyberspace venture step-by-step. Slaunwhite looks at the basics of doing business online and then helps you identify online trends, create a game plan and a website, and market your site, and then he provides tactics for turning clicks into customers. Find out how to use website analytics and search engine optimization. Appendix B helps you locate free and nearly free online tools and resources. Well written and organized, use this reference to help you with day-to-day issues.

Solis, Brian. *Engage, Revised and Updated: The Complete Guide for Brands and Businesses to Build, Cultivate, and Measure Success in the New Web,* rev. ed. Wiley, 2011. 336p. ISBN 1-11800-37-64. $18.95.

Solis analyzes the social media environment and identifies ways to effectively use social media in business. He looks at one network and one tool individually. Follow him through the specific steps required for conceptualizing, implementing, managing, and measuring a social media advertising campaign. Find out about the psychology, behavior, and influence of the new social consumer. Using Solis's techniques, your business will gain the ability to increase visibility, build communities of loyal brand enthusiasts, and increase profits. Learn how to create a space online that really represents your business and cultivates customer loyalty and trust.

Strange, C.A. *How to Start and Run an Internet Business,* 2nd ed. How to Books, 2010. 230p. ISBN 1-84528-356-2. $30.

Strange has written a practical guide to establishing a profitable online business. She includes case studies, business ideas, ways to create a visible and usable web presence, and ideas for gaining and keeping a good customer base. She provides checklists and secrets for online business success. Learn how to create an appealing virtual shop window for retail sales. She covers many aspects of selling to the international market, too. If you have the right idea, Internet access, and enthusiasm for working until you get it right, a career as an Internet entrepreneur may be right for you.

Szetela, David. *Pay-Per-Click Search Engine Marketing.* Sybex, 2010. 432p. ISBN 0-470-48867-0. $29.99.

Learn how to develop, implement, measure, and manage successful pay-per-click ad campaigns by following this hour-a-day plan for success. Many topics discussed here may be new to you, such as mastering the tactics of bidding for position and for keywords, seeing why content and search advertising complement each other, leveraging Google's content network to make your strategy a success, and understanding the differences between search engines Google, Yahoo!, and Bing. Also very useful from Szetela are the templates and tools from the book's website.

Tasner, Michael. *Marketing in the Moment: The Practical Guide to Using Web 3.0 Marketing to Reach Your Customers First.* FT Press, 2010. 256p. ISBN 0-137-0810-09-X. $24.99.

Tasner will help you derive the most value from next-generation web, online, mobile, and social marketing tools and techniques with proven tactics and successful ground-level execution. Learn how to use action plans practically and how to use virtual collaboration to accomplish marketing projects. Learn how to use sites and tools you have never heard of, such as Plurk, UStream, Joost, Tumblr, and iGoogle. No one business can use or do it all, but Tasner may give you enough information to pick and choose what to pursue.

Travis, Tom. *Doing Business Anywhere: The Essential Guide to Going Global.* John Wiley, 2007. 202p. ISBN 0-470-14961-2. $24.95.

Travis presents his six tenets of global trade and illustrates them in the context of real stories of global trade. He emphasizes the importance of international trade in the economy of all nations. If you want to expand your present venture, Travis helps you organize, plan, operate, and execute with a global mind-set. Learn how to navigate international laws and deal with many cultures. He also explains how to utilize the benefits of free trade agreements to begin and operate a competitive business. Also highlighted is brand protection through patents, copyrights, and trademarks. Security concerns and measures are also discussed. Travis will convince readers that embracing his six tenets is key to doing business anywhere.

Turner, Krista. *Start Your Own Import/Export Business,* 3rd ed. Entrepreneur Press, 2010. 240p. ISBN 1-59918-37-57. $17.95.

This book contains insights and practical advice for entering global markets. It covers aspects of the startup process, including collecting money from overseas transactions, using the Internet to simplify your transactions, accessing trade law information to keep your business in compliance, how to find contacts in the United States and abroad, and choosing a customs broker. Chapters on market research, working online, employees, pricing, and insurance will help run a business efficiently and effectively. A brief appendix on international trade resources may also prove useful. Interviews with successful importer/exporters and an updated resource list will help show the way to success.

Urquhart-Brown, Susan. *The Accidental Entrepreneur: The 50 Things I Wish Someone Had Told Me about Starting a Business.* AMACOM, 2008. 178p. ISBN 0-8144-0167-8. $17.95.

This title includes two outstanding chapter. "What Is an Entrepreneur, Anyway?" asks you to define yourself, your business, and your goals. "What Do You Bring to the Party?" asks important questions about accountability and procrastination. Real-life examples are often included to illustrate the author's points. One other valuable and interesting chapter is "Get Connected to the Web for Profit." Also, learn what to avoid in starting your new venture.

■ Online Resources

About.com: entrepreneurs.about.com/ (Accessed Spring 2011).

This large site has many parts and is at times a bit difficult to navigate. Use the search feature if you have trouble. On the left side of this main page, you will find "Business Ideas on a Budget," "Choosing a Business to Start," "Business Plan Outline," "Step-by-Step," "Business Legal Organizational Structures," and a "How to Library." Further down, topics like "Financing," "Case Studies and Interviews," and "Resources" provide more links to information. The About.com large website also covers the biotech/biomedical, composites/plastics, metal, insurance, and retail industries. The Retail Industry (http://retailindustry.about.com/), which is notoriously difficult to locate information about, is especially well done; articles provide information on current retail trends, retail statistics, retail industry profile, apparel trends, consumer trends, and more. The entire site is fully searchable, so put in your keywords and find information. Under "Business and Finance," users will find articles on, for example, various industries, selling to the government, store operations, retail trends, advertising costs, branding, and more. International information on global trade shows and industry trends is also available through a simple search.

All About Market Research: www.allaboutmarketresearch.com/ (Accessed Spring 2011).

This directory is a guide to outstanding tools, tips, resources, and services for your e-commerce Internet marketing research. This well-organized site has areas listed across the top, including "Blog," "Academic Market Research," "Associations," "Directories," "Internet Growth," "Library," "e-Commerce," and "Links." The "Library" has coaching-type articles on search engine optimization, Internet writing, Internet online advertising, and more. "Associations" has a lengthy list of links to international market research organizations. "Internet Growth" has a wealth of informative statistics. Use this site to improve your online marketing efforts.

BEOnline: Business and Economics Online: www.loc.gov/rr/business/beonline/ (Accessed Spring 2011).

Compiled by the Library of Congress Business Reference Services for researchers, under "Subject Guides," you will find a lengthy list of business topics, such as associations, business plans (forms), companies by industry, data sets, e-commerce, economic indicators, international trade, legal resources, and more. If you click on "Associations," you will find a short list of associations. Clicking on an association takes you to its website. Under the "International Trade Listing," you will find foreign trade statistics and the Trade Compliance Center.

BizMove.com: www.bizmove.com (Accessed Spring 2011).

The wealth of information covers a variety of topics, including general management, small business marketing, Internet business, and international trade. Worksheets and sample plans will help guide users. "Growing a Business on the Internet" covers topics like search engine positioning, website promotion, and e-mail marketing methods. The "International Trade" section centers on exporting but covers many diverse topics, including how to export a service and how to sell overseas.

Bplans.com: www.bplans.com (Accessed Spring 2011).

This well-established, frequently updated site, sponsored by Palo Alton Software, Inc., is the best for help in writing your business plan. The section entitled "Write a Business Plan" contains articles, calculators on cash flow, starting costs, break even, a business plan template, executive summary, and mission statement help, plus access to expert advice. Currently 60 free plans are viewable online for free. Another nice feature is a "Business Planning Audio" for auditory learners. The section on "Running an Online Business" includes great articles for setting up and running an e-commerce site. Find ideas on marketing your site and how to improve sales as well as measuring key performance factors. Bplans.com is a useful, practical site that also offers fee-based experts and assistance.

Business Owners Idea Café: www.businessownersideacafe.com (Accessed Spring 2011).

Developed by successful entrepreneurs and authors of published guides on starting a business, the large site presents short articles on all aspects of small business or entrepreneurial life. The main divisions include "CyberSchmooz," "Starting Your Biz," "Running Your Biz," "Take Out Info," "Classifieds," "The 'You' in Your Biz," "De-Stress and Have Fun," "About Idea Café," and "Join Idea Café." The large "Running Your Biz: eCommerce" section has excellent coverage on all things e-commerce plus links to outside information on e-commerce. Here you can find experts to answer your questions or discuss your current business crisis. You'll find sample business plans, financing help, business forms, and business news.

Buyusa.gov: www.buyusa.gov/home/export.html (Accessed Spring 2011).

This simple-to-use government website offers to help businesses get into international sales through market research, trade events, introductions to buyers and distributors, and counseling for every/any step of the export process. One part of the website helps importers to the United States and another helps exporters from the United States, and both parts cover products and services. When you click on a country, you get the "Country Commercial Guide," a calendar of events, employment opportunities, market information, and services for U.S. exporters and suppliers. Also part of this site is *Commercial News USA,* the "official export promotion magazine of the U.S. Department of Commerce." This online publication also contains a wealth of information, including franchising, trade shows, a company index, and more. Under "Our Worldwide Sites," you can search for "Export Assistance Centers" and "Find Export Information by Country."

ClickZ Stats: www.clickz.com/stats (Accessed Spring 2011).

This large site has sectors for statistics on business-to-business, demographics, hardware, marketing channels, tools, security issues, and ad industry metrics. Categorized by month, year, and subsection, the "Statistics Toolbox" was set up as a resource that lets users find statistics, numbers, and tables that have been incorporated into ClickZ Stats articles. The "Web Worldwide" is a look at current and projected Internet users with links to some related articles on different countries. Use the information here to understand the Internet business environment and make informed business decisions.

Commercial News: www.thinkglobal.us/ (Accessed Spring 2011).

Commercial News USA is the official export promotion magazine of the U.S. Department of Commerce and it showcases U.S.-made products and services. You will find lists of companies already exporting grouped in various different industries. Trade show opportunities are highlighted and described, often letting businesses know who attends and who should attend. Also an excellent source for trade leads and to advertise your products or services to find customers or partners, subscribe online or by mail. Issues may be read online for download in PDFs. Franchising information is available as well as success stories to inspire new exporters.

**E-Commerce Guide—SBDCNet: www.sbdcnet.org/e-commerce-guide.html (Accessed Spring 2011).

The Small Business Development Center National Information Clearinghouse provides timely, web-based information to entrepreneurs. Small Business Development Centers are located in all 50 states and offer free, confidential business counseling. This website provides information on business start-up, international trade, e-commerce, industry research, marketing, trends, and more. The E-Commerce Guide contains online training in building your website, managing a digital business, writing an Internet business plan, and more. A free newsletter will help you keep up on trends in small business. Small and medium-sized business owners will find plenty of links and information here to help them plan, expand, and run their new business.

Ecommerce-Guide to Building a Successful Ecommerce Site: www.ecommerce-guide.com (Accessed Spring 2011).

Jupiter Corporation's large e-commerce site has different channels for "News & Trends," "Solutions," "Resources," "Forums," "Products," "Glossary," and "Events." In the section on building a successful site, users will find advertising/marketing, technology, Twitter marketing, web design, and customer relation areas to help build a better, growing business. White papers and case studies are also available. Trends and product reviews are provided as well as company information. Videos provide visual information. The articles on international e-commerce are practical and informative. Additionally, an "E-Commerce Webopedia" is provided with definitions of old, new, and upcoming e-commerce terms, like business VOIP, e-discovery, Netcheque, and key fob. The "eBiz FAQ" is a particularly useful section.

Ecommerce Times: www.ecommercetimes.com (Accessed Spring 2011).

This commercial website sponsored by the Triad Commerce Group offers short news articles, columns, a products and service guide, *TechNewsWorld, MacNewsWorld,* and *LinuxInsider* in an easy-to-read format. Under "Ecommerce Times Archives," you'll find news items dating from 1999. White papers and case studies are also available. When you click on a particular article, related articles are listed below it. Several other channels present many news options.

eMarketer: www.emarketer.com/Welcome.aspx (Accessed Spring 2011).

This excellent site for Internet economy statistics is large and frequently updated. While eMarketer's purpose is to sell expensive competitive business reports, it also provides a good amount of free, information, including a free newsletter. The *eMarketer Daily Newsletter* provides current information every business day. The eStat Database is a subscription service that provides links to current and past articles with statistical breakdowns of specific markets and emerging technologies.

Export.Gov: www.export.gov (Accessed Spring 2011).

Created as a government-to-business initiative, Export.Gov is the government's portal to exporting and trade services. It is designed to simplify the exporting process by being a single point of access to export-related services and thus reducing the need to view multiple government sources. Over 19 U.S. departments and agencies contribute to the information the site provides, including the U.S. International Trade Administration, the U.S. Commercial Service, the Department of Commerce, the Export-Import Bank, the Agency for International Development, and the U.S. Trade and Development Agency. Companies new to exporting will find step-by-step help through the export process. To facilitate international trade, companies can also find references on foreign tariff and tax information, search foreign and domestic trade events, subscribe to receive trade leads and industry-specific market intelligence, and gain access to federal export assistance and financing. Export.Gov is fully searchable and allows you to globally search the contents of all of its contributing entities. Use this site to start market research, international statistics searches, and for getting advice and counseling.

The Export Yellow Pages: www.exportyellowpages.com (Accessed Spring 2011).

The Export Yellow Pages are administered by the Export Trading Company Affairs of the International Trade Administration in partnership with the U.S. Department of Commerce. Containing information on U.S. business products and suppliers, this site is designed to promote and connect small-and medium-sized entertripses (SMEs), improve market visibility, help establish international contacts, simplify sales sourcing, and solve language barriers. This site is often used by foreign buyers as a reference tool to find U.S. goods and services. U.S. firms can register their businesses without charge at www.myexports.com.

Also, export intermediaries such as freight forwarders, sales agents, and other service companies that help export businesses can register at no charge in the U.S. Trade Assistance Directory. Find trade leads and other resources here in a wide variety of industries. Products and services are offered by over 27,000 U.S. companies.

ExportHelp, your online export helpdesk: www.exporthelp.co.za/index.html (Accessed Spring 2011).

This large export assistance site from South Africa has an abundance of information and advice for new exporters. Find information on documentation, marketing, an initial SWOT (strengths, weaknesses, opportunities, threats) analysis, country selection, and more. A lengthy article on trade fairs and getting the most out of them is also a highlight. The section on e-commerce is also practical.

Federation of International Trade Associations (FITA): http://fita.org (Accessed Spring 2011).

This huge, very useful site covers all areas of importing and exporting. Users will find help with market research, transportation and logistics, documentation, trade finance and currencies, trade law, directories, a trade show calendar, and worldwide trade leads. Find here a user-friendly introduction to the fundamental aspects of exporting, links to practical sites from other countries, a trade information database, and much more. FITA has International Trade Business Operations Software listed on its site. The "E-commerce Toolbox" is practical and useful. This site is well organized, annotated, and easy to use.

FedStats: www.fedstats.gov (Accessed Spring 2011).

The official website of the Federal Interagency Council on Statistical Policy is a gateway to statistics from over 100 U.S. federal agencies and is well organized and easy to use. Users can find information under "Links to Statistics," "Topic Links A–Z," "MapStats," and "Statistics by Geography from U.S. Agencies." "MapStats" provides statistical profiles of states, counties, cities, congressional districts, and federal judicial districts. The "Statistical Reference Shelf," a bit further down on the home page, is a large collection of online reference sources such as the *Statistical Abstract of the United States*. You will find a variety of other sources, such as the *State and Metropolitan Area Data Book* and *Digest of Education Statistics*, which will provide statistics on many topics of interest to entrepreneurs. On the other half of the page, "Links to Statistical Agencies," under "Agencies by Subject," click "Economic" on the drop-down arrow to lead you to a list of "Periodic Economic Censuses." Below this area, you'll find "Data Access Tools," which link users to agency online databases.

GlobalEDGE: http://globaledge.msu.edu (Accessed Spring 2011).

Managed by Michigan State University's Center for International Business Education and Research, this site links to a broad selection of international trade data, including globalization, statistical data sources, government resources, trade portals, journals, and mailing lists. The "Global Resources" section provides access to more than 5,000 online resources. You will also find a wealth of information on all countries, information on all U.S. states, in-depth analysis of selected industries, and an international business blog with insights on business around the world.

Global Technology Forum: www.ebusinessforum.com (Accessed Spring 2011).

This excellent site from the Economist Intelligence Unit targets senior executives and offers an international selection of e-commerce news. "Global News Analysis," updated daily, is organized by region of the world and links to recent, full-text articles from a variety of respected sources. See "Best Practices" for company-focused discussions organized by telecommunications, pharmaceuticals, media/entertainment, professional services, consumer products, energy/chemicals/utilities, and more. The research module contains in-depth material from respected analysts in market trends and benchmarking.

Ideas-for-Marketing.com: www.ideas-for-marketing.com/ (Accessed Spring 2011).

This large site presents an overview of Internet marketing by entrepreneur Paul Taylor. Here you will find ideas about a systematic approach to Internet marketing, detailed step-by-step guides to some of the most important actions that you need to take, tools to help automate your electronic marketing activity, and templates for organizing and tracking your marketing. There is a wealth of information here, but it is a commercial site that also offers things for sale.

The Industry Standard: www.thestandard.com (Accessed Spring 2011).

This site provides complete coverage of the news, analysis, trends, and events that shape the tech economy every day. Companies, people, products, and technologies that impact the direction of the e-economy are covered. The news section looks at technology news, trends, and products. "Tech Watch" covers the major players that capitalize on using the Internet providing music, video, games, content, marketing, and publishing. "Money" details mergers, venture capital activities, bankruptcies, and initial public offerings, while "Politics" covers government regulations and laws domestically and internationally. "Cloud Computing" covers current trends, events, and resources in the cloud. The blog provides daily updates from the best journalists to keep up with daily news events, market trends, and the future of the Internet economy.

KnowThis.com: www.knowthis.com/index.php (Accessed Spring 2011).

This large site is a smorgasbord of data and guidance on marketing, including how to conduct market research, promotion versus advertising, using current technologies, and a large section on marketing tutorials, divided into marketing management, promotion, and marketing research. Find guidance on creating marketing plans as well as sample plans. Find lots of information on data collection as well as primary and secondary research. New topics include selling virtual clothes for avatars and reviews of software to enhance small e-commerce sites. Tutorials on managing customers, personal selling, targeting markets, and more are available.

The List: The Definitive ISP Buyer's Guide: www.thelist.com/ (Accessed Spring 2011).

This large commercial site will help you find an Internet service provider (ISP), find a broadband ISP, find a web host, find a web designer, and even find an ISP or a tech job. It covers the United States and Canada, letting you search by area code or location. It provides FAQs on various items and also leads users to other business information.

MoreBusiness.com: www.morebusiness.com (Accessed Spring 2011).

Sections on this site include "Startup," "Running SmallBiz," "Templates," and "Tools." The "Templates" section provides sample business contracts and agreements, business and marketing plans, press releases, and business checklists. A large collection of articles and advice under "Business Technology" will help you understand the Internet, online shopping, website technology, hacking, and even laptop issues. The section on "Build Your

Own Website" is very useful. Many of the articles are lengthy and thorough. Use this site to help improve your marketing and management skills.

New York Public Library, International Trade Research Guide: www.nypl.org/research/sibl/trade/trade.html (Accessed Spring 2011).

This wonderful guide produced by the Science, Industry and Business Library provides invaluable information in learning how to conduct business between the United States and another country. Guides, business directories, periodicals, and trade statistic sources can be located through this large and practical site. Well organized, and easy to navigate, this site contains information grouped under market research, trade leads, shipping and logistics, and cross-cultural business communication.

Online Business: http://onlinebusiness.about.com (Accessed Spring 2011).

This really practical, useful introductory site contains "Online Business 101," "Find Products to Sell Online," and "Web Site Check List," all under "Essentials." The "Articles and Resources" section lists subjects such as "Starting Up," "Web Hosting," "Auctions," "Search Engines," and "Success Stories." Find website guides, newsletters, FAQs, discussion forums, and chat, plus build a web store, or learn about banner advertising or portal sites. Other topics include associations, business issues, broadcasting, domain registration, history of the Internet, innovations, legal resources, news resources, online journals, reference services and trading, trade fairs, and statistics. Find articles about improving your ranking in search engines, hiring a web designer, marketing offline, and more. Use the Google-like search box to find relevant articles. You will probably find About.com's Online Advertising site helpful as well, at http://advertising.about.com/. Constantly updated, users can search to find practical advice and guidance for all aspects of e-commerce.

Open Directory Project: E-Commerce: http://dmoz.org/Business/E-Commerce (Accessed Spring 2011).

This excellent gateway leads users to entry points to many articles, periodicals specializing in e-commerce, government and standards sites, and organizations. This site is updated frequently, and most links are active. Links cover a wide variety of topics, such as website promotion, sales agents, shopping carts, technology vendors, and Internet law. Links are not annotated. Some of the sites linked to may charge fees.

Red Herring: www.redherring.com/ (Accessed Spring 2011).

Red Herring, a media company, covers innovation, entrepreneurial activity, the business of technology, and venture capital and capital markets worldwide. By analyzing all of these areas, it evaluates the probable success or failure of companies and technologies. Each major area is divided into subtopics; for instance, capital is further subdivided into economy and policy, public markets, venture capital, and private markets. The site publishes profiles of notable companies, briefings, metrics and statistics, and opinions. Free registration is required to access much of the content.

Small Business Administration (SBA): www.sba.gov (Accessed Spring 2011).

This official government site offers a wealth of resources and programs for starting and growing a small business. Under "Starting and Managing a Business," check out the areas you need help with while doing your business planning. Other major sections cover business planning, financing, international trade, managing, marketing, employees, taxes, legal aspects, and business opportunities. Find here online forms, sample business plans, loan information, and many publications. Under "Exporting and Importing," you will find articles on international trade, export working capital, and export financing. Some contents are available in Spanish. Also part of the SBA program are the Small Business Development Centers (www.sba.gov/sbdc), which are located in every state and deliver counseling and training for small businesses in the areas of management, marketing, financing, and feasibility studies.

Smarta.com: www.smarta.com/ (Accessed Spring 2011).

Under "Advice, Guides," you will find over 40 useful guides on things like how to prove your business idea will work, how to start a toy shop, five reasons to start a business at university, and more. More than 600 videos and 343 guides are available on many topics. Case studies are provided also. The "Tools Directory" covers ideas like finding a franchise, creating your brand identity, building and managing a website, expanding internationally, shipping goods, and more. The slight British bent is not a barrier.

Social Media Examiner: www.socialmediaexaminer.com/ (Accessed Spring 2011).

This free online magazine will help you learn how to use social media tools like Twitter and Facebook to increase sales and generate more brand awareness. Find here current articles and tools along with case studies, reviews of industry research, and advice from industry experts. Find out about Foursquare, Facebook Places, Gowalla, and others. Learn how to use automation tools and which ones are better and why. Also download the "2011 Social Media Marketing Industry Report" by Michael A. Stelzner (www.socialmediaexaminer.com/social-media-marketing-industry-report-2011/) and use it to maximize your social media activities and learn about trends in social media marketing.

TechWeb: E-Business: www.techweb.com/e-business (Accessed Spring 2011).

Lots of advertising but beyond that, this site contains the latest in e-business news, trends and analysis, and product reviews. E-business white papers and reports are also available. Users have access to a huge variety of information by using different "Pipelines"—for example, InternetWeek, Small Business, Web Services, and many more. Each Pipeline has trends, a blog, security issues, a glossary, newsletter, services, and more.

U.S. Bureau of Industry and Security: www.bis.doc.gov (Accessed Spring 2011).

This agency of the Department of Commerce is responsible for advancing U.S. national security, foreign policy, and economic objectives by ensuring an effective export control and treaty compliance system and promoting continued U.S. strategic technology leadership. It issues export licenses, prosecutes violators of export control policies, and implements the Export Administration Act's antiboycott provisions. Export license requirements are triggered by the actual item (commodity, software, or technology) being exported, where it is going, who is going to use it, and what they will be using it for. The FAQs on export licensing will answer many questions. Another important section is entitled "E-Commerce," where you will find regulations on orders processed using the Internet, intangible downloads, the transfer of funds to certain entities, prohibited activities, and more. Check this site before you fill your first Internet order.

**U.S. Census Bureau: www.census.gov (Accessed Spring 2011).

This web page is the best place to start searching for the multitude of data produced by Census programs, publications, and statistics. The home page groups the data under

"Census 2000," "People," "Business," "Geography," "Newsroom," "At the Bureau," and "Special Topics." Under "Business," you can click on "Foreign Trade," "Economic Census," "NAICS," "E-Stats," and "Survey of Business Owners." Under "Foreign Trade," learn directly from the Census Bureau how to properly classify your products for export and how to file your shippers' export declaration online. The bureau also processes, tabulates, and releases the data collected by the Bureau of Customs and Border Protection on exports and imports of goods. The "Catalog," a search feature, and links to related sites are also accessible on the left side of the home page. Another important part of the Census Bureau's website is the International Data Base (IDB) at www.census.gov.ipc/www/idb/. The IDB presents estimates and projections of basic demographic measures for countries and regions of the world. Country summaries, country rankings, and population pyramids all provide useful data. U.S. export and import statistics by commodity, country, customs district, and method of transportation provide value and quantity on a monthly, year-to-date, and annual history basis. U.S. state export data and port statistics for imports and exports are also available. Use this site frequently to help start and grow your business.

USA.gov: www.USA.gov (Accessed Spring 2011).

"Explore Topics" will interest and amaze first-timers. Topics include "Defense and International Relations," "Environment, Energy and Agriculture," "Money and Taxes," "Reference and General Government," and "Science and Technology." Clicking on "Business and Nonprofits" brings up lots of informational links on selling and buying from the government, data and statistics, international trade, and more. Also under "Businesses and Nonprofits" is a section on "Exporting," where you will find trade data, export finance information, doing business in … guides, and much more. Trade mission information is also available here. Spanish translation of the site is also available. You can e-mail questions about the site and the statistics or telephone for help. Your taxes pay for the collection, compiling, and publishing of these statistics and information, and they are available for your use.

VerticalResponse Marketing Lounge: http://lounge.verticalresponse.com/ (Accessed Spring 2011).

This large site includes groups, case studies, articles, business tools, and videos to help you successfully market your small company. Learn how to increase your social media clicks, how to blog as a marketing tool, use e-mail marketing, how to improve your search engine optimization, and more. Learn about new software through webinars, live demos, and other events.

Yahoo! Small Business Ecommerce: http://smallbusiness.yahoo.com/ecommerce/ (Accessed Spring 2011).

This large site is packed with articles and links to information on all aspects of starting, marketing, and running an online business. Fully searchable and easy to navigate, users will find information and help on web connectivity, domain names, and even an "eBay Center." The annotated links lead users to other well-respected sites such as Entrepreneur. com, AllBusiness.com, and Inc.com, for example, and are divided by subject area. Also check out "Reaching Beyond Borders" for international business suggestions and additional insights in implementing a successful e-commerce site.

MANAGEMENT

9

Many people seem to think that success in one area can compensate for failure in other areas. But can it really? . . . True effectiveness requires balance.
—Stephen Covey

Effective management necessarily begins with planning, which implies goal setting. Planning is the essence and most important function of managing and maintaining a business. Management is responsible for the accomplishment of the mission of an organization. The manager directs and integrates all the components (e.g., equipment, techniques, people, and practices) of the business. Management involves problem solving, decision making, speculating on the future, setting objectives, and considering alternatives. The importance of good management skills cannot be overemphasized. Poor management and poor planning can put you out of business very quickly. You must continually exercise one of the four functions of managing: planning, organizing, leading, and controlling.

Managers decide such matters as what and how much to produce, which markets to serve and pursue, how much to advertise, and what prices to charge. A manager is the person responsible for planning and directing the work of a group of people, checking their work, and taking corrective action if necessary. In a small business, sometimes one person—you—plans and directs the work of outside sources or contractors in order to accomplish delivery of the product or service. Keeping better track of your money, staff, and paperwork will result in a more successful business.

PRINCIPLES OF MANAGEMENT

As stated above, the four principles or functions of management are planning, organizing, leading, and controlling. Good managers accomplish the entire management process efficiently and effectively. Remember that your business will be the accumulation of the management decisions you make. Your business will accomplish its work under the guidelines that you establish. You need a vision of what you want your business or organization to be and accomplish. Also, remember that your customers are the real judges of how good your management decisions are. Base your decisions on how you want your customers to view your products or services.

Let's run through each principle of management to understand it a bit more:

1. *Planning* is the intellectual process that determines the anticipated use of resources, methodology, and projected outcome on a given time line. Based on an organization's mission, planning begins with setting goals and objectives. A small business develops and uses its business plan to begin the challenge of managing the business. Look at your goals and plan how to achieve them.

2. *Organizing* involves decisions concerning the best allocation and utilization of resources for implementing the business or strategic plan. Managers coordinate the use of capital, information, physical resources, and people as part of this process. Choosing an organizational model is important and can determine the success or failure of your business. Are you ready to go into business? Make lists and make sure everything is in place and ready to begin.

3. *Leading* involves directing the people of the organization or staff and therefore is a complex function. Managers with leadership ability get employees to willingly follow in the achievement of the organization's goals. Motivation is extremely important. Building a team is one method of leading an organization effectively. Good managers lead by example, so organize your work and keep everyone involved in your business informed about your needs and decisions. Communication skills are vital to good leadership. Although leadership is sometimes considered an art, it involves skills that can be learned. If your leadership skills are less than top-notch, take time to learn and cultivate them.

4. *Controlling* involves monitoring, evaluating, and correcting whatever is necessary to achieve the established goals. Planning and controlling are closely linked; controlling involves comparing accomplishments at different intervals of time against the set goals and taking corrective action if necessary. When things are not going according to your plan, you need to step back and adjust. Problems will occur. Supplies won't be delivered on time, or someone will get sick. Learn to improvise and revise, continue monitoring your business functions, and make changes to improve how it works.

To learn more about management techniques, organization, managing technology, and more, try the "Management Channel" of the SmallBusinessTV.com website at sbtv.com. These short videos cover a wide range of topics and can get you started in the right direction. The following book is also a wonderful resource to help guide you through your management challenges.

Gegax, Tom. *The Big Book of Small Business.* HarperBusiness, 2007. 448p. ISBN 0-06120-669-5. $29.99.

This lively, practical guide will help you start, fund, and get your new business off the ground as well as create a mission statement and create processes for continuous innovation. Gegax will explain and illustrate the importance of effective leadership. The business plan can easily be adapted to a web-based company as well as retail or service bricks-and-mortar. Great for the beginner and also useful to those who have started a successful company but want to expand and enjoy their business life.

ACTION PLANS

How do you, the entrepreneur, accomplish everything and still do what you really need to do? Three action plans can help build a framework or strategy for you to operate and manage your business by organizing the necessary activities, such as obtaining and working with suppliers and other vendors to get necessary supplies, materials, and services; filling orders; providing customer support and service after the sale; and dealing with unexpected occurrences. These action plans are really to-do lists and can be just for your use or you can add them as supporting documents in your business plan package. Many of the large small business sites, such as the Small Business Administration's, provide start-up to-do lists to help small businesses organize their openings.

These action plans explain what you, the owner, need to do to get your business open. As your business evolves, you will move from doing things yourself to doing things through others. The success of your business may depend on how well you can make this transition.

1. Set up an *Operations Plan.* Figure out how you will create and deliver your product or service to your customers. What materials, software, hardware, equipment, and so on do you need? Where will it be set up? Does it work? Do you need a phone line or more than one phone line? Do you need a fax machine or copier? What type and how many computers do you need? Do you or others need new skills or expertise? Locate and sign up for workshops or classes. More about managing technology will be presented later in this chapter.

   Make a sketch of the work area—whether it's an office or complex of offices, a factory, a restaurant, a mail order packaging line, whatever. As thoroughly as you can, plan every step of the operation from raw material to delivery to the customer.

2. Create a *Management Plan*. Part of this will be managing employees—which we'll discuss more thoroughly in the next chapter, but consider what employees you need to start and what jobs they will perform. As we learned above, part of managing is organizing. Delivery of products or services must be kept on schedule or customers will not return, and business will decline instead of grow. A good manager monitors all the diverse activities of the business and intervenes if things aren't happening or aren't happening in a timely fashion. Set up processes for getting things done, including accounting, payroll, and deliveries. Recognize if some activities are a major drain on your time and resources, preventing you from getting more important things done. Value your time as your most valuable asset; you can always make more money but not more time. We'll talk more about time management later in this chapter.

3. Create a *Contingency Plan*. Even with careful planning, Murphy's Law (if anything can go wrong, it will) may intervene. Your contingency plan will help you avoid disruptions in your operation when industry, economic, or business conditions change beyond what you are prepared to handle— perhaps you'll have more customers than you had dreamed possible, or your supplier cannot provide the materials you need or goes out of business completely. Basically, here you try to identify the areas in your business that are susceptible to variable factors. Contingency planning is a prearranged method of changing the direction of your business or retrenching in the face of less-than-hoped-for results. So if things go much better or worse than expected, you have considered your responses and are prepared to react, perhaps more quickly than your competitors, thus presenting you with an opportunity or competitive advantage.

Action plans can also be part of strategic planning or developing a strategy for your business to grow and develop. If you want to learn more about growing your business, check out the Small Business Administration website (www.sba.gov). Under "Running a Business," select a category and it will lead you to many articles that can help you develop ways to continue planning your business moves after your initial business plan. Planning should not consume the business owner's time, but it is a necessary element in developing a successful business.

STRUCTURING YOUR ORGANIZATION

How you design your organization plays a big part in your success in making your business plan work. Whether you have 2 or 2,000 employees, you need to understand your employees' roles in carrying out the business plan and achieving company goals and objectives. In the beginning, your organizational chart will probably have you at the top as owner, and everyone else below, doing all the jobs that have to be done. This model works until you have over 20 employees. As your business grows, remember that the core of any organization is its people and their functions. Duties, tasks, and responsibilities often evolve in an expedient manner. As the firm develops, others are hired to fill specific roles, often on a functional basis. Roles that were handled by consultants and specialists outside the firm now are handled internally. As new needs emerge, new roles develop.

At this time, you want to consider investigating a functional model where different functions such as financial, customer service, and production are in subgroups or teams; a divisional model where divisions are based on products, or markets, or something else; or a matrix model where everyone wears two hats, maybe one function group and one special project group. These models call for different management skills and often work well based on management training and leadership skills. Keep in mind that a simple organizational structure keeps costs under control and is more flexible. Be willing to change your organizational structure as your business grows, and keep exploring options as you go about creating and recreating your organization. To explore more ideas on organizational structure, check out the Edward Lowe's Entrepreneurs Resource Center website (www.edwardlowe.org/ERC).

ORGANIZATION CHART

The management process is a key ingredient throughout the business life cycle, and related to the organizational structure is another management tool that is used to further the organization's goals: the organization chart, or org chart for short. Org charts illustrate the intended structure of the organization or company and reflect the power structure of the company. The entrepreneur may need to incorporate strong working relationships with outside consultants into the structure of everyday operations to form a management team for the organization or business. This team should be shown on your org chart and might consist of an accountant, lawyer, banker, and other consultants who provide needed expertise to assist in running the business. Develop an org chart that reflects where you want the organization to go and how it will grow rather than simply reflecting how it is now. For more help on building an org chart, take a look at "Organization Charts as a Management Tool" on About.com's Small Business Information page (http://sbinformation.about.com). Here you will find advice and examples representing different types of small and larger businesses.

Along with the org chart, develop a list of key personnel with a job description listing responsibilities and authority level. Planning in advance will help you grow your business in an organized manner, resulting in less last-minute decision making. When an organization has structure, employees feel they know where the company is going and what their role is in getting there. A structured organization has a better chance at success.

ACCOUNTING/BOOKKEEPING

Even if you have no intention of keeping your own books, you need to have a basic knowledge of accounting to monitor your accountant or bookkeeper and determine if she or he is doing a good job. Accounting is the method by which financial information is gathered, processed, and summarized into useful financial statements and reports like cash flow, balance sheets, and income statements; simply put, it monitors how much money is being paid out and how much is coming in. To learn many of the basics of accounting and financial management, check out BusinessTown.com at www.businesstown.com. Besides an entire section on accounting, you will find a section on finance. Use this site to increase your knowledge of financial statements in general.

Right from the start, you need to set up a system to track, record, and store your source documents for internal management and external taxation purposes. You need to track transactions such as supplier invoices and customer sales orders, pay taxes, develop capital and operating budgets, and manage and value product inventory. The best advice is probably to hire an accountant to set up an efficient, cost-effective bookkeeping system that you can follow. In today's business world, that system will probably be software on a computer. Software options today vary in function and cost, and many are designed for small businesses. If your accountant suggests using a software package, use that package because your information will be organized so that the accountant can work directly from your electronic files, saving her or him time and you money.

If you are able to manage your personal finances, you can probably learn to work with a small business accounting software package to enter and store your important financial data. To learn more about bookkeeping and accounting, try Angie Mohr's book *Bookkeepers' Boot Camp: Get a Grip on Accounting Basics*. The advice in her guide will help you understand budgeting, accounting, and taxes. Also find help here on finding a good accountant to help your business grow.

Mohr, Angie. *Bookkeepers' Boot Camp: Get a Grip on Accounting Basics*, 2nd ed. Self-Counsel Press, 2010. 204p. ISBN 1-55180-449-2. $14.95.

This handy title walks users through the essentials of recordkeeping for a small business and explains why it's so necessary to track this information. Learn how to sort through paperwork, how to record and file what is important for your business, and how to use that information to help your business succeed. The basics of balance sheets, income statements, cash flow statements, inventory management, and monitoring budgets and cash flow are thoroughly explained. Also covered are tax planning, choosing an accountant, and the role of an accountant in running your small business. Learn how to manage the financial part of your business and personal life.

In chapter 2, we talked a bit about industry ratios. Industry ratios are used to help you see what the financial condition of your business is compared to the averages of other businesses in your industry. You need to know the financial ratios of your business in order to compare yourself with the industry. Ratios also help you spot financial patterns that might threaten the health of your business. At the American Express Open Forum at www.openforum.com, under "Money," find the article "Know Your Ratios." Even if you hire an accountant, you will want to know as much as you can about operational and profitability ratios as well as liquidity, efficiency, and solvency ratios. Another good site for learning about ratio analysis is Edward Lowe's Entrepreneurs Resource Center at www.edwardlowe. org/ERC. Under "Acquiring and Managing Finances," you will find "Ratio Analysis" as a heading and articles on how to analyze profitability and using financial ratios. Check out these two sites to improve your knowledge of these important management tools.

TECHNOLOGY

A website today often functions much like a business card. In many industries, it is virtually impossible for entrepreneurs to function without a web presence. To many young people, using the Internet is as natural as using the telephone (or cell phone today). For some entrepreneurs, conducting business on the Internet is also taken for granted, while others are new to cyberspace. At the very least, as a small business owner you will want to use the Internet to gather information about your industry and competitors and exchange e-mail to facilitate networking with customers or suppliers or mentors. Decide how using the Internet will benefit your particular business.

The personal computer sits at the center of this technology. Purchase the best desktop computer that you can afford, and some software will be available with the purchase or at reduced cost. Purchase software that can help you with your managerial duties such as word processing, a spreadsheet or bookkeeping or accounting package recommended by your accountant, and software to manage the communications connection to the server computer. Your telephone company, cable or satellite television company, or a local Internet company can explain ways to connect and the costs. Be sure to read the small print because there are many restrictions in the services offered by any company; talking to other business owners who have used the service is as important here as it is in other areas of doing business. With a computer, you can manage your inventory, track customer accounts, monitor your competition, and keep in touch with business associates and customers. If you are new to doing business on the Internet and the web, you might want to read a very good article on the Small Business Administration's website, www.sba.gov. Under "Starting & Managing a Business" select "Running a Business" and then "Using Technology." Here you will find e-commerce resources and online advertising information. Under the "e-Commerce Resources" is a long list of information links to help you explore the possibilities. Chapter 8 in this book covers the Internet and e-commerce very thoroughly.

▌Websites

Many entrepreneurs today are developing websites to enlarge their customer base and boost profits. Clearly define why you want or need a website and determine if you can afford it. Study websites of businesses similar to yours and make note of what you like and don't like about them. Are they well organized, how do you contact someone with a question, can you place an order quickly, are you planning to offer that service on your site? Then, you will want to research locally and on the Internet different companies that can help in the design, development, and implementation of your site. As in other phases of starting a business, research and preparation will help make your website project a success. Use the same criteria for hiring a professional website developer, if you go that route, as you did when hiring an accountant or lawyer. Study their work, check references, talk to colleagues, ask for bids, and shop around for the best price without sacrificing quality. Remember that you only have one chance on the Internet to make a good first impression. In your contract with a web designer, be sure to specify a work schedule, desired results, and payment terms as well as a termination clause. A good print resource on a business website and e-commerce in general is McFadyen's *Ecommerce Best Practices.*

McFadyen, Thomas. *Ecommerce Best Practices: How to Market, Sell, and Service Customers with Internet Technologies.* McFadyen Solutions, 2008. 366p. ISBN 0-9815951-0-3. $34.95.

This title provides tools for companies in any stage of developing a web presence to market and sell its products or services to global customers. McFadyen is a frequent speaker and consultant on e-commerce matters. Learn how to make navigation easy for your customers, the latest in shopping carts, and how to make visitors into buyers. Use this well-written and well-organized resource to improve your website.

Now that you have a website, you will need a web hosting service. Some issues to consider when choosing a web host include the following:

1. Ask what uptime it will guarantee in writing and shoot for 95%. Ask the host to sign an agreement to the effect that if the site is not up 95% of the time, it will lower your monthly fee.

2. Ask about the host's connection to the Internet and insist on connections directly to the Internet, not through someone else's network. Ask about its servers to make sure they are fast and reliable.

3. Check on what type of technical support is provided. Call at various evening and weekend hours to be sure there's a person to help you and not an answering machine. Send its customer service an e-mail and see how fast the host responds.

4. Of course, you will want to find out the costs and compare them with competitors. A simple site with one domain name might cost $50 per month, while those taking up lots of disk space and large amounts of data transfer

will drive the costs up. A very simple brochure online-type website may only cost $10 to $15 per month or even less.

5. Ask if the web host can handle the software used to design your site; the designer may suggest a host. This question may narrow your choices.

6. Be sure the web host uses special security programs to conduct online transactions safely and protect the privacy and security of customers and their credit cards.

Work with your web designer to find a web host that works for you. This relationship will probably be a long-term relationship, and you will want to keep that in mind. Take a look back at chapter 8 for more information on websites and technology as well as chapter 7 to learn how to use your website as a marketing tool. Another good book for helping you learn the basics about websites and e-commerce is:

Holden, Greg. *Starting an Online Business for Dummies,* 6th ed. For Dummies, 2010. 432p. ISBN 0-4706-0210-4. $24.99.

As in other books of this series, readers find the basics of starting a business on the Internet. E-commerce survival stories, best practices, and other resources to help you develop your new business are provided. The book contains good tips on selecting an online host, understanding website design, establishing a graphic identity, providing customer service, and providing various payment options. Some coverage of legal matters, trademarks, copyrighting, and taxes is included.

TIME MANAGEMENT AND ORGANIZATION

If you don't manage your time, time will manage you. There are never enough hours in the day to complete all the work associated with your small business, so learn some time management solutions. Efficiency is vital to any business, especially if it is a one-person operation. Use the website Time-Management-Guide. com to develop skills needed to manage your time successfully. Find more about the website in the e-resources list at the end of the chapter. The following rules will help you save time and use it wisely:

1. *Track your time usage.* Make a copy of a page from your day planner and record the time you spend doing things for a week. Now you will see the pattern of how you are spending your time.

2. *Allocate and prioritize your time.* This step is very personal. Identify your most productive time. If you are a morning person, you may want to start the day with the most difficult or worrisome task and then mix in easy tasks as breaks. Or if it takes you a while to get going in the morning, you may want to return phone calls, check e-mail, and so on until you are wide awake and ready to tackle difficult tasks. Whenever possible, complete projects with deadlines first, for this will please your customer, win you repeat business, and you'll get positive reinforcement.

3. *Stick to the schedule and control your agenda.* Take time each afternoon to write a prioritized list of the next day's tasks and projects so you can start your day in a productive manner. Often by lunchtime, your plans may be shattered, but try to complete as many tasks on the list as possible and then move what can't be finished to the next day's list. Also make to-do lists for the week and one for things to do during the month. As you accomplish these goals, cross them off for a feeling of accomplishment and moving forward.

If you are constantly interrupted, you must make it clear that you can only be interrupted by dire emergencies—which you define. Turn on the answering machine, don't answer the door, whatever it takes. If you are unable to do this in your workplace, take a day or an afternoon away from the workplace each week to catch up on whatever is being pushed aside or tasks that need your entire concentration to finish. If you are still having trouble, investigate day-timer software to help you organize and manage your time.

4. *Stay or get organized.* This item is extremely important. Keep your desk and work space tidy. Completed projects should be filed; answered phone messages filed or tossed; new orders filed. A neat space allows you to concentrate on the task at hand. A good filing system allows you to retrieve information you need quickly, without wasting time looking for things. Set aside time for planning, and, when planning, also schedule time for organizing.

5. *Delegate what you can.* You should delegate work to others in your organization (if there are others), particularly to those who may have more time or more skill in a particular area. Delegate routine administrative tasks, special projects, and tasks that an employee has a special talent for accomplishing. Explain fully what is expected of the employee and encourage him or her to ask questions at any time. Once the task or project has been completed, don't forget to evaluate the final product and discuss the results with the employee. As your business grows, you'll spend more time strategizing and less time on the daily components of running a business.

Remember to avoid the big day wasters. Talking on the telephone, surfing the web, and checking e-mail are all great things when done in moderation, but you can lose hours of your day with them. Limit your day wasters to your least productive hour or so each day. Also, don't forget that saying no can help you from being overburdened.

Managing paperwork is another daunting task. Every day it accumulates, but try to handle each piece of paper only once. File paperwork as diligently as you schedule meetings and appointments. Buy a weekly or daily planner and write things down. Have an address book or contact management software on your PC where you record contact information and toss piles of business cards. Buy different-colored folders for different topics and segments of your business. Retire files as soon as possible, but separate and retain any information needed for tax purposes or other financial matters. Remember, there is no statute of limitations for reviewing business tax forms. Most importantly, purge files at the end of every year. Barbara Hemphill's book *Taming the Paper Tiger at Work* provides many ideas for helping you keep your desk and your office organized and ready to do business.

Hemphill, Barbara. *Taming the Paper Tiger at Work,* 3rd ed. Kiplinger Books, 2002. 170p. ISBN 0-9387-2198-4. $14.95.

If you need help in getting organized, Hemphill will help you. She clearly states the principles involved in organizing the mounds of paperwork and files filling most offices. Learn how to use action and reference files as well as preparing and using to-do lists effectively. In this new edition, readers will find website links, advice on how to work efficiently and effectively in virtual offices, and expanded information on computer safety tips, e-mail etiquette, and other electronic time-savers. Also learn how long you need to keep your files. Get organized and use your computer to help.

If you need more help with time management skills or organizing your work and workplace, check out the Business Know-how website at www.businessknowhow.com. The resources listed below will provide more help in all the areas covered in this chapter.

REFERENCES

Starred titles are discussed in the chapter.

■ Print Resources

Bromage, Neil. *100 Ways to Business Success: A Resource Book for Small Business Managers,* 3rd ed. How to Books, 2006. 222p. ISBN 1-84528-135-7. $20.

This slim volume covers the basics of running and growing a small business. Learn how to manage yourself as well as your employees, promote yourself and the business, use the Internet, and succeed in managing a growing enterprise. Get advice to help you face and master the challenges of every day in the business world. Find out how to get better deals from suppliers and reduce bad debt. Discover how to manage effectively and efficiently.

Burton, Virgil L., III. *Encyclopedia of Small Business,* 4th ed. Gale Cengage, 2010. 2v. 1,414p. ISBN 1-4144-2028-5. $631.

Arranged alphabetically, over 500 essays cover topics such as advertising media on the web, business start-up, employee compensation, franchising, health insurance options, e-commerce, product development, and tax planning. How those topics affect small business is, of course, emphasized. Bibliographic citations at the end of each topic point to additional sources of information. The master index at the end of volume 2 provides additional subject, organization, government agency, and legislation access. Written in a relevant and accessible format and manner, all types and ages of entrepreneurs will find this a useful reference.

Chandler, Steve and Black, Steve. *The Hands-off Manager: How to Mentor People and Allow Them to Be Successful.* Career Press, 2007. 223p. ISBN 1-564-14950-1. $19.99.

This new system of managing shows managers how to coach and mentor employees rather than hover and micromanage. Each employee's strengths are honed and honored in a work climate of mutual goal setting and respect. Chapter 11, "Letting Go of Judgment," is very insightful, as is "Living in Three Worlds." Let the authors convince you that mentoring is a much better goal than managing. With stories, examples, and practical activities, learn how to motivate and lead your employees to success.

**Gegax, Tom. *The Big Book of Small Business.* HarperBusiness, 2007. 448p. ISBN 0-06120-669-5. $29.99.

This lively, practical guide will help you start, fund, and get your new business off the ground as well as create a mission statement and create processes for continuous innovation. Gegax explains and illustrates the importance of effective leadership. The business plan can easily be adapted to a web-based company as well as retail or service bricks-and-mortar. Great for the beginner and also useful to those who have started a successful company but want to expand and enjoy their business life.

Good Small Business Guide 2010, 4th ed. A & C Black, 2010. 581p. ISBN 978-1-4081-2370-6. $24.99.

Besides helping you answer the question "how can I be sure I've got what it takes to run a business?" this large reference work has sections on "Refining and Protecting Your Idea," "Finding Premises," "Communicating with Customers," "Managing Yourself and Others," and "Working Online." A large section on calculating ratios and creating financial statements as well as amortization, asset turnover, and more, is also very useful for the new business owner. This edition has a British slant but has a great deal of useful information for all English-speaking entrepreneurs. The directories in the back present a collection of print and online resources in a wide variety of business areas. This well-organized resource is a bargain.

Gottry, Steve. *Common Sense Business: Starting, Operating, and Growing Your Small Business—In Any Economy!* HarperBusiness, 2005. 368p. ISBN 0-06-077838-5. $19.95.

Gottry started and ran a large Minneapolis-based ad agency and video production firm, which failed after 22 years in business. You can learn from his mistakes. Well-organized and clearly written, Gottry's book includes specific how-tos, such as ways to prioritize bills for payment when cash flow is limited. He explains how to find solutions to the questions and challenges you're facing daily and even how to manage your day. Learn how to begin to understand yourself, your employees, your vendors, and your customers. Using humor, Gottry will help you successfully manage your business through good times and bad.

Harvard Business School Press. *Manager's Toolkit: The 13 Skills Managers Need to Succeed.* Harvard Business School Press, 2007. 352p. $29.99.

This comprehensive guide is a valuable resource for experienced managers and a wonderful primer for new managers. The first section addresses five basic skills necessary to build a foundation for becoming a high-performing manager, such as setting goals that others will pursue. The second part builds on the skills of part one, and part three focuses on financial tools needed by managers such as budgeting and reading and interpreting financial statements. Each chapter concludes with key topics and a summary. References to books and articles are also listed at the end of the book.

Hatcher, Diane A. *Don't Agonize, Organize Your Office Now!* BookSurge, 2007. 83p. ISBN 1-41965-866-2. $10.99.

This short, practical guide to organizing your office uses a nautical theme for the journey to decluttering your work space. Hatcher believes that clutter creates an emotional response of feeling drained and de-energized. The basis of her method is RAFT: R for read or refer; A for act; F for file; and T for toss. Additional chapters cover reducing paper, filing 101, organizing receipts and the office supplies, and two chapters on time management. Hatcher's work is short and surprisingly useful.

**Hemphill, Barbara. *Taming the Paper Tiger at Work.* Rev. ed. Kaplan Business, 2005. 208p. ISBN 0-9387-2198-4. $14.95.

If you need help in getting organized, Hemphill will help you as she explodes the myth of the paperless office. She clearly states the principles involved in organizing the mounds of paperwork and files filling most offices. Learn how to use action and reference files as well as how to prepare and use to-do lists effectively. In this new edition, readers will find website links, advice on how to work efficiently and effectively in virtual offices, and expanded information on computer safety tips, e-mail etiquette, and other electronic time-savers. Also learn how long you need to keep your files. Develop your own personal style for getting organized and use your computer to help.

Hess, Edward. *So, You Want to Start a Business?* Pearson Education, 2008. 194p. ISBN 0-13-712667-0. $18.99.

This practical, well-organized work begins with a chapter entitled "Can You Be a Successful Entrepreneur?" Learn what it takes and what defines an entrepreneur. Other chapters cover basic rules for success in business, identifying a good business opportunity, hiring and keeping good employees, and how to manage growth. Learn about management by objectives and exceptions as well as the power of simplicity. A lengthy list of books by subject and some web resources conclude the work. Use this guide to be successful in any enterprise you undertake.

**Holden, Greg. *Starting an Online Business for Dummies,* 6th ed. For Dummies, 2010. 432p. ISBN 0-4706-0210-4. $24.99.

As in other books of this series, readers find the basics of starting a business on the Internet. E-commerce survival stories, best practices, and other resources to help you develop your new business are provided. Learn how to create an e-business plan. The book contains good tips on selecting an online host, understanding website design, establishing a graphic identity, providing customer service, and providing various payment options. Some coverage of legal matters, trademarks, copyrighting, and taxes are included. The book also has good coverage of using social media for advertising and how to identify a market need.

Little, Steven S. *The 7 Irrefutable Rules of Small Business Growth.* John Wiley, 2005. 256p. ISBN 0-471-70760-0. $18.95.

Find out Little's real and powerful principles for helping a small business expand and develop new business. Little acknowledges the difficulties small businesses have in today's global economy, where competition comes from the Internet as well as the business down the street. Learn more about how topics like technology, planning, hiring and firing, and globalization relate to small business today. An entire chapter is devoted to each of the author's seven rules. For example, he explains why it is essential to have a thorough understanding of the marketplace, why processes must be customer driven, and how to attract and keep the best and brightest employees. Practical solutions and strategies are presented to achieve and sustain a competitive advantage. Simply but effectively written, Little teaches entrepreneurs to have a realistic view of the marketplace and their place in it.

Manheim, Sheldon. *Exit Strategy: The Art of Selling a Business.* USPublication.com, 2010. 368p. ISBN 1-5959-4378-1. $29.95.

Manheim explains why all businesses must develop an exit strategy in the beginning of their operations and then must revise it regularly, as dictated by its maturation and changes in the economy. With an exit strategy in place, business owners are then ready to exit rapidly and profitably. Present or potential business owners will find Manheim's book to be a thought-provoking and invaluable resource, providing all the information you need to either sell a business in the shortest period of time, or to buy the right business at the best price.

**McFadyen, Thomas. *Ecommerce Best Practices: How to Market, Sell, and Service Customers with Internet Technologies.* McFadyen Solutions, 2008. 366p. ISBN 0-9815951-0-3. $34.95.

This title provides tools for companies in any stage of developing a web presence to market and sell their products or services to global customers. McFadyen is a frequent speaker and consultant on e-commerce matters. Learn how to make navigation easy for your customers, the latest in shopping carts, and how to make visitors into buyers. Use this well-written and well-organized resource to improve your website.

**Mohr, Angie. *Bookkeepers' Boot Camp: Get a Grip on Accounting Basics,* 2nd ed. Self-Counsel Press, 2010. 204p. ISBN 1-55180-449-2. $14.95.

This handy title walks readers through the essentials of recordkeeping for a small business and explains why it's so necessary to track this information. Learn how to sort through paperwork, how to record and file what is important for your business, and how to use that information to help your business succeed. The basics of balance sheets, income statements, cash flow statements, inventory management, and monitoring budgets and cash flow are thoroughly explained, so readers can understand what their accountant is telling them. Brief case studies illustrate the use of financial data in your business. Also covered is tax planning, choosing an accountant, and the role of an accountant in running your small business. Chapter summaries highlight important concepts in each chapter. Learn how to manage the financial part of your business and personal life as an entrepreneur.

Pakroo, Peri. *The Small Business Start-Up Kit,* 6th ed. Nolo Press, 2010. 368p. ISBN 1-41331-099-0. $29.99.

Besides comprehensively covering the basics, chapter 3, "Picking a Winning Business Name," is a well-written collection of information and advice on trademarks, names, and domain names. The undated chapter on financial management is also very useful and thorough, as is the chapter on choosing a legal structure. Chapters on federal, state, and local start-up requirements; on insurance and risk management; and on taxes are also treasure troves of practical, useful information for every new business owner. The updated e-business chapter covers how to use social media to promote business, and information on search engine optimization strategies will help readers drive traffic to their websites. A CD-ROM is included with the book and contains useful forms and a partnership agreement. Pakroo's outstanding book is mentioned many times throughout this book because it really provides essential advice to new entrepreneurs in many areas of starting a new business and is a worthwhile purchase.

Reiss, Bob. *Bootstrapping 101: Tips to Build Your Business with Limited Cash and Free Outside Help.* R&R, 2009. 190p. ISBN 0-57-802413-6. $19.95.

Reiss presents a variety of ideas to kick-start a new enterprise without spending a lot of cash. Follow his advice to learn about getting and keeping customers, bartering, outsourcing, and networking. Detailed and clear, the book offers many resources that illustrate the concepts and applications. Learn more about government help to gain success and other resources such as universities and business incubators. A short case study using bootstrapping techniques is also included. From spreadsheets and advertising to fiscal management and meeting hard-to-reach contacts; this book is useful for all small business owners and managers.

Scarborough, Norman M. et al. *Effective Small Business Management: An Entrepreneurial Approach,* 9th ed. Prentice Hall, 2008. 928p. ISBN 0-13-615170-5. $133.

One of the highlights of this volume is the use of numerous real-life examples; concepts covered are explained with illustrations of how entrepreneurs are using them. Learn about e-commerce, strategic management, guerrilla marketing techniques, finding sources of equity and debt financing, and how to conduct business internationally. Learn how to build a customer database, how to determine the value of an existing business, and cash management techniques. Purchasing, layout, and inventory decisions are discussed. A boxed feature, "Gaining the Competitive Edge," is designed to provide practical advice on a particular topic so readers can develop a competitive edge in their business or industry.

Sharp, Seena. *Competitive Intelligence Advantage: How to Minimize Risk, Avoid Surprises, and Grow Your Business in a Changing World.* John Wiley, 2009. 304p. ISBN 0-470-29317-9. $39.95.

This practical resource explains what competitive intelligence (CI) is, why data is not intelligence, when to use CI, how to find the most useful information and make it actual intelligence, and how to present findings in a compelling manner. Sharp thinks businesses should view CI as an investment, not a cost. The highlight of Sharp's book is the more than 60 examples of when to use CI. Sharp presents a clear case for how and why CI is one of the best management tools for business success and growth.

Strauss, Steven D. *The Small Business Bible,* 2nd ed. John Wiley, 2008. ISBN 0-470-26124-2. $19.95.

Strauss's massively expanded and updated edition teaches an entrepreneur what steps to take to start, run, and grow a successful business. Included here are proven strategies, tips, tools, and forms to fill out. The first chapters concentrate on how to choose and do what you love, and new chapters cover green businesses, online advertising and marketing, mobile technology, and many aspects of e-commerce. Learn how to write an outstanding business plan and how to conduct financial planning for your start-up. Thorough coverage of this complex challenge is presented clearly.

Tracy, Tage C. *Small Business Financial Management Kit for Dummies.* For Dummies, 2007. 384p. ISBN 0-470-12508-X. $24.99.

Tracy will help you plan a budget, streamline your accounting process, raise capital, and generally keep your business solvent. Learn how to avoid common management pitfalls and use the bonus CD's reproducible forms, checklists, and templates. Find out how to choose your legal structure for income tax purposes. Tracy explains the financial foundations of a sound business. Find out what are the 10 rules for small business survival.

Yerkes, Leslie and Decker, Charles. *Beans: Four Principles for Running a Business in Good Times and Bad.* John Wiley, 2003. 176p. ISBN 0-7879-6764-5. $19.95.

From the true story of a small Seattle coffee bar, the authors distill universal business truths, such as maintain a consistent, quality product; view both customers and employees as friends; and be passionate about what you do. Each chapter is divided into scenes and contains lots of dialogue. Also stressed is the importance of intention in striving for and achieving success: you have achieved success when your results match your intentions. Learn good management skills by example.

■ Online Resources

About.com Small Business Information: http://sbinformation.about.com (Accessed Spring 2011).

Clearly, management and management skills is a huge topic and vitally important to a successful business. This site provides a treasure trove of information, links, books, and other assorted help in learning new management skills and improving those an entrepreneur has already developed. Sections cover "Management 101," "Management Tips," "How to Manage," and more. Learn best business practices and leadership skills from experts. A related area of the site is "Human Resources," which helps users learn about human resources issues and managing employees.

AllBusiness: www.allbusiness.com (Accessed Spring 2011).

This huge site contains articles and advice on any area of business law, including legal structure, property leases, patents, trademarks, employment law, taxes, and even how to work with your lawyer. Articles on exiting your business are thorough and helpful. The articles on green businesses are also very useful. Links to many directories are also provided as well as news and business information sites. The "Sales and Marketing" section has many articles on techniques, advertising, and publications. The tax articles discuss topics such as barter tax and accounting issues and tax strategies for keeping the family business in the family. Use this well-organized, functional website often.

American Express Open Forum: www.openforum.com/ (Accessed Spring 2011).

Small business owners will find help here on management, technology, and marketing. This outstanding site has information on managing debt, business plans, and loans. Under the "Managing" heading, learn how to communicate with customers, learn how to be a leader in your industry, and more. "Technology" includes articles on using social media and emerging technologies. Explore this site for insights into many areas important to businesses today.

BusinessKnow-How.com: www.businessknowhow.com (Accessed Spring 2011).

This large site has an abundance of articles on starting and managing a small business. Different areas cover incorporating online, business loans, human resources training and tools, and web design and tools. Users will find many articles on job descriptions, cash management and accounting, a break-even calculator, and a job or product pricing system. Franchising and marketing strategies are also covered. Find basic business information here on a wide range of topics.

**BusinessTown.com: www.businesstown.com (Accessed Spring 2011).

This extensive business information site has sections on "Managing a Business," "Home Businesses," "Internet Businesses," "Accounting," "Selling a Business," and more. The articles are not lengthy but quite thoroughly cover their subjects. Under "Home Business," you will find ideas for home businesses, how to set one up, and articles on getting started right. Under "Accounting," you will learn basic concepts, how to budget, how to plan and project, and more. The site also has links to a variety of financial calculators at www.dinkytown.net. Useful site and not commercial, use it to help you in any area where you need more information.

Bloomberg Businessweek: www.businessweek.com/small-business/ (Accessed Spring 2011).

This large, timely site has an abundance of current articles on many phases of starting and running a small business. Financing, sales and marketing, management and more are covered as well as research and special reports. Users will find tools and services needed to understand and manage all aspects of technology in running their own business as well as how it affects the business world in general. Also find business and government forms, legal training courses, and information on business structure laws. The "Small Business" and "Management" areas provide articles on business plans, target market research, and health insurance basics. Also available are articles on other specific areas of business development, including human resources, finance, technology, and sales. Keep current on all areas of business and economic news here.

**Entrepreneurs' Resource Center: www.edwardlowe.org/ERC (Accessed Spring 2011).

This nonprofit organization promotes entrepreneurship by providing information, research, and education. The "Acquiring and Managing Finances" section will help new entrepreneurs learn about all aspects related to their business's financial situation. The section of this useful site entitled "Building and Inspiring an Organization" will lead you to articles on crisis management, communication skills, management development, organizational structure, and more. Use this site also to find practical articles on marketing, finances, human resources management, and legal issues and taxes. Networking possibilities include conferences and educational seminars listed here.

Entrepreneur.com: www.entrepreneurmag.com (Accessed Spring 2011).

Maintained by *Entrepreneur Magazine,* this site supports new businesses and growing companies. Two important areas of this page are listed at the top: "Management" and "Business Coaches." Here you'll find lists of articles covering various topics in management such as trends in management, time management, managing employees, and more. "Business Coaches" can help you through difficult times in your business life. "Start Up Topics" include organization and managing, finding a location, naming your business, and business structure. Find ready-made business forms here, too. Use this site whenever you need help in determining what to do next.

Entrepreneur's Guidebook Series: www.smbtn.com/businessplanguides/ (Accessed Spring 2011).

Defining real entrepreneurs as managers who adopt key behaviors developed by understanding key market concepts and theories and who are successful because of their planning and researching skills, this site covers a wide variety of subjects in its "Small Business Plan Guides." Here you will discover articles on managerial and leadership skills and time management. Explore this website for more good ideas.

Financial Calculators for Business: www.dinkytown.net/business.html (Accessed Spring 2011).

This lengthy list of calculators will help you with break-even analysis, cash flow, inventory, taxes, business valuation, ratios, and more. Use to help you with payroll deductions, self-employment taxes, and more.

Free Management Library: www.managementhelp.org/ (Accessed Spring 2011).

The large site provides easy-to-access and comprehensive resources about the leadership and management of yourself, other individuals, plus groups and organizations. This library has become one of the world's largest and best-organized collections of resources for small businesses. Approximately 600 topics are included here, with over 4,500 articles and almost 10,000 links. Topics range from best practices to start, develop, operate, evaluate, and resolve problems in for-profit and nonprofit organizations. Each topic includes a list of recommended books and related articles. Content is particularly pertinent to most small and medium-sized organizations. Grouped alphabetically by subject, the "E-Commerce" collection is particularly noteworthy.

GS1 US: www.gs1us.org/ (Accessed Spring 2011).

This site was formerly called the Uniform Code Council, and its mission remains the same. The new name encompasses the family of subsidiaries and partnerships it now represents. The bar code or 12-digit, all-numeric universal product code is essential for anyone selling a product in today's global marketplace. The UPC identifies each product and the company that makes it and where it is warehoused, sold, delivered, and billed, either through wholesale or retail channels. To obtain a UPC, you must become a member of the Uniform Code Council, Inc.; it's a two-step process. First, you have your numbers and then you go to one of the UCC's Solution Partners to produce the bar code symbols themselves. On the left side of the home page, under "EAN.UCC System," you will find "I Need a Bar Code," where you can quickly get to the explanation. Cost is based on how many products you have and your annual sales. This site is easy to navigate and thoroughly explains the process of obtaining a bar code.

Internal Revenue Service: www.irs.ustreas.gov (Accessed Spring 2011).

Find useful information about keeping good records here. Learn about what kinds of records to keep and how long to keep them. A sample record system is presented. Under the "Businesses" tab, a great deal of information on small business taxes of all kinds can be found. Also available through a link is the IRS's site for small business/self-employed at www.irs.gov/businesses/small. This site provides information and links on many issues such as employment taxes, paperwork reduction for employers, changes to IRS Schedule C-EZ, small business forms and publications, and more. Tax scams and tax education information is also included.

MoreBusiness.com: www.morebusiness.com (Accessed Spring 2011).

Sections on this site include "Startup," "Running SmallBiz," "Templates," and "Tools." The "Templates" section provides sample business contracts and agreements, business and marketing plans, press releases, and business checklists. A large collection of articles and advice under "Business Technology" will help you understand the Internet, online shopping, website technology, hacking, and even laptop issues. The section on "Build Your Own Website" is very useful. Many of the articles are lengthy and thorough. Use this site to help improve your marketing and management skills.

National Association for Women Business Owners (NAWBO): www.nawbo.org (Accessed Spring 2011).

This group has chapters located throughout the United States and sponsors national and regional conferences, provides networking opportunities, and sponsors awards. The Center for Women's Business Research, part of the National Foundation for Women Business Owners, produces original, groundbreaking research to show the economic and social contributions of women-owned firms. This site's list of resources for taking your product or service to an international market is outstanding.

SBDCNET: http://sbdcnet.org/ (Accessed Spring 2011).

The Small Business Development Center National Information Clearinghouse provides timely, web-based information to entrepreneurs. Small Business Development Centers are located in all 50 states. This website provides information on business start-up, e-commerce, industry research, marketing, trends, and more. Entrepreneurs will find plenty of links and information here to help them plan and run their new business.

Small Business Administration: www.sba.gov (Accessed Spring 2011).

This official government site offers a wealth of resources and programs for starting and growing a small business. The "Emerging Business Series" covers topics including strategic planning, management issues, and human resources management. Other articles cover business planning, financing, managing, marketing, employees, taxes, legal aspects, and business opportunities. Under "Loans and Grants," you will find articles on grants, loans, and bonds. Also find here online forms, business plans, and loan information. Some contents are available in Spanish.

Small Business and Entrepreneurship: http://libguides.unm.edu/small_business (Accessed Spring 2011).

This web page was created and is maintained by me. Some of the resources, especially under the "I need to find . . ." tab, are specific to the University of New Mexico. However, under the tab "Selected Internet Resources," you will find links to many free small business gateways and legal and government sites. Use my guide as a gateway to many of the websites—such as Business Owners Idea Café, Entrepreneur.com, and MoreBusiness—listed in this resource. My colleagues and I also publish other research guides on business topics such as marketing and advertising, company and industry information, and business and management. Use all of these guides to help you find more information to start and run your new business.

**Small Business Notes: www.smallbusinessnotes.com (Accessed Spring 2011).

Here you will find articles on starting or buying your first business as well as merging, planning, management, and legal issues. Explore articles on business management and planning. Under "Management" are articles on the planning process, sample plans, business plan resources, strategic planning, and more. Basic articles contain links to fuller explanatory articles on a wide variety of topics, such as business models and recordkeeping. The articles on "Why Merge" and "Merge Wisely" are enlightening and provide the owner with information and food for thought when considering a merger. Come to this useful site for many topics related to small business and entrepreneurship and for answers to basic and more complex questions.

**SmallBusinessTV.com: sbtv.com (Accessed Spring 2011).

This web-based network provides information and advice of interest to entrepreneurs and small business owners and managers. Various channels such as "Money," "Marketing," "Legal," "Real Business," "Women," and "Technology" contain a list of short videos where experts present practical advice. Sign up for the newsletter to keep current on what's happening. A high-speed Internet connection is a real bonus for viewing the videos.

SmartMoney Magazine's Small Business site: www.smsmallbiz.com/ (Accessed Spring 2011).

This large site covers small business by identifying the entrepreneur as a quick-thinking individual who easily turns a passion for a product or a service into a successful business. Regular columns focus why and how you should run your own show. Sections include "Work & Life," which advises entrepreneurs on challenging issues such as getting away from the business or dealing with illness or finding family time. "Starting Up" helps entrepreneurs through the early stages of writing a business plan and finding financing with case studies and articles. Other sections cover marketing, technology, taxes, best practices, and more. Each month streaming video reports from SmartMoney TV identify a special topic of interest to entrepreneurs; these topics might include raising capital or disaster planning. Special attention is provided for women and minorities because they make up the fastest-growing area of entrepreneurs.

Time-Management-Guide.com: www.time-management-guide.com (Accessed Spring 2011)

This large, well-organized site has a wealth of tips and information on managing your time, making smart decisions, teamwork, using meeting time wisely, and more. Additionally, you will find thoughts on procrastination, goal setting, coping skills, and burnout. No large visual ads on this site make the information seem more expansive and easier to find.

PERSONNEL/HUMAN RESOURCES   **10**

Motivation is the art of getting people to do what
you want them to do because they want to do it.
—*Dwight D. Eisenhower*

Not every small business needs or should hire employees. According to recent surveys, nearly 80% of sole proprietorships do not have more than one employee, the owner. However, maybe during your setup phase, you find yourself overwhelmed with work, or as your business grows, it's impossible to manage it efficiently by yourself; then it's time to add staff. It's important to make decisions and have policies and procedures in place before you hire anyone in order to avoid personnel problems later. In this chapter, various types of employees will be considered and described. Also, you will find out how you can learn how to write and establish job descriptions to enable you to find and hire the right people. Your expectations must be realistic, and you must be able to communicate them to prospective employees.

DETERMINING WHAT YOUR NEEDS ARE

Before taking the step of hiring anyone, carefully consider creative solutions to staffing that might work for the short term. Try to project into the future and determine if current demand and workload will keep outstripping your personal ability to cope.

Make a list of what you would like another person or persons to do, and then add a second section of what the person might do in the future after mastering the first list. Look beyond your immediate needs. Consider which tasks can easily be taught to someone else, or think about skills you don't have that someone else could provide to help build your business. Take into account what qualifications a person would need to be able to complete your list of job duties. With those lists in mind, consider whether any of the following types of employees could fill your need:

1. *Independent contractors.* These workers complete projects for you as well as other clients on their own terms; you just specify what you want them to do, the quality required, and when delivery is due. This worker is not someone who works on your site during business hours to greet visitors and answer the telephone. Usually contract employees are used for specific projects or consulting services. A couple of caveats must be mentioned. First, independent contractors are not bound by the contract they sign to complete the job; and, second, if you treat an independent contractor like an employee and fail to pay employment taxes, you could face a tax bill that might bankrupt your business. The Internal Revenue Service (IRS) has very specific guidelines for identifying independent contractors, and these can be found at its website: www.irs.gov.

2. *Leased employees.* This type of worker is employed by another company that handles the payroll and administers benefits, and you pay the company a fee plus expenses to do so. Employment-leasing companies remove many employee problems from the owner's shoulders, because the owner does not have to understand and pay workers' compensation, state and federal unemployment taxes, FICA (Federal Insurance Contributions Act) tax and Medicare, pension plans, health care, and other benefits. Because this employment-leasing company has many workers leased to different companies, it can often offer better benefits at a lower cost than your small business can offer. This arrangement may be cheaper for your company even if you need several employees.

3. *Temporary help.* Especially useful if you can't determine that you need an employee or employees for the long term, it may be prudent and less costly to hire someone through a temporary help agency that takes care of the payroll administration and fringe benefits. The agency will also recruit and send you qualified applicants, saving you time and possibly money. However, if your needs continue, you may have to train a stream of workers who leave at unpredictable times. On the other hand, you may find a good temp who can work for you permanently and save recruiting time and expenses.

For more thorough coverage of all these topics, Lin Grensing-Pophal's book *Employee Management for Small Business* is an excellent resource. Grensing-Pophal details the ins and outs of all types of employees, and how to manage each type.

Grensing-Pophal, Lin. *Employee Management for Small Business,* 3rd ed. Self-Counsel Press, 2010. 265p. ISBN 1-55180-863-3. $20.95.

Small businesses especially must select and nurture employees who mirror the company's culture and performance objectives. Included here are checklists and samples of all the forms necessary as well as real-world examples to maintain an efficient, productive workforce. Find hints on developing interview and questioning skills, selecting the best candidate, conducting performance reviews, motivating your employees, and managing dismissals and departures. Learn to find and retain good employees, what should be in your employee handbook, and how to protect your business from litigation. The basics of employment law are also thoroughly covered. This title is a one-stop manual for hiring, firing, and keeping employees for your small business and maintaining an effective human resources plan.

HIRING EMPLOYEES

Once you have looked at your needs, created a job description and qualifications, and determined that you need a full-or part-time employee, take some time to scrutinize the issue further. Be sure to consider and investigate all the costs involved—not just salary but insurance, workers' compensation, withholding taxes, equipment, office furniture, supplies, and so on. You also need to decide what kind of salary or hourly wage to offer. Check want ads in the local paper to see what other companies are offering. If you can't afford to pay as much as others, think of low-cost or no-cost benefits you might offer, such as flexible working hours, job sharing, time off for classes, telecommuting, or working part-time from home. As you can probably already tell, hiring employees takes your time and attention away from core business activities. This investment of your time is an ongoing commitment to hiring, training, compensating, and motivating good employees to help your business succeed.

It's not always easy to find qualified employees. Placing a want ad is a start. Also, try contacting your state's department of employment or labor to see if you can place your help-wanted position on an online site or office bulletin boards or whatever mechanism it uses. You might want to try local colleges or schools to get recent graduates or part-time or summer help. Asking friends, family, former coworkers, and business associates to refer potential employees is still the hands-down best source of employees.

GOOD HIRING PRACTICES

Though not required by law, it's good business practice to develop a written job description and application form. Since you've already decided what the position involves and have identified the skills and qualifications needed to do the job, write a job description that blends these two elements. List each essential function, rank the functions in order of importance, list the activities involved with completing each function, and list the skills and abilities needed to perform the activities. For example, for a receptionist, the number one function or task might be greeting customers; activities would include in-person and telephone greetings and answering questions, and skills would include good speaking skills, pleasant dress and manner, and working knowledge of good customer service skills. Be sure to state where this job fits in your organization's structure and to whom the employee reports. Have a salary range in mind for the position. For more information on job titles and duties as well as wages, check out the *Occupational Outlook Handbook* from the U.S. Department of Labor at www.bls.gov/oco/home.htm.

The job application form helps you gather the same essential information from all applicants and allows you to make a fair decision. A basic application should contain the applicant's name, address, Social Security number, education, previous employment (past 10 years is standard), and signature with date. Next, you should verify some of the information presented to check its accuracy. Speak with former employers and other references listed.

Once you have a pool of applicants, you must select the interviewees. Remember that not only are you interviewing the job applicant, but that the applicant will interview you. You both need to agree to work together before a solid working relationship can develop.

Before beginning the interviews, develop a list of interview questions focused on the position that you are trying to fill, on the applicant's previous job experiences, and on your company or industry. Some common interview questions include:

1. Why did you apply for this position and where did you hear about the opening?

2. Why did you leave your last job?

3. What are your strengths? Weaknesses?

4. Describe a situation where you made a mistake and how you resolved it.

5. Why should I hire you?

6. What motivates you?

7. Do you have any questions for me?

Take notes and retain your notes for your records, whether the individual is hired or not. People often bring lawsuits. If you have doubts about the legality of a question, please check one of the resources at the end of the chapter or simply search "illegal interview questions" on the Internet. Often the difference between a legal question and an illegal one is the wording. Retaining complete records on everyone will protect you, and give you a defensive position. Also be aware of body language and other nonverbal cues when interviewing. Consider dress, eye contact, posture, facial expressions, and tone of voice as clues to the applicant's character, attitudes, and emotions.

Depending on the current job market in your area, you may have many qualified applicants or you may not. If a nearly qualified candidate comes along who isn't quite what you had in mind but who is enthusiastic and appears to be a quick learner, perhaps you can negotiate a slightly lower pay, hire on a probationary basis, and challenge the person to discover whether he or she is right for the job. Follow your instincts on picking the right person for your business and to work with you.

Note: Don't assume millennial generation employees will perform exactly like baby boomers and Generation Xers. The millennial generation, in general, likes to enjoy life, may not be ready for long-term commitments, and may not even mind quitting their jobs despite the investment you made to hire them. This new generation of workers is spending more time "finding themselves" than any past generation. They often delay postsecondary education, enter the workforce later or enter on a part time basis, and start families years later even than their baby boomer parents. They are very savvy with new and developing technologies, thrive on learning new job skills, and have an abundance of self-confidence. Some of these things may be great characteristics for your small business, but you should be aware of these generalizations about the attitudes of millennials. Be sure to always use good hiring practices.

Getting back to probationary employment, good hiring practice requires all employees to work on a probationary basis for the first 60 or 90 working days. A probationary employment policy must be in writing and should state the length of the probationary period. Probationary employees may be terminated without explanation. A probationary period gives you—the employer—time to observe and evaluate the new employee. The probationary employment policy statement should be included on the application form that every applicant signs. At the end of the probationary period, review the employee's performance with him or her. Annual performance reviews are a good time for both parties to share concerns. This annual discussion is an opportunity to review the employee's personal and career goals and to discuss possible opportunities for promotion and expansion of responsibilities.

UNSATISFACTORY EMPLOYEE PERFORMANCE

When there is a problem with an employee's performance, it's best to try and find the root cause. If he or she has been performing well and suddenly there's a noticeable change, like calling in sick once a week or arriving late every day, a discussion with the employee about why this change happened may work toward solving the problem. Communication with employees will go a long way toward solving many problems. Listen to employees when problems occur.

It never hurts to be prepared. Common disciplinary problems include absenteeism, alcohol or drugs on the job, inability to get along with others, lack of productivity, tardiness, and sloppy or inappropriate dress. Consider when you would give a warning—verbal or written—about these behaviors, when and what action you might take, and when you would terminate or fire for not changing behaviors or conforming to expectations.

Try to use discipline as an opportunity to motivate your employee or employees to better performance. Never correct or discipline an employee in a public or even semipublic place. Try never to be angry when disciplining an employee, but realize that the sooner you bring the problem or behavior to the employee's attention, the sooner the improper behavior will be stopped. Conduct the corrective meeting in private, stay on topic, remain calm, and try to be as positive as possible. Remember, it's a dialogue or discussion, not a speech. Concentrate on the behavior you want to change, not the person or personality. End on a positive note, and be sure to schedule a follow-up meeting.

It's important to recognize good work, and improvement is definitely worthy of praise and acknowledgment. When you hire employees, you must work with a variety of personalities and cultures different from your own. It's always useful to get another perspective, and Pincus, in her book *Managing Difficult People,* provides advice and techniques for working with a wide range of employees. Read her book to find help in dealing with different personality types.

Pincus, Marilyn. *Managing Difficult People.* Adams Media, 2004. 224p. ISBN 1-59337-186-1. $9.95.

Discover and identify the 10 most common types of difficult people, including sneaky slackers, resident workplace tormentors, whiners, social butterflies, and manipulators. Pincus details positive, proactive measures to target these behaviors and put an end to workplace tension and the stress they cause. Employees with negative attitudes can disrupt and bring down the morale of the entire staff. Understand your employees and deal with bad behavior in creative ways.

KEEPING GOOD EMPLOYEES

Employee motivation is a key management skill. Whether you have one employee or one hundred, it is important to work to create a motivating workplace. Employees who feel valued and rewarded naturally have fewer performance problems and issues. Recognizing good work at a staff meeting can help build morale. Keeping lines of communication open throughout the organization is also important to encourage new ideas. A competitive salary is a key ingredient for keeping and building morale. Benefits are optional and not required by law, but benefits packages that include paid vacation and sick time, conference attendance, paid education or training, bonuses, flex time, and surprise small rewards can increase job satisfaction. Make employees feel important and recognized. Focus on the individual's strengths to motivate her or him to do better work. Be creative and find out what works for your employees. For many good articles on the subject of motivating employees, use the Motivation Center at http://humanresources.about.com. For an excellent book on employee reward ideas, look at *The 1001 Rewards and Recognition Fieldbook* by Bob Nelson and Dean Spitzer. It contains excellent plans, ideas, and checklists for implementing your program.

Nelson, Bob and Spitzer, Dean R. *The 1001 Rewards and Recognition Fieldbook.* Workman, 2003. 384p. ISBN 0-7611-2139-0. $17.95.

Using the basics of motivation, learn how to develop and manage a rewards or recognition program in your workplace. Topics covered include how to recognize an individual or group and how to develop and implement a low-cost recognition program. Discover how to improve attendance, increase retention, and improve morale. The case studies from companies like Starbucks, IBM, FedEx, Pizza Hut, and Southwest Airlines illustrate important points made by the authors. Unique ideas are presented for employee rewards, such as a secret Happiness Committee and asking each employee to write down 10 things that motivate them so you have an individualized motivation checklist for each employee. The 1,001 low-cost and no-cost recognition ideas are sure to be of interest to any small employer.

EMPLOYEE RETIREMENT INCOME SECURITY ACT (ERISA)

ERISA protects employees' rights to employer-provided pension and health and welfare plans. It is often easier to keep employees if you can offer some benefits. Neither the federal government nor ERISA requires that employers provide such benefits, but when benefits are provided, ERISA outlines the rules employers must follow. Enforced by both the IRS and the Department of Labor, see one or both of the following websites for more information: www.benefitslink.com/erisa/index.html or www.dol.gov/dol/topic/retirement/erisa.htm. In order for your business to receive a tax deduction for its benefit plan contributions, you must comply with the tax code provisions under ERISA. Small businesses are sometimes discouraged from offering qualified retirement plans because of the administrative costs related to ERISA.

FIRING AN EMPLOYEE

Needless to say, when an employee just doesn't work out, following the correct procedures is critical. This situation is difficult and uncomfortable for even the most experienced manager and owner. However, it is sometimes unavoidable. It's not fair to the employee, the other employees, your business, or yourself to keep an employee who's not performing up to your standards. Muster your courage; be sensitive and kind but honest. Be sure you have a legitimate and unbiased reason and explain it thoroughly and calmly to the employee in a private termination meeting. Be sure you have paper documentation to show previously discussed warnings, meetings, and actions. If you'd like more information on how to terminate, check out the Business Town website at www.businesstown.com/people/firing.asp.

The following references and resources will further explain and amplify employment management issues and procedures.

REFERENCES

Starred titles are discussed in the chapter.

■ Print Resources

Alessandra, Tony. *The New Art of Managing People, Updated and Revised.* Free Press, 2008. 368p. ISBN 1-416-5506-23. $18.

Find here the practical strategies, guidelines, and techniques to develop specific interpersonal skills needed to begin and maintain good relations with employees, to understand different types of people, and to create trust between employees and managers. A good manager guides, directs, and motivates, but energetic, enthusiastic workers also need to express their own personalities in order to create a positive spirit throughout the organization.

American Bar Association. *Legal Guide for Small Business,* 2nd ed. Random House Reference, 2010. 496p. ISBN 978-03757-2303-2. $17.

This handy little guide will help small businesses understand their legal responsibilities and options. It thoroughly covers the legal aspects of topics like employees, franchising, contracts, taxes, and start-up basics. Highlights of the employee section include a short course on law in the workplace, terminating employees, maintaining a safe place of business as well as dealing with customers and customer credit.

Armstrong, Sharon and Mitchell, Barbara. *The Essential HR Handbook.* Career Press, 2008. 224p. ISBN 1-5641-4990-9. $14.99.

Find here tools, tips, checklists, and roadmaps to help managers learn to individually manage employees, manage a multigenerational workforce, develop rewards strategies, and identify legal pitfalls to stay out of court. Case studies and sample documents are used to illustrate important issues and challenges. Human resources managers or small business managers will refer to this well-written and well-organized work often.

Bagley, Constance E. and Dauchy, Craig. *The Entrepreneur's Guide to Business Law,* 3rd ed. South-Western College/West, 2007. 784p. ISBN 0-32-420493-0. $73.95.

This comprehensive resource helps new entrepreneurs select and work with an attorney, determine the legal structure of their business, learn about contracts and leases as well as legal issues involved with e-commerce, identify needed insurance, and much more. The chapter on human resources is very useful; here you will find a sample work agreement form as well as other information to work with a variety of employees. Seventeen chapters cover every aspect of start-up, growth, and buying a business as well as international legal issues when appropriate.

Broadsky, Norm and Burlingham, Bo. *The Knack: How Street-Smart Entrepreneurs Learn to Handle Whatever Comes Up.* Portfolio, 2008 (and Kindle). ISBN 1-59-184221-2. $18.99.

This thoughtful guide stresses the thinking necessary to deal with many different situations and uses engaging examples or case studies to illustrate how the authors' advice works. Learn the basics of accounting, how to establish goals, spot problems in the numbers, why you need cash to survive, and keep your perspective when dealing with challenges. Chapters on being the boss and selling as a team sport are very practical and useful.

Chandler, Steve. *The Hands-off Manager: How to Mentor People and Allow Them to Be Successful.* Career Press, 2007. 223p. ISBN 1-564-14950-1. $19.99.

Using examples, stories, and activities, Chandler demonstrates how any manager can learn to coach and mentor employees rather than micromanage them. Find out how to honor each individual's strengths and develop a climate of mutual goal setting and partnership. At the end of each chapter are exercises to move you ahead to becoming a better manager for today's workforce. Transform your company's culture from one of judgment and criticism to one where work is fun and rewarding as well as productive.

Daily, Frederick W. *Tax Savvy for Small Business,* 14th ed. Nolo Press, 2010. 380p. ISBN 1-4133-1279-9. $39.99.

One section covers fringe benefits very thoroughly, and another discusses retirement plans and ERISA. Learn how to manage employee benefits. Discover how to pay payroll taxes on time, use retirement funds as a tax break, keep records, and negotiate payment for late taxes. If you are faced with an audit for any reason, Daily will help you prepare in advance. This handy reference guide will help you plan employee benefits and work with your accountant or lawyer.

DelCampo, Robert G. *Human Resource Management DeMystified.* McGraw Hill, 2011. 224p. ISBN 07-173724-1. $22.

DelCampo will help you start to understand what essential skills are needed to be a human resources manager. Using short quizzes, you can test your knowledge as you work your way through the book. Use the chapter about equal employment opportunity and the law to help your business run legally. Get some hints on managing difficult employees, disciplining employees, working with organized labor, and find out what workplace safety really is today. Learn how to write job descriptions and recruit good applicants. Detailed examples and explanations make the material easy to grasp.

Dion, James E. *The Complete Idiot's Guide to Starting and Running a Retail Store.* Alpha Books, 2008. 368p. ISBN 1-592-57726-1. $19.95.

With over 30 years of experience in retail, Dion provides practical, hands-on tips and advice on all aspects of retailing. Dion explains human behavioral principles and delves deeply into key topics like recruiting the right people, motivating a team, and how to motivate. Find practical examples and case studies to help your business be successful.

Encyclopedia of Small Business Legal Forms and Agreements. Atlantic, 2010. 288p. ISBN 1-60138-248-1. $29.95.

This encyclopedia and companion CD-ROM focus on the issues, situations, and tasks that you, as a small business owner, face every day when running your business, such as incorporation, insurance, employee applications, employment policies, termination, job descriptions, sales and service contracts, bills of sale, invoices, press releases, employee benefits, license agreements, letters of intent, domain names, e-commerce contracts, and release forms. Over 250 essential documents—including checklists, worksheets, forms, contracts, and human resource documents—are included to help your business succeed. Organize your business and manage it while increasing your bottom line.

Fleischer, Charles H. *HR for Small Business,* 2nd ed. Sphinx, 2009. 432p. ISBN 1-572-48690-2. $16.95.

This handy guide explains in concise language what employers need to know in order to comply with the law when dealing with their employees. This new edition includes everything from recruiting and hiring to discipline and termination. It covers employment law from federal statutes and the general principles of state law. Useful appendices include "Employee Handbook Outline," "Legal Holidays," "Employer Tax Calendar," and "Required Postings in the Workplace." Useful Internet resources plus a complete glossary are also provided.

**Grensing-Pophal, Lin. *Employee Management for Small Business,* 3rd ed. Self-Counsel Press, 2010. 265p. ISBN 1-55180-863-3. $20.95.

Small businesses especially must select and nurture employees who mirror the company's culture and performance objectives. Included here are checklists and samples of all the forms necessary as well as real-world examples to maintain an efficient, productive workforce. Find hints on developing interview and questioning skills, selecting the best candidate, conducting performance reviews, motivating your employees, and managing dismissals and departures. The basics of employment law are also thoroughly covered. This title is a one-stop manual for hiring, firing, and keeping employees for your small business and maintaining an effective human resources plan.

Grensing-Pophal, Lin. *Managing Off-site Staff for Small Business.* Self-Counsel Press, 2010. 280p. ISBN 1-55180-865-9. $19.95.

The changing face and pace of today's workplace allows employers to seek alternative solutions to housing more staff and accommodate the needs of workers. Expand your business by providing a more flexible work environment and not a larger physical space. Learn here how to set up and maintain a productive telecommuting program to attract and keep the best employees. Learn how to properly use technology to communicate and motivate your distance workers.

Guerin, Lisa, J.D. and DelPo, Amy, J.D. *Create Your Own Employee Handbook: A Legal and Practical Guide,* 5th ed. Nolo Press, 2011. 432p. ISBN 1-41331-385-X. $49.99.

Geared to employee and labor laws for each state, the authors, both lawyers, walk you through sample policies that you may change to meet your company's individual needs. The CD lets you cut and paste into your own handbook. This edition has been updated to comply with the latest developments in federal and state law, covering many emerging workplace issues like lactation breaks, instant messaging, and dealing with victims of domestic violence and stalking. This comprehensive kit will help you complete the task of creating an employee handbook quickly and easily.

Hess, Edward G. and Goetz, Charles F. *So, You Want to Start a Business?* FT Press, 2008. 224p. ISBN 0-137-12667-0. $21.99.

Using real-life experiences, case studies, and research, the authors present 55 simple but indispensable rules for success. Especially important is their insight into the art and science of managing people, operations, and growth. Learn to set priorities, know your competitors, and create practical and efficient processes. The chapter on human resources is very practical and useful to help you evaluate and keep your best employees. Written in a simple but academic style, you will find help here to realize your business goals.

Holzschu, Michael. *Complete Employee Handbook,* rev ed. Acorn Alliance, 2007. 256p. ISBN 1-55921-256-X. $39.95.

This comprehensive resource guides employers in the development of a cohesive personnel program to fit their business's unique needs and goals. Discover how to deal with personnel issues before they become problems. Policy areas covered include hiring, benefits, standards, terminations, job descriptions, and personnel files. Sample forms are included on the CD as well as sample employee handbooks, federal regulations and laws, and worksheets for assessing personnel needs and goals. A key piece of wisdom is to remind employers to have a lawyer review their handbook before implementing it in their workplace.

Meister, Jeanne C. and Willyerd, Karie. *The 2020 Workplace: How Innovative Companies Attract, Develop, and Keep Tomorrow's Employees Today.* HarperBusiness, 2010. 304p. ISBN 0-06-176327-6. $26.99.

Learn how to harness the potential of the millennial generation in your business. This collection of case histories, significant statistics, global surveys, and personalized anecdotes will help you understand and use Web 2.0 technologies in your workplace, with your staff, and to market your business appropriately. The chapter entitled "Twenty Predictions for the 2020 Workplace" is fascinating, as is the prediction that "A 2020 mind-set will be required to thrive in a networked world." The authors provide useful, thoughtful tips, the latest in corporate training, and advice for negotiating this new workforce for businesses of any size.

Muller, Max. *Manager's Guide to HR: Hiring, Firing, Performance Evaluations, Documentation, Benefits, and Everything Else You Need to Know.* AMACOM, 2009. 304p. ISBN 0-8144-1076-6. $24.95.

This step-by-step guide to human resources includes training and development, employment law, and records retention. Learn how to deal with conflict, privacy issues, COBRA (Consolidated Omnibus Budget Reconciliation Act) compliance, and more. The discussion of ways to prevent sexual harassment is especially relevant and important in today's workplace.

**Nelson, Bob and Spitzer, Dean R. *The 1001 Rewards and Recognition Fieldbook.* Workman, 2003. 384p. ISBN 0-7611-2139-0. $17.95.

This now classic resource will help you use the basics of motivation and learn how to develop and manage a rewards or recognition program in your workplace. Topics covered include how to recognize an individual or group and how to develop and implement a low-cost recognition program. Discover how to improve attendance, increase retention, and improve morale. The case studies from companies like Lands' End, FedEx, and Southwest Airlines illustrate important points made by the authors. Unique ideas for employee rewards—such as a secret Happiness Committee and asking each employee to write down 10 things that motivate them so you have an individualized motivation checklist for each employee—are explained. Learn how to use Recognition Technique Reminder Cards and Recognition Planning Worksheets, for example. The 1,001 low-cost and no-cost recognition ideas are sure to be of interest to any small employer.

**Pincus, Marilyn. *Managing Difficult People.* Adams Media, 2004. 224p. ISBN 1-59337-186-1. $9.95.

Discover and identify the 10 most common types of difficult people including sneaky slackers, resident workplace tormentors, whiners, social butterflies, and manipulators. Pincus details positive, proactive measures to target these behaviors and put an end to workplace tension and stress they cause. Employees with negative attitudes can disrupt the entire staff and bring down the morale of the staff. Understand your employees and deal with bad behavior in creative ways.

Sitarz, Daniel. *Small Business Legal Forms Simplified,* 5th ed. Nova, 2011. 304p. ISBN 0-892949-6-28. $29.95 includes CD-ROM.

This comprehensive resource not only provides the forms to handle a multitude of legal situations but straightforward instructions explain what forms are necessary, how to prepare them, and the legal effect of each form. The CD-ROM contains the forms with Adobe Acrobat Reader software. Over 130 forms, including contracts, deeds, collection documents, leases, receipts, employment forms, and releases, are provided. Most of the forms are valid in all 50 states and the District of Columbia.

Steingold, Fred S. *Legal Guide for Starting and Running a Small Business,*11th ed. Nolo Press, 2009. 275p. ISBN 9-78141-3-559. $39.99.

This helpful approach to the start-up process is written in a clear, practical manner that most small business owners can understand. Learn to negotiate a favorable lease, hire and fire employees, understand the tax laws, insure your business, create contracts and agreements, and cope with financial problems. Appendix A also lists state offices that provide small business start-up help for every state.

Waldrop, Sharon Ann. *Everything Human Resource Management Book.* Adams Media, 2008. 304p. ISBN 1-598-69-624-6. $14.95.

Waldrop's practical guide will help you identify the benefits more employees want and use, plan and present useful performance evaluations, and deal with difficult employees. Understand federal labor laws and create accurate, useful human resources policies. Also learn techniques for identifying and firing poor performers.

Willams, Beth and Murray, Jean. *The Complete Guide to Working for Yourself: Everything the Self-Employed Need to Know about Taxes, Recordkeeping, and Other Laws.* Atlantic, 2008. 288p. ISBN 1-601-38048-8. $29.95 includes CD-ROM.

Starting your own business is a genuine, attainable, and gratifying goal. Williams and Murray will help you make the right choices and prevent you from choosing the wrong ones. If you truthfully answer a few questions at the beginning of the book, you can fore-cast your own success. Other areas covered include legal concerns, tax consequences, li-ability, naming your business, hiring, firing, marketing, and location. Also presented is where and how to look for help when needed. It covers the basic and the more advances challenges to starting your own business. Find ready-to-use forms, ideas on cutting costs, and a sample business plan here.

Yerkes, Leslie. *Fun Works: Creating Places Where People Love to Work,* 2nd ed. Berrett-Koehler, 2007. 235p. ISBN 1-5767-5408-5. $17.95.

Many managers have not yet learned that fun as a value of the company's culture and as a set of daily behaviors can mean success both financially and personally. Yerkes details how 11 successful companies such as Pike Place Fish, Southwest Airlines, and Pruden-tial have brought fun into the workplace and demonstrates how this has improved the company's results. Using these stories, Yerkes demonstrates the 11 principles of what she calls the "Fun/Work Fusion." These principles include give permission to perform, chal-lenge your bias, capitalize on spontaneous, and hire good people and get out of the way. Though Yerkes used large companies in general, the strategies, resources, tools, tips, and techniques presented will motivate you to unleash the power of fun in your workplace so your company will be a success.

Online Resources

About.com: http://humanresources.about.com (Accessed Spring 2011).

The Motivation Center is a highlight of the large human resources section. This large website provides articles and resources on policies with samples and topics such as manag-ing performance, salary and benefits, training and education, team building, work relation-ships, employment law, coaching and mentoring, and recruiting and staffing. Employee recognition ideas and empowerment suggestions are presented. Some very good advice on working with difficult people is provided as well as information on terminating or firing an employee. Outsourcing is also thoroughly covered. Refer to this site often for new ideas on managing employees.

AllBusiness: www.allbusiness.com (Accessed Spring 2011).

This huge site contains articles and advice on any area of business law, including legal structure, property leases, patents, trademarks, employment law, taxes, and even how to work with your lawyer. The human resource articles look at workers' compensation and workplace health and safety. The articles on green businesses are also very useful. Links to many directories and to news and business information sites are also provided. The tax articles discuss topics such as barter tax and accounting issues and tax strategies for keep-ing the family business in the family. Use this well-organized, functional website often.

BenefitsLink: http://benefitslink.com/index.html (Accessed Spring 2011)

This site provides users with everything they want to know about employee benefits. "Authorities" will link you to employee benefit plan compliance matters like inflation-ad-justed limits, audit guidelines, deferred compensation, ERISA, and more. The "Directory" links to vendors and human resources software. This large site will help answer questions and solve problems related to employee benefits.

**Bureau of Labor Statistics (BLS): www.bls.gov/oco/home.htm (Accessed Spring 2011).

Find here publications like the *Dictionary of Occupational Titles* and the *Occupational Outlook Handbook* online. The handbook provides training and education needed, earnings, and expected job prospects for a wide range of jobs. Use this site to locate information on all aspects of the legalities of employees. If you follow the federal guidelines, you're likely to be in compliance with state regulations as well.

**BusinessTown.com: www.businesstown.com (Accessed Spring 2011).

This extensive business information site has sections on managing a business, home businesses, Internet businesses, accounting, selling a business, and more. The articles are not long but thoroughly cover their subjects. Under "Home Business," you will find ideas for home businesses, how to set one up, and articles on getting started right. The "Hiring and Firing Topics" are also very useful for new business owners. Under "Accounting," you will learn basic concepts, how to budget, how to plan and project, and more. The site also has links to a variety of financial calculators at www.dinkytown.net. Useful site and not commercial, use it to help you in any area where you need more information.

Entrepreneur's Resource Center: www.edwardlowe.org/ERC/ (Accessed Spring 2011).

This nonprofit organization promotes entrepreneurship by providing information, research, and education. Use this site to find practical articles on marketing, finances, human resources management, and legal issues and taxes. The "Human Resources Management" section contains articles and resources on interviewing, employee retention, benefits, diversity, morale, motivation, and performance appraisals. Networking possibilities include conferences and educational seminars listed here.

Employers of America: www.employerhelp.org (Accessed Spring 2011).

This large website can help you work with your employees toward common goals. Find information on writing job descriptions, human resources manuals, employee reviews, how to coach and train new employees, safety tips, and more. If you have concerns about sexual harassment, you'll find tools to help you here. Top stories keep you up to date on human resources trends such as ways to motivate your employees. The well-organized, easy-to-navigate site can help you with personnel issues.

FindLaw's Small Business Center: http://smallbusiness.findlaw.com (Accessed Spring 2011).

Chock-full of articles and guides on all aspects of business development, the "Employment & HR" section is particularly outstanding. Find out how to write good job descriptions and advertisements, avoid discrimination during hiring, and learn good interviewing techniques. Safety for employees, termination procedures, and links to relevant regulatory agencies are also provided. Forms and contracts are discussed and samples provided. An entire section is devoted to workers' compensation. Taxes and immigration sections also provide help for the new employer. If you have legal questions, check this site for advice and discussion.

Health Insurance Association of America (HIAA): www.hiaa.org (Accessed Spring 2011).

This site offers various consumer guidebooks. Here you will find information on group health insurance, tips on choosing quality coverage, and a checklist to help evaluate the different types of coverage available. Other guides discuss long-term care insurance and disability income insurance. Included are many articles on the political side of health care. Get accurate insurance information here.

HRTools.com: www.hrtools.com (Accessed Spring 2011).

Good information and articles are presented in sections about staffing, legal compliance, training and performance, and benefits and compensation. Free registration is required, and a free newsletter is available with registration. "Legal Updates" and "HR News" are highlighted. An "eTools" section provides especially good information on federal and state coverage for workers' compensation.

**Internal Revenue Service: www.irs.ustreas.gov (Accessed Spring 2011).

Find here a detailed description of independent contractors and how they differ from employees of a business. Before you hire your first employee, read the section on "Businesses with Employees" for advice and assistance. Also find information on self-employment and employment taxes. The IRS publication *Employer's Supplemental Tax Guide* is also available from the site. Common employment tax forms for small businesses can also be accessed. A great deal of information on small business taxes of all kinds can be found here.

MoreBusiness.com: www.morebusiness.com (Accessed Spring 2011).

Basic sections on this site include "Startup," "Running SmallBiz," "Templates," and "Tools." The templates provide sample business contracts and agreements, business and marketing plans, press releases, and business checklists. A large collection of articles and advice on employees can be found under "Running SmallBiz." Learn how to motivate employees and how good coaching can improve attitudes. Articles on technology and your employees are very useful. Learn about customer service training for your employees, too. Many of the articles are lengthy and thorough. Use this site to help improve your people management skills.

Nolo Press: www.nolo.com (Accessed Spring 2011).

This commercial site has a good collection of free articles written by lawyers generally. The "Business and Human Resources" section has many interesting articles on topics such as "Abiding by Wage and Hour Laws," "Ensuring Privacy in the Workplace," and "Firing Employees." The main article on "Employers' Rights and Responsibilities" is very thorough and easy to understand. You'll also find help on writing your own employee handbook. Nolo's legal self-help books, now often accompanied by CD-ROMs, are outstanding, and you will find useful information and advice on the site as well as invitations to buy its products.

Smartbiz.com Small Business Resource: www.smartbiz.com (Accessed Spring 2011).

This large site is organized into six major sections: "Smart Moves," "Heads Up," "Network," "Tech Center," "Form Fetcher," and "Smart Links." Users will find business forms for daily cash flow, employee disciplinary action, employee time sheets, sample business and marketing plans, and collection letters. Interesting articles cover "Secrets to Organizational Greatness" and "Keeping a Staff Motivated through Training and Development." One exceptional article is entitled "Minimize Negativity." Sample policies regarding drug tests, smoking, safety, time off, and workplace AIDS are also provided. The "Network" section will prove useful to many new entrepreneurs.

SmartMoney Small Business: www.smsmallbiz.com/ (Accessed Spring 2011).

This large site covers small business by focusing on the entrepreneur as a quick-thinking risk taker who can turn a passion for a product or a service into a thriving business. Regular columns focus on why and how you should run your own show. Sections include "Work & Life," which advises entrepreneurs on tricky issues such as taking vacations, dealing with illness, and creating family time, and "Starting Up," which helps entrepreneurs through the early stages of launching a business with case studies and articles. Other sections thoroughly cover marketing, technology, taxes, best practices, and more. The "Benefits" section covers employee benefits, retirement issues, retaining employees, and more. Each month, streaming video reports from SmartMoney TV focus on a special topic of interest to business owners, whether that's raising capital or dealing with disaster. Special attention is provided for women and minorities, who make up the fastest-growing subset of entrepreneurs.

LEGAL AND TAX ISSUES

11

It might send shivers up your spine or make your head spin, but running a business involves many legal and financial decisions, and your business's performance depends on your ability and expertise to make those decisions. Some areas we've already discussed and we'll just recap or connect those decisions to other legal implications such as taxes. Much of this chapter will deal with various taxes that you, as a small business owner, must be aware of and be careful to understand. If at any time, you are confused or can't grasp the legal implications, please seek the advice of a lawyer. As we all know, "ignorance of the law is no excuse" and "knowledge is power." Every unique situation cannot be covered here, just the basics. Understanding your legal rights and responsibilities and being aware of your options are key factors in business success. Doing it right the first time will save you and your business time and money.

KNOW THE LAW

Knowledge is power, and, as a small business owner, you need to understand some basic legal issues to avoid legal problems. Listed below are citations for a couple of good basic small business legal resources. Read and understand the sections that apply to your small business.

American Bar Association. *Legal Guide for Small Business*, 2nd ed. Random House Reference, 2010. 496p. ISBN 0-3757-2303-2. $16.99.

This handy little guide will help small businesses understand their legal responsibilities and options. It thoroughly covers the legal aspects of topics such as financing, employees, franchising, contracts, taxes, and start-up basics. Highlights include chapters on home-based businesses, franchises, insurance, and maintaining a safe place of business as well as dealing with customers and customer credit. If you are still in doubt about which legal structure—sole proprietorship, corporation, or limited liability company—is best for your business, this book has a chapter on each one. Then, a chapter titled "So What's the Best Business Form for You" discusses the options using real-life examples to help you consider all the options with more information. The chapters on when you need a lawyer and how to choose a lawyer are also very useful.

Steingold, Fred S. *Legal Guide for Starting and Running a Small Business,* 11th ed. Nolo Press, 2009. 275p. ISBN 9-78141-3-559. $39.99.

This helpful approach to the start-up process is written in a clear, practical manner that most small business owners can understand. Learn to negotiate a favorable lease, hire and fire employees, understand the tax laws, create contracts and agreements, and cope with financial problems. "Representing Yourself in Small Claims Court" is a unique and thorough chapter if that situation arises. Appendix A lists state offices that provide small business start-up help for every state.

Some of the areas that were discussed earlier include selecting a name and deciding on a legal structure for your business. Both of the above resources list ways to register your name, provide explanations of trademarks and copyright, and cover the legal implications of selecting each of the different legal structures (refer to chapter 3 for more discussion on these topics, as well as later in this chapter).

COMPLYING WITH THE LAW

Regulations vary by state and locality and depend on the type of business you start. For a local tax registration certificate or business license, check with your city or county clerk. In most states, any business that sells any type of tangible goods to the public needs a seller's permit. In some states, businesses that only sell services are exempt from obtaining a seller's permit. Even if you don't need to collect sales tax, you may need a seller's permit. Check with local authorities.

If you're starting a home-based business, don't assume that licensing and zoning laws or regulations don't apply to your small business. Check first and avoid unpleasant surprises. Be flexible, use common sense, and negotiate with neighbors or local authorities if necessary. For more information on home-based businesses, check Jim Blasingame's website, www.smallbusinessadvocate.com/.

If your business is open to the public, get information from your city's or state's economic development office on the Americans with Disabilities Act. Environmental regulations affect some businesses with rules on water and air pollution, toxic chemical disposal, and so on, so check with local officials. A gateway website that may help you is the U.S. Environmental Protection Agency, www.epa.gov/smallbusiness/. Also check on local building codes and zoning ordinances. As you can see, many agencies get involved with small businesses. Be as thorough as you can and obtain all necessary licenses, permits, and permissions. Also, keep records of who you contacted, on what date, and what you were told in case at a later date you are told something different. Regulations do change, and it's always good to document that you have tried to follow the rules.

LEGALITIES OF BUSINESS NAMES

As has been alluded to several times, naming your business may not be as simple as you might think. You want a short, easy-to-remember, somewhat descriptive, attention-getting, and appealing name. Do not be misleading in any way—this is a kiss of death to a small business. To register your business name and receive approval from the local and state government where you are located or organized, there are a few specific requirements to follow depending on the type of business structure you have chosen. You'll want to research them thoroughly.

1. *Sole proprietorships.* Usually, it is assumed that you operate under the owner's name, but if you choose a fictitious name, you must file a fictitious owner affidavit and indicate the assumed name and identify the owner. This affidavit notifies the public and the local government that you are the owner and that your company is operating under an assumed name. Contact the county recorder of deeds office to get specific information on proper filing procedures and the necessary forms. You will need a copy of this affidavit when you open your business bank account under the fictitious name. You will also want to get your business license in the fictitious name.

2. *Partnerships.* A general partnership follows the same procedure as a sole proprietorship. However, limited partnerships need to file a certificate of limited partnership (usually with the secretary of state's office), and a unique name is required. Call the secretary of state or use its website to see if your selected name has been used or reserved by someone else.

3. *Corporations.* Again, the name must be filed with the secretary of state's office and must not be used or reserved for another corporation. Be sure the name you choose does not closely resemble another name already in use, because this can cause major problems for your business in the future. Also, the name must include one of the words *corporation* (or *Corp.*), *incorporated* (or *Inc.*), *limited* (or *Ltd.*), *company* (or *Co.*), *chartered*, or some other phrase indicating the entity is truly a corporation. S corporations do not have to indicate their status as such in their names, only when filing federal and possibly state income tax returns. Usually you can reserve an available name with the secretary of state's office in your state for at least 100 days if you are not yet ready to incorporate your business but are performing the name search.

4. *Limited liability companies (LLCs).* Laws governing LLCs differ in each state. Generally, this name must also be registered with the secretary of state's office (usually when the articles of organization are registered), it must be

unique, and it must include the words *limited liability company* (or *LLC*), limited liability partnership (or *LLP*), or some phrase indicating its status.

Performing the name search for your new company will be somewhat unique in each state. However, some general resources to search can be mentioned besides your secretary of state's listings. Check with your local public or college library to see if you can access Lexis/Nexis, a legal research database. Search its corporate name database for the state where you will incorporate or form an LLC. Try using several web search engines such as Google, Yahoo!, and AltaVista to search the name and see whether it is being used elsewhere. Because you will probably want to register a domain name for your business, it's probably useful to search InterNIC.com, a large website established to provide public information regarding Internet domain names at www.internic.com. Another large public or university library resource that searches millions of business names in yellow pages across the country is *ReferenceUSA*. In this database, you can search just your state, several states, or across the nation to see if the business name you're thinking about is used in the yellow pages. One final place to check is the United States Patent and Trademark Office website at portal.uspto.gov. If you turn up a very similar or identical name, you probably want to think of something else. Remember, if your business name diminishes or disparages the reputation of a famous trademark, the owners of the famous trademark, which is probably a larger and wealthier business, may stop you from using the name, even if it's highly unlikely that your company and theirs would be confused.

Before you begin your naming process and search, a good resource to consult is the chapter "Picking a Winning Business Name" in Peri H. Pakroo's book *The Small Business Start-Up Kit*.

Pakroo, Peri. *The Small Business Start-Up Kit*, 6th ed. Nolo Press, 2010. 368p. ISBN 1-41331-099-0. $29.99.

Besides covering the basics, the chapter on financial statements is very useful. Chapters on federal, state, and local start-up requirements, on insurance and risk management, and on taxes are treasure troves of practical, useful information for every new business owner. A CD-ROM is included with the book and contains useful tax forms and a partnership agreement.

TAX BASICS

For some entrepreneurs, the laws governing taxation of business and personal income can be difficult to understand. If you have a solid recordkeeping system, a good accountant, and a basic awareness of tax law, taxes just become a part of doing business. Remember that there is no statute of limitations on business taxes. Keep all tax records as long as the business is in existence. As with bookkeeping, never abandon your responsibility even when you hire a professional to assist you in accounting and preparing your tax returns. You are ultimately responsible for your tax obligations and should have a basic knowledge of the tax system. Tax laws change constantly, so keep in touch with your accountant to learn if changes affect your business. If you are in doubt at any time, check with your local Internal Revenue Service (IRS) office for advice; it will be more than happy to tell you what you owe.

Your federal and state tax requirements include, but are not limited to, the following:

1. *Federal tax identification number.* If you are a sole proprietor with no employees, you can use your Social Security number, but it's best to get a federal tax identification number (or employer identification number, EIN) from the IRS to keep business finances separate from personal finances. You file an IRS Form SS4 obtained either from your local IRS office or online at www.irs.ustreas.gov to get your EIN. At this time, you might also request the IRS's packet of forms and publications, which contains a great deal of information about federal business taxes.

2. *State sales tax registration.* You are required to collect sales tax if your state has sales tax, and you must register with the appropriate state agency in your state, even if you are running an e-commerce business. Also obtain a resale tax certificate if you buy materials or products from wholesalers. Each state has its own filing requirements and deadlines, but usually you submit sales tax monthly.

3. *Withholding requirements.* If you have employees, you need to withhold federal and state income taxes from their wages as well as Social Security and Medicare (also known as FICA, from the Federal Insurance Contributions Act) taxes and remit these funds regularly to the IRS and appropriate state agency.

4. *Unemployment insurance tax.* Again, this tax is required for all businesses with employees and has a state and federal component. Check with your accountant.

5. *Self-employment tax.* If you operate as a sole proprietorship or partnership and earn at least $400 per year from your business, you will need to pay self-employment taxes. This tax is imposed on your net self-employment income and is reported on Schedule SE of Form 1040.

6. *Federal and state income tax.* Of course, we all know about personal income tax, but based on your legal structure, you will also be obligated to file annual federal business income tax return and possibly a state form.

   a. *Sole proprietor* files taxes as an individual, using a Schedule C or C-EZ. Here you figure net profit or loss by entering gross receipts minus returns and allowances, then subtract deductible expenses and the cost of inventory, supplies, and labor other than your own. Profit or loss is reported on your 1040.

b. *Partnership* files a Form 1065 with Schedule K-1. The K-1 divides the income (or loss) of the partnership between you and your partners. It is then included on your Form 1040.

c. *C corporation* is a separate legal entity. It files a Form 1120 Corporate Income Tax Return and pays corporate income taxes on its income. Shareholders then pay tax on their dividends, so the income is double taxed. Federal corporate tax brackets are different from individual ones and are not adjusted each year for inflation.

d. *S corporation* is a tax status similar to a partnership and is computed in a similar fashion. It reports its income on Form 1120S but does not pay tax. Shareholders must pay taxes on their share of the income.

e. *Limited liability company* combines the best of partnerships and corporations, and it can choose to be taxed as a partnership or a C corporation. As a member of an LLC, you are a partner, not an employee, and, as such, are not subject to self-employment tax.

Obviously, this has been a very brief coverage of basic taxes that small business owners are faced with when they begin their business. An excellent source for a more thorough explanation of taxes is Barbara Weltman's *J. K. Lasser's Small Business Taxes*. Weltman is an expert in taxation for small businesses and details coverage of new tax laws and IRS rules, including deductible expenses, employment taxes, and tax planning strategies.

Weltman, Barbara. *J. K. Lasser's Small Business Taxes,* Kindle ed.; rev. ed. John Wiley, 2010. 578p. ISBN 0-470-59725-9. $19.95.

Discover how to take advantage of every tax break you are entitled to by reading Weltman's complete explanation and using the tax advice and strategies she suggests. A chapter is dedicated to each deductible expense and includes dollar limits and documentation requirements. She includes sample forms and checklists to help you prepare for tax time. The guide to informational returns you may need to file is very comprehensive. Well organized and well indexed, use this book to lower your tax bill.

Since taxes may be one of the most challenging parts of starting and running a small business and you'll certainly want to try and avoid an IRS audit, consult a tax adviser or accountant early in your start-up phase. Maintain a well-annotated set of books in which you document your income, losses, gains, expenses, and other information required by your tax preparer. Remember that you can deduct many start-up costs, so keep accurate records concerning your investigation of your new business or business ideas. Keep all records that document information on your tax returns organized and in a safe place. Document all business deduction expenses by saving receipts and canceled checks.

HOW AND WHEN TO USE A LAWYER

Do you need a lawyer when you first organize your small business? Here are some considerations when you are concerned about legal issues. If your business started out with just you as sole proprietor and begins growing and expanding, and if you want or need other investors, you'll likely want to change your legal structure. Discussing the various forms in relation to your situation with a lawyer would be prudent. One way to save some money is to ask your attorney to suggest how work on a legal matter could be divided between him or her and you. Instead of the lawyer handling the legal matter from beginning to end, you would gather some information, fill out some forms, write some letters, and the lawyer would coach you, offer suggestions, and check to be sure everything is completed legally. This procedure is called unbundling, and it could save you money. When more money and risk are involved in a business transaction, it's best to get legal advice and help to make good decisions.

An annual legal audit, a time to sit down with your lawyer and review the legal side of your business, can pinpoint omissions or changes in documents brought about by new laws or regulations and changes in the business. This meeting provides an opportunity for the business owner to discuss potential problems concerning him or her. Year-end tax planning issues could also be discussed. Legal help is important before problems occur and before you sign that big contract.

FINDING AN ACCOUNTANT AND/OR A LAWYER

As discussed earlier, hiring a professional is like hiring any other employee for your business. Look for someone who has experience in organizing and representing small businesses. Find someone who is intelligent, competent, and trustworthy. Use referrals from other businesspeople, perhaps through the local chamber of commerce, insurance agent, or friends. State and national certification programs can provide a list of lawyers experienced in commercial and corporate law or tax law. For an accountant, contact the American Institute of Certified Public Accountants, 1211 Avenue of the Americas, New York, NY 10035-8775, or at www.aicpa.org. State or local certified public accountant groups or the Better Business Bureau may also provide information. Prepare a list of questions to ask as if it were an interview to see whether the lawyer or accountant fits your needs and budget. Call several lawyers and accountants, and ask the same questions about previous experience, availability, and fees. Whenever you meet with a professional, it's always good to prepare a list of questions you have regarding the current situation. It will save you time and money. Don't forget to consider your comfort level when hiring a lawyer or accountant. Does his or her personality, office location and environment, and staff make you feel at ease and that you will receive the time and attention you need? Remember that lawyers charge for their time, so you can reduce the necessary time spent on your legal matters by preparing in advance. Find a lawyer who will let you unbundle some of the legal services you need. Check out the article "Handling Legal Concerns" at http://sba.gov to help you find a lawyer.

Fees should be negotiated with accountants in advance so that there are no surprises. An accountant is instrumental in establishing good recordkeeping practices for your small business and for providing you with the information you need for taxes and many business decisions; a lawyer can help you make good management decisions before you open your business and provide important legal counsel if some unforeseen situation arises. By clearly organizing your business and the needs of your business, you will make it easier and quicker for professionals to provide the services you need.

The resources listed below will help you make business decisions that are legal and expedient. Good management skills are necessary to run a successful business, and developing better skills is a long-term task of education and practice.

REFERENCES

Starred titles are discussed in the chapter.

■ Print Resources

**American Bar Association. *Legal Guide for Small Business,* 2nd ed. Random House Reference, 2010. 496p. ISBN 0-3757-2303-2. $16.99.

This handy little guide will help small businesses understand their legal responsibilities and options. It thoroughly covers the legal aspects of topics such as employees, franchising, contracts, taxes, and start-up basics. Learn about types of business organizations/structures, business taxes, state and city taxes, and knowing your rights and responsibilities as an employer. Contract law and protecting your intellectual property rights are covered. Home-based businesses, extending credit, and getting help from a lawyer when you need it are also discussed. Exit strategies such as retirement, selling, or a death are described with the various legal ramifications. Learn how to spot problems before they become major legal issues, minimize the time and expense you spend on legal problems, and learn how to protect your business. Refer to this handbook whenever you are faced with legal decisions.

Bagley, Constance E. and Dauchy, Craig. *The Entrepreneur's Guide to Business Law,* 3rd ed. South-Western College/West, 2007. 784p. ISBN 0-32-420493-0. $73.95.

This comprehensive resource helps new entrepreneurs select and work with an attorney, determine the legal structure of their business, learn about contracts and leases as well as legal issues involved with e-commerce, identify needed insurance, and much more. Seventeen chapters cover every aspect of start-up, growth, and buying a business as well as international legal issues when appropriate.

Cagan, Michele. *Streetwise Incorporating Your Business: From Legal Issues to Tax Concerns.* Adams Media, 2007. 352p. ISBN 1-598-6909-49. $19.95.

This collection of instructional advice is user friendly. Use this work to introduce readers to ways to launch their own businesses. This resource will ensure a small company's successful launch through effective recordkeeping and explains the possible benefits of incorporation. Cagan covers many issues involved in whether an S corporation or a C corporation would be best for a particular business and which state and federal regulations will affect a corporation. Tax planning strategies and necessary accounting practices when incorporated are also presented. Learn how to avoid hidden costs that are sometimes associated with incorporating a company.

Daily, Frederick W. *Tax Savvy for Small Business,* 14th ed. Nolo Press, 2010. 380p. ISBN 1-4133-1279-9. $39.99.

Learn the ins and outs of the tax code and avoid trouble with the IRS from Daily, who translates the tax code into plain English. Discover how to write off up to $100,000 long-term assets each year, compare the tax advantages of different legal structures, pay payroll taxes on time, use retirement funds as a tax break, and negotiate payment for late taxes. Understand how your legal structure affects your tax bill. What do you do if you can't pay the taxes you owe? If you are faced with an audit, Daily will help you prepare in advance. Understand penalties, interest notices, and how to get penalties reduced. The last chapter, "Answers to 25 Frequently Asked Tax Questions," will answer many questions you have or will have in the future. A glossary, appendix, and index provide access to and more information about business tax issues. This handy reference guide will help you work with your accountant or lawyer.

Duboff, Leonard. *The Law (in Plain English) for Small Business,* rev. ed. Sphinx, 2007. 320p. ISBN 1-572-4859-X. $19.95.

Duboff covers all the areas of concern when an entrepreneur begins his or her first business venture. He explains choosing a legal structure and the steps to take to legally structure the business and how to write a business plan. Insurance options and tax deductions are discussed. Also included are legal issues involved with product liability and how to protect your trademarks and patents. Very complete and easy to understand, this title will help you navigate the complex world of laws relating to small businesses.

Elias, Stephen. *Trademark: Legal Care for Your Business and Product Name,* 9th ed. Nolo Press, 2010. 464p. ISBN 1-4133-1256-X. $39.99.

Learn the correct procedures to register your name or other mark with the U.S. Patent and Trademark Office (USPTO), and find here all necessary forms and step-by-step instructions. Discover how to protect your marks from use by others and maintain their legal strength. Changes to the USPTO's electronic trademark programs and new electronic forms for various marks are also included. Uniquely and especially important to online businesses, Elias also explains how to apply trademark law to domain names and web pages.

Encyclopedia of Small Business Legal Forms and Agreements. Atlantic, 2010. 288p. ISBN 1-60138-248-1. $29.95.

This encyclopedia and CD-ROM identify the issues and problems that you, as a small business owner or manager, may face daily. Covered are the issues of incorporation, partnerships, business plans, insurance, employment policies, employee termination, job descriptions, sales and service contracts, bills of sale, invoices, venture capital, license agreements, letters of intent, domain names, and even e-commerce contracts. Over 250 important business documents, including lists, forms, sample contracts, and human resources procedures, are included to help your business succeed. Organize your business and manage it while increasing your bottom line.

Fishman, Stephen. *Deduct It: Lower Your Small Business Taxes,* 7th ed. Nolo Press, 2010. 560p. ISBN 1-4133-1276-4. $34.99.

Help your small business make more money by paying less in taxes. Maximize all the business deductions that you and your business are entitled to legally. Fishman describes how different business structures are taxed and how tax deductions work. He explains how to keep audit-proof records and avoid most common mistakes made by entrepreneurs and small businesses. The information on deductions is organized by category and utilizes all the latest tax laws possible. Not a replacement for professional help, but it is an excellent reference guide.

Hazelgren, Brian and Covello, Josep. *The Complete Book of Business Plans: Simple Steps to Writing Powerful Business Plans,* 2nd ed. Sourcebooks, 2006. 512p. ISBN 1-4022-0763-8. $24.99.

The authors present step-by-step instructions for writing business plans as well as tips on avoiding common mistakes. They help you understand the challenges in owning and running your own business and how to plan for them. They teach readers how to read and understand financial statements and explain how they are developed. Sales taxes and payroll or self-employment taxes need to be collected, forms need to be completed and filed with the appropriate authorities, and bank deposits and paying debits must be done in a timely manner. Understand how starting a business will impact your family, your income, your personality, and generally your life.

Kamoroff, Bernard B. *422 Tax Deductions for Businesses and Self-Employed Individuals,* 9th ed. Bell Springs, 2010. 240p. ISBN 0-917-510-3-13. $18.95.

Arranged alphabetically, this book walks you through a collection of legal deductions, not tax avoidance schemes or questionable areas of law. Kamoroff uses everyday language, not accounting jargon, to discuss deductions from the cost of buying, feeding, and maintaining a watchdog and the depreciation of athletic facilities to the creation of medical savings accounts. Most will appreciate the deductions the IRS does not list on its tax forms. Inspiring quotes, cartoons, and little-known facts are interspersed throughout the book to make the subject less intimidating.

Mancuso, Anthony. *Incorporate Your Business: A Legal Guide to Forming a Corporation in Your State,* 5th ed. Nolo Press, 2009. 272p. ISBN 0-07140-983-1. $49.99.

The nuts and bolts of incorporating your business are presented in this comprehensive guidebook. Organized chronologically, chapters cover whether you should incorporate, whether you should form a C or S corporation, protecting your corporate name, preparing articles of incorporation with examples, creating corporate bylaws, and how to get money out of the corporation. The necessary forms and instructions plus rules and laws for each state are also included. An index provides more access points, and a glossary explains unfamiliar terms.

Mancuso, Anthony. *Nolo's Quick LLC: All You Need to Know about Limited Liability Companies,* 6th ed. Nolo Press, 2011. 224p. ISBN 1-41331-324-8. $29.99.

This easy reference guide describes the advantages and drawbacks of forming an LLC. The articles of organization are filed with the state and must conform to state regulations.

Mancuso thoroughly explains the operating agreement, tax options, paperwork, and how LLCs differ from corporations, partnerships, and sole proprietorships. Thorough and easy to understand, another good reference from Nolo.

**Pakroo, Peri. *The Small Business Start-Up Kit,* 6th ed. Nolo Press, 2010. 368p. ISBN 1-41331-099-0. $29.99.

Besides comprehensively covering the basics, chapter 3, "Picking Winning Business Names," is a well-written collection of information and advice on trademarks, names, and domain names. The undated chapter on financial management is also very useful and thorough, as is the chapter on choosing a legal structure. Chapters on federal, state, and local start-up requirements, on insurance and risk management, and on taxes are also treasure troves of practical, useful information for every new business owner. The updated e-business chapter covers how to use social media to promote business and search engine optimization strategies that will help readers drive traffic to their websites. A CD-ROM contains useful forms and a partnership agreement. Pakroo's outstanding book is mentioned many times throughout this book because it really provides essential advice to new entrepreneurs in many areas of starting a new business and is a worthwhile purchase.

Pinson, Linda. *Keeping the Books: Basic Recordkeeping and Accounting for the Successful Small Business,* rev ed. Kaplan Business, 2007. 224p. ISBN 1-4195-8438-1. $22.95.

Pinson, an expert on business planning and financial management, explains how to set up an effective bookkeeping system and how to keep good records. She walks readers through preparing projected and historical financial statements to show where your business is headed. Use her system to maintain required records and prevent tax disasters. Prepare and analyze financial statements to stay in touch with the heartbeat of your business. Numerous samples and worksheets are included. Good records will enable you to examine trends, make decisions, and implement changes to help your business prosper and grow.

Rosenberg, Eva. *Small Business Taxes Made Easy,* 2nd ed. McGraw-Hill, 2010. 304p. ISBN 0-07-174327-8. $19.

This guide will help you understand the taxes your small business must pay. Rosenberg walks you through the process and shows you how to reduce the amount of taxes you pay each year. Find out the tax benefits of various forms of financing your business. Her analysis of the home-office deduction enables taxpayers to take full advantage of this tax break with a clear conscience. Learn about the tax benefits of various forms of financing and how to spot errors in 1099s. The chapter titled "Special Considerations for Online Businesses" covers Internet sales tax issues, sales tax case law, and legal issues on the Internet. What special tax breaks do independent truckers have? What are mixed-use assets, and are they deductible? Learn how to keep good records and how long you should keep them on file. Chapters conclude with a list of web resources for more information on the topic covered in the chapter. Comprehensive information on tax notices, audits, and collection notes is also provided. Useful checklists, forms, and to-do lists can be accessed through the book's companion website to efficiently help you organize your many responsibilities as a small business owner.

Sitarz, Daniel. *S-Corporation: Small Business Start-up Kit*, 4th ed. Nova, 2010. 304p. ISBN 1-892949-53-0. $19.99.

Sitarz provides everything necessary to set up a new S corporation with clear instructions, business plans, marketing worksheets, financial planning tools, federal tax forms, and payroll guidelines. The updated fourth edition also includes state-specific incorporation forms on the enclosed CD. Well written and organized, Sitarz's work will help many entrepreneurs make the decision about how to incorporate.

Sitarz, Daniel. *Small Business Legal Forms Simplified*, 5th ed. Nova, 2011. 304p. ISBN 0-892949-6-28. $29.95 (with CD-ROM).

This comprehensive resource not only provides the forms to handle a multitude of legal situations but straightforward instructions explain what forms are necessary, how to prepare them, and the legal effect of each form. The CD-ROM contains the forms with Adobe Acrobat Reader software. Over 130 forms, including contracts, deeds, collection documents, leases, receipts, employment forms, and releases, are provided. Most of the forms are valid in all 50 states and the District of Columbia.

**Steingold, Fred S. *Legal Guide for Starting and Running a Small Business*, 11th ed. Nolo Press, 2009. 275p. ISBN 9-78141-3-559. $39.99.

This helpful approach to the start-up process is written in a clear, practical manner that most small business owners can understand. Learn to negotiate a favorable lease, hire and fire employees, understand the tax laws, insure your business, create contracts and agreements, and cope with financial problems. Understand how your business's legal structure can help you and your business. Find answers to questions about naming your business and naming your products. Let Steingold walk you through the process of buying a business or a franchise. Discover how to save money on insurance. Find out how to extend credit and solve collection problems. "Representing Yourself in Small Claims Court" is a unique and thorough chapter if that situation arises. Appendix A lists state offices that provide small business start-up help for every state. Steingold wants to put the power of the law in your hands.

Stephenson, James and Mintzer, Rich. *Ultimate Homebased Business Handbook*, 2nd ed. Entrepreneur Press, 2008. 404p. ISBN 1-599-18185-1. $29.95.

This handy guide will help you start your own venture in your kitchen or spare room. Every stage of business creation is covered, but the chapter on setting up your business legally is especially noteworthy. Also learn how to create an effective online presence. Stephenson and Mintzer provide how-to tips, ideas, and tools to organize and develop a winning business strategy. Operations, collections, taxes, licenses, and increasing sales are presented thoroughly and in layperson's language. And, if you haven't determined what kind of business to start, good ideas are available here. This useful book will help many new entrepreneurs.

Stern, W. Rod and Brittain, Carol A. *Tax Planning for Business*. Entrepreneur Press, 2007. 304p. ISBN 1-599-18137-1. $32.95.

All the common tasks and decisions in setting up a small business can impact the tax burden for your business. Decisions on legal structure, hiring employees and independent contractors, and leasing and buying equipment will affect your taxes this year and for years to come. The accompanying CD has IRS forms and sample documents such as a fringe benefits chart, a recordkeeping checklist, and other miscellaneous recordkeeping forms. Current and cost-effective legal and tax advice can help you resolve business and legal issues you face daily.

Strauss, Steven D. *The Small Business Bible,* 2nd ed. John Wiley, 2008. ISBN 0-470-26124-2. $19.95.

Strauss's massively expanded and updated edition teaches an entrepreneur what steps to take to start, run, and grow a successful business. Included here are proven strategies, tips, tools, and forms to fill out. The first chapters concentrate on how to choose and do what you love, and new chapters cover green businesses, online advertising and marketing, mobile technology, and many aspects of e-commerce. Understand how to organize your records to pay taxes and complete all your legal obligations. Thorough coverage of this complex challenge is presented clearly.

Thaler, John. *The Elements of Small Business: A Lay Person's Guide to the Financial Terms, Marketing Concepts, and Legal Forms That Every Entrepreneur Needs.* Silver Lake, 2005. 354p. ISBN 1-56343-784-4. $24.95.

Specializing in small business law, this lawyer and small business owner presents tools, tips, and advice to help you get your business off to a smooth and legal start. Chapters are thorough and cover topics such as business formation, franchises, business plans, insurance, computers and e-commerce, and marriage and divorce. Each chapter concludes with a list of resources. Over 20 appendices provide forms and sample reports, such as registration for a fictitious business name, operating agreement for an LLC, financial statements, and so on. This well-written book will help many entrepreneurs.

**Weltman, Barbara. *J. K. Lasser's Small Business Taxes,* Kindle ed.; rev. ed. John Wiley, 2010. 578p. ISBN 0-470-59725-9. $19.95.

Discover how to take advantage of every tax break you are entitled to by reading Weltman's complete explanation and using the tax advice and strategies she suggests. A chapter is dedicated to each deductible expense and includes dollar limits and documentation requirements. She includes sample forms and checklists to help you prepare for tax time. The guide to informational returns you may need to file is very comprehensive. Also included is information on reporting farm expenses and losses, home office deductions, deductions for insurance premiums, and capital gains and losses. Find out the tax advantages to C and S corporations and more. Use this well-organized and well-indexed book to lower your tax bill.

Willams, Beth and Murray, Jean. *The Complete Guide to Working for Yourself: Everything the Self-Employed Need to Know about Taxes, Recordkeeping, and Other Laws.* Atlantic, 2008. 288p. ISBN 1-601-38048-8. $29.95 (with CD-ROM).

Starting your own business is a genuine and attainable goal. Williams and Murray will help you make the right decisions and prevent you from making the wrong ones. If you truthfully answer a few questions, you can forecast your own success. Other areas covered include legal concerns, tax implications, liability, naming your business, marketing, location, and human resources issues. The authors cover the basic and the more advances challenges to starting your own business. They cover self-employment taxes, employer identification numbers, and dealing with independent contractors. Find ready-to-use forms, ideas on cutting costs, and a sample business plan here.

■ Online Resources

About.com Small Business Information: http://sbinformation.about.com/ (Accessed Spring 2011).

This large website provides articles and resources on business legal structures, business plans, naming your business, e-commerce, and more. Taxes are covered, and ideas for recordkeeping are included. Legal issues affecting small businesses are discussed in several sections. A section on financial planning tips for business owners discusses deferring your taxes and other financial considerations. Articles on creating a business name and filing your trade name are especially noteworthy. Refer to this site often for new ideas on managing employees and other financial considerations.

AllBusiness: www.allbusiness.com (Accessed Spring 2011).

This huge site contains articles and advice on any area of business law, including legal structure, property leases, patents, trademarks, employment law, taxes, and even how to work with your lawyer. Links to many directories and to news and business information sites are provided. Forms and agreements are covered in detail. The checklists—including a contract checklist, issuing stock checklist, and more—are very thorough. The tax articles discuss topics such as barter tax and accounting issues and tax strategies for keeping the family business in the family. Use this well-organized, functional website often.

**American Institute of Certified Public Accountants: www.aicpa.org (Accessed Spring 2011).

This site is geared toward certified public accountants (CPAs) but does provide some information on accreditation and finding a good CPA for your business. Business valuation and auditing are also covered. The FAQ section provides information on local chapters, charges for the services of a CPA, and more.

BFI Business Filings Inc.: www.bizfilings.com (Accessed Spring 2011).

This large site provides detailed information on incorporating, listing advantages and disadvantages, forms needed, advice on where to incorporate, and publication requirements. LLCs are also discussed in detail. Learn why many corporations file their incorporation papers in Delaware and each state's requirements for incorporating. The "Starting Your Business" section covers many subjects related to start-up, taxes, and legal issues. Helpful business tools throughout the site provide sample forms and agreements. Learn how to select an accountant and an attorney.

Business Owner's Toolkit: http://toolkit.com (Accessed Spring 2011).

Commerce Clearinghouse, now a Wolters Kluwer business, started the *Small Business Guide,* which provides information and tools to help individuals start, run, and grow a successful small business. Business tools provided include sample letters, contracts, forms, and agreements ready for you to customize for your business. Financial spreadsheet templates are available as well as checklists to help you stay organized in completing necessary tasks. IRS tax forms, state tax forms, employee management forms, and more are all linked to this site. Also find articles on how tax law changes could affect your business.

Entrepreneurs' Help Page: www.tannedfeet.com (Accessed Spring 2011).

Find here help with business plans, financial statements, legal structure and legal forms, marketing and public relations, human resources, and strategy. Entrepreneurs Help Page does not claim to substitute for professional advice and judgment but provides information to entrepreneurs to get them started in the right direction. "Legal" and "Legal Forms" are buttons at the top of the home page that lead you to information on LLCs, incorporating, and partnerships as well as sole proprietorships. Articles are usually short and up to date and ask questions to help the new business person start thinking about what is needed and what questions will be asked of him or her.

Entrepreneur's Resource Center: www.edwardlowe.org/ERC/ (Accessed Spring 2011).

This nonprofit organization promotes entrepreneurship by providing information, research, and education. Use this site to find practical articles on marketing, acquiring and managing finances, human resources management, and legal issues and taxes. Under "Legal Issues and Taxes," you will find articles on sexual harassment, intellectual property, discrimination, and more. Networking possibilities include conferences and educational seminars listed here. Now aimed at entrepreneurs, the Edward Lowe Foundation, which sponsors this site, provides good basic help too.

Financial Calculators for Business: www.dinkytown.net/business.html (Accessed Spring 2011).

This lengthy list of calculators will help you with break-even analysis, cash flow, inventory, taxes, business valuation, ratios, and more. Use this site to help you with payroll deductions, self-employment taxes, and more.

FindLaw's Small Business Center: http://smallbusiness.findlaw.com (Accessed Spring 2011).

Chock-full of articles and guides on all aspects of business development, the "Employment & HR" section is particularly outstanding. However, legal information on business structure, finance, and intellectual property is also covered thoroughly. The article entitled "Ten Things to Think About—Picking a Business Form" is very thought-provoking. Information on a wide variety of small business legal issues is covered, including forms and contracts and starting a business. The "LLC Formation Packages and Forms" section is very practical. The tax issues area offers help in preparing for an audit. A directory of lawyers by zip code is also available. Links to relevant regulatory agencies are also provided.

**Internal Revenue Service: www.irs.ustreas.gov (Accessed Spring 2011).

Find here a detailed description of independent contractors and how they differ from employees of a business. Employer identification numbers and their importance are fully explained. Also find information on self-employment and employment taxes. Publication 583, "Starting a Business and Keeping Records," is available on this site and will help you get started right. Other publications online include *Business Use of Your Home.* A great deal of information on small business taxes of all kinds can be found here. Also available through a link is the IRS's site for Small Business/Self-Employed Tax Center at www.irs.gov/businesses/small/index.html. This site provides information on and links to many issues such as employment taxes, paperwork reduction for employers, changes to IRS Schedule C-EZ, small business forms and publications, and more.

**InterNIC.com: www.internic.com (Accessed Spring 2011).

This website was established to provide public information in regard to Internet domain name registration services and is updated frequently. A directory lists ICANN-accredited

(Internet Corporation for Assigned Names and Numbers) registrars; for more information on ICANN, go to its website at www.icann.org. InterNIC's FAQs will answer many of your questions about registering a domain name and the competitive registration environment.

Nolo Press: www.nolo.com (Accessed Spring 2011).

This commercial site contains a good collection of free articles written by lawyers generally. Three particularly good sections are "Choosing a Business Name," "Doing Business Online," and "Business Taxes." Nolo's legal self-help books, now often accompanied by CD-ROMs, are outstanding, and you will find useful information and advice on the site as well as invitations to buy its products.

SmallBusinessTV.com: http://sbtv.com (Accessed Spring 2011).

This web-based network provides information and advice of interest to entrepreneurs and small business owners and managers. Various channels such as "Money," "Marketing," "Law for Business," "Real Business," "Women," and "Technology" contain a list of short videos where experts present practical advice. Sign up for the newsletter to keep current on what's happening.

**Small Business Administration: www.sba.gov (Accessed Spring 2011).

This official government site offers a wealth of resources and programs for starting and growing a small business. Major articles cover business plans, financing, managing, marketing, employees, taxes, legal aspects, and business opportunities. Also find workplace issue information on interviewing, working environments, training, hiring procedures, and employing minors. Green businesses and energy efficiency information for businesses is also readily available. The site map acts like a table of contents and takes you right to the information you need. Some contents are available in Spanish.

Small Business Advisor: www.isquare.com (Accessed Spring 2011).

This large site has lots of articles and advice for entrepreneurs just getting started in business. The "Small Biz FAQs" answer many basic questions, such as should I incorporate in Delaware, and why do so many businesses do; do I need a federal ID number; and do I need a business license. "Tax Advice" and "Checklists for Success" are other major sections. Find articles on pricing your product or service, steps to improve sales, and how to build customer loyalty. Sections on books, business services, and a glossary add value. The U.S. government and state information are also very helpful. Use this site to help you get started right.

**Small Business Advocate: www.smallbusinessadvocate.com/ (Accessed Spring 2011).

This website is part of Jim Blasingame's large website. Here you will find articles on starting a home-based business, what's hot in home-based businesses, zoning information, insurance, and more. Articles are grouped into categories such as "Startup," "Marketing," "Online Strategies," and "More Hot Topics." Learn about managing and growing your small or home-based business here.

Small Business and Entrepreneurship: http://libguides.unm.edu/small_business (Accessed Spring 2011).

This web page was created and is maintained by me. Some of the resources, especially under the "I need to find . . ." tab, are specific to the University of New Mexico. However, under the tab "Selected Internet Resources," you will find links to many free small business gateways and legal and government sites. Use my guide as a gateway to many of the websites listed in this resource, such as Business Owners Idea Café, Entrepreneur.com, and MoreBusiness. My colleagues and I also publish other research guides on business topics like marketing and advertising, company and industry, and business basics. Use all these guides to help you find more information to start and run your new business.

SmartMoney Small Business: www.smsmallbiz.com/ (Accessed Spring 2011).

This large site covers small business by focusing on the entrepreneur as a quick-thinking risk taker who can turn a passion for a product or a service into a thriving business. Regular columns focus on why and how you should run your own show. Sections include "Work & Life," which advises entrepreneurs on tricky issues such as taking vacations, dealing with illness, and creating family time, and "Starting Up," which helps entrepreneurs through the early stages of launching a business with case studies and articles. Other sections thoroughly cover marketing, technology, taxes, best practices, and more. The taxes section covers many aspects of taxes, including employee, self-employment, incentives, and more. Each month, streaming video reports from SmartMoney TV focus on a special topic of interest to business owners, whether that's raising capital or dealing with disaster. Special attention is provided for women and minorities, who make up the fastest-growing subset of entrepreneurs.

**United States Environmental Protection Agency (EPA): www.epa.gov/smallbusiness (Accessed Spring 2011).

The Small Business Gateway does more than inform small businesses about environmental information and assistance. The section entitled "The Bottom Line: Saving and Finding Money" provides information on grant writing, environmental accounting, doing business with the EPA, and more. The "Small Business Ombudsman" provides documents on EPA small business initiatives, a source book on environmental auditing, and a directory of small business environmental assistance providers.

**United States Patent and Trademark Office: http://portal.uspto.gov (Accessed Spring 2011).

If you need or think you need to obtain a patent or trademark for your business, this site can help you. An online guide for trademark guidance as well as searchable databases for patents and trademarks are available here. FAQs as well as a tutorial, "How to Use USPTO.gov," are easy to find. You can apply for patents and trademarks online, too, but seeing an attorney first is probably advisable.

WORKING WITH THE GOVERNMENT

12

Qualifying to sell to the federal government can be complicated and time-consuming given the amount of paperwork and large number of potential agencies to approach. Any contracts falling between $3,000 and $150,000 are reserved for small, small disadvantaged, small women-owned, and small veteran-owned businesses. Thus, the Small Business Act established for federal executive agencies an annual goal of awarding 23% of prime contract dollars to small businesses. In fiscal year 2009, small firms won a record $96.8 billion in federal prime contracts, representing almost 22% of all federal spending. In fiscal year 2006, small businesses won $77 billion in direct prime contracts, $65 billion in subcontracts, and over $142 billion in total federal contracts.

In reality, the same basic business principles and strategies apply in selling your products or services to commercial customers and selling them to government entities. You need to know your customers' needs and wants, how they buy, and who buys what. It's market research, but for a different market. So, how do you begin? Research what types of goods and services are purchased by the hundreds of federal agencies at www.usaspending.gov. Initially you might select one or two agencies and study their operations and needs. Also remember to check FedBizOpps (www.fbo.gov) to learn about buying opportunities at targeted federal agencies; all planned purchases of more than $25,000 must be listed at this site.

SMALL BUSINESS ADMINISTRATION

The simplest place to start is at the Small Business Administration's (SBA's) website, at the "Government Contracting" area: www.sba.gov/category/navigation-structure/contracting. The "Getting Started" section will answer many of your initial questions. Am I a small business? How do I identify my industry code? How can I get a DUNS number? DUNS stands for data universal numbering system and is used to identify contractors and their locations for all procurement-related activities. Assigned and maintained solely by Dun and Bradstreet, this unique nine-digit identification code has been assigned to over 84 million businesses worldwide. A small business can also obtain a DUNS number from Dun and Bradstreet at no cost by calling 866-705-5711 or more quickly on the web at http://fedgov.dnb.com/webform. This number is also used to register with the Central Contractor Register and the Electronic Commerce/Electronic Data interchange system called FACNET. FACNET, the Federal Acquisition Computer Network, enables the entire procurement process, from solicitation through award and payment, to be done electronically.

If this all sounds complicated, just step back and understand that if you're dealing with 8 million contracts, there will be some complications; but you can move through them one at a time. Use the SBA.gov site to find a wide variety of other links under "Contract Opportunities," such as green contracting and federal business opportunities. The SBA has also created SUBNet: www.sba.gov/subnet, a tool to help small firms search for and find subcontracting opportunities from prime contractors.

Under "Working with the Government," you will find "Small Business Certifications and Audiences," "Small Business Innovation Research," "Contracting Support," and the "Contracting Rulebook." Investigate the SBA's certification programs developed to assist specific groups in securing federal contracts: the Historically Underutilized Business Zone Program, known as HUBZones; the 8(a) Business Development Program; and the Small Disadvantaged Business Certification Program.

The *CCR Handbook,* in both PDF and HTML formats, is available through a link from this site. Under the "Government Contracting" section again, you will find articles on "How the Government Buys" and "Preparing Bids and Proposals" plus "Government Contracting FAQs." Learn to use the SBA.gov site to help you in your bids to sell to the government.

FEDBIZOPPS.GOV

Under "Federal Acquisition and Procurement Opportunities" is a link to FedBizOpps.gov (FBO), which is the single most important point of entry for federal government procurement opportunities over $25,000. Vendors use FBO to search, monitor, and retrieve opportunities to sell to the federal government, and agency

Figure 12.1 Screenshot of Small Business Administration (www.sba.gov/category/navigation-structure/contracting)

procurement officers use it to identify potential contractors for open bids and to publicize their business opportunities to private companies. The FBO portal site has a great list of FAQs to help businesses new to working with the federal government. Various questions are answered, including how to reach the FBO help desk, what are procurement classification codes, what is a special notice, and how do I get on the General Services Administration (GSA) schedule.

To further facilitate your entry into the world of selling to the federal government, seek out a Small Business Development Center (SBDC) at the website www.asbdc-us.org/. The SBDC can help facilitate this process by showing you how to contact agencies, get on bid lists, understand solicitations, and explain other parts of the process that you do not understand. Using the FBO or the SBDC is the best way to get involved in doing business with the government, so be sure to understand the processes and procedures.

CENTRAL CONTRACTOR REGISTRATION

Another entry point for selling to the federal government can be gained when you register with the Central Contractor Registration (CCR) website at www.ccr.gov. This site provides information to small businesses and vendors as well as federal agency buyers. The CCR is an online government-maintained database of companies wanting to do business with the federal government, and agencies search the database to find prospective vendors. Create a profile in the CCR and keep it current to ensure your company has access to federal contract opportunities. Enter your profile information also on the "Dynamic Small Business Search" (DSBS) page to help government agencies find you. Some state and local governments also use this database to find vendors. Several government programs use CCR data, so you are adding more agencies and programs to the customer base for your business. The CCR registration form contains both mandatory and optional fields, but fill in as much information as possible so more government buying offices will identify your business as one that can provide the products and services they need. Analyze the profiles of firms in your area of expertise, and use them as a guide to develop your profile because they will likely be your competitors.

Be sure to have your DUNS number, Standard Industrial Classification, and North American Industry Classification System codes, information about electronic funds transfer, and point of contact information ready to fill in the form completely.

When you meet with federal contracting officers and other buyers, ask them for an appraisal of your CCR/DSBS profile.

A great print resource on selling and working with the federal government is Scott Stanberry's *Federal Contracting Made Easy,* where you will learn about the CCR process, invitation for bids (IFBs), request for proposals (RFPs), and more.

Stanberry, Scott A. *Federal Contracting Made Easy,* 3rd ed. Management Concepts, 2008. 376p. ISBN 1-56726-231-7. $35.

This practical guide explains the process of selling to the government in easy-to-understand language that is simple to follow. Learn how to identify new contracting opportunities, find the 2,500 buying offices in the nation, enhance your efficiency in preparing bids and RFPs, and improve your profitability by doing business with the government. Stanberry includes sample government forms, rate calculations, sample cost formulas, and bid formulas. Also described is the SBA's subcontracting program that pairs small businesses with prime contractors. Proven marketing strategies used to obtain government business are outlined in a lengthy chapter. This book is a good investment if you're new to trying to sell to the government.

NETWORKING

Besides using the web, you can take other steps to make contact with purchasing representatives:

1. Attend procurement conferences, trade shows, and workshops.

2. Set up appointments to meet with purchasing agents in your area.

3. Advertise in trade journals read by purchasing agents.

4. Find a procurement officer trade association and join or attend industry expos and professional meetings.

5. Seek out a mentor, someone who has successfully worked with the federal government as a supplier or contractor.

Personal contacts and networking are always important methods for gaining access to the right people and good information.

REQUEST FOR PROPOSALS OR NEGOTIATED PROCUREMENT

When a government entity identifies a product or service it needs, it often issues an RFP or request for proposal, sometimes now referred to as negotiated procurement. RFPs are issued to companies on the agency's bid list and advertised in the FBO. Remember, the FBO website is the public notification media that U.S. government agencies now use to identify proposed contract actions and contract awards. To learn more about agency requirements, you can also request a copy of the entire RFP. All RFPs have a due date, and be absolutely sure to submit all necessary materials by the deadline. If you decide not to bid on an RFP, send a "no bid" letter as a courtesy to the contracting officer before the deadline stating that you will not be submitting a proposal. If you don't withdraw your bid, your company will be deleted from the bid list. On the other hand, you, the bidder, can withdraw a proposal at any time before an award is made.

The sealed bid process requires that invitation for bids be issued by the purchasing officer or office. "IFBs usually include a copy of the specifications for the particular proposed purchase, instructions for preparation of bids, and the conditions of purchase, deliver, and payment schedule. The IFB indicates the date and time of bid opening. Each sealed bid is opened in public at the purchasing office at the time designated in the invitation. Facts about each bid are read aloud and recorded" (www.rfpbids.com/RFP). The lowest bidder, whose bid meets with all the IFB's requirements and is most advantageous to the government, is then awarded.

WRITING BIDS AND PROPOSALS

Generally there are two types of offers: bids and proposals. Bids are part of the sealed bidding purchases process, while proposals involve awards to be made following negotiation.

Some general guidelines for writing bids or proposals are listed below:

1. Before preparing a bid offer, closely study the specifications to understand the requirements, and pay special attention to the instructions to offerors

and to conditions of purchase, delivery, and payment. Read the complete RFP several times to fully understand what is required.

2. For bids, be careful to include all costs of material, labor, overhead, packaging, and transportation. Always follow the requirements of the bid solicitation or the RFP instructions as closely as possible. If you don't understand some of the information in the RFP, submit written questions to the contracting officer.

3. Be sure to professionally package your RFP or bid using a quality cover and good paper. You want your business and your bid or proposal to exceed expectations.

4. Always, always mail your offer in sufficient time to reach the purchasing office before the closing date, with all materials properly tagged and marked. Also mail any samples well in advance of the opening date. Bids or proposals received even one minute after the deadline are considered nonresponsive. On the other hand, if you want to change or withdraw a sealed bid, send a letter or telegram to that effect to the purchasing office; it must reach the office prior to the time set for opening the bids.

The RFP or negotiated procurement proposal process is a bit more flexible than the sealed bid process, because there is greater opportunity to seek modification of specifications, conditions of purchase, or delivery and payment. If the contracting officer will negotiate on a firm's proposal, he or she will require a complete cost analysis, so be prepared to support your quotation with facts and figures.

If the above information has aroused your curiosity and you want to know more about RFP writing, try Deborah Kluge's website at www.proposalwriter.com. She gives visitors many pointers on writing proposals with tips and a checklist of things to do and include and other hints on how to do business with the government. Or, depending on how large and important to your business the RFP is, you could also hire her to write the RFP. If you're interested in a good book on writing proposals, want to learn how to do it yourself, or want to make sure whoever prepares it does a good job, see the citation below:

Porter-Roth, Bud and Young, Ralph. *Request for Proposal: A Guide to Effective RFP Development.* Addison-Wesley Professional, 2001. 288p. ISBN 0-201-7757-5-1. $39.99.

Offering several templates that you can adapt for your own organization's RFP efforts, the authors provide pointers and advice to help you avoid common pitfalls and explain RFP best practices. Learn how to plan and organize each and every section of an RFP and develop, write, and review all the requirements. Walk through the entire life cycle of the RFP process. A variety of checklists and illustrations reinforce concepts and advice. Vendors who understand a buyer's requirements will win awards from their well-constructed RFPs.

More resources at the end of this chapter can help you in your attempts to market and sell to the federal government.

STATE GOVERNMENTS

All the federal rules and regulations may seem a bit overwhelming to you as a new business owner. Why not start with selling to your own state government? To find a directory of purchasing or procurement officers for your state, start at the website of the National Association of State Procurement Officials at www.naspo.org. Listed alphabetically, each state provides the name of someone to contact and a link to the state's website for purchasing or procurement.

Many of the resources listed below will help you get started in selling to federal, state, or local governments. Face-to-face meetings and contacts are often the best way to find out what services or products you can sell.

REFERENCES

Starred titles are discussed in the chapter.

■ Print Resources

DiGiacomo, John. *Win Government Contracts for Your Small Business,* 5th ed. Toolkit Media Group, 2010. 480p. ISBN 0-808-02281-7. $24.95.

DiGiacomo, director of the Procurement Technical Assistance Center at Rock Valley College, provides the techniques necessary to discover, negotiate, and win government contracts. He lists 10 easy steps for entering a small business into the federal government system, receiving bids for lucrative federal contracts, and competing successfully for government contracts in general. Learn how to write and submit a proposal.

Hamper, Robert and Baugh, L. *Handbook for Writing Proposals,* 2nd ed. McGraw-Hill, 2010. 256p. ISBN 0-071-4648-9. $19.95.

The authors walk you through the entire proposal-writing process from initial contact through completion and follow-up. Learn how to set up a proposal team, evaluate potential projects, identify tasks for team members, and deliver a show-stopping proposal or client presentation. Their nine-step proposal-writing process is unique. The case study presented is helpful and practical. Chapters contain checklists, samples, and summaries to keep you on track and on budget. Downloadable forms are also provided. Use this book to help you write all types of proposals.

Parvey, Malcolm and Alston, Deborah. *Winning Government Contracts: How Your Small Business Can Find and Secure Federal Government Contracts Up to $100,000.* Career Press, 2008. 236p. ISBN 1-564-14975-7. $19.95.

The authors use easy-to-understand, clear language to take you through the registration and bidding process. Learn how to download drawings and specifications, understand shipping and packaging requirements, and how much the government is currently paying for an item before you submit your bid. Learn how to find the results of the bidding process as well as the names and prices of all the other bidders.

**Porter-Roth, Bud and Young, Ralph. *Request for Proposal: A Guide to Effective RFP Development*. Addison-Wesley Professional, 2001. 288p. ISBN 0-201-7757-5-1. $39.99.

This classis offers several templates that you can adapt for your own organization's RFP efforts, and the authors provide pointers and advice to help you avoid common pitfalls and explain RFP best practices. Learn how to plan and organize each and every section of an RFP and develop, write, and review all the requirements. Walk through the entire life cycle of the RFP process. A variety of checklists and illustrations reinforce concepts and advice. Vendors who understand a buyer's requirements will win awards from their well-constructed RFPs.

Sant, Tom. *Persuasive Business Proposals: Writing to Win More Customers, Clients, and Contracts*, 2nd ed. AMACOM, 2004. 248p. ISBN 0-81447-153-6. $17.95.

Sant scrutinizes the entire proposal development process and brings possible pitfalls to the reader's attention. He presents tips, tricks, and techniques to improve anyone's business proposal writing expertise and art of persuasion. Learn to organize your thoughts and your proposals. Real-life examples are a bonus. He reminds writers to keep the focus on what the customer needs. The chapter on word choice will particularly delight wordsmiths and help those who are constantly searching for a better word. This unique and useful book on business writing will help everyone write more effectively.

**Stanberry, Scott A. *Federal Contracting Made Easy*, 3rd ed. Management Concepts, 2008. 376p. ISBN 1-56726-231-7. $35.

This practical, easy-to-follow guide explains the process of selling to the government in easy-to-understand language. Learn how to identify new contracting opportunities, find the 2,500 buying offices in the nation, enhance your efficiency in preparing bids and RFPs, and improve your profitability by doing business with the government. Stanberry includes sample government forms, rate calculations, sample cost formulas, and bid formulas. Also described is the SBA's subcontracting program that pairs small businesses with prime contractors. Websites are provided to help you learn more about selling to a particular agency or area of the government. Proven marketing strategies used to obtain government business are also included. This book is a good investment if you're trying to sell to the government.

U.S. Government, GSA, and Small Business Administration (SBA). *2011 Essential Guide to Federal Business Opportunities—Comprehensive, Practical Coverage—Bidding, Procurement, GSA Schedules, Vendors Guide, SBA Assistance, Defining the Market*, Kindle ed. Progressive Management, 2010. 133KB. $9.99.

This valuable e-book provides an up-to-date digest of federal publications on selling products and services to the federal government. The introduction for this guide describes how the government buys products and services, plus data on regulations, policies, and best practices. A discussion of small business size standards and regulations governing this topic is included, as well as a step-by-step process on how to register your small business for various contracting programs. Also included is a review of small business certification programs. Learn how government contracting officials use procedures that conform to the

Federal Acquisition Regulation (FAR) to make purchases. Understanding the responsibilities of contractors and recognizing subcontracting and procurement opportunities are the first steps to navigating this complex world of contracting. The FAR System consists of the Federal Acquisition Regulation (FAR), which is the primary document, and agency acquisition regulations that implement or supplement the FAR. The contents of this digest includes for example: "How to Get on GSA Schedules; How to Register Your Business; Defining the Market; Contract Negotiation; and Central Contractor Registration (CCR) Specifications."

Online Resources

American FactFinder: http://factfinder2.census.gov/home/ (Accessed Spring 2011).

This federal government source for information on population, housing, economic, and geographic data is easy to use and well designed. You can get a fact sheet for your community by just entering town, county, or zip code. A quick link gets you to the Decennial Census of Housing and Population, American Community Survey, the Economic Census, or the Population Estimates program. A couple of clicks under the "Subjects A to Z" will get you to *County Business Patterns,* information on NAICS codes, statistics about small business from the Census Bureau, the characteristics of business owners' database, and more. A glossary, FAQs, and a search feature will help you use this great, free resource.

Business Owner's Toolkit: http://toolkit.com (Accessed Spring 2011).

The section of this large site under "Small Business Guide" entitled "Win Government Contracts" tells small businesses what the government needs, defines the rules, and presents case studies of small businesses that have been successful in their efforts to sell to the federal government. One company began supplying fasteners to the military 16 years ago, and another precision machine shop makes tools for the aerospace and pharmaceutical industries. An artist in Oregon was awarded an indefinite federal contract for wildlife artist services, paintings portraying a variety of subjects. An array of government contracting forms, such as a sample request for quotation and the central contractor registration form, are also available here under "Business Tools." If you think the government doesn't need or want your products or services, you might want to think again.

**Central Contractor Registration (CCR): www.ccr.gov (Accessed Spring 2011).

This website provides another entry point for selling to the federal government. This site provides information to small businesses and vendors and federal agency buyers. Several government programs use CCR data, so you are adding more agencies and programs to the customer base for your business. The CCR registration form contains both mandatory and optional fields, but fill in as much information as possible so more government buying offices will identify your business as one that can provide the products and services they need. Be sure to have your DUNS number, SIC and NAICS codes, information about electronic funds transfer, and point of contact information ready to fill in the form completely.

**FedBizOpps.gov (FBO): http://fedbizopps.gov (Accessed Spring 2011).

FedBizOpps.gov is the single most important point of entry for federal government procurement opportunities over $25,000. Vendors use FBO to search, monitor, and retrieve opportunities to sell to the federal government, and agency procurement officers use it to identify potential contractors for open bids and to publicize their business opportunities to private companies. The FBO portal site has a great list of FAQs to help businesses new to working with the federal government. Questions answered include how to reach the FBO help desk, what are procurement classification codes, what is a special notice, and how do I get on the General Services Administration (GSA) schedule.

GovPro.com: www.govpro.com (Accessed Spring 2011).

This website provides news, articles, and other information about state and local government procurement. Designed to meet the needs of government professionals and featuring information from the publication *Government Product News,* vendors will find information on what is being sold to the government. An article archive and a list of events are available in the "GovPro Procurement Topics and Resources" area. Products for the office, technology, green solutions, parks and recreation, and facilities are showcased. The *GPN Government Product Guide,* available in print and online, is a directory of products and services purchased by local, state, and federal government officials. Sign up to receive free e-newsletters, too.

Michigan Electronic Library (MEL): http://mel.org (Accessed Spring 2011).

This huge small business portal from the Michigan Department of Education has links to dozens of sites. Under "Business and Jobs," and then the "Business" section, you will find links under topics such as "Entrepreneurs," "Finance and Venture Capital," "Import/Export," and "Small and NonProfit." Related topics include "Associations," "Doing Business with Federal Government," and "Planning and Business Models."

National Association of Small Business Contractors: www.nasbc.org (Accessed Spring 2011).

This trade association supports the interests of small business suppliers who provide goods and services to governments, prime contractors, and corporate buyers. It also houses the National Small Business Supplier Registry. Membership is not required to register. Besides the registry, find here news on government procurement, a knowledge center, "Government Ready," which provides training and certification sessions and more.

**National Association of State Procurement Officials: www.naspo.org (Accessed Spring 2011).

This nonprofit association strengthens the procurement community through education, research, and communication. This group wants to improve the quality of purchasing and procurement, provide leadership in professional public purchasing, and exchange information and cooperate to attain greater efficiency and economy for state governments. A directory provides links to state procurement or purchasing offices and the names of procurement officers in each state. Many states have publications or websites to help businesses sell to them.

**Proposal Writer: www.proposalwriter.com (Accessed Spring 2011).

Deborah Kluge has prepared and maintains an outstanding website designed to help visitors write proposals for U.S. and international government contracting. She provides RFP tips, the proposal outline, and a proposal preparation checklist. She includes long lists of links to different government agencies, sources of government loans and grants, international development and grants, and more.

**Small Business Administration: www.sba.gov/category/navigation-structure/contracting/working-with-government (Accessed Spring 2011).

The SBA provides articles and information under the heading of "Contracting"; subsections include "Contracting Support" and "Contracting Opportunities." A guide in plain English called "Getting Started" explains government contracting, and information on the Federal Register and Federal Government Contract Center is provided also. Find out how to locate the *CCR Handbook.* The SBA will help you get started and be successful in your efforts to sell to the federal government.

Small Business Advisor: www.isquare.com (Accessed Spring 2011).

This large site has lots of articles and advice for entrepreneurs just getting started in business. The "Small Biz FAQs" answer many basic start-up questions. The "U.S. Gov Biz" section discusses doing business with the U.S. government and provides links to many government sites. A useful guide on the site is entitled "United States Government—New Customer!" State-specific information provides data on procurement offices and state fiscal years. "Tax Advice" and "Checklists for Success" are other major sections. Use this site to help you get started selling your products or services to the government.

**SBDCNet National Information Clearinghouse: www.sbdcnet.org/ (Accessed Spring 2011).

The Small Business Development Centers are partners with the SBA in providing education and assistance to small businesses in the United States. This large site tries to meet the information needs of the SBDC community and provides a great deal of information. Under "Procurement" are links to federal government websites such as the Department of Defense Procurement Gateway, the Federal Acquisition Jumpstation, the SBA Office of Government Contracting, and the FedBizOpps.gov site. Also provided is a link to the State Procurement Office Directory with links to state procurement offices. Well organized and easy to use, this site will help you sell to the government.

**USAspending.gov: www.usaspending.gov (Accessed Spring 2011).

Provided by the Office of Management and Budget, this interesting site provides information about each federal award. Sections include "News," "Summaries," "Trends," "Data Feeds," "Opportunities," "Sub-award Documents," "FAQs," and more. Fully searchable, locate the information you need here on federal spending. It also links to many other useful government websites.

Winning Government Contracts: www.singov.com (Accessed Spring 2011).

Sponsored by the Procurement Technical Assistance Program, this large site connects to many state and federal government sites concerned with government procurement. A library of articles helps you find information on many parts of the process, including bonding, letters of credit, accounting issues, claims, and more. Find information on many of the SBA programs, working with the military, and more. Use this site to answer your many questions about selling to the government.

COMPETITIVE ANALYSIS

13

CHAPTER HIGHLIGHTS

Identify Your Competitors

Data Gathering

Monitor the Competition Constantly

Analyze Competitive Intelligence

SWOT Analysis

Competitive Advantage

The world of business is one of competition and volatility. It is very important to know and understand your competition and keep track of their activities. Competitive intelligence (CI), also known as market intelligence and business intelligence, is the information about another company that a company accumulates and analyzes. This information is systematically and ethically gathered from public sources and effective interviewing skills. Competitive analysis (CA) uses CI to make good business plans and decisions or strategy. As an entrepreneur, you must begin this process when you begin making your business plan. Competitive analysis is part of the business plan procedure, but it doesn't end once the business is open. Similar to planning and strategizing, CA is an ongoing process and continues while the business exists. Most businesses gather information about competitors and the external business environment informally. If a more formalized method for collecting, assimilating, and converting the competitive information into knowledge is developed, it can be used to increase the competitive advantage of the business, and a successful business will result, thereby beating the competition.

The most competitive businesses transfer data relating to competitors into insights for their business strategy. A critical element of the CI process is positioning or attempting to raise the position of your company's products or services to current and potential customers relative to competitors' offerings in the marketplace. To learn more about gathering and using CI, read Seena Sharp's book, *The Competitive Intelligence Advantage*.

Sharp, Seena. *The Competitive Intelligence Advantage: How to Minimize Risk, Avoid Surprises, and Grow Your Business in a Changing World.* John Wiley, 2009. 304p. ISBN 0-470-29317-9. $39.95.

This practical resource explains what competitive intelligence is, why data is not intelligence, when to use CI, how to find the most useful information and make it actual intelligence, and how to present findings in a compelling manner. Sharp thinks businesses should view CI as an investment, not a cost. This overview of best practices in the field of CI is worth reading. The highlight of Sharp's book is the more than 60 examples of when to use CI. Sharp presents a clear case for how and why CI is one of the best management tools for business success and growth.

IDENTIFY YOUR COMPETITORS

By now, it is hoped that you can answer the following questions:

1. Who are your three or four nearest direct competitors?
2. Do you have indirect competitors and who are they?
3. How does your product or service differ from your direct and indirect competitors'?
4. What do you know about your competitors' operations or advertising that could improve your business?
5. List your strengths and weaknesses and your competitors' strengths and weaknesses.

By knowing what your competitors are doing, you will gain a better understanding of what products or services you should be offering, how to market your products or services effectively, and how you can position your business in the marketplace. Sometimes businesses devote too much attention to the current large–market share competitors and overlook smaller potential competitors. Critical insight can be gained in customers' buying behaviors by analyzing smaller rivals or the "substitute" rivals. Businesses with products or services that could be alternatives are substitute rivals.

DATA GATHERING

Start a file on each of the three or four competitors you named and a similar one for your company. Research your own company right along with all your competitors. CA can help you reflect on and learn about your own business and its vulnerabilities, limitations, and capabilities in relation to the competition. Develop a list of items it would be helpful to know about each competitor. This list might include how the competitor is structured; its area of specialty or niche; its level of service or quality of its product; values and practices; financial strength; market share; and what the competitor is likely to do next. Increase your awareness of the market in general. Watch your competitors and market for customers' perceptions and loyalty, promotional campaigns, product quality and service levels, and changes in products or services. Understand how your competitors provide value to customers. The following resource will help you begin gathering data and understand how to use what you find on the Internet:

Vibert, Conor. *Competitive Intelligence: A Framework for Web-based Analysis and Decision Making*. South-Western, 2003. 264p. ISBN 0-324-20325-X. $39.95.

Vibert explains how to conduct competitive research using the Internet. Part 1 contains a chapter on "Strategically Searching the Web and Differentiating Good Online Information from Bad." Part 2 has chapters on "Analysis: Why It Is Important" and "Web-Based Research Mission—Incorporating the Internet into Analysis." Part 3's best chapter is "Using Web CI to Understand the Online Music Business, A Case Example." The contributors all focus on free, publicly available information sources rather than expensive commercial databases. Learn about Internet research on competitors and how it can be used to help your business.

Don't limit yourself to just using free resources on the Internet, but consider all of the following, including the Internet:

1. *Advertising.* Collect competitors' product literature or business brochures. Closely read and analyze their ads. Make note of prices, the publication, frequency, special offers, product features, and style. What audience is it targeting? If you see a competitor's ad in an industry publication neither of you are currently selling to, it indicates that it is trying to expand its customer base or reach a new market segment. Take note of the design and tone of ads. Are competitors' ads in black and white or color? Why does the ad attract attention? What do you like or dislike about it?

2. *The Internet.* This huge, powerful tool can help you find information on competitors, the industry, and your market. Use search engines, periodical databases, and government sources. Diverse types and sources of information on competitors are readily available on the Internet; use it to see what you can find, or ask someone who's more familiar with searching to see what they can find. Besides the book mentioned above, check back to chapter 2 on "Research, Statistics, and Information Gathering" for more ideas on industry and market resources. Don't forget government websites. Visit your competitors' websites and take notes on what's included, how often it's updated, and how they are advertising their products or services, and keep track of how often the websites change. Perhaps they have some type of annual report online. Don't forget to take an impartial look at your own website, too. Do you have too little or too much company information available?

3. *Direct observation.* Buy one of your competitor's products, if that's feasible, and compare it with your own. Is something better about it? Is it a better price, or does it give the customer better value for the money? Let friends or

relatives try it, and collect opinions on it. Compare it to your own product. Can you draw any conclusions about your competitor's capabilities or technological innovations?

See how competitors present themselves at trade shows. If possible, listen to a sales presentation. Observe how they talk to prospective clients or customers. Are there new companies who will soon be competitors to your business? Do they have a print annual report available? If a competitor is speaking at the show, attend to hear what she or he has to say.

4. *Published sources.* Read your industry's trade publications to see if your competitors are mentioned and what is said about them. Does the trade association have any published statistical sources or surveys? Visit the library and search a large periodical database for newspaper and general business magazine articles on your competitor. Are there press releases indicating that the competitor is opening a new location or adding employees? Has a journalist written a favorable or unfavorable article about the competitor? Can you find product reviews? Use the commercial sources to compare financial ratios (sources covered in chapter 2).

5. *Customer service.* If possible, visit your competitor's store or sales location. Observe how much stock is available, placement of products, or any special displays. Ask questions. How does the customer service compare with yours? Call or ask a friend to call the toll-free number with questions or problems to see how those are handled. Don't use an alias when collecting competitor intelligence, because it may come back to haunt you. Do an informal survey of your customers to see what they think about your competitors. You might even consider holding a focus group to gather the impressions and experiences customers have had with your company and your competitors.

6. *Employees.* Probably one of the best sources for CI is your employees; they gather immense amounts of information through dealings with suppliers, customers, and other industry contacts. CI should be a regular topic in staff meetings, and all members of the organization are valuable intelligence agents. Also check your competitors' job postings; recruiting technical or marketing specialists might indicate where the company is heading in the future. Job competencies required will also indicate a company's abilities and intentions.

7. *Business network.* Talk to mutual suppliers and industry experts. Don't forget trade shows and seminars. Training seminars are sometimes useful opportunities for ethical CI gathering. Perhaps you even see your competitors socially or at chamber of commerce events. Simple, everyday conversations can provide useful information about business successes or new customers. Listening is an important skill in any business interaction.

A good book to use to help you organize and start analyzing your CI gathering effort is called *The Manager's Guide to Competitive Intelligence*.

McGonagle, John J. and Vella, Carolyn M. *The Manager's Guide to Competitive Intelligence.* Greenwood, 2003. 272p. ISBN 1-56720-571-2. $74.95.

This practical resource covers basic topics, including what CI means to a manager/ owner, legal and ethical issues, an overview of managing data gathering, effectively communicating CI, and measuring the impact of CI on the company. Readers will find checklists and forms that can be used to gather and analyze CI. Also included is the best way to set up a CI unit, including hiring, managing, salary scales, and so forth.

MONITOR THE COMPETITION CONSTANTLY

Why should you monitor the competition? Because by knowing your competitors, you can predict their next moves, exploit their weaknesses, and undermine their strengths. If you track your competition, you will see the big picture (or at least most of it), and you will recognize changes as they occur. Figure out what the changes in a competitor's strategy indicate about the current, emerging, and potential marketplace. Assess how well a competitor's performance is changing, gaining, or losing market share compared to your company or other competitors.

How does one continually monitor competitors? Frequently review the files you have on your competitors, and constantly compare your company to them. See how often your competitors have discount sales. Review and study any new advertising copy and promotional materials. Use this information to plan or change your own marketing efforts. Also, keep in mind and monitor the strength of your market; is it growing or shrinking? Are there enough customers for both you and your competitors to reach your sales targets? What's happening in the industry as a whole? Personal traits you will want to cultivate in order to become a good CI analyst include being a good listener, being creative and persistent, and being a good interviewer and writer. Communication and people skills are real assets in the business world. Also, you will want to read national, regional, and local business journals and newspapers to keep up with industry and economic news. The *Wall Street Journal* is an excellent source, and a subscription should be considered to keep up with trends and current events in the business world. *Business Week* is also an excellent source of business and economic trends and news. *Money* or *Smart Money* magazine are oriented toward investing but carry interesting articles on business. Don't forget to read the publications of the trade association you have chosen to join to help keep abreast of news in your industry.

Don't forget to keep an eye out for potential and emerging competitors— companies that may be moving into your market. Businesses that complement each other can also become competitors. For example, books provide content for magazines, and magazines print publicity and reviews for books. These businesses complement each other but can become competitors if they begin selling the same products or provide similar services. Perhaps you run a coffee shop and the convenience store across the street decides to offer "gourmet" coffee with lattes and espresso; try to think about whether this new competition is serious and how you can counter some of the effect. Should you change prices? Should you add new products or services? Could your product or service be offered on the Internet by a competitor? How would that affect your business? Conversely, if you're opening or running an Internet business, what happens if a brick-and-mortar operation opens in your town? Always be aware of what's happening in your industry and market. Know the triggers that indicate that you should step up or institute a CI project, including a lost contract bid, a competitor's new product launch, pending legislation, or supply shortages.

Every business has competitors. Even if your product or service is truly innovative, you need to determine what product or service customers are currently using to accomplish the task or fill their needs. Keep in mind that success breeds competition. Competitors often create new technologies or expand market opportunities. Competitors force you to constantly improve your business to get, satisfy, and keep your customers. Customers make market choices, deciding what to buy and where to spend their money based on needs and willingness to pay. Find out why customers buy from your competitors. Is it price or value, service or convenience? Focus on perceived as well as real strengths and weaknesses. Customer perception is sometimes more meaningful than reality. For help on profiling your competitors and researching your market and industry, read the "Plan for the War with Your Competitors" and "Devise a Winning Strategy" chapters in *Trump University Entrepreneurship 101*.

Gordon, Michael E. *Trump University Entrepreneurship 101: How to Turn Your Idea into a Money Machine*, 2nd ed. Wiley, 2009. 304p. ISBN 0-470-4671-83. $24.95.

Gordon, an entrepreneur, shares his lifetime of wisdom and covers all the bases. Pertinent topics in this new edition include Web 2.0, cloud computing, technopreneurship, and opportunity recognition in turbulent economic times. Also new in this edition, various analysis tools briefed in charts and exhibits can be downloaded from the website for personal use. An "Action" section follows each chapter to motivate new small business owners to begin using what they learn.

ANALYZE COMPETITIVE INTELLIGENCE

Now it's time to analyze the data you've gathered. From the competitive intelligence you've gathered, build a grid, including your own company, so you can easily review and compare these four or five companies. List the name, product or service information, market share, strengths, and weaknesses. If you can, list expected strategies or what competitors' next moves are in the marketplace. What are the opportunities and threats in the industry or your locations?

SWOT ANALYSIS

A SWOT analysis—strengths, weaknesses, opportunities, threats—is a marketing and management tool used to evaluate a company's competitive position.

Strengths	Weaknesses
1. New equipment	1. Poor location for public access
2. Plentiful capital	2. No PR staff
Opportunities	Threats
1. Growing market	1. New government regulations
2. Strengthening local economy	2. Low consumer confidence

Figure 13.1 SWOT (Strengths, Weaknesses, Opportunities, Threats) Analysis

A SWOT analysis diagrams your present business situation. Market research works hand-in-hand with CA, so review chapter 7 on marketing and consult your marketing plan as you continue through your CA. This process focuses on the strengths and weaknesses of you, your products or services, your business, and your staff; plus it looks at the external opportunities and threats that impact your business such as market and consumer trends, changes in technology, government legislation, and financial issues. Let's define these terms further:

1. *Strengths.* Look at what your firm does well; what competitive advantages your firm has over competitors; and your resources, including staff, customer loyalty, products, location, packaging, hours, and so on. Strengths are defined as your company's core competencies. However, if you and your major competitor both have very friendly staff, it can't be considered a strength for your company. If your delivery is friendlier and faster than your competitor's, then that is a strength. Education, experience, and reputation in your area of expertise are strengths. As you list your strengths, be as honest and realistic as possible. The analysis of strengths provides ideas for future expansion for your business.

2. *Weaknesses.* Again being as objective as possible, describe what you could do better. What are your company's drawbacks? Could your product or service be improved in some way? How reliable is your customer service? Does your supplier deliver exactly what you want and exactly when you want it? Do you need more staff to provide better customer service? Look at your business from the customer's perspective. Look at the big picture of your company. You might survey your customers or several big or frequent customers.

3. *Opportunities.* These are favorable situations or characteristics within the larger marketplace that could create benefits or competitive advantage to your company if pursued. Examples would be competitors who are not performing very well, legislation favorable to your industry or affecting your customers, technological developments in hardware or software, or market

trends or changes in consumer buying habits or even changes in the state or local economy. Quick action before your competitors could help you develop a niche market or expand your current market. Creative managers/owners are constantly looking for opportunities and trying to capitalize on them ahead of the competition. Think about ways to turn weaknesses into opportunities, too. An experienced staff member leaving for a better job or retiring is a loss, which creates a weakness, but if you can hire someone with new skills your company needs, it becomes an opportunity.

4. *Threats.* Obstacles or conditions that prevent your company from achieving its objectives are threats. Similar to opportunities, competitors' actions, demographic changes, environmental issues, changing technology, legislation, or your own limited financial resources can all be threats to the success of your business. Often threats are intuitive guesses that never happen, but being vigilant means that you can react quickly if a threat does materialize. What happens if a new competitor moves into your market? What if a new product outperforms yours or can be sold cheaper through new technology? Consider how your company could respond.

An excellent website to help in your SWOT analysis is at www.websitemar-ketingplan.com. The article "SWOT Analysis—Beyond the Text Book" by Bobette Kyle is enlightening, and other articles are also available. A SWOT analysis also is a method of presenting knowledge about your business to others who need to know and who can help advance the quality of the knowledge it imparts. This visual communication of key learning or business intelligence stimulates dialogue and promotes action. Another good site to learn more about SWOT analysis and how to perform and present it visually is the Bplans.com website at www.bplans. com. Use the SWOT analysis to identify potential and critical issues affecting your business on an ongoing basis.

As with your CA, you must learn from your SWOT analysis. Build on your strengths and use them to your full potential. Determine how financial resources, staff, and capacity should be allocated to create an exploitable advantage. Minimize the risk your weaknesses represent or overcome them if possible. If you find a weakness that undermines an opportunity, you can work toward correcting that situation or problem area. Now that you can see some opportunities, plan how to capitalize on them. Try to turn threats into opportunities, and counter any threats as they come up.

The SWOT analysis presents an overview of how your business is functioning and evaluates the external and internal forces that can help your business succeed and grow. Similar to other parts of running a business, a SWOT analysis is not a one-time event but an ongoing good business practice. Plan to update it and refer to it on a regular basis as one of your management tools. Another good site for SWOT analysis help is About.com Small Business Information (http://sbinformation.about.com). Just search "SWOT analysis" and you will see a list of articles describing it and how it can be used to help run and market your company.

COMPETITIVE ADVANTAGE

Competitive advantage is found in the differences between competitors. In order to succeed, each competitor must be different enough to have a unique advantage. Competitive advantage creates superior value above its rivals. A competitive advantage can be achieved through product, service, people, or image differentiation, and the foundations of competitive advantage are efficiency, quality, or innovation. If there are two small restaurants on the same street, the one that differentiates itself through price, product mix, customer service, or ambiance plus good food is more likely to survive and prosper. A competitive strategy means deliberately choosing a different set of activities to deliver a unique mix of value. Look at two airlines and see what distinguishes one from the other. Is it more frequent flights, lower fares, or more leg room? eBay created a unique way to sell and acquire used and new items. The company serves the same purpose as classified ads, flea markets, or formal auctions but made it global, simple, and efficient.

Look at your competitors and learn from them through CA to create competitive advantage. Gordon, in *Trump University Entrepreneurship 101*, lists four basic approaches to gaining competitive advantages: becoming the low-cost supplier, developing differentiated and innovative products or services, targeting a niche by geography, industry, or product/service, or employing differentiated business methods and approaches. Look at his examples and see what you can use. Once you've identified your competitive advantage, work to convey it to your customers through advertising and promotions.

Listed below are many resources to help you expand your knowledge of CI and CA and to learn how to use them to help your business prosper and grow in the competitive world of business.

REFERENCES

Starred titles are discussed in the chapter.

▉ Print Resources

Burwell, Helen P. *Online Competitive Intelligence: Increase Your Profits Using Cyber-Intelligence,* 2nd ed. Facts on Demand Press, 2004. 400p. ISBN 1-889150-41-X. $25.95.

This well-written guide to where to find and how to use the best commercial and Internet resources will help your small business remain profitable. Use the data Burwell helps you access to develop company strategies to beat your competitors in your market. Learn how to build and retain market share by targeting new and emerging markets and anticipating industry changes. Learn how to evaluate the information you find. Discover how to save money and maximize your profits. Her chapter on the "Invisible Web" is thorough and includes many choices for searching deeper for competitive information. Use the techniques Burwell explains to see what competitors can find out about your business. Use the references to more than 1,500 websites to help your company keep ahead of the competition. Section 4 divides Burwell's list of bookmarks and favorites into categories such as "Demographics," "European Union," "Financial Information Sites," "Industry Research," "Market Research," "People Locators," and many, many more.

Carr, Margaret Metcalf. *Super Searchers on Competitive Intelligence: The Online and Offline Secrets of Top CI Researchers*. Information Today, 2003. 336p. ISBN 0-910965-64-1. $24.95.

Find out how to use CI resources, analytical techniques, and models from 15 leading CI researchers. Monitoring competitive companies and keeping on top of industry trends, opportunities, and threats is vital in business today, and Carr will help you learn how to do it. Each chapter ends with "Super Searcher Power Tips," which will help novice and experienced CI researchers alike learn the tricks and tips of this useful skill.

Dion, James E. *The Complete Idiot's Guide to Starting and Running a Retail Store*. Alpha, 2008. 368p. ISBN 1-59-257726-1. $19.95.

The retail industry is particularly attractive to entrepreneurs and small business owners. Dion is a well-known expert and consultant for companies like Maytag and Harley-Davidson. Provided here are practical, hands-on tips for many aspects of retail business, including choosing the right business model and finding an ideal location. The pages on a SWOT analysis in the chapter on "Know Thy Competition" are simple and succinct, and the "Know Thy Industry" chapter is useful as well. The chapter on measuring your store's performance is outstanding. Well-organized and thoughtful, this book will help readers learn some of the psychology and human behavior connected to buying and selling.

Fleisher, Craig S. and Bensoussan, Babette. *Business and Competitive Analysis*. FT Press, 2009. 528p. ISBN 0-13-216158-3. $70.

Fleisher and Bensoussan examine the wide variety of techniques used in analyzing business and competitive data, including environmental analysis, industry analysis, benchmarking analysis, competitor analysis, and temporal analysis models. Over 24 analytical models are discussed and evaluated with examples to illustrate the best application. This practical primer shows how to transform raw data into compelling, actionable business recommendations and thus will help small business owners and managers learn the theory and application of competitive analysis.

Fuld, Leonard M. *The Secret Language of Competitive Intelligence*. Dog Ear, 2010. 326p. ISBN 1-608-44553-4. $19.95.

Fuld helps you understand a customer's strategic thinking, your rival's cost structure, and a competitor's new product plans. Learn how to introduce a new product effectively, when it's best to outsource, and how and when to form strategic alliances. Every market is full of distortions, rumors, and smoke screens, and Fuld provides some potential solutions to this pervasive problem with practical tools for separating fact from fiction. His diverse examples help to explain techniques and reasons for gathering competitive intelligence.

Gilad, Ben. *Early Warning: Using Competitive Intelligence to Anticipate Market Shifts, Control Risk, and Create Powerful Strategies*. AMACOM, 2003. 272p. ISBN 0-8144-0786-2. $27.95.

Gilad explains and makes a case for his Competitive Early Warning (CEW) system. Discovering that other companies are ahead of yours is not a good thing in any industry. CEW combines strategic planning, CI, and management action to meet new realities. Each chapter ends with a "Manager's Checklist" of key points. Using wry humor and providing lots of charts, tables, and tools, Gilad reveals how to read the signs that indicate a change is coming. Case studies illustrate important points. Learn to use your competitive analysis to help your business succeed.

**Gordon, Michael E. *Trump University Entrepreneurship 101: How to Turn Your Idea into a Money Machine,* 2nd ed. Wiley, 2009. 304p. ISBN 0-470-4671-83. $24.95.

Gordon, an entrepreneur, shares his lifetime of wisdom and covers all the bases. Pertinent topics in this new edition include Web 2.0, cloud computing, technopreneurship, social networking, and opportunity recognition in turbulent economic times. Gordon puts short lines of pithy wisdom in boxes, like "Sustainable traffic is THE source of competitive advantage on the Web." Also new in this edition, various analysis tools briefed in charts and exhibits can be downloaded from the website for personal use. An "Action" section follows each chapter to motivate new small business owners to begin using what they learn.

Halliman, Charles. *Business Intelligence Using Smart Techniques,* rev. ed. Information Uncover, 2009. 230p. ISBN 0-96-749066-9. $69.95.

Halliman, a business intelligence consultant, provides a pragmatic approach to converting business information into business intelligence for sound marketing strategies and production policies. He suggests manageable strategies and processes to uncover possibilities to break out of the status quo. Find here tools to learn about your current business climate and competitors' activities and to examine the external environment for opportunities and threats. Real examples and case studies are provided.

**McGonagle, John J. and Vella, Carolyn M. *The Manager's Guide to Competitive Intelligence.* Praeger/Greenwood, 2003. 272p. ISBN 1-56720-571-2. $91.95.

This practical resource covers basic topics, including what CI means to a manager/owner, legal and ethical issues, an overview of managing data gathering, effectively communicating CI, and measuring the impact of CI on the company. Readers will find checklists and forms that can be used to gather and analyze CI. Also included is the best way to set up a CI unit, including hiring, managing, salary scales, and so on. The importance of CI is identified, and ways to use it are presented in a clear, organized manner.

Mohr, Angie. *Financial Management 101: Get a Grip on Your Business Numbers.* Self-Counsel Press, 2004. 176p. ISBN 1-55180-448-4. $14.95.

Mohr helps new entrepreneurs plan the financial end of their business from the first financial statements through budgeting for advertising. Learn to measure your business success and how to find new opportunities. Follow her examples to create sales and marketing plans as well as to learn about analyzing the competition. The chapter on ratio analysis will help readers learn what basic ratios tell them, what to do when ratios indicate a problem, and how to integrate ratios into a management reporting system. Case studies are presented throughout to help readers understand the importance of the concepts presented.

Mullins, John. *The New Business Road Test: What Entrepreneurs and Executives Should Do Before Writing a Business Plan,* 3rd ed. FT Press, 2010. 336p. ISBN 0-273-73279-X. $19.99.

Before writing a business plan or investing any money, use Mullins's new version of the seven domains model for assessing new business ideas. Learn how to run a customer-driven feasibility study to assess that new business opportunity. Updated case studies use real businesses like Honda and Starbucks to illustrate industry trends and opportunities. What are critical success factors and niche markets? Avoid the "me too" trap and more. Chapter 13 has been rewritten to make the Industry Analysis Checklist more understandable. Use his practical advice and guidance to help your new business succeed.

Porter, Michael. *Competitive Strategy: Techniques for Analyzing Industries and Competitors.* Free Press, 1998. 432p. ISBN 0-684-84148-7. $37.50.

Porter is a leading authority on competition and strategy, and this work is a standard in modern business education. Part 1 discusses the structural analysis of industries, competitive strategies, a framework for competitor analysis, and structural analysis within industries. Part 2 presents competitive strategy within various industry environments, including emerging industries, mature industries, and global industries, for example. Part 3 discusses various strategic decisions such as vertical integration and expansion of companies in their industries. Particularly noteworthy and useful are Appendix A, "Portfolio Techniques in Competitor Analysis" and Appendix B, "How to Conduct an Industry Analysis." If you find you enjoy Michael Porter's writing, you might also read *Competitive Advantage: Creating and Sustaining Superior Performance* (Simon & Schuster, 1998, ISBN 0-684-84146-0).

Prescott, John E. and Miller, Stephen H. *Proven Strategies in Competitive Intelligence.* John Wiley, 2001. 288p. ISBN 0-471-4017-8-1. $24.95.

The highlight of this collection is the case studies. Learn how large companies collect competitive information. Discover and understand the philosophy, tactics, and concepts behind CI. Learn how CI techniques are used and applied in market research and forecasting and product development. Though not always applicable to a small business, the real-life examples illustrate CI's importance to success.

Rothbert, Helen and Erickson, G. Scott. *From Knowledge to Intelligence: Creating Competitive Advantage in the Next Economy.* Elsevier Science and Technology Books, 2004. 368p. ISBN 0-7506-7762-7. $39.95.

Competitive intelligence—or the strategic gathering of knowledge about competitors, climate, trends, and new products—generates competitive advantage. Topics include how to develop a strategy for sharing and gathering information, best CI practices, and using internal and external intelligence to gain a competitive advantage. Real examples from the corporate world are provided. This well-written book has become a competitive intelligence classic.

**Sharp, Seena. *The Competitive Intelligence Advantage: How to Minimize Risk, Avoid Surprises, and Grow Your Business in a Changing World.* John Wiley, 2009. 304p. ISBN 0-470-29317-9. $39.95.

This practical resource explains what competitive intelligence is, why data is not intelligence, when to use CI, how to find the most useful information and make it actual intelligence, and how to present findings in a compelling manner. Sharp thinks businesses should view CI as an investment, not a cost. This overview of best practices in the field of CI is worth reading. The highlight of Sharp's book is the more than 60 examples of when to use CI. Sharp presents a clear case for how and why CI is one of the best management tools for business success and growth.

Smith, Jaynie L. and Flanagan, William G. *Creating Competitive Advantage: Give Customers a Reason to Choose You over Your Competitors.* Crown Business, 2006. 240p. ISBN 0-3855-1709-2. $19.95.

This down-to-earth book is filled with practical advice, insightful stories, and specific steps on how to pinpoint your competitive advantages, develop new ones, and get the message out about them. The authors tell small business owners to stop focusing on cost as your advantage. To compete with your competitors, you must come up with competitive advantages that are unique to your business. This title helps you define what these competitive advantages are and gives you insight on how to develop your own advantages that will set you apart from the rest. Learn how to set your business apart from your competitors.

**Vibert, Conor. *Competitive Intelligence: A Framework for Web-based Analysis and Decision Making.* South-Western, 2003. 264p. ISBN 0-324-20325-X. $39.95.

Vibert explains how to conduct competitive research using the Internet. Part 1 contains a chapter on "Strategically Searching the Web and Differentiating Good Online Information from Bad." Part 2 has chapters on "Analysis: Why It Is Important" and "Web-Based Research Mission—Incorporating the Internet into Analysis." Part 3's best chapter is "Using Web CI to Understand the Online Music Business, A Case Example." The contributors all focus on free, publicly available information sources rather than expensive commercial databases. Learn about Internet research on competitors and how it can be used to help your business.

Waters, T.J. *Hyperformance: Using Competitive Intelligence for Better Strategy and Execution.* Jossey-Bass, 2010. 272p. ISBN 0-47-053364-1. $27.95.

Waters has turned his experience collecting and analyzing competitive intelligence into strategies for helping businesses stay on the leading edge of their industries. He describes his practical process and turns it into a step-by-step process beginning with planning (identifying competitive threats and determining what resources are needed to counter them), through implementation (how to create a real-world organizational strategy), to execution (collect the key information needed and turn it into bottom-line results). The key is that after collecting and analyzing competitor, market, and customer information, businesses must act on the information in a timely fashion to gain the competitive advantage. Waters teaches his method through extensive case studies on businesses—from start-ups to multinational corporations—that have successfully used his strategies.

■ Online Resources

About.com: http://sbinformation.about.com/ (Accessed Spring 2011).

Under the "Manage and Grow" section of the huge About.com site, you will find several good articles on gathering competitive intelligence or you can just search the site for articles. In addition to suggestions about public or commercial sources of information are links to companies that will track a company or industry for you and provide periodic updates. Also, you will find articles on competitive analysis and SWOT analysis by searching the site. Analyzing the competition is important when you prepare your business plan, but it is essential to continue monitoring the competition as long as you are in business.

AllBusiness: www.allbusiness.com (Accessed Spring 2011).

This huge site contains articles and advice on researching and writing about your competitors. Competitive intelligence is thoroughly explained as well. The articles on green businesses are very useful. Links to many directories are also provided as well as news and business information sites. The "Sales and Marketing" section has many articles on techniques, advertising, and publications. The tax articles discuss topics such as barter tax and accounting issues and tax strategies for keeping the family business in the family. Use this well-organized, functional website often.

**Bplans.com: www.bplans.com (Accessed Spring 2011).

This well-established, frequently updated site, sponsored by Palo Alto Software, Inc., is the best for help in writing your business plan, and it also contains articles on a wide range of small business topics. Fully searchable, users can quickly find topics that they need, such as business structure, SWOT analysis, cash flow, starting costs, and business plan legalities. Other sections include "Finance and Capital," "Marketing & Advertising," "Buying a Business," "Market Research," and a monthly newsletter. The article on "Your Online Competitive Analysis" is excellent. The section titled "Write a Business Plan" contains articles, calculators for cash flow, starting costs, breakeven and more; a business plan template; executive summary and mission statement help; and access to expert advice. Bplans.com is a useful, practical site that also offers fee-based experts and assistance.

Edward Lowe's Entrepreneurs Resource Center: www.edwardlowe.org/ERC/ (Accessed Spring 2011).

This well-known small business site contains a large section on "Defining and Serving a Market." One of the articles here is "Gathering Market Research," and it walks users through identifying data sources, gathering customer and competitor information, and gathering information on suppliers with real-life examples of successful marketing. Additional resources are often provided at the end of the articles. Find also information on branding, direct mail marketing, social media, and providing a promotional mix for your new business. An outstanding article under the topic of "Defining and Serving a Market" is on "How to Conduct and Prepare a Competitive Analysis." It is an excellent place for new entrepreneurs to begin learning about how to monitor the competition. Use this site frequently when you need help running or marketing your business.

Entrepreneur.com: www.entrepreneurmag.com (Accessed Spring 2011).

Maintained by *Entrepreneur Magazine,* this site supports new businesses and growing companies, and you are probably familiar with it by now. Under "First Steps," learn how to evaluate your idea and determine whether there's a market for your business. "Start Up Topics" include location, naming your business, and business structure. Another important article discusses competitive analysis, its advantage in relation to your business plan, and explains that examining competitors' strengths and weaknesses can help you determine how to succeed and stay competitive. Find ready-made business forms here, too, in the "FormNet" section.

Inc.com: www.inc.com (Accessed Spring 2011).

The publishers of *Inc.* magazine present a large directory of articles by topic targeting many problems, concerns, and decisions confronting new business owners and managers. The "Start-Up" section on business plans is precise and practical. Particularly strong is the article on writing your business description; write out the problem your business solves for its customers, and then describe how your business solves your customers' problem. As stated earlier, the executive summary is a critical section in the business plan, and the article here is right on target. Get advice on what not to include in the executive summary. Another useful section on competitive analysis contains a worksheet to help evaluate and compare your products or services with competitors. Simple but effective advice is the hallmark of this outstanding, easy-to-use site.

Small Business Administration: www.sba.gov (Accessed Spring 2011).

This official government site offers a wealth of resources and programs for starting and growing a small business. Under "Starting and Managing a Business," users will find an "Is Entrepreneurship for You?" quiz that will help them conduct a personal evaluation of possible success in their own business. Other major articles cover business plans, financing, managing, marketing, employees, taxes, legal aspects, and business opportunities. Learn more about a competitor analysis here. A wealth of information and links will help you develop your marketing strategy and develop your competitive advantage. Find here online forms, business plans, financing and loan information, and many publications. Some contents are available in Spanish.

Society of Competitive Intelligence Professionals: www.scip.org (Accessed Spring 2011).

This international, nonprofit organization, established in 1986, provides CI publications and annual conferences. You can find names of CI consultants and CI training firms in your area. The FAQs answer many questions about CI, how it makes a difference in your bottom line, and how it is changing, plus tips on getting started collecting CI. Ethical and legal issues are covered as well.

**WebSite Marketing Plan: www.websitemarketingplan.com (Accessed Spring 2011).

This large website on online marketing contains a wealth of articles on a variety of topics relating to small business, including Bobette Kyle's "SWOT Analysis—Beyond the Text Book." Featured directory categories include articles grouped under "Search Engine Marketing," "Marketing Strategy," "Marketing Plan," and "Public Relations." Many commercial links but plenty of free help for the new entrepreneur, too. This site is especially helpful for those interested in e-commerce. The wealth of articles at this well-organized and easy-to-use site will help you develop your competitive advantage through marketing.

GROWING YOUR BUSINESS AND MOVING ON

14

When the horse dies, get off.
—Kinky Friedman

When you first start your business, it may appear that expanding the business will be a terrific sign that you're a success. In the early days, things will be hectic, but you will still feel that the business is under your control. However, as you begin to juggle more tasks, decisions, and responsibilities and delegate some of these items to your staff and still you don't have enough time to get everything done, you may decide it's time to expand your business. Be careful when planning this important step, because success and expansion, if done improperly, can quickly bankrupt the entire business. Because business growth rarely occurs predictably and smoothly, fast growth can destabilize a successful business and provide a false sense of security, while additional operating dollars quickly eat up any new revenues.

GROWING YOUR SMALL BUSINESS

Don't forget the main lesson from chapter 3, "Start Up": plan for growth. Have a strategic reason to expand and pay careful attention to financial management. Unplanned growth can result in loss of current customers if you and your staff are spread too thin. Also, remember from chapter 9, "Management," that good management is the root of business success and growth.

An excellent resource to help you identify how to expand your business is Tom Gegax's *The Big Book of Small Business*. This well-organized, clearly written guide presents guidelines to help determine the state of your business as it matures while helping you find solutions for challenges you will encounter.

Gegax, Tom. *The Big Book of Small Business.* HarperBusiness, 2007. 448p. ISBN 0-06120-669-5. $29.99.

This lively, practical guide will help you start, fund, and get your new business off the ground as well as create a mission statement and create processes for continuous innovation. Gegax explains and illustrates the importance of effective leadership. His business plan guidance can easily be adapted to a web-based company as well as retail or service brick-and-mortar. Great for the beginner but just as useful to those who have started a successful company but want to expand and enjoy their business life. This practical reference tool for best practices gives you a good idea about what should be on your task list, how to prioritize the tasks based on your situation, plan growth, and where to get the details when growing your business.

What are possible ways that your business could grow and expand? Consider these ideas:

- Add more products or services.

- Adapt your current products or services to meet the need of another niche market.

- Market your products or services to a new geographic area.

- Compete with larger companies.

What should you consider when planning for expansion and growth? Remember that unplanned growth is destined to fail. The main rule to keep in mind is that you expand when there is an untapped opportunity, such as a new niche you can fill or a location that is not being served. Other factors to consider include the financial ramifications of expansion; the logistics—especially if more than one location will be needed; and your emotional or personal readiness for the stress and additional work. Bluntly consider whether you can afford to expand and whether your cash flow can support the additional investment. Keep in mind that growth or expansion does not immediately result in more profit, because when handling more volume or an added location, there will be additional overhead as well. Keep your overhead as low as possible. Watch your profit margin.

Also be prepared to play a less hands-on role as your business grows. You may need more staff and even a manager for a new location. New players in your business mean new ideas, and you should be open to them. This loss of control can be an emotional issue for some entrepreneurs. An excellent resource for helping you plan for growth is Gottry's *Common Sense Business*, which will help you make a plan to operate and grow your small business.

Gottry, Steve. *Common Sense Business: Starting, Operating, and Growing Your Small Business— In Any Economy!* HarperBusiness, 2005. 368p. ISBN 0-06-077838-5. $19.95.

Gottry started and ran a large Minneapolis-based ad agency and video production firm, which failed after 22 years in business. You can learn from his mistakes. Well-organized and clearly written, Gottry's book includes specific how-tos, such as ways to prioritize bills for payment when cash flow is limited. He explains how to find solutions to the questions and challenges you're facing daily. Learn how to begin to understand yourself, your employees, your vendors, and your customers. He discusses feasibility studies, business plans, cash management, websites, legalities, finding and keep good employees, and planning and managing growth. Using humor, Gottry will help you successfully manage your business through good times and bad.

When considering expansion, you should also analyze the strategies of your competitors. Refer to chapter 13 and your competitive analysis. If your competitors are tapping into new opportunities, they may have stumbled onto a good idea, and you may consider waiting to see how it works for them or you may want to jump in and follow their lead. Maybe their new approach can stimulate your own thinking about how to fill a developing niche or provide a needed new service or product related to your current business operation. You may want to revisit and revise your SWOT analysis. As your business environment changes, you can use the SWOT analysis to analyze your business and its potential. Ask yourself how to prepare your business for change.

Hopefully you have been reading trade journals and newspapers and have joined a trade association to keep abreast of trends in your field. Becoming an authority on issues related to your business is necessary for the success and growth of your business. Look for trends and opportunities in your industry and your local business climate. Remember to keep focused on what brought you success in the first place. If you're the best at closing the sale, then hire staff for other support functions such as marketing and recordkeeping, and keep doing what you're best at doing.

Also, think about the reaction of your current customers. Timing is crucial in the decision to expand a business. Look at the overall outlook for the U.S. economy and your state's economic situation. Can your customers afford more services or products at this time? Keep in mind various alternatives and find the most appropriate vehicles for expansion for you and your business.

A terrific website to help you focus and plan the growth of your business is Business Know-How (www.businessknowhow.com) under the section "Growth and Leadership." Another good resource is the U.S. government's Small Business Administration website (www.sba.gov). This site will provide you with information you need to finance and grow a business. Under "Starting and Managing" are many resources that will help you plan for expansion and growth in your business and industry. Learn how important it is to take calculated risks. This section also will help you learn how to make good decisions, an essential part of business expansion.

Keep in mind that growth and expansion are not inherently good or desirable; remember your own definition of success. Be realistic and don't spread yourself too thin. If expansion takes you away from the passion and vision of your original dream and you lose control over your business and your life, expansion may make you richer but also unhappy.

EXIT STRATEGIES TO CONSIDER

Some entrepreneurs start a business believing that they will keep working in it "til death do us part," while others are serial entrepreneurs. Most businesses do not last forever. In fact, research has shown that entrepreneurs who have a well-planned harvest option are more successful, because they have developed specific goals besides creating a job and a living for themselves. While your business is still growing, you will want to begin planning how, if, and when you will move on.

There are many reasons why an entrepreneur decides to harvest the monetary value he or she has created in the enterprise. The reasons behind selling your business will determine how you approach the task and will also affect your expectations of the transaction. Ideally, you should plan to sell your business three to five years in advance of the actual sale.

Retirement is one reason for selling a business. If that is your reason, you can probably sell at any time over a range of years to choose the best offer available. If you have all your net worth tied up in the business and have become overly cautious, you might lose market share to more aggressive competitors. Then you may feel the need to diversify to prevent the loss of everything you've worked for to date. If you are in poor health, you might have to sell quickly. If you sense your business has reached its summit under your leadership and needs an infusion of new ideas, skills, or resources to expand, you might decide to sell. Maybe the partner in your business wants to dissolve the partnership, and you need to buy out him or her. If a financial crisis arises, selling quickly at a low price may be the only way for you to avoid losing your entire investment. A death in your family or the death of a partner also might precipitate selling the business. Or you may be a serial entrepreneur and feel the need to start a new venture.

ALTERNATIVES TO SELLING

If raising cash is your motive for selling your business, you may elect to sell only a portion of the business to raise some capital and use the cash to strengthen the part you keep. If you are experiencing financial problems, a partner might bring expertise and needed cash into the company.

How can you change the way you're doing business to cut expenses? Compare the costs of selling your business with the costs of continuing. Even if you get an offer that seems too good to refuse, you probably want to take a long look at the value of your business and at what your life will be like after the sale. Selling a business is a major, life-changing event and should not be rushed.

SELLING STRATEGY FOR YOUR BUSINESS

Just as you needed a plan to start your small business and a plan to grow your business, you need a plan for selling the business and reaping the rewards of your work. Once again you will probably want to put together a team of professionals that includes your attorney, banker, and accountant. You can sell your business yourself, but contracting with a business broker is a good idea. Legal, tax, ethical, and accounting considerations are all involved in selling a business, and a savvy broker knows how to reach the business buyer market. Good sites to look at before you start this process are the Wall Street Journal Online (http://online.wsj.com/public/page/news-small-business.html) and the Small Business Administration (www.sba.gov). Search "selling a business" or "valuing a business," and you will find articles about different ways to find buyers, calculate value, and get the most value from your business.

■ Valuing Your Business

Selling your business will probably be one of the most important things you'll ever do, because, unlike most other business decisions you've made, this one you'll only do once. One of the first considerations your new team will have to make is to value something that you have poured years of time, energy, and money into and that may feel like an extension of yourself. Most brokers will talk about fair market value, which generally means "the highest price the property would bring free of any encumbrances at a fair and voluntary private sale for cash" (*Black's Law Dictionary*). Generally, there are four main methods of valuing a business: cash-flow-based, net assets, multiple earnings, and standard formulas. Cash-flow-based information and net assets can be found on the financial statements. The multiple earnings calculation is based on the price/earnings ratio or P/E ratio, which is more complicated to calculate for a privately held company. Standard formulas have been established for some industry sectors and can be investigated through trade and professional associations. Remember, all of these methods are only as good as the information provided. Valuing an ongoing small business is not easy, nor is it an exact science. Entire books have been written on this subject, and one good title is Wilbur M. Yegge's *A Basic Guide for Valuing a Company*. Yegge uses real-life examples and presents the information on valuing a business in an organized manner, and the full citation is listed at the end of this chapter. Thomas Horn's book is more current and presents the information in a slightly different manner.

Horn, Thomas W. *Unlocking the Value of Your Business: How to Increase It, Measure It, and Negotiate an Actual Sale Price—In Easy Step-by-Step Terms*, 3rd ed. Charter Oak Press, 2008. 273p. ISBN 0-8752-1016-3. $39.95.

A good way to really examine how your business is doing is to analyze it in simple, everyday language. Horn explains how to calculate the value of your business and how to maximize its market value. This book contains practical advice on negotiating the acquisition contract and how to prepare and present your business to potential buyers. Buyers and sellers of a business will use this knowledge to negotiate price much more effectively. Horn clearly presents tried-and-true formulas for valuing your business.

Learn as much as you possible can about this technical area before you put your business up for sale, and you will be able to make intelligent decisions when you work with a professional or your professional team. A few points to keep in mind when starting to value your business include:

1. Be realistic in setting your price, and don't forget that negotiations will be involved once you have an interested buyer.

2. Cash flow is usually more important than profits when valuing a small business.

3. Buyers will consider values other than financial considerations—that is, psychological value versus dollar value.

4. The ownership of a trade secret, proprietary process, or ownership of a patent may increase the value of a business. License agreements and long-term contracts are sometimes considered.

5. Physical location can be an important component of value. High-traffic spots, tourist destinations, and other proximity factors may affect the business value.

6. An intangible known as goodwill is sometimes a key consideration. Reputation or a long-established customer base can be considered part of goodwill. Often the amount paid above the net asset value of a small business is called goodwill.

The price you settle upon is extremely important; and with so many things to consider in valuing your small business, you may want to find a trained, certified expert. The National Association of Certified Valuation Analysts at www.nacva.com

will help you find an expert. A directory where you can enter a zip code and find an analyst is found under the "Resources" tab. The website also provides some very basic information on valuation.

Present and Prepare Your Business for Sale

Another thing that most small business owners do to present their business for sale is prepare a comprehensive documentation package, sometimes referred to as a selling prospectus. The selling prospectus highlights the important features of your business and documents its value and your reasons for selling. Included are the business history, location, operations, employees, financial statements, and competition. Also include in your package a confidentiality statement, justification for your price, and terms of sale.

Because many small business owners operate their business in a way calculated to minimize taxes, you may have taken perks and benefits and plowed profits back into capital improvements in order to keep your profits low. Now you must consider maximizing the company's value. Your accountant can adjust or recast your past income statements to reflect what would have happened if you removed your perks and your family members' salaries, removed nonoperating expenses, and removed interest payments on business loans. Your accountant can also adjust your balance sheets to remove assets that won't be sold with the company, value current inventory at current replacement cost, value assets at current fair market value, write off any loans the company made to you, and remove any debt that will not be assumed by the buyer. These changes should be documented clearly on the financial statements so the buyer knows you aren't covering anything up but just clarifying how the financial statements would look with a new owner. Your accountant should then prepare projected financial statements for the next five years with reasonable assumptions about future growth or decline in income and expenses using trends established in the past several years.

Besides the documentation package, you should also prepare your business for sale. Reduce discretionary expenditures such as travel and entertainment; maintain your property and business assets, including machinery and office equipment; improve your cash flow if possible; and maintain good relations with suppliers and customers.

MERGERS AND ACQUISITIONS

If you can't or don't want to sell your business to another small business owner, sometimes you can transfer ownership to another business in a merger or acquisition. Mergers usually involve two similar-sized firms, while acquisitions involve larger firms taking over smaller businesses. Another business might buy your business in order to reduce its cost per unit, increase its market share, decrease competition, acquire new technology or new customers, acquire a unique distribution channel, or increase its presence in your location. When two companies combine or merge, sometimes current management is allowed to stay on to help run the new company, either permanently or for a limited amount of time; but mergers involve new partners or bosses, and the former owner may have less control.

Mergers and acquisitions are very complex transactions. If you have no experience with them, enlist experienced legal and financial professionals to help you with this type of transaction. If neither of the two companies are publicly held, the complexity is further complicated. Be particularly aware of what method is used to value your business, how payment is to be structured, and what your relationship will be to the new company.

For excellent articles and advice on mergers and business valuation, check out the Small Business Notes website at www.smallbusinessnotes.com.

EMPLOYEE STOCK OWNERSHIP PLANS

An employee stock ownership plan (ESOPs) is a vehicle for owners to realize some liquidity through sale of their stock to the plan and employees. Because an ESOP creates ownership of stock among employees, it can be seen as a positive motivational device for the company, too. The owner may or may not exit the company, but in either case he or she is able to obtain a considerable amount of money. ESOPs were originally created to provide retirement benefits for employees, but many are now used to help current owners harvest capital or increase their cash flow.

ESOPs are designed to allow employees invest in their company's stock. The U.S. government encourages this by providing significant tax advantages for ESOPs. An ESOP covers all employees, and the company needs to disclose a great deal of confidential information. Because of the many legal and tax implications, be sure to seek professional legal and financial advice when considering an ESOP. For more information on ESOPs, check out the website of the National Center for Employee Ownership at www.nceo.org.

CLOSING

Under some circumstances, it is best to simply sell your inventory and fixtures, pay your creditors and employees, close the door, and walk away. If your business is failing, isn't valuable enough to invite a merger or acquisition, or depends on you personally for success, closing may be the best choice. Depending on your financial circumstances, filing for voluntary liquidation or declaring bankruptcy are also options. Small businesses are failing at record rates; in 2008, 43,000 filed for bankruptcy, and this trend continued in 2009 and 2010. Bankruptcy is supposed to give you a second chance, "wipe out your debts and get a fresh start!" However, it may result in the end of your business. Read the Elias and Laurence book below before you take any steps toward bankruptcy.

Elias, Stephen and Laurence, Bethany. *Bankruptcy for Small Business Owners: How to File for Chapter 7.* Nolo Press, 2010. 344p. ISBN 1-4133-1080-X. $39.99.

The authors help you assess the financial condition of your business to determine whether you should declare bankruptcy. Follow step-by-step instructions for completing all of the bankruptcy forms and filing them in court. Find out what business debt and assets (if any) would be impacted by bankruptcy, and learn about automatic stays and how business assets like goodwill and intellectual property are evaluated. Learn the various bankruptcy options that are available (such as Chapter 7, Chapter 13 and Chapter 1). The authors explain the eligibility factors and downsides of each. They want to help small business owners avoid the mistakes that can cost them their business and other property. Educate yourself to better understand the bankruptcy process, protect yourself, and deal with the aftermath of bankruptcy.

If you're closing down because there's little or no chance of getting back in the black, it may be time to close down in an orderly fashion. Check out chapter 12 in Warner and Laurence's book *Save Your Small Business*:

Warner, Ralph E. and Laurence, Bethany. *Save Your Small Business: 10 Crucial Strategies to Survive Hard Times or Close Down and Move On.* Nolo Press, 2009. 316p. ISBN 1-4133-1041-9. $29.99.

The basic thrust of this book is covered by chapters about concentrating on what is really profitable for your business, controlling your cash flow, minimizing your liability, bankruptcy and its alternatives, and not wasting money on ineffective marketing. Chapter 12 is about closing down your business and is very thorough. If you feel the business has run its course, learn how to shut down operations while protecting your personal assets. The appendix, "How to Prepare a Profit and Loss Forecast and Cash Flow Analysis," is very well done.

INITIAL PUBLIC OFFERING

Few small firms ever qualify for an initial public offering (IPO), because they are too small, too limited in their potential, or are in an industry that doesn't attract investor interest. An IPO is also expensive and involves close public scrutiny of all the firm's operations. The advantage of an IPO is the higher price the entrepreneur will obtain for the business. Opportunities to reap large harvests for a small business through an IPO occur very infrequently.

FAMILY SUCCESSION

When a small business is the main component of family wealth, the desire to perpetuate it in one form or another is strong. However, the paramount management challenge may be an orderly succession to family members. Issues involved include business legalities, family dynamics, tax considerations, and estate issues. If you perceive the succession of ownership as a process, not an event, it will ease the course of the change. This process requires planning, teamwork, compromise, and constant reevaluation. If you don't plan the succession, it may be done in a crisis with many unintended consequences. The book *Family Business Succession* can help you plan and implement a successful family succession, passing on assets and power smoothly and efficiently.

Aronoff, Craig E., McClue, Stephen L. and Ward, John L. *Family Business Succession: The Final Test of Greatness*, 2nd ed. Palgrave Macmillan, 2010. 112p. ISBN 0-230-1110-09. $23.

Learn how good succession management is like good strategic planning and how to divide succession planning into manageable pieces. The authors identify different types of leadership transitions, how to prepare the family for a successful transition, how to develop outstanding successors, and how to implement succession. Post-succession mistakes and problems are also discussed. Real-life case studies and practical tips are provided as well as practical guidance on tough family business issues. If you're planning to have a family member succeed you in your small business, this book will help you work through the process smoothly.

RETIREMENT

The keys to a happy retirement are financial security, good health, and physical and mental activities that interest you. You'll have more time to do the things you enjoy most. Before you decide how to spend your retirement, it must be funded. As in every other step of business, retirement should be planned. The earlier you start planning and saving money, the better off you'll be when the time comes to retire. And, of course, the best way to accumulate funds is through a steady process of saving that starts early. The source that was mentioned earlier in this chapter and is listed at the end, *Unlocking the Value of Your Business* by Thomas W. Horn, should be useful to help small business owners put together a thoughtful, practical plan for selling their business and retiring. AARP (www.aarp.org) and several other nonprofit organizations provide good information on retirement options for every retiree's situation.

In sum, a well-thought-out plan for exiting a business is just as important as the planning required when starting a business. Save time, money, and frustration by putting together a good exit strategy. The resources below will help you prepare and develop different contingency plans for whatever stage of your business life you are in today.

REFERENCES

Starred titles are discussed in the chapter.

▮ Print Resources

American Bar Association. *Legal Guide for Small Business*, 2nd ed. Random House Reference, 2010. 496p. ISBN 0-3757-2303-2. $16.99.

This handy little guide will help small business owners understand their legal responsibilities and options. Getting help and choosing a lawyer are also useful chapters. Exit strategies such as retirement or selling and death are described with the various legal ramifications. Learn how to spot problems before they become major legal issues, minimize the time and expense you spend on legal problems, and learn how to protect your business. Refer to this handbook whenever you are faced with legal decisions.

**Aronoff, Craig E., McClue, Stephen L. and Ward, John L. *Family Business Succession: The Final Test of Greatness*, 2nd ed. Palgrave Macmillan, 2010. 112p. ISBN 0-230-1110-09. $23.

Learn how good succession management is like good strategic planning and how to divide succession planning into manageable pieces. The authors identify different types of leadership transitions, how to prepare the family for a successful transition, how to develop outstanding successors, and how to implement succession. Post-succession mistakes and problems are also discussed. Real-life case studies and practical tips are provided as well as practical guidance on tough family business issues. If you're planning to have a family member succeed you in your small business, this book will help you work through the process smoothly.

Cooper, Ian, et al. *Smarta Way to Do Business*. John Wiley, 2011. 334p. ISBN 1-907312-52-8. $34.95.

This British title is brought to you by Smarta.com, the United Kingdom's ultimate resource for business advice, networking, and tools. The emphasis here is tied to the consumer's and the company's online experience; learn how to use networking and interactive tools such as giveaways, vouchers or coupons, and codes to access restricted areas of the website. Discover here strategies for survival, expansion, and exiting your business. This step-by-step guide provides practical advice and tips to help you start and grow a successful business.

Dini, John F. *11 Things You Absolutely Need to Know about Selling Your Business*. iUniverse. com, 2010. 128p. ISBN 1-450-250-246. $14.95.

This book offers a step-by-step guide to the process of selling your business. It provides you with the tools you need to prepare, market, and sell at the best price possible. The information in this book eye-opening, and readers will gain a better perspective on the mechanics of selling a business.

**Elias, Stephen and Laurence, Bethany. *Bankruptcy for Small Business Owners: How to File for Chapter 7*. Nolo Press, 2010. 344p. ISBN 1-4133-1080-X. $39.99.

The authors help you assess the financial condition of your business to determine whether you should declare bankruptcy. Follow step-by-step instructions for completing all of the bankruptcy forms and filing them in court. Find out what business debt and assets (if any) would be impacted by bankruptcy, and learn about automatic stays and how business assets like goodwill and intellectual property are evaluated. Learn the various bankruptcy options that are available (such as Chapter 7, Chapter 13, and Chapter 1). The authors explain the eligibility factors and downsides of each. Educate yourself to better understand the bankruptcy process, protect yourself, and deal with the aftermath of bankruptcy.

Finnell, Kelly O. *The ESOP Coach: Using ESOPs in Ownership Succession Planning*. Executive Financial Services, 2010. 212p. ISBN 0-578-04699-7. $30.

Finnell thoroughly and concisely covers the topic of ESOPs as a way to sell your business in clear, natural language. As you near retirement especially, you will face a dilemma in selling your business; instead of paying a huge amount of tax and walking away from your life's work, an ESOP might work for you. The ESOP also allows you to sell to your kids, work until you die, and more, but with a little planning to keep tax expenses lower and reward the employees with ownership. An ESOP is a great exit strategy and can be a great tool for giving your employees an ownership stake and possibly raising more capital for expansion and growth.

**Gegax, Tom. *The Big Book of Small Business.* HarperBusiness, 2007. 448p. ISBN 0-06120-669-5. $29.99.

This lively, practical guide will help you start, fund, and get your new business off the ground as well as create a mission statement and create processes for continuous innovation. Gegax explains and illustrates the importance of effective leadership. The business plan can easily be adapted to a web-based company as well as retail or service brick-and-mortar. Great for the beginner and also useful to those who have started a successful company but want to expand and enjoy their business life. This practical reference tool for best practices gives you a good idea about what should be on your task list, how to prioritize the tasks based on your situation, and where to get the details when growing your business.

**Gottry, Steve. *Common Sense Business: Starting, Operating, and Growing Your Small Business—In Any Economy!* HarperBusiness, 2005. 368p. ISBN 0-06-077838-5. $19.95.

Gottry started and ran a large Minneapolis-based ad agency and video production firm, which failed after 22 years in business. You can learn from his mistakes. Well-organized and clearly written, Gottry's book includes specific how-tos, such as ways to prioritize bills for payment when cash flow is limited. He explains how to find solutions to the questions and challenges you're facing daily. Learn how to begin to understand yourself, your employees, your vendors, and your customers. Using humor, Gottry will help you successfully manage your business through good times and bad.

Holton, Lisa and Bates, Jim. *Business Valuation for Dummies.* For Dummies, 2009. 360p. ISBN 0-470-34401-6. $21.99.

Another well-written, clearly organized work from the For Dummies series explains how to conduct due diligence and increase your company's value when selling, incorporate valuation into prep work before negotiating to buy a business, and when to seek assistance from experts. The authors present numerous case studies on buying and selling businesses, which will help you discover what to build into partnership agreements and why pause before transforming your business into an ESOP. In general, this title will help anyone understand business valuation and why it's challenging and how to analyze historical performance and grasp key valuation tools.

**Horn, Thomas W. *Unlocking the Value of Your Business: How to Increase It, Measure It, and Negotiate an Actual Sale Price—In Easy Step-by-Step Terms,* 3rd ed. Charter Oak Press, 2008. 273p. ISBN 0-8752-1016-3. $39.95.

Often a good way to really examine how your business is doing is to analyze it in simple, everyday language. Horn explains how to calculate the value of your business and how to maximize its market value. Practical advice on negotiating the acquisition contract and how to prepare and present your business to potential buyers is included. Buyers and sellers of a business will use this knowledge to negotiate price much more effectively. Horn clearly presents tried-and-true formulas for valuing your business.

Hunter, J. Scott and Wiese, Matt. *How to Sell a Business in Good and Bad Times.* BusinessZone Press, 2010. 178p. ISBN 0-98-428220-3. $19.95.

This readable handbook walks you through the complex process of selling your small business. Learn the basics of business valuation, how to find buyers, how to make your business more marketable, and the fine points of seller financing. Sample documents are included in the appendix.

Kaplan, Jennifer. *Greening Your Small Business.* Prentice Hall, 2009. 304p. ISBN 0-7352-0446-1. $19.95.

This practical guidebook will help your company become more competitive, profitable, and eco-conscious. Find ideas on reducing waste, saving energy, and green marketing. Find out how to tell your customers and stakeholders about your sustainable mission and keep your core customers happy while finding a whole new group of eco-conscious consumers for your service or product. Learn about 50 ways to make your workplace greener as well. Develop a green business plan and be part of saving the planet. Learn ways to green your office supplies and shipping services as well as utilizing green information technology.

Little, Steven S. *The 7 Irrefutable Rules of Small Business Growth.* John Wiley, 2005. 256p. ISBN 0-471-70760-0. $18.95.

Find out Little's real and powerful principles for helping a small business expand and develop new business. Little acknowledges the difficulties small businesses have in today's global economy, where competition comes from the Internet as well as the business down the street. Learn more about topics such technology, planning, hiring and firing, and globalization as they relate to small business today. An entire chapter is devoted to each of his seven rules. For example, he explains why it is essential to have a thorough understanding of the marketplace, why processes must be customer driven, and how to attract and keep the best and brightest. Practical solutions and strategies are presented to achieve and sustain a competitive advantage. Simply but effectively written, this book teaches entrepreneurs to have a realistic view of the marketplace and their place in it.

Lyon, Thomas W. *Exit Strategy: Maximizing the Value of Your Business.* Sales Gravy Press, 2008. 144p. ISBN 0-98-18004-08. $24.95.

Selling your business can be an emotional and overwhelming event. Lyon walks you through the complete process of demonstrating profitability, maintaining confidentiality, transfer of title, price negotiations, and more. He also explains how to keep your business operating efficiently during this process. Lyon will help you avoid costly mistakes and exit your business with less stress and more success.

Manheim, Sheldon. *Exit Strategy: The Art of Selling a Business.* USPublication.com, 2010. 368p. ISBN 1-5959-4378-1. $29.95.

Manheim explains why all businesses must develop an exit strategy in the beginning of their operations and revise it regularly, as dictated by the business's maturation and changes in the economy. With an exit strategy in place, business owners are ready to exit rapidly and profitably. Present or potential business owners will find Manheim's book to be a thought-provoking and invaluable resource, providing all the information needed to either sell a business in the shortest period of time or to buy the right business at the best price.

Pease, Tom. *Going Out of Business by Design: Why Seventy Percent of Small Businesses Fail.* Morgan James, 2009. 188p. ISBN 1-60037-672-X. $29.95.

Pease is very good at analyzing business processes and procedures and determining how to creatively deal with all manner of business trouble. He explains the owner's responsibility to the success and failure of his or her small business. His book guides you through important topics such as how to establishing positive cash flow, correct pricing and selection of products, various legal troubles, and leadership methods. Learn what Pease considers to be the great secret to making a small business last and retain employees.

Phibbs, Bob. *Growing Your Business: A Step-by-Step Approach to Quickly Diagnose, Tread, and Cure.* John Wiley, 2010. 272p. ISBN 0-470-58717-2. $19.95.

Find here the action steps you need to make change happen for your new business; learn practical yet simple tactics to differentiate your company from competitors. Discover how to decipher financial reports and discover why things are not going as planned. Find advice and insight into human resources management, sales training, merchandising methods, and marketing. Easy to read, well-written, and easy to implement, use Phibbs's guidance to help your small business grow and succeed.

Richards, Rene V. *How to Buy and/or Sell a Small Business for Maximum Profit.* Atlantic, 2006. 288p. ISBN 0-910-6275-35. $24.95 (with CD).

Richards's book is a roadmap of suggestions, insights, and techniques for both buyers and sellers. Covered here is the entire selling process step-by-step, from making the decision of when to sell or buy, through determining how to market the company, to understanding the various legal and financial documents involved in a sale, and on to closing the deal and handling the transition afterward. The novice entrepreneur who wants to buy a small business will find plenty of help here. Areas Richards covers include finding and evaluating a business to buy or sell, how to value a business, raising the funds for purchase, evaluating a business financial condition, asset valuation and income capitalization, leveraged buyouts, letters of intent, and legal and tax concerns.

Rosen, Corey and Rodrick, Scott. *Understanding ESOPs.* National Center for Employee Ownership, 2008. 142p. ISBN 1-932-92447-7. $35.

Both authors work for the National Center for Employee Ownership. Their book will teach you how ESOPs work in both C and S corporations, what their uses are, what the valuation and financing issues are, how to set them up, and more. Especially important is that this book is about the U.S. ESOP, not the various types of plans called ESOPs in other countries. Chapters cover topics like selling to an ESOP in a closely held company, things to do with an ESOP in addition to buying out the owner, how to finance an ESOP, and ESOP valuation issues.

Rodrick, Scott S. and Rosen, Corey. *Leveraged ESOPs and Employee Buyouts,* 4th ed. National Center for Employee Ownership, 2001. 218p. ISBN 0-926902-75-X. $35.

The National Center for Employee Ownership is a nonprofit membership and research organization serving as the leading source of accurate, unbiased information on ESOPs. This title is a guide to the complex issues involved in setting up and using an ESOP for a leveraged buyout. ESOPs provide new capital and a tax-advantaged employee benefit, which may help your company's cash flow and help you retain employees. Learn about contribution limits, valuation issues, and employee buyouts in plain English. Included are changes in ESOP rules brought about by the Economic Growth and Tax Relief Reconciliation Act of 2001.

Sampson, John E. *How to Sell Your Business: And Get the Best Price for It.* Beaver's Pond Press, 2003. 212p. ISBN 1-59298-000-7. $24.95.

This roadmap leads a business owner through the process of selling a business from preparing the business for sale through the negotiations and closing. Suggestions, insights, and techniques cover everything from when and how to tell employees about a forthcoming sale through the related legal documents and what the definitive sale agreement must include and why. Find out about legal representations and warranties, earn-outs, and how to handle the transition after the sale. Use this book to prepare you for the selling process.

Sargent, Dennis J. and Sargent, Martha S. *Retire—And Start Your Own Business.* Nolo Press, 2008. 316p. ISBN 1-4133-0765-5. $24.99.

Highlighted here are important financial and personal issues you should consider during your preretirement and retirement years. Exercises, checklists, and reality checks as well as worksheets are provided to help you organize your ideas and plans. The book is full of examples, anecdotes, and simple exercises to help you work through all the important considerations in starting a business. The authors present a very logical process using clear, jargon-free language. Highlighted boxes present practical ideas and leads on where to go for more information. If you're planning to retire early or if you're already retired, this handbook will help you work with the time and money you have to pursue your retirement goals and dreams and enhance your lifestyle in retirement.

Schenck, Barbara Findlay and Davies, John. *Selling Your Business for Dummies.* For Dummies, 2008. 384p. ISBN 0-470-38189-2. $24.99 (with CD).

Another well organized and well written title from the For Dummies series that will give you tips on pricing and presenting your business for sale, advice on how to evaluate and locate potential buyers, ways to improve your business before selling, and a look at the business marketplace's trends and truths. Also learn the "ten deal-killers to avoid." The CD/DVD is full of practical questionnaires, worksheets, and forms to help with sale details as well as an outline for gathering information into a sales presentation.

Shaw, Kelly and Rasmussen, Trevin. *The Complete Guide to Selling Your Business.* Business Brokerage Services, 2009. 133p. ISBN 0-69-2003851. $14.95.

Shaw and Rasmussen cover every aspect of selling a business, including how to structure the sale, liability issues, how to keep your business improving while selling, and more. Template agreements, forms, and checklists are also provided. Understand the process, timing, and sequence of events in selling any business, and learn how to maximize your business value and increase personal wealth.

Sigmon, Patricia. *Six Steps to Creating Profit: A Guide for Small and Mid-Sized Service-Based Businesses.* John Wiley, 2010. 208p. ISBN 0-470-55425-8. $34.95.

Learn how to change your business and measure the results of each change so your business is more profitable. Learn more about cash flow, management costs, and how important selling is for all your employees. Find out more about visibility in the marketplace, marketing, and financing. Sigmon presents useable, practical, and easily implemented tactics to improve your bottom line.

Simmons, Chad. *Business Valuation Bluebook: How Successful Entrepreneurs Price, Sell, and Trade Businesses,* 4th ed. Facts on Demand Press, 2009. 336p. ISBN 1-88915-055-X. $25.95.

Tools provided here include valuation techniques to determine a fair market value price, sellers' techniques to negotiate from strength, and buyers' tactics to pay less. A business valuation expert for over 20 years, Simmons presents the information on valuing a business in an organized, logical manner. Learn about trading businesses and how to defer capital gains taxes. Useful valuation models are included.

Sperry, Paul and Mitchell, Beatrice H. *The Complete Guide to Selling Your Business,* 2nd ed. Kogan Page, 2005. 192p. ISBN 07-4944-457-6. $35.

This guide to the complicated process of selling a business uses a case study to illustrate important concepts. Samples of a confidentiality agreement and a letter of intent are included. The authors discuss many issues, including reasons to sell, estimating the value of the business, and negotiating and closing the sale. Learn how to determine when the time is right to sell from both financial and personal points of view.

Steingold, Fred S. *The Complete Guide to Selling Your Business,* 3rd ed. Nolo Press, 2007. 496p. ISBN 1-4133-0706-X. $34.99 (with CD-ROM).

This overview of the sales process covers all the key concerns, including price and payment terms, liability protection, and restrictions on future competition. Learn how to get your business ready to sell. Specific advice is presented on the tax consequences of selling a business, how to set a realistic price, how to create a marketing plan to attract buyers, how to investigate prospective buyers, and how to create sales agreements and confidentiality letters. Each chapter is complete with checklists and a list of tasks to accomplish. The sales agreement, confidentiality letter, promissory notes and security agreements, noncompeting and consulting agreements as well as closing checklists are available on the CD-ROM. Steingold, an attorney and prolific author, presents the material in a well-organized, concise manner.

Thaler, John. *The Elements of Small Business: A Lay Person's Guide to the Financial Terms, Marketing Concepts, and Legal Forms That Every Entrepreneur Needs,* 21st ed. Business Brokerage Press, 2011. 354p. ISBN 0-97485-188-4. $127.

Specializing in small business law, this lawyer and small business owner presents tools, tips, and advice to help you get your business off to a smooth and legal start. Chapters are thorough and cover topics such as business formation, insurance, computers and e-commerce, marriage and divorce, retirement planning, and exit strategies. Each chapter concludes with a list of resources. Over 20 appendices provide forms and sample reports, such as registration for a fictitious business name, an operating agreement for an LLC, financial statements, and more. This well-written book will help many entrepreneurs.

Thomson, David G. *Mastering the 7 Essentials of High-Growth Companies.* Wiley, 2010. 201p. ISBN 0-470-61062-6. $19.95.

Thomson's "7 Essentials" include value proposition along high growth market segment, marquee customers, big brother alliances, exponential returns, inside/outside leadership, and essential board experts. This book is the timely answer to the search for what it will take to propel a company's growth through these challenging times. Growth companies grow through recession and recovery periods to become the new growth leaders, and Thomson's case studies and the numbers in this book prove it. Thomson is known as America's growth expert on what it takes to transform a small business into a billion-dollar one, and his book will help you and your business overcome challenges and thrive in today's challenging business world.

Tracy, Tage C. *Small Business Financial Management Kit for Dummies.* For Dummies, 2007. 384p. ISBN 0-470-12508-X. $24.99.

Tracy will help you plan a budget, streamline your accounting process, raise capital, and generally keep your business solvent. Learn how to avoid common management pitfalls and use the bonus CD's reproducible forms, checklists, and templates. Tracy explains the financial foundations of a sound business. You will also learn about putting a market value on your business as well as how to invest company money wisely. If you are closing your business, chapter 15, "Hanging Up the Spikes and Terminating Your Business," will help you make some of the final decisions.

Trugman, Gary R. *Understanding Business Valuation,* 3rd ed. AICPA, 2008. 210p. ISBN 0870517488. $124 (with CD).

This third edition covers topics such as valuation standards, theory, methods, discount and capitalization rates, S corporation issues, and more. A new chapter addresses the emerging topic of intangible asset valuation, and another chapter gives websites to locate economic, industry, financial, and business information. Trugman provides tables, boxes, and figures to illustrate and emphasize important issues in each chapter. The CD includes sample reports and a comprehensive bibliography of business valuation practice.

Ward, John L. *Perpetuating the Family Business: 50 Lessons Learned from Long Lasting, Successful Families in Business.* Palgrave Macmillan, 2004. 256p. ISBN 1-4039-3397-9. $29.95.

Ward, an international expert on family business, draws the best practices from some of the most successful family businesses, such as Ford Motors and Marriott Hotels. He has developed a framework of five insights and four principles in which to place his 50 lessons learned for business longevity. Tools and checklists are included to help readers apply these best practices to their own family businesses.

**Warner, Ralph E. and Laurence, Bethany. *Save Your Small Business: 10 Crucial Strategies to Survive Hard Times or Close Down and Move On.* Nolo Press, 2009. 316p. ISBN 1-4133-1041-9. $29.99.

Businesses that make it through a severe economic downturn emerge more competitive and more focused. The basic thrust of this book is covered by chapters about concentrating on what is really profitable for your business, controlling your cash flow, minimizing your liability, bankruptcy and its alternatives, and not wasting money on ineffective marketing. Chapter 12 is about closing down your business and is very thorough. If you feel the business has run its course, learn how to shut down operations while protecting your personal assets. The appendix, "How to Prepare a Profit and Loss Forecast and Cash Flow Analysis," is very well done. Use this book to learn how to keep your best employees and share costs and resources with competitors.

West, Tom. *The Business Reference Guide,* 21st ed. Business Brokerage Press, 2011. 767p. ISBN 0-97-4851-88-4. $125.

Loaded with information, this superb guide provides pricing guidelines, expanded industry trend information, and extensive benchmarking data for business expenses, including rent, labor costs, sales per square foot, and so on. The detailed table of contents and lengthy index enables readers to find specific information quickly and easily. The "Industry Expert Listing" is a unique highlight of West's new edition.

**Yegge, Wilbur M. *A Basic Guide for Valuing a Company*, 2nd ed. John Wiley, 2002. 294p. ISBN 0-471-15047-9. $24.95.

This down-to-earth guide features an abundance of case studies from real companies, presents common valuation techniques, and contains tips for determining tangible and intangible values. Sample balance sheets and valuation exercises illustrate the author's thoughts about valuation for 10 different types of businesses, including small retail stores, a small manufacturer, a wholesaler, and a restaurant. Besides brick-and-mortar companies, approaches to valuing start-up technology firms and dot-com businesses are also discussed. Yegge walks readers through data collection to arrive at a saleable figure for many types of businesses, both privately held and publicly traded.

■ Online Resources

About.com Small Business Information: http://sbinformation.about.com/ (Accessed Spring 2011).

Under the "Manage and Grow" section of the huge About.com site, you will find good articles on growing and developing your small business. In addition to suggestions about public or commercial sources of information are links to companies that will track a company or industry for you and provide periodic updates so you can follow competitors. Also, you will find articles on competitive analysis and SWOT analysis by searching this site. Find articles on selling your business or exit strategies by searching these keywords. Analyzing the competition is important when you prepare your business plan, but it is essential to continue monitoring the competition as long as you are in business.

AllBusiness: www.allbusiness.com (Accessed Spring 2011).

This huge site contains articles and advice on any area of business law, including legal structure, property leases, patents, trademarks, employment law, taxes, and even how to work with your lawyer. Articles on exiting your business are thorough and helpful. The articles on green businesses are also very useful. Links to many directories and news and business information sites are provided. The "Sales and Marketing" section has many articles on techniques, advertising, and publications. The tax articles discuss topics such as barter tax and accounting issues and tax strategies for keeping the family business in the family. Use this well-organized, functional website often.

BizBuySell: www.bizbuysell.com (Accessed Spring 2011).

This very useful, practical website not only lets you list your business for sale on the Internet but provides a wealth of articles on valuing and selling a business. The "Common Questions and Answers" section covers items such as seller financing, how you can help your business sell, and what business brokers really do. Business brokers can be located from the site. Under "Seller Resources," you'll find the fundamentals of selling a business as well as information about valuation and financing. Of course, you can search for a business or a franchise to buy here as well.

BizQuest: www.bizquest.com (Accessed Spring 2011).

Billing itself as "A Business For Sale Marketplace," this site lists businesses for sale and includes resources for buying or selling your business online. Users can search for businesses by industry or location or for a franchise for sale. A fee is charged for listing a business for sale. Under both tabs "Buy a Business" and "Sell Your Business," free information and links to free information are provided. Several newsletters are also available.

**BusinessKnow-How.com: www.businessknowhow.com (Accessed Spring 2011).

This large site has an abundance of articles on starting and managing a small business. A large department titled "Growth and Leadership" covers many issues involved in business growth and individual management skills development. Find advice on ways to expand your business incrementally and safely. Different areas cover incorporating online, business loans, human resources training and tools, and web design and tools. Users will find many articles on job descriptions, cash management and accounting, a break-even calculator, and a job or product pricing system. Find basic business information here on a wide range of topics.

Business Owners Idea Café: www.businessownersideacafe.com (Accessed Spring 2011).

Developed by successful entrepreneurs and authors of published guides on starting a business, this large site presents short articles on all aspects of small business and entrepreneurial life. The main divisions are "CyberSchmooz," "Starting Your Biz," "Running Your Biz," "Take Out Info," "Classifieds," "The 'You' in Your Biz," "De-Stress and Have Fun," "About Idea Café," and "Join Idea Café." Here you can find experts to answer your questions or discuss your current business crisis. You'll find sample business plans, financing help, business forms, and business news. The "Running Your Biz" section contains articles about business services, marketing and sales, running a business, and worldwide business information. Everything involved in operating a growing business is discussed. A search feature takes you to relevant articles that may be of interest.

Business Owner's Toolkit: www.toolkit.com/ (Accessed Spring 2011).

Commerce Clearinghouse's Small Business Guide provides pages of information and tools to help individuals start, run, and grow a successful small business. Business tools provided include sample letters, contracts, forms, and agreements ready for you to customize for your business. Several good articles on the fine points of selling your business, including recasting your financial statements, are included. An article called "Valuation of Small Business" is also quite thorough. Financial spreadsheet templates are available as well as checklists to help you stay organized in completing necessary tasks. IRS tax forms, state tax forms, employee management forms, and more are all linked to this site. Also find articles on how tax law changes could affect your business.

Entrepreneur's Guidebook Series: www.smbtn.com/businessplanguides/ (Accessed Spring 2011).

Defining real entrepreneurs as managers who adopt key behaviors developed by understanding key market concepts and theories and who are successful because of their planning and researching skills, this site covers a wide variety of subjects in its Small Business Plan Guides. A lengthy article on determining the proper valuation for a business walks readers through how financial statements are used to determine fair market value. Rule-of-thumb formulas are also presented for various specific types of businesses. Explore this website for good ideas.

MergerNetwork: www.mergernetwork.com (Accessed Spring 2011).

This large site facilitates the search for a business to buy. Users can search MergerNetwork's database of businesses for sale or create a business wanted ad. Basic membership is free. You can browse businesses by location, size, relocation capability, franchises for sale, industry, and size. A partner site, SellerWorks at www.sellerworks.com, provides listings for sellers of businesses. Business for sale ads are free, or a featured ad is available for $1 per day.

**National Association of Certified Valuation Analysts (NACVA): www.nacva.com (Accessed Spring 2011).

The NACVA will help you find a trained, credentialed expert to help you place a value on your business. Under the "Resources" tab is a directory that you can search by industry and zip code or just zip code to locate a professional in your area. Some PDF forms and informational publications are available, such as the IRS Business Valuation Guidelines.

**National Center for Employee Ownership (NCEO): www.nceo.org (Accessed Spring 2011).

The NCEO, a private, nonprofit membership and research organization, has a large site with many articles on employee stock ownership plans. Hot issues such as legislation and Securities and Exchange Commission decisions are presented and discussed. Articles cover steps to setting up, a history of the ESOP, selling a closely held business to an ESOP, and ESOP distribution and diversification rules. Links to ESOP books, seminars, webinars, and consulting are also provided. A "Reference Desk" provides basic information and statistics. Use this site to learn more about ESOPs.

PowerHomeBiz.com: www.powerhomebiz.com/ (Accessed Spring 2011).

This large site has an outstanding guide to "Growing a Business." Featured articles include "Managing Your Business," "Developing Strategic Alliances," "Small Business Technology," and "Managing Customers." This established, well-organized site will help new entrepreneurs with growing, financing, managing, and other aspects of starting a new business or expanding one. Regular visitors to this frequently updated site will identify trends in small and home-based businesses.

**Small Business Administration: www.sba.gov (Accessed Spring 2011).

This official government site offers a wealth of resources and programs for growing a small business. Under "Starting and Managing Your Business," you will find advice and articles on managing for growth, forecasting the future, sharpening your management skills, and managing employees. Here you will also find online business training. Another vital area for growing businesses is leading change, and many articles on this topic are also included. Strategic planning articles explain how to match the strengths of your business to available, new opportunities. Other major sections cover business planning, financing, managing, legal aspects, and business opportunities. Some contents are available in Spanish.

Small Business Notes: www.smallbusinessnotes.com (Accessed Spring 2011).

This site contains articles on buying or selling a business as well as merging, planning, management, and legal issues. The articles on "Why Merge" and "Merge Wisely" are enlightening and provide business owners with information and food for thought when considering a merger. Common business valuation methods are also discussed. With many topics related to small business and entrepreneurship, come to this useful site for answers to basic and more complex questions.

Smarta.com: www.smarta.com/ (Accessed Spring 2011).

Under "Advice, Guides," you will find more than 40 useful guides on topics such as how to prove your business idea will work, how to start a toy shop, five reasons to start a business at university, and more. More than 600 videos and 343 guides are available on many short topics. Case studies are provided also. The "Tools Directory" covers ideas like finding a franchise, creating a brand identity, building and managing a website, expanding internationally, shipping goods, and more. The slight British bent is not a barrier.

**Wall Street Journal Online: http://online.wsj.com/public/page/news-small-business. html (Accessed Spring 2011).

WSJOnline is an authoritative site that has a section entitled "How-To," where entrepreneurs will find a great deal of help deciding if they are entrepreneurs, how to get started in business, and how to prepare for leaving a business. Collected here are many articles about different aspects of selling a business. Learn how to get top dollar when you sell and how to prepare for a death in the business. Find articles on important issues, such as why and how to continue to use the financial statements an accountant prepares when you sell your business. Continually updated and well-written, this site is useful to all entrepreneurs.

GLOSSARY

This glossary lists only terms in this book that may be new or used in a new way to readers. A larger and more complete small business dictionary is available on the web at www.small-business-dictionary.org.

Advertising: paid communication about a product or service through various media.

Angel investor: high-net-worth individual who provides early-stage or start-up businesses with capital in the form of debt, ownership capital, or both.

Assets: balance sheet items in which a business invests in order to conduct business.

Balance sheet: summary or snapshot of all of a company's assets, liabilities, and equity as of a specific date.

Benchmarking: process of identifying and learning about best business practices in a company, an industry, or the world.

Better Business Bureau (BBB): national organization dedicated to protecting consumers from unscrupulous businesspeople.

Blog: short for Weblog, essentially an online journal.

Bounce rate: percentage of visitors who leave a website after visiting only one page.

Brand: proprietary name, symbol, or trademark that differentiates a particular product or service from others of a similar nature.

Break-even analysis: analysis that determines how much a company needs to sell in order to pay for the investment or the point at which a company's revenue will equal expenses.

Brick-and-mortar: describes a traditional business not involved in e-commerce and incurring the cost of physical structures.

Browser: software program that reads hypertext markup language (HTML) and allows web users to find and view information anywhere on the Internet.

Budgeting: process of developing financial plans that project inflows and outflows for a future specific time period.

Business incubator: facility that provides help for new businesses by providing a package of services, often affiliated with a college or university.

Business plan: detailed summary of a business including objectives and projects over a three-to five-year period.

Business structure: legally recognized organizational framework for conducting business, including, but not limited to, a sole proprietorship, general or limited partnership, limited liability company, or corporation.

GLOSSARY

Capital: represents the investment in the company or business.

Cash flow statement: details the reasons for changes in cash during the accounting period.

CI: competitive intelligence, also known as market intelligence and business intelligence, refers to the information a company gathers about another company from public sources and effective interviewing skills.

Clicks-and-bricks: e-commerce organization with a physical facility that also operates online combining a brick-and-mortar location with the click technology of the internet.

Collateral: property that is promised by a borrower as security for a loan.

Corporation: legal entity owned by stockholders that is authorized by law to act as a single person.

Cyberspace: the Internet when seen as the electronic medium of computer and communication networks in which online communication takes place.

DBA or doing business as: fictitious business name or any name used to do business other than the owner's own name.

Demographics: population measures such as age, race, income, sex, and occupation.

Domain name: name given to a specific computer and address on the Internet; most include.com,.net, or.gov at the end of the name.

Dot-coms: businesses that operate primarily or completely on the Internet.

Early stage: stage in business development in which a firm is usually expanding and already producing and delivering products or services but is less than five years old.

E-business: all the internal processes of a company or organization that become digitally based functions.

E-commerce: a company or organization that conducts business transactions via the Internet.

Ecopreneur: entrepreneur who is concerned with environmental issues.

E-government: government initiatives to provide information and services electronically over the Internet through e-mail and websites.

Economic indicators: statistical measures associated with business cycles.

EIN: employer identification number, or federal employer tax identification number, assigned by the Internal Revenue Service.

E-mail newsletters: electronic version of a print newsletter sent to a subscriber's inbox.

Employee: person hired by a business to perform work under the control, direction, and supervision of the employer.

Entrepreneur: creative individual willing to risk investing time and money in a business activity that has the potential to make a profit or incur a loss.

Equity: value of a piece of property after deducting liens.

ERISA (Employee Retirement Income Security Act): legislation that imposes requirements on covered employers to manage employee pension funds for the benefit of their workers.

ESOP (Employee Stock Ownership Plan): a tax-qualified benefit plan designed to invest primarily in company stock.

Executive summary: part of a business plan that compellingly explains the opportunity, shows why it is timely, describes how the company plans to pursue it, outlines the entrepreneur's expectation of results, and includes a short sketch of the business.

Exit strategies: methods used by businesses to discontinue businesses, products, or relationships with customers or suppliers.

E-zine: electronic or e-mail magazine.

FACNET: Federal Acquisition Computer Network; enables procurement process to be completed electronically from solicitation through award and payment.

FICA: Federal Insurance Contributions Act, which requires employers to withhold Social Security and Medicare taxes from employees' wages.

Fictitious business name: *see* **DBA or doing business as.**

Financial ratio: the result of dividing one financial statement item by another. Ratios help interpret financial statements by focusing on specific relationships, and they allow comparisons between companies and within the industry.

Financial statement: record of financial data needed to plan the future of a business.

Forecasting: analysis of past and current situations in order to anticipate the future.

Franchise: an agreement by which a person permits the distribution of goods or services under his or her trademark, service mark, or trade name, during which time the franchisor retains control over others or renders significant assistance to others (from the Federal Trade Commission rules).

Global economy: the economic relations between countries, where markets in individual countries have now spread beyond national boundaries and are more integrated with those of other countries.

Home equity loan: loan secured by an interest in the borrower's home that creates a mortgage against the home.

Home page: default URL or beginning page of a website.

Human resources (HR): a collection of related activities pertaining to the management of personnel within a company.

Hypertext: generic term describing any media format—such as graphics, sound, text, and links to other documents—not limited to the Internet but used extensively there.

Income statement or profit and loss statement: compares revenues and expenses to illustrate how well a business is performing.

Independent contractor: person who is hired to perform a specific task or project and is typically paid on a per-project basis.

Industry: group of businesses that produce a similar product or provide a similar service.

Initial public offering (IPO): an event in which the stock of a closely held corporation, proprietorship, or partnership is offered for sale to the public for the first time in hopes of raising cash for expansion and growth. Also know as going public.

Internal Revenue Service (IRS): national tax collection agency for the U.S. government, under the auspices of the Treasury Department.

Internet: complex matrix of globally connected computer networks.

Internet security: means used to protect websites and other electronic files from attack by hackers and viruses.

Job description: describes functions of a job for a particular business, needed to hire and evaluate employees.

Landing pages: page through which users enter a website, not always the home page.

Limited liability company (LLC): business structure that allows a business owner to limit personal liability without all the paperwork and expense of forming a corporation.

Line of credit: unsecured loan that allows you to use what you need and is replenished whenever you pay back into it.

Link: connection made between two websites.

Management: people who are responsible for the accomplishment of the mission of an organization, using planning, organizing, leading, and controlling behaviors.

Market analysis: the study of a market to identify and quantify business opportunities.

Market research: the development, interpretation, and communication of decision-oriented information, such as assessing the size and nature of a market for business owners or managers.

Market share: percentage of market sales a company controls.

Marketing: a plan or strategy designed to let current and potential customers know what you have to sell and why they should buy it from your business.

Marketing mix: the main factors of marketing, comprised of product, price, placement, promotion, and people.

Mergers and acquisitions: joining together of two or more businesses.

Microloan: a small loan available to novice entrepreneurs with poor credit to enable them to start a small business.

Mission statement: memorable statement of the reasons for a company's existence.

NAICS: North American Industry Classification System developed by the United States, Canada, and Mexico to categorize businesses by the type of goods and services they provide in their principal activity using a six-digit coding system.

Networking: the art of making connections with other business people to help you generate new business, find working capital and new employees, and keep an eye on your competitors.

Niche market: very specialized market segment within a broader segment satisfying specific market needs.

Online community: way to allow web users to engage with one another and an organization through the use of interactive tools such as e-mail, chat, and blogs.

Outsourcing (or subcontracting): transfer of the provision of services formerly or generally performed in house to an external organization with a contract of agreed-upon standards, costs, and conditions.

Partnership: two or more persons associated for the purpose of conducting business, with each contributing money, property, skill, or labor and with all expecting to share in profits or losses.

Patent: protective right given to inventors by the federal government to prevent others from copying an invention or improvement to a product or process.

Pay per click: auction-style Internet advertising model used to direct traffic to websites and where advertisers pay a hosting service when the ad or link is clicked.

Performance review: structured, formal interview between a supervisor and employee in which the employee's work is evaluated and discussed, held at least annually.

Personalization (e-commerce): process by which a website presents customers with information or products and services tailored to individual users' characteristics or preferences.

Positioning: method by which a company uses its marketing strategy to create and maintain a unique image in the minds of consumers.

Press release: news about a business, product, or service that is sent to reporters or editors as a source of material for news articles.

Profit and loss statement: *see* **Income statement or profit and loss statement.**

Profit margin: amount by which income is greater than expenditure.

Publicity: technique aimed at raising public awareness of a business, product, or service.

Public relations (PR): process of influencing one's image in the media.

Recordkeeping: organizing and tracking information that helps a person understand how and if a business is growing.

Retirement plan: provides income to an employee after retiring or results in a deferral of income by employees during their employment.

Return on investment (ROI): the simple ratio of net profits to total assets.

Request for proposal (RFP): asks for offers from suppliers for products or services needed by an organization.

Revolving credit: set amount of credit from a financial institution.

Search engine: database of website addresses and page contents that can be used to search for information on a particular topic.

Seed money: the amount of capital needed to get a business up and running.

Service: any activity with a mix of tangible and intangible outcomes offered to a market with the goal of satisfying a customer's needs.

Sexual harassment: form of employment discrimination in the workplace; this form of sex discrimination violates Title VII of the Civil Rights Act of 1964, which applies to employers with 15 or more employees, including federal, state, and local governments, and includes any behavior that affects an individual's employment, work performance, or that creates an intimidating, hostile, or offensive work environment.

Social media: use of web-based and mobile technologies to turn communication or user-generated content into interactive dialogue between users.

Social media marketing: programs used by businesses and organizations to create content that attracts attention and encourages readers to share it with their social networks; an organization's message is spread from user to user and presumably resonates because it is coming from a trusted, third-party source as opposed to the brand or company itself.

Software: program that a computer runs to control the functioning of the hardware and direct its operations.

Sole proprietorship: individual engaged in a trade or business without any protection against legal liability.

Start-up: a new business of any size but usually small.

Statistics: the classification, tabulation, and study of numerical data.

Subcontracting: *see* **Outsourcing (or subcontracting).**

SWOT analysis: (strengths, weaknesses, opportunities, threats), a marketing/management tool used to evaluate a company's competitive position.

Target market: group of buyers toward whom a business or company directs its marketing efforts.

Teleworker: employee who spends a substantial amount of work time away from the employer's main premises and who communicates with the company through the use of computing and telecommunications equipment.

Temporary workers: people who are hired through another company that is responsible for making payroll deductions, hiring, firing, and paying; generally not considered employees.

Time management: controlling the use of one's most valuable asset: time.

Trade association: industry group used for networking and valuable business contacts.

Trademark: A name, symbol, or other device identifying a product, officially registered and legally restricted to the use of the owner or manufacturer.

Trade publication: medium that carries articles and advertising targeted at the specific needs of businesses in a certain industry.

Turnover: the rate at which staff leave and are replaced in an organization.

Tweet: a post on Twitter, which is a microblogging service.

Uniform franchise offering circular (UFOC): disclosure document containing required information supplied by the franchisor to the franchisee.

URL (universal resource locator): the identifier of a web page or file on the Internet.

Valuation: entire perceived worth of a company's assets.

Venture capital: money invested in a business by professional investors, often with the expectation of high risk and high return.

Vision statement: statement giving a broad, aspirational image of the future that a company is aiming to achieve.

Web 2.0: interactive websites and tools that promote two-way communication and connect people.

Web 3.0: next phase of the web, which will be similar to having a personal assistant who knows practically everything about a user and can access all the information on the Internet to answer any question and will connect the user to information.

Webinars: web-based seminars or tutorials.

Wholesaler: business that purchases goods from a manufacturer and sells them to a retailer or distributor.

INDEX

INDEX

INDEX

INDEX

INDEX

ABOUT THE AUTHOR

Professor of Librarianship Susan C. Awe is Director of Outreach for the University Libraries at the University of New Mexico. Besides this second edition of *The Entrepreneur's Information Sourcebook,* she is the author of *Going Global* (ABC-CLIO, Libraries Unlimited, 2009) and a frequent contributor to such professional publications as *Booklist/ Reference Books Bulletin* and *Choice* magazine. She was a contributor to the American Library Association's *Guide to Reference* online edition in 2009–2010, and she edited *ARBA Guide to Subject Encyclopedias and Dictionaries,* second edition (Libraries Unlimited, 1997).